Deweaponizing Interdependence

Deweaponizing Interdependence

Bringing the Idea of International Clearing Union into the Twenty-First Century

Edited by Jamie Morgan and Heikki Patomäki

BLOOMSBURY ACADEMIC
LONDON · NEW YORK · OXFORD · NEW DELHI · SYDNEY

BLOOMSBURY ACADEMIC
Bloomsbury Publishing Plc, 50 Bedford Square, London, WC1B 3DP, UK
Bloomsbury Publishing Inc, 1359 Broadway, New York, NY 10018, USA
Bloomsbury Publishing Ireland, 29 Earlsfort Terrace, Dublin 2, D02 AY28, Ireland

BLOOMSBURY, BLOOMSBURY ACADEMIC and the Diana logo are trademarks of
Bloomsbury Publishing Plc

First published in Great Britain 2026

A catalogue record for this book is available from the British Library.

Library of Congress Cataloging-in-Publication Data available

ISBN: HB: 978-1-3505-7480-9
PB: 978-1-3505-7484-7
ePDF: 978-1-3505-7482-3
eBook: 978-1-3505-7481-6

Typeset by Deanta Global Publishing Services, Chennai, India
Printed and bound in Great Britain

For product safety related questions contact productsafety@bloomsbury.com.

To find out more about our authors and books visit www.bloomsbury.com and
sign up for our newsletters.

Contents

Figures

Contributors

Nicolás Aguila is a research assistant in the Department of Philosophy, Politics and Economics at the Witten/Herdecke University. His research interests include monetary theory, monetary history (focus on Argentina) and financing sustainable and just transformation.

Massimo Amato is Associate Professor of Economic History and History of Economic Thought at Bocconi University in Milan. He is the author of numerous books and articles, co-authored with Luca Fantacci and Lucio Gobbi. He is also the author of *Le radici di una fede* (B. Mondadori, 2008) and *L'enigma della moneta* (2010; *L'énigme de la monnaie*, Cerf, 2015). He coordinates two research teams, working on the project of a European Debt Agency and on an algorithmically based clearing facility for trade credit.

Nathaniel Cline is Associate Professor of Economics and Associate Dean for Curricular Affairs at the University of Redlands. He has published in the fields of macroeconomics, international finance, economic history as well as regional economic development.

Luca Fantacci is Associate Professor of Economic History at Università degli Studi di Milano. Together with Massimo Amato he wrote *The End of Finance* (Polity, 2012), *Saving the Market from Capitalism* (Polity, 2014) and *A Fistful of Bitcoins: The Risks and Opportunities of Virtual Currencies* (Bocconi UP, 2020). He is a consultant for the Committee on Finance and Banking at the Italian Senate.

Adrien Faudot is an associate professor of economics at the Université Grenoble Alpes (France). He is a co-editor of the *Revue d'Histoire de la Pensée Économique*. His research focuses on international monetary economics from a history of economic thought and an economic history perspective.

David Fields is an economist for the Utah Department of Commerce. He has published in the fields of macroeconomics, money and banking, international political economy, stratification economics, sociology and community planning.

Lucio Gobbi is an assistant professor at the University of Trento. His research focuses on macroeconomic issues. He has published numerous articles in scientific journals such as the *Cambridge Journal of Economics, Journal of Macroeconomics and Structural Change* and *Economic Dynamics*.

Paula Haufe is a PhD researcher at Witten/Herdecke University, Germany, and part of the sustainable finance research project 'Climate change and global finance at the crossroads'. Her PhD focuses on the political economy of international climate finance and green EU policymaking. She also works as a research analyst at the German Advisory Council on Global Change (WBGU).

Lauri Holappa is the director of Finnish Centre for New Economic Analysis (UTAK) and a visiting researcher at the University of Helsinki. His research has focused on international political economy, macroeconomics and monetary theory.

Niina Kari is a doctoral researcher at the University of Helsinki. Her research focuses on the international monetary system and economic policy space. She has also written about the eurozone crisis and the role of public affairs agencies in Finnish politics. Kari is currently working as an economic policy advisor for the Left Alliance parliamentary group in the Finnish parliament.

Haider A. Khan is John Evans Distinguished University Professor and Professor of Economics at the Joseph Korbel School of Global and Public Affairs, University of Denver. He has published more than twenty books and over two hundred articles in professional journals and received many international awards.

Konsta Kotilainen is a postdoctoral researcher at the University of Helsinki. He works at the intersections of world politics, economics, and philosophy. Kotilainen's doctoral dissertation *From Monetary Sovereignty to Macroeconomic Policy Autonomy?* (2024) has been awarded the University of Pavia's Supranational Political Economy PhD Thesis Prize. Kotilainen is a chief editor of the *Finnish Review of Political Economy*.

J. A. Kregel is Professor of development finance at Tallinn University of Technology, adjunct Professor at the New School for Social Research, and co-editor of the *Journal of Post Keynesian Economics*. His most recent publication is *Financial Macroeconomics*, Anthem Press, 2024.

Jamie Morgan is Professor of Economics at Leeds Beckett University. He co-edits the *Real-World Economics Review* with Edward Fullbrook. He has published widely in the fields of economics, political economy, philosophy, sociology and international politics.

Heikki Patomäki is Professor of World Politics and Global Political Economy at the University of Helsinki. His most recent monographs are *World Statehood* (2023) and *The Three Fields of Global Political Economy* (2022). Patomäki's research interests include philosophy and methodology of social sciences, peace and security studies, futures studies, and global political economy.

Matías Vernengo is Full Professor at Bucknell University and Director of the Bucknell Institute for Public Policy (BIPP). He was formerly Senior Research Manager at the Central Bank of Argentina (BCRA) and he has been an external consultant to several United Nations organizations. He specializes in macroeconomic issues for developing countries, in particular Latin America, international political economy and the history of economic ideas. He is also the emeritus founding co-editor of the *Review of Keynesian Economics* (ROKE), and co-editor in chief of the *New Palgrave Dictionary of Economics*.

Joscha Wullweber is Professor of Political Economy, Transformation and Sustainability at Witten/Herdecke University, Germany. His recent books include *Central Bank Capitalism* (2024) and *Critical Political Economy and Public Policy* (coauthor, 2023). He is a member of the *German Advisory Council on Global Change* (WBGU) and Director of the *International Center for Sustainable and Just Transformation* [tra:ce].

Preface

The scope and scale of globalization has been in question for a number of years now. One very obvious reason for this has been the increase in tensions over trade, of which the most high-profile example has been the conflict between China and the United States. Trade conflicts of this kind ultimately stem from a basic contradiction: while trade surpluses and deficits balance out globally, surplus countries usually amass savings, and deficit countries tend to accumulate debt. A fallacy of composition – the mistaken belief that what one actor can achieve at a given moment can be achieved by all actors at once – lies behind this state of affairs. It is not possible for every country to run a trade surplus at the same time, although this is encouraged by the kind of international trade and monetary system we currently have.

For the deficit countries, a possible individual response is to resort to unilateral measures, the kind that the Trump II administration has begun to apply bilaterally to most countries in the world. However, this can trigger a spiral of retaliation, as it did in the 1930s, and this simply exacerbates the situation. In the 2020s, we are witnessing the weaponization of interdependence, the securitization of commodity chains, and growing divisions between differently aligned blocs of states. Not only is this combination highly volatile, but also, at a time when the world confronts numerous existential challenges, it impedes cooperative action to the benefit of all. It is, however, possible to establish behaviour-shaping rules and principles and create more suitable common institutions. An International Clearing Union (ICU) is one potentially constructive way forward.

This book is a result of the Academy of Finland-funded project 'How to avoid tendencies toward trade wars? A multi-method study about institutional designs for an International Clearing Union (ICU)', which ran from September 2021 to August 2025 and was led by Heikki Patomäki. This historically informed but future-oriented project explored the economic-theoretical and normative foundations, as well as the political feasibility, of various ICU proposals. As part of the project a workshop on ICU proposals was organized at the University of Helsinki from 15 to 16 March 2024. Most of the chapters in this book were developed based on papers discussed at the workshop. The notable exception is the chapter by Nicolás Aguila, Paula Haufe, and Joscha Wullweber, 'The ecor as global special purpose money: towards a green international monetary system to finance sustainable and just transformation'. This was first published in *Sustainability Science* (20, pp. 1245–57) and is included here because it resonates with the themes of the workshop and fills a gap from the original discussions. The original article is republished here with the kind permission of the authors and Springer.

This book is also, in part, the result of collaboration between the two of us over the past two decades. In addition to numerous discussions over the years in Helsinki, Standish (Greater Manchester), and Cambridge, the process of editing the book has been facilitated by modern technologies that enable real-time video discussions.

Jamie Morgan and Heikki Patomäki

1

Introduction

The idea of an ICU and its relevance in the twenty-first century

Jamie Morgan and Heikki Patomäki

Introduction

The concept of an International Clearing Union (ICU) is usually traced to debates in the 1940s and is typically associated with John Maynard Keynes. However, Keynes was not the first to propose the idea, and discussion predates this period. Proposals for clearing systems of one kind or another date back to at least the 1890s and were widely discussed in the 1920s and 1930s. Moreover, during the early 1940s, as war raged in and beyond Europe, there were several clearing union proposals on the table and not just Keynes's. Still, Keynes's particular conception is usually taken as a point of departure. For him, an ICU involved an impartial system for managing currencies and a world central bank governing a common currency, the bancor. Financial positions would be defined against the rest of the world and obligations made systemic and equitable between debtors and creditors. The resultant plan was intended to achieve several aims. In principle, it would avoid problems associated with a dominant international currency belonging to one state, it would reduce and mitigate conflicts between states in trade and monetary matters, and insofar as it functioned effectively, it would enable the pursuit of rational economic policies for the mutual benefit of all states. The plan, of course, was not without its problems, several of which were quickly identified by E. F. Schumacher and then Michał Kalecki and Schumacher. In any case, Keynes's plan was not implemented. Instead the system eventually agreed upon at Bretton Woods in 1944 mainly reflected American views and the US dollar became the dominant currency of the world economy.

Since Bretton Woods, and especially since the 1960s, there have been various attempts to revisit the concept of an ICU. As the world-historical context has changed over the years, these attempts have involved reconsiderations of its institutional form, function and justification.[1] Some proposals have offered novel ethical and political principles drawing on Kalecki and Schumacher, as well as Keynes. Others have focused on mechanisms to redefine the role of a proposed clearing house or world central bank, and most have tried to improve the feasibility of the idea under the circumstances of the late twentieth or early twenty-first century. While many of the more innovative plans bear the imprint of post-Keynesian theory, it is also the case that different understandings of economic theory have informed perspectives on prospective ICUs.

We suggest that in the 2020s, discussion of proposals for some version of an ICU remains highly relevant. This is because:

- increasing globalization has intensified the need for adequate mechanisms to govern the world economy
- major imbalances in the world economy continue to generate policy problems within states and conflicts among states and to cause underdevelopment
- the current monetary system remains vulnerable to multiple sources of instability and crisis, as the 2008–9 Global Financial Crisis highlighted
- developments in world politics, especially since the 'conservative turn' in the early 2000s, signify the continued importance of Keynes's analysis of the economic causes of peace and war
- since the 2010s, the world has been characterized by disintegrative tendencies and by potential and actual trade wars; these have been accompanied by contestations over the position of the US dollar and attempts to find alternatives, especially among members of the BRICS group
- in the 2020s, rising prices, debt, and interest rate levels associated with the recent pandemic and ongoing wars have intensified long-standing debates about the role of the US dollar as the global reserve and trade currency
- since the beginning of 2025, the second Trump administration's rhetoric and policies have accelerated concerns regarding the sustainability of the current global monetary order and his imposition of tariffs has led to renewed attention on trade deficits and their significance (in the context of widespread discussion of the collapse of the existing order)

Despite the importance and contemporary relevance of the topic, the literature on the ICU concept remains relatively scant. With this in mind, one key purpose of the book is to revitalize the debate regarding an ICU. This is something that has clear traction, given we are in a regressive phase in world history characterized by 'polycrisis' and the threat of major catastrophe, and given that trade wars and disputes over the role of the US dollar are prominent in the media and characteristic of the dynamics of the world political economy.

An ICU-style arrangement could, for example, go a long way towards eliminating trade wars and related conflicts. This is because a simple practical contradiction lies behind many trade disputes, such as the ongoing China-US trade war and the expansion of trade wars to include more and more countries. Trade deficits and surpluses cancel each other out. Countries with trade surpluses tend to have savings surpluses, whereas countries with trade deficits tend to accumulate debt. The contradiction arises from the fact that many policymakers fall into a 'fallacy of composition', that is, a (tacit) assumption that what is possible for a given actor at a given time is possible for all actors simultaneously. Every country cannot target and achieve a surplus. For the deficit countries, a possible individual response is to resort to unilateral measures. For smaller countries, this often means devaluations or austerity policies. The United States, meanwhile, currently has at least two options. On the one hand, it can continue accumulating debt and, on the other hand, it can try to pressure other countries into trade relations on its terms to its advantage. The problem with the latter, preferred by the Trump II administration, is that it can easily lead to a spiral of tit-for-tat retaliations, further aggravating the situation. It seems desirable, therefore, to create more adequate common institutions to avoid suboptimal and contradictory outcomes, which can have far-reaching adverse political consequences. Hence the relevance of the idea of an ICU – though as we shall see there are other reasons too.

In this introduction, we first discuss the historical context of the emergence of the idea of an ICU. Second, we briefly summarize some of the key moments that led to the establishment of the Bretton Woods system in 1944 and its subsequent transformations. Third, we tentatively outline the development of the ICU concept since the crises of the 1960s and 1970s and into the 2010s. Finally, we summarize the main contents of the chapters of the book. Each chapter sheds light on some aspect of current prospects, possible transitional organization, preferred forms and/or future potentials of the ICU concept. Questions asked concern the mechanisms of political economy, real-historical processes and the institutional and political conditions of the ICU, as well as its normative desirability.

Historical context of the emergence of the idea of an ICU

A world monetary system can emerge and evolve over several decades as a collective result of changing practices and various individual decisions and agreements. Alternatively, it may also arise from a grand architectural vision and its implementation. The nineteenth-century international gold standard is more of an example of the first possibility. The scheme was meant to be evolutionary: the self-interest of states would lead each to adopt the gold standard rules voluntarily, and once in place, the balancing mechanisms would appear natural – though clearly there is an institutional history involved. The system took more than half a century to evolve. Britain officially adopted the gold standard in 1821, gradually spreading related practices through its trade, finance and empire. When the Germans adopted the gold standard in 1871 following the Franco-Prussian War and the influx of gold from France, some other countries followed suit, yet the United States only adopted the standard in 1900. The basic understanding of the system followed from David Hume's 1752 essay 'Of the balance of trade'. This sets out an adjustment mechanism in terms of price-specie-flow and while Karl Polanyi was to argue that the gold standard was an institutional innovation that put the theory of self-regulating (i.e. self-balancing) markets into practice, it was also clear from early on that it deviated significantly from its theoretical ideal (Polanyi 2001).[2] As Charles Kindleberger was to later argue, the system was essentially a Sterling hegemony rather than a simple metallic standard (Kindleberger 1973, 1984).[3] The important point for our purposes, however, is that as various problems manifested, the concept of multiparty clearing was put forward as a possible means to resolve difficulties.

In the context of the gold standard, it was widely accepted by the end of the nineteenth century that multiparty clearing could reduce risks, reduce the number of transactions and associated costs, and that clearing could also ease access to liquidity and capital, thus facilitating trade. The first plan to establish a clearing system for interstate balances was proposed in the early 1890s. From the 1890s to the 1920s, various versions of such plans emerged in the contemporary literature and at international conferences.[4] These proposals were tailored to issues arising from the design faults of a system that used a commodity as an anchor.[5] For obvious reasons, discussion often focused on economizing (i.e. minimizing) the actual exchange of gold, although access to liquidity and overdraft facilities were also discussed. It is, however, also important to note that while the existence of the gold standard was intended to lead to price stability to the benefit of trade, the reality of the policies required to maintain the gold standard encouraged protectionism and coincided with colonial expansion and ultimately conflict (Polanyi 2001). In any case, the First World War led (formally or informally) to the suspension of the gold standard by combatants and restoring some version of a gold standard was a major constituent in post-war debates. As Barry Eichengreen charts, there was a basic split between countries that attempted to restore the gold standard at pre-war exchange rates and who opted for domestic fiscal contraction and deflation, such as Britain, Sweden and the Netherlands and those that depreciated and inflated, such as France, Belgium and Italy (Eichengreen 1996: 153–86; see also Patalano 2023: 299–302). Both had consequences for domestic and world economy.

From its earliest discussions there was already potential to connect clearing unions to conflict avoidance. The events that followed in the first half of the twentieth century and after can only have reinforced this potential, although it was left to Keynes and other later thinkers to articulate the connection. The idea of a worldwide clearing union assumed new relevance in the early 1930s, after the breakdown of post–First World War attempts to restore a version of the gold standard.[6] Against the backdrop of fragmenting international trade and the Great Depression various countries had turned to bilateral clearing agreements and it was a short step from there to proposals for multilateral clearing. In 1932 the London Chamber of Commerce and Industry proposed the establishment of a new international payment system based on a multilateral clearing mechanism. Proposals were also made outside the English-speaking world, many of them based on turning the already existing bilateral clearing systems into a multilateral system. University of Geneva professor Edgard Milhaud (1873–1964) published a series of texts (from 1932 onwards) in which he developed the idea of a system based on existing institutions with a view to developing multilateral compensation from existing bilateral agreements. According to the proposals, the then-recently established Bank for International Settlements (BIS) would execute international payments through certificates in national units of account that could be exchanged at the BIS (or wherever an International Compensation Office was eventually located).[7]

It is also worth noting here, given some of the arguments later in the book, that many of the 1930s proposals for a world clearing union were based on a gradualist or evolutionary approach. Paul Einzig, a columnist for *The Financial Times*, for example, wrote several works on international exchange and clearing between 1934 and 1936 in which he proposed, not unlike Milhaud, that effective coordination of bilateral clearing systems could lead to the gradual transfer of responsibilities to a global body (possibly the BIS).[8] According to Einzig, with a multilateral clearing system it would be possible to turn external imbalances into a mere accumulation of debts and credits without affecting the internal monetary stability of the countries, that is, without inducing inflation or deflation. Surplus countries could actively strive for rebalancing by investing in deficit countries.

Einzig's ideas were not particularly popular in Britain. However, their existence is an important reminder that the period was one in which the automatic steering mechanism of the gold standard was being questioned and the possibilities of more managed approaches were being raised (see Patalano 2023: 305–7).[9] This had particular pertinence in the context of militarization and then war. Soon after the rise of the Nazi dictatorship in 1933–4, Germany started to conclude bilateral clearing treaties with several countries, especially in South-East Europe and Latin America. By 1938, about half of Germany's trade was conducted through bilateral clearing; only one-fifth was settled through the 'free' foreign exchange market. When the Second World War started, Britain developed a similar system. (Skidelsky 2001: 194–5, 228–30).

In July 1940, Germany's economic minister Walther Funk proposed a European clearing system as part of the 'new order' of the Axis powers set against the 'old liberal order' (Hofmann 2017). This proposal may have been part of Nazi Germany's broader economic strategy to dominate Europe and establish a German-led economic bloc, but it also resonated with many of the earlier clearing union proposals, not least with Einzig's.[10] Funk's proposal can also be interpreted as a German response to Britain's Sterling area. The German plan laid out by Funk was opposed to the use of gold as the basis of the system. The new European system would have the German mark as an international unit of account, but in this plan, there was no central bank. Funk assumed that trade would, at least initially, be planned so that surpluses and deficits would not arise in the clearing accounts, though Funk envisaged some liberalization over time.[11]

As all of the above ought to indicate, however briefly, Keynes's plan did not arrive from nowhere.

Keynes's plans for an international clearing union

In November 1940 Harold Nicholson, from the British Ministry of Information, asked Keynes to respond to Funk's proposal. Nicholson originally envisaged a debunking of Funk's proposal and an endorsement of both laissez-faire and the pre-war monetary system based on British Sterling. Keynes, however, rejected the suggestion and in a letter to Nicholson dated 20 November 1940, he instead agreed with many of Funk's ideas (and those of similar proponents of an ICU):

> I am not the man to preach the beauties and merits of the pre-war gold standard. In my opinion about three-quarters of passages quoted from the German broadcasts would be quite excellent if the name of Great Britain were substituted for Germany or the Axis, as the case may be. If Funk's plan is taken at its face value, it is excellent and just what we ourselves ought to be thinking of doing. (Keynes 2013: 2)

The issue, of course, was not new to Keynes. He had participated in discussions on Britain's post-war economic policy, return to the gold standard and more broadly the form and functioning of the world monetary system throughout the 1920s. Volume II of his *A Treatise on Money*, first published in 1930, is subtitled 'The Applied Theory of Money' and its final chapter is a discussion of 'Problems of Supranational Management'. Here he sketches a system with a world central bank at its core. The primary aims of that central bank would consist of the stability of the value of gold (although Keynes envisaged gold's role diminishing over time) and countercyclicality ('its second duty should be the avoidance, as far as possible, of general Profit Inflations and Deflations of an international character'; Keynes 1930: 401). The letter to Nicholson in 1940 is, however, sometime after the publication of his *General Theory* in 1936 and his subsequent elaboration and defence of it in the *Quarterly Journal of Economics* in 1937 (which post-Keynesians make much of) and, as such, it and his ICU proposal belong to his 'mature internationalism' (Markwell 2006: 178–89).

Keynes saw Funk's proposal as a step in the right direction but, given the historical circumstances, this was tempered by rejection of Nazi ambitions for supremacy. At this time Britain was also embroiled in war financing negotiations with the Americans and the United States had yet to enter the war. This was still the case when Germany invaded the Soviet Union in June 1941. The invasion changed the British situation and war prospects (Germany having now committed to war on several fronts), but the immediate situation for Britain remained dire and the United States outside the war. However, in a leap of faith, Keynes began to believe that cooperation with the United States was sufficiently likely to make it worthwhile to design a sustainable multilateral system. In September 1941, while at his Sussex farmhouse he drafted the first version of his proposals for an ICU (Bollard 2020: 127–35). He went on to write four drafts over 1941 to 1942 before a White Paper on the topic was published on 7 April 1943.[12]

Interpreting Keynes's work has become something of an industry and his ICU proposals can be analysed and interpreted in many different ways. What seems relatively uncontroversial is that his holistic or 'macro' viewpoint – based on seeing economic developments from the standpoint of all actors and countries at once – was tempered by a need to convince the Americans (as the world's main creditor) and the British (who were still keen to preserve the Empire) about the merits of the plan. While the general goal was to equalize the rights and obligations of surplus and deficit countries and creditors and debtors, Keynes was willing to compromise. This can be seen in how the proposals developed in relation to the feedback he received. For example, the first two drafts included the idea of confiscating (taxing) excessive credit balances but this idea was later replaced with voluntary adjustments. In the fourth draft, Keynes introduced more stringent conditions on debtors and proposed a new Governing Body structure, in which the United States and United Kingdom could outvote everyone else.

While not wholly original and despite the compromises, Keynes's final ICU proposal was a far-reaching and in some sense radical proposal regarding how world trade and the monetary system should be reformed after the war. Against the backdrop of his and others' analysis of the economic causes of war and peace, it provided institutional means that favoured the latter. The goal of Keynes's ICU plan was to guarantee, with the help of a fair system of clearing, adjustments and lending, the continuation of trade in almost all conditions at a level that enabled full-employment policies in each country (Keynes 1969/1942). Adjustments may be gradual and are undertaken by both debtors *and* creditors (rather than placing special onus on debtors in the form of adverse and punitive deflation). The system had to be multilateral so that only overall net balances would matter and, as previously noted, Keynes called the systems' world currency the 'bancor'. Clearing would occur through 'clearing accounts' held by member central banks in the world central bank and this organization would become a focal point for institutional action (instead of piecemeal chaotic adjustments in a more fragmented system). By minimizing unemployment and policy-driven rapid changes in prices as far as possible, the ICU was supposed to mitigate interstate military conflicts by averting trade wars. In the context of the time it was also conceived as a bulwark against the attractions of state-socialist (Bolshevik) and reactionary (fascist) types of political responses to the inequalities, fluctuations and crises of the capitalist market economy.

In Britain, at the beginning of the 1940s, the clearing union was initially only discussed within the confines of government and the central bank. Several well-known economists took part in these discussions and made comments on Keynes's plans. After the publication of the White Paper in April 1943, three critics went public. These were Thomas Balogh, Schumacher and Kalecki.[13] Of these three, Schumacher had already begun sketching ideas for a multilateral clearing union in 1941. He sent his first draft to Keynes as early as 16 September that year and this brought him to Keynes's attention (he was also to go on to be employed at Balliol College, Oxford – Kalecki, meanwhile, had been working at the Oxford Institute of Statistics since 1940). Schumacher's proposal was eventually published in *Economica* in 1943 but prior to this he had raised the subject with Keynes of its publication in the *Economic Journal* and been advised to delay.[14] According to Leopold Kohr's 1980 obituary of Schumacher:

> [when the proposal] was published in the spring of 1943 in *Economica*, it caused some embarrassment to Keynes who, instead of arranging for its separate publication, had used the essay almost *verbatim* in his famous Plan for an International Clearing Union which the British Government issued as a White Paper a few weeks later. (Kohr 1980)

A short joint article by Kalecki and Schumacher entitled 'New plans for international trade: international clearing and long-term lending' was also published a few months after the White Paper in 1943. Keynes's approach targets an overall balance among current accounts, that is, an equilibrium of the system, but this does not make much sense in a world where different countries are at different stages of development. Some will have more need for imports of capital goods than others in order to 'catch-up' and will thus have legitimate reasons to run larger deficits than otherwise allowed. Others will be further along in the process of developing a successful strategy of export-led growth, and these may have legitimate reasons to run higher surpluses. For Kalecki and Schumacher, taking these differences into consideration meant taking a broader point of view than Keynes seemed to have in mind. Thus, while Keynes may well have been thinking in terms of a fair and equitable system with a target of full employment everywhere, achieving this goal in a dynamic context required greater attention to institutional design and historical circumstances. This was necessary so that the system suit diverse countries (the examples given at the time included Britain, Poland and China).

An effective ICU proposal also required more attention be given to dynamics of power and to unintended consequences. For example, in Keynes's plan, the total amount of liquidity is given, and so acting strategically the surplus countries might well ration their exports and deficit countries their imports, resulting in overall counterproductive deflationary tendencies. Kalecki and Schumacher argued that developing countries should be allowed to borrow funds for full-employment policies and investment, and that the surplus countries should be allowed to invest in those countries for this purpose. To achieve this goal they proposed an additional fund for long-term investment – an International Investment Board. This differed from other available plans (even those that included an investment agent), since it is only by combining current trade and investments 'into one organization [that] a satisfactory solution [can] be found for the problems of both' (Kalecki and Schumacher 1943: 32).

Moving on, the important points to bear in mind as we turn to Bretton Woods are that Keynes was not the first to propose an ICU, Keynes's conceptualization quickly attracted constructive criticism and there were in fact alternatives available.

The Bretton Woods system and its transformation and partial demise

Bretton Woods is a tourist destination in New Hampshire in the United States, known for its skiing. It is the location of the Mount Washington Hotel and resort, and it was here that the United Nations Monetary and Financial Conference was held in July 1944 (hence the 'Bretton Woods system' or just Bretton Woods). Forty-four allied nations took part, as well as other interested parties and observers, and hundreds of delegates participated, although less than a hundred directly took part in the negotiations. The goal was to establish the international monetary and financial system that would prevail after the conclusion of the Second World War. The standard story typically portrays Bretton Woods as a struggle between Harry Dexter White (the main negotiator on the US side) and Keynes (leading the British delegation). In this simple struggle story, the US side and thereby White's vision, prevailed, albeit subject to a few modifications (e.g. Steil 2013: chapters 6–8; Hirai 2024: 136–51). However, during 1942 and 1943, there were in fact several monetary schemes – including French, Norwegian and Chinese – circulating among the Allies and competing with American and British schemes (Markwell 2006: 233–5). In any case, the White Plan was written and completed in March–May 1942. Most of this plan was adopted two years later at Bretton Woods, including:

(a)   the creation of a modest-scale International Monetary Fund (IMF) and a world bank[15]

(b) the confirmation of the US dollar as the world's money, anchoring a fixed exchange rate system and with the dollar, in turn, convertible to gold[16]

(c) the implementation of some capital controls, but with encouragement of gradual liberalization[17]

(d) the establishment of a quota system for member countries contributions to the fund and the apportionment of relative voting rights based on those quotas

The eventual agreement then, placed the US dollar at the heart of the world's monetary system and gave significant voting power and hence influence to economically powerful countries, especially to the United States as the largest contributor. From an ICU design and implementation perspective, Bretton Woods, whatever else is said in its regard in contrast to later neoliberalism, is remembered as a lost opportunity. The Bretton Woods system was not a clearing union proper, yet it was a modification of and improvement on nineteenth-century liberalism based on institutions of free trade and the gold standard.

While the White Plan aimed to reduce trade barriers and liberalise capital flows over time, and in that sense, it aimed to return to some of the basic tenets of nineteenth-century liberalism, the system was in other respects qualitatively different than what had come before. John Ruggie (1982) captures this nicely. He refers to the Bretton Woods system as the compromise of 'embedded liberalism':

> unlike the economic nationalism of the thirties, it would be multilateral in character; unlike the liberalism of the gold standard and free trade, its multilateralism would be predicated upon domestic interventionism [. . .] to assure domestic economic growth and social security [. . .]. Indeed, progress on multilateralism seemed to be made contingent upon progress in expanding domestic production, employment, and the exchange and consumption of goods. (Ruggie 1982: 393–4)

Modifiable but fixed exchange rates and capital controls were intended to stabilize trade and shield states and their domestic policies in order to facilitate growth, and where problems arose the International Monetary Fund was empowered to offer loans. According to Ruggie, moreover, Bretton Woods shared some basic tenets with Keynes's ICU plan, namely multilateralism, collaboration to facilitate balance-of-payments equilibrium, and an attempt to make domestic full employment possible for the participating states. So, while falling short of a system of multilateral clearing, the system enabled domestic Keynesianism and the building of social democratic welfare states under the circumstances that prevailed in the 1940s–1960s, though only 'within acceptable center-left bounds' (Ruggie 1982: 394).[18]

While, as noted, standard accounts of the Bretton Woods negotiations focus on only two countries and above all on their chief negotiators, more nuanced accounts stress that many countries and negotiators attending the meeting – especially from Latin America – actively participated in the discussions. These countries advocated state-led developmental goals for poorer countries, and even got some proposals through. According to Eric Helleiner (2014) they achieved their goals to some extent in two areas. First, the importance of the World Bank's development mandate was emphasized and strengthened from the one originally conceived. Second, a 'waiver clause' was introduced, providing scope for more generous IMF balance of payments support for commodity-exporting countries than would otherwise have occurred. Commodity-exporting countries were also promised a future international agreement relating to relevant marketing and pricing. Overall, however, it would be misleading to overstate the practical significance of these achievements.[19] In any case, soon after the war, US officials downplayed the developmental content of Bretton Woods and according to Helleiner (2014: 259) this was because of 'changing US priorities in the context of domestic political shifts and new strategic priorities' as the Cold War started.

Given the purpose of this edited collection (highlighting the lost opportunity represented by not implementing an ICU, exploring the potentials an ICU may offer today) and given the eventual partial demise of Bretton Woods, it is also important to highlight the system's intrinsic vulnerabilities. The most important of these was, of course, the central role played by the US dollar. Although White's plan talks about clearing, the Bretton Woods system was based on actual multilateral clearing only to the extent that states trade in the same national currency. This typically was the US dollar and a fixed link between the US dollar and gold stood behind this. As Benn Steil (2013: 133) puts it, White's system was 'a halfway house between state-controlled trading [. . .] and free trade under a mechanical gold standard'. The role of the US dollar was, however, from its inception unsustainable within the system's design. As White was clearly aware, under Bretton Woods expanding trade required the availability of increasing amounts of dollars for use outside of the United States, and this creates pressure for the money supply to rise, which creates a further tendency for it do so relative to gold reserves. If this occurs in a fixed exchange system without adjustment then it can become profitable for investors to start exchanging dollars for gold, creating pressures on reserves. However, while White was aware of this problem, he was not overly concerned by it. On the one hand, he put his trust in the superiority of US gold reserves, and on the other hand, he believed in the possibility and powers of multilateral regulation and stabilization. This was to prove overly optimistic and the problem was to resurface in a slightly different guise later as the Triffin Dilemma.[20] As White well knew, the United States was likely to find itself running balance of payments deficits in order for dollars to be available to the rest of the world but would face other economic pressures to reduce any deficits it ran. As Triffin was to point out in the 1960s, if the United States stops running balance of payments deficits, the world economy loses its largest source of additions to liquidity and reserves and this might result in shortage of liquidity which could pull the world economy into a contractionary spiral. The onus would seem, therefore, to be on the United States to continue to run deficits to provide a steady stream of dollars to stimulate world economic growth and yet the very existence of those 'necessary' deficits can become a signal of the weakness of the US economy leading to erosion of confidence in the US dollar.

Without confidence the dollar cannot fulfil its role as the world's reserve currency. The implication being that eventually a fixed exchange rate system built around the dollar is likely to break down. Various other sources of vulnerability follow from this central role of a national currency in an international system – not least the continual potential for conflict of interest between domestic concerns of the source of the main currency and the needs of the other countries in an international system dependent on that national currency. These could be mitigated for some time in the early post-war period. But the very point of Bretton Woods was to facilitate economic growth and trade among many countries while allowing some market liberalizations to develop. This highlights another intrinsic vulnerability of the system. Its 'halfway house' and 'embedded liberalism' fostered changes the system itself was not able to contain.

The original Bretton Woods system was developed when the world economy was in a state of disintegration and during a time when the United States accounted for half of the world's GDP and controlled two-thirds of the world's gold. At the same time, as previously noted, liberalization of trade and finance was built into the Bretton Woods system. From early on the IMF adopted the practice of conditionality for its loans, allowing it to require domestic policy changes facilitating liberalization, though until the 1970s this only applied to a few debtor countries. More immediately significant, between 1947 and 1964 there were six GATT rounds and these covered more and more countries and tariffs and this progressively liberalized world trade (or rather re-liberalized it if we take a longer historical perspective). Against this backdrop, by 1957, the

United States was running deficits. Moreover, at the end of the 1950s payment systems were liberalized and in the early 1960s capital controls were loosened. All of this, while consistent with the aims set out at Bretton Woods to facilitate economic growth and to allow for liberalization, meant growing tensions in the system based on its mechanisms of adjustment and on the role of the US dollar within those mechanisms. In the 1960s new opportunities to exploit problems and exacerbate tensions started to arise. For example, tax havens were established in connection with the City of London, offshore dollar strategies were developed and so on. A whole host of developments occurred involving changing relations of production and increasingly easy exit options for capital, and these started to change power relations. In the 1970s this started to tip the balance in some settings in favour of neoliberal local or national solutions. As readers are likely aware, neoliberal responses became increasingly dominant in the 1980s and 1990s (see Patomäki 2001: chapters 2 and 3; 2008: chapter 6).

So, while the context of the decades after the Second World War was in many ways different from that of the nineteenth century, gradually the post–Second World War world slid towards a new manifestation of nineteenth-century economic liberalism. The partial demise of the original Bretton Woods system further contributed to these developments. By 1968, the dollar had become in effect non-convertible into gold; it was declared formally non-convertible in 1971. The subsequent unilateral decisions by President Richard Nixon in 1973–4 instituted a system of floating exchange rates and expanded and deepened the liberalization of financial markets. This was *not* a return to the nineteenth-century gold standard, rather the world adopted a fiat monetary system for the first time. Yet, while *not* a return, many of the central mechanisms of the world monetary and trade system that have emerged are analogous to the nineteenth-century system of free trade and the period up to the First World War.

Given its historical echoes of a period in which the original idea for multilateral clearing originated, one might expect that the transition to neoliberalism and the subsequent problems of neoliberalism would provoke lively debate regarding an ICU. This, however, did not and has not happened. Rather, there have been only a few main interventions. These interventions have included: the World Bank initiated Brandt Commission; a series of more academically focused discussions and policy proposals in the West; and discussions in China following the sitting governor of the People's Bank of China, Zhou Xiaochuan's 2009 call for a new 'supranational currency' (these discussions have been mostly in Chinese and are little known outside China). We now turn briefly to these three main attempts to reopen debate regarding an ICU.

The Brandt Commission: a first attempt to reopen debates on an international clearing union

The most politically significant attempt to reopen discussion of an ICU took place in 1977–80, when an Independent Commission on International Developmental Issues was led by former West German Chancellor Willy Brandt. The Brandt Commission produced two main reports, *North-South, A Programme for Survival* in 1980 and *Common Crisis, North-South: Cooperation for World Recovery* in 1983. The Commission undertook its work against the backdrop of the turmoil of the 1970s – the Cold War and proxy wars, concerns over the possibility of devastating nuclear war, issues arising from environmental harms, population growth (the 'population bomb'), food security concerns, resource dependency and fears over eventual depletion, oil crises, the growing sense of structural economic inequality among UN member states (much of it deriving from unfair commodity trading and lack of investment), and so on.[21] With these kinds of issues in mind it took as its task the construction of a new international economic system able to forestall a contemporary variation on the conditions of the Great Depression of the 1930s (and the war that followed). A new monetary and credit system formed part of this new international economic system discussed in the first report and this includes a version of the ICU idea (Independent Commission 1980: 201–20).

According to the report, the monetary system of the future should not be based on the currency of any particular country, rather it should be founded on a jointly approved global currency. Future currency reserves would be held in this currency and this could be used to manage global liquidity (total combined world supply of money) and manage arising deficits and surpluses between countries.[22] It was suggested that the IMF Special Drawing Rights (SDRs) system could be developed and extended as a first step towards this eventual end. The SDR system was established at the IMF in 1969 in the form of supplementary foreign exchange reserve assets, the value of which is set by the organization and central banks of member states each held a specific amount. The SDR system has undergone various changes since the time of the Brandt Commission. However, it should be easy to understand the underlying attraction of the SDR system to the Commission. A universal accounting unit commonly recognized by member central banks could form the basis of a more active approach to global economic management of deficits and surpluses between countries, as well as management of associated issues of debt, investment and development.[23] According to the report, SDRs could lead to a global currency, reallocation and distribution of SDRs could be used to balance out surpluses and deficits and the IMF could take a longer-term and less onerous approach to any lending it provides to countries for development.[24]

Several chapters of this book discuss SDRs and the possibility of extending their use, either as a substitute for establishing a proper global clearing union or as a transitional step. This, of course, creates various issues regarding feasibility of reforming the IMF and, whatever one's opinion on this matter (see later discussions), reform of the IMF was a key concern of the Brandt Commission – not least giving a greater role in decision-making to developing countries in order to even out existing power relations – and in its own context the first Brandt Report puts forward an ambitious range of proposals of which an ICU is just one small part. The report's authors, moreover, are far more interested in recognising and addressing inequalities of development than Keynes was but they do so in the spirit of Keynes's commitment to economic management for mutual benefit.

For example, the report recognizes that the accumulation of debt in developing countries of the Global South following the oil crises of the 1970s has contributed to maintaining demand in the industrialized northern countries, but notes that this is not a sustainable way of ensuring sufficient levels of overall demand (Independent Commission 1980: 67). According to the report the transfer of resources could contribute to the Global South's economic development and industrialization, and at the same time act as a common stimulus package for the entire world economy (through development aid, transfer of funds through taxation, and debt arbitration). Based on this rationale expansion of balanced markets would contribute to growth in all parts of the world economy. This, however, would also create problems of adjustment in the affluent North that required management insofar as the import of products from the Global South might replace domestic industrially produced equivalents in some parts of the Global North.

To be clear, there is far more to the first Brandt Report than just a version of an ICU. It sees its task as more fundamental – hence the subtitle 'a programme for survival'. While not radical, the report explores various sources of systematic differences in power and opportunity between the Global North and Global South. Mechanisms proposed included:

- price stabilization mechanisms for primary products, benefiting developing countries above all

- global taxes, the revenue from which would be used in efforts to eradicate poverty and to promote economic development of the Global South
- common legally binding regulations on the investments and other activities of transnational companies
- a controlled and actively supported transition towards renewable energy sources

In accordance with its goals the Commission considered it the task of states to actively facilitate adjustment to maintain full employment, support alternative sources of employment, and implement or maintain active regional policies (Independent Commission 1980: 172–86). It thus articulated concerns rooted in what later came to be called 'global Keynesianism' – a term that began as criticism but was adopted by those it was targeted at (Mead 1989). Although most of its proposals were not new as such, as a whole, the Commission provided a qualitatively new kind of approach to tackling a variety of global, including environmental, problems.[25] However, while at the time the Commission began its work there was some sense that a genuine choice existed between social democratic and neoliberal policy frameworks to guide global futures, by the time the first report was published in 1980, power dynamics had started to more decisively favour neoliberalism. While the shift to full-scale neoliberal hegemony in world politics took a few more years, self-regarding protection of the interests of the Global North was already in full swing. As such, hardly any of the proposals of the Commission were ever implemented and the immediate impact of the report was limited (Wionczek 1981: 104–8).

After the work of the Brandt Commission came to an end, the idea of an international or global clearing union more or less disappeared. During the next two decades, the main significant contribution in the West towards developing and innovating the idea came from Paul Davidson (1992–93, 2002, 2004), a leading post-Keynesian economist. There was, however, also an intervention from Joseph Stiglitz which achieved a wider readership, but no greater traction than Davidson's work.

Critical academic explorations 1990–2010: Paul Davidson and Joseph Stiglitz

The end of the Cold War further reinforced neoliberalism (Gerstle 2022: 141–9) and by the early 1990s the public sphere was ripe with talk of 'globalization' (as though scale itself was an explanation of anything). Like many others, Davidson was deeply sceptical regarding the benefits of the system that had emerged in the wake of the decision to switch the United States and the world to floating exchange rates in 1973. As a post-Keynesian, however, he was well placed to orient his critique on the role of the monetary system and issues of aggregate demand management and was, of course, well aware of Keynes's work on an ICU. The opening sentence of his first paper on the subject in the early 1990s states that '[t]he current international payments system does not serve the emerging global economy well' (Davidson 1992–93). He argues that the system of floating exchange rates has meant recurrent unemployment and inflationary crises and that post-1973 developments have been characterized by slow growth in OECD countries and debt-burdened growth or stagnation (often involving falling real GNP per capita) in developing countries. As such he states, quoting from an issue of *The Economist* from January 1990, that the decade of the 1980s will be:

> noted as one in which 'the experiment with floating currencies failed ... [W]hen macropolicies are inconsistent and when capital is globally mobile, floating rates cannot be relied upon to keep current accounts roughly in balance'. (Davidson 1992–93: 153)

He points out that the original Bretton Woods system, combined with Marshall Aid, laid the foundation for unprecedented economic growth and increased welfare, while the subsequent system increased uncertainty, placed the demand for adaptation unilaterally on debtors' shoulders, and reduced aggregate demand and thus increased unemployment.

The book *Financial Markets, Money and the Real World* (Davidson 2002) and article 'The Future of the International Financial System' (Davidson 2004) return to the subject a decade or so later. In these he argues that returning to the original Bretton Woods system is not a solution. Instead Keynes's 1940s ICU plans could serve as the basis for a better system in changed circumstances. The core issue he highlights, however, is that 'the ubiquitous desire of all nations (except the United States) to pursue export-led growth policy for the purpose of accumulating additional dollar foreign reserves' is contradictory (Davidson 2004: 594). The sum of deficits and surpluses is zero and so not every country can achieve export-led goals at the same time. Moreover, for Davidson, the widespread pursuit of surpluses leads to economic policies that result in a collective decrease in total aggregate efficient demand in the world economy.

In response to the problems he sets out Davidson advocates what he considers to be a more realistic and cautious, essentially moderate, version of an

ICU which takes into account the political situation at the time of writing. His proposal is more nationally oriented than Keynes's original plan and requires neither a gold-based currency system nor a world central bank. For Davidson, a supranational central bank is 'at this stage of economic development and global economic integration [. . .] not politically feasible' (Davidson 2002: 209).

Like Keynes's original, Davidson's proposal involves a spectrum of different capital controls. Based on the proposal, if a member country accumulates excessive credit balances by running current account surpluses it has three options to spend its credits:

> (1) on the products of any other member of the clearing union, (2) on new direct foreign investment projects, and/or (3) to provide unilateral transfers (foreign aid) to deficit members. (Davidson 2004: 600)

His thinking is that a country can only be living beyond its means if it is at full employment, but even then, its deficit may be due to poverty, in which case richer countries are obliged to help it. The system is thus at least modestly redistributive. However, it relies on, at least partly, voluntary state-compliance with articulated principles of fiscal policy and falls short of a regime which taxes a slice of the surpluses. It also raises questions about public/private control over trade and investments. To what extent can and should governments control cross-border flows of trade or investments and what sorts of common institutional arrangements would that require? These were and remain important questions given that institutional arrangements and the positioning of economically and politically powerful countries (and corporations) has tended to work against constructive solutions able to benefit all, and has increasingly done so against the background of cumulative climate change and ecological breakdown.

In any case, Davidson's work attracted little attention. The articles were published in *Journal of Post Keynesian Economics*, a specialist heterodox journal with relatively few readers, and the book was published by Edward Elgar with little publicity. According to Google Scholar Davidson (now deceased) is one of the better-cited of the post-Keynesians but his work has never had the reach and visibility afforded to the best-known mainstream economists. Joseph Stiglitz, however, has had a stellar career as a (New-Keynesian) straddling academia, policy and practice. As Ben Fine notes, he wielded significant influence during his time as chair of the President's Council of Economic Advisers (1995–7) for the Clinton administration, and as chief economist at the World Bank (1997–2000) and being fired from the latter does not seem to have done his career any harm – he shared the 'Sveriges Riksbank Prize in Economic Sciences in

Memory of Alfred Nobel' with George Akerlof and Michael Spence in 2001 'for their analyses of markets with asymmetric information' (Fine 2024; Morgan 2024).[26] He went on to be what passes in mainstream economics circles for a critical public intellectual, discussing a wide range of issues of the day and publishing a series of popular books. As readers are no doubt aware, the turn of the millennium witnessed a high tide of 'anti/alter-globalization' sentiment, and highly media-visible demonstrations and 'shadow summits' were organized as protests against various world economic summits (G8, WTO, and others), including, for example, the 1999 'Battle of Seattle'.[27] Against this backdrop and the attention it drew to structural inequality and adverse debt relations between countries in the early 2000s, Stiglitz's interest turned to reforming the global monetary system, a subject he returned to with Bruce Greenwald in the wake of the Global Financial Crisis.

Stiglitz's first proposal for a system inspired by Keynes's ICU, 'Dealing with Debt. How to reform the global financial system', was published in the *Harvard International Review*, a relatively obscure journal. This was followed by discussion in the book *Making Globalization Work* a few years later, and this sold more than two million copies (see Stiglitz 2003, 2006: 245–68). The article 'Towards A New Global Reserve System' published in the *Journal of Globalization and Development*, revisits the subject and outlines several possible ICU models (Greenwald and Stiglitz 2010). Stiglitz holds the current dollar system partly responsible for the prevailing situation of global financial instability and argues that a jump to a new system based on an alternative national currency such as the euro or yuan renminbi would not solve the problem. Rather a global system is needed. Across the three publications, the two authors propose a Global Monetary Authority and 'global greenbacks'. According to the proposal, global money issuance capacities would be used for purposes of global macroeconomic stabilization and the common good, involving, in effect, elements of global fiscal policy and redistribution for the purposes of development, as well as to expedite responses to climate change. If we compare the proposal to the first Brandt Report and to Davidson's work, then the mechanism or framework seems closer to Keynes's original concept, while the remit is more ambitious and closer to the global Keynesianism of the Brandt Commission.

However, despite the success of *Making Globalization Work*, and despite the furore created later by the Global Financial Crisis and despite the issues arising from the need for global responses to climate emergency, Stiglitz (and Greenwald) has been no more successful than the Brandt Commission or Davidson. The part of the book dealing with the proposal for a new global reserve system did not attract widespread attention or debate and nor did the articles. Moreover, while the Global Financial Crisis prompted some relatively novel central bank responses, and despite numerous subsequent regulatory changes to banking and finance, the main consequence of the crisis was to augment processes of financialization (see, e.g. Baker and Morgan 2021; Morgan 2022). As such the crisis ultimately involved no significant deviation from the prevailing neoliberalism in most dimensions of policy (Patomäki 2009: 436–40; 2021).

As far as we are aware, since publication, none of the central civil society organizations involved in the alter-globalization movement have adopted some version of an ICU proposal as part of their programme of reform or transformation and none have made significant use of it in their campaigning. Nor have countries or the main international organizations made much of the issue. There have, however, over the years been various restricted or regional clearing and monetary system initiatives in Europe, Africa and among members of the BRICS group of countries that have drawn to varying degrees on the idea as means to address problems of the prevailing global system. These are taken up and discussed by contributors to this edited collection and form part of its thematic structure.[28] However, since the Global Financial Crisis, and especially since 2009, there has been discussion in China about reforming the world's monetary system and a supranational currency. This was initially quite lively and is barely known about in the West. We now turn to a brief summary of this discussion.

Chinese discussions on reforming the world monetary system through a supranational currency 2009–24

The 2008 Global Financial Crisis spurred significant Chinese interest in international monetary reform and a supranational currency. While the initial wave of Chinese enthusiasm for international monetary reform and supranational currencies waned by the 2020s before Trump's second administration, the intellectual groundwork laid during the period prior to this waning remains significant. Future reform efforts might benefit from revisiting these discussions, particularly in light of ongoing global challenges and the recent resurgence of these discussions in China. Much of the following summarizes the survey of the literature by Elmer (2025).

Among the more high-profile discussions was a proposal by Zhou Xiaochuan in 2009. Zhou was Governor of the People's Bank of China (China's central bank) from 2002 to 2018. He states that the Global Financial Crisis:

> calls for creative reform of the existing international monetary system towards an international reserve currency with a stable value, rule-based issuance and manageable supply, so as to achieve the objective of safeguarding global economic and financial stability. (Zhou 2009: 1)[29]

At the heart of Zhou's proposal, with issues such as the Triffin Dilemma, liquidity, systemic risk and unequal influence in mind, was the aim of reducing the global financial system's reliance on the US dollar. To be clear, however, Zhou did not propose a fully formed international clearing union but rather a new international currency unit, inspired by Keynes's bancor, for the purposes of serving as a (to use the commonly translated phrase) super-sovereign reserve currency. This would then be used to manage global trade imbalances. The proposal suggested expanding the use of the IMF's Special Drawing Rights (SDRs) as a pragmatic first step. Among other things, Zhou argued that:

> A super-sovereign reserve currency not only eliminates the inherent risks of credit-based sovereign currency, but also makes it possible to manage global liquidity. A super-sovereign reserve currency managed by a global institution could be used to both create and control the global liquidity. And when a country's currency is no longer used as the yardstick for global trade and as the benchmark for other currencies, the exchange rate policy of the country would be far more effective in adjusting economic imbalances. This will significantly reduce the risks of a future crisis and enhance crisis management capability. (2009, §II.2: 2)

Unsurprisingly, the proposal faced strong opposition from the United States and despite initial international attention was not pursued further by Zhou. The proposal was, however, part of (and in part instigated) a broader wave of Chinese scholarship exploring alternatives to the dollar-dominated system. Other notable interventions include Ma Guoshu's book *Global Independent Money*, also published in 2009. Ma's interest in, and research on, the subject appears to date back to at least the East Asian Crisis of 1997.

Following on from the title of his book Ma proposes a Global Independent Money (GIM) system. GIM is designed to function as a non-sovereign, global currency system that can coexist with national currencies while offering a more stable, non-inflationary alternative for international trade and finance.

He envisages its establishment through a series of agreements, starting from a 'GIM Founding Community' (this is similar to the coalition of the willing approach we discuss later). The community would consist of participating nations that agree to issue GIM alongside their national currencies, initially in a dual system. As more countries adopt GIM for international settlements, the system would transition into a single global monetary framework. Further Treaties provide the mechanisms for the system: a 'Global Trade Surplus Community Treaty' and 'Global Foreign Exchange Reserve Community Treaty'. These would align global monetary practices and phase out the dependency on sovereign currencies for international reserves. GIM thus intends to provide a comprehensive proposal to address the structural issues in global finance and trade, backed by global trade surpluses. This stands in sharp contrast to a system of separate sovereign states, whose interactions are frequently zero-sum. Instead, it purports to offer win-win based global mechanisms and institutions.

Between 2009 and 2014, several Chinese scholars participated in discussions, including Li Ruogu, Xie Ping and Li Chong, each making their own proposals. By the early 2020s, there were about ninety publications focused on supranational currency and many more on international monetary reform, although the frequency and prominence of these publications declined significantly after 2015. This decline was partly due to the US opposition to international monetary reform, which hindered the dissemination of such ideas abroad. Additionally, China faced a series of domestic financial stability issues that garnered more attention. As a result, Xi Jinping's administration has prioritized national stability and incremental reforms, like renminbi internationalization, over radical changes in global monetary policy.

However, it is worth noting that, according to Elmer's survey, much of the Chinese literature has stressed the importance of worldwide cooperation and inclusivity in order to achieve effective global monetary reform. There is, it seems, a shared pragmatic orientation that includes scope to accommodate US interests and different means to use incremental strategies – such as positioning RMB internationalization as a stepping stone. More latterly, reform proposals have begun to consider the potential inherent in new technologies such as blockchain (underpinning interoperable digital currencies and so on, for international payments). In any case, the material discussed in this section illustrates that there is discussion of relevant issues that many Western readers may be only dimly aware of.

A brief guide to the contributions to the collection and its thematic structure: ICU proposals for the 2020s and 2030s

The purpose of this edited collection is to spark widespread discussion of the ICU concept in the current world-historical context and we provided a bullet point list of why the concept remains highly relevant now at the beginning of this introduction.

Where are we now? In contrast to Chinese policymakers and scholars, global civil society did not become particularly vocal on world monetary reforms during or after the Global Financial Crisis of 2007–9. Despite the brief rise of the Occupy movement at the time of the Global Financial Crisis and despite the rise of various climate movements since then, global civil society remains more marginal than it was in the aftermath of the 1997–8 Asian crisis or the early 2000s; no new worldwide transformative movement has emerged. Politically, it has been mostly nationalist and authoritarian populism that has gained ground (for an explanation, see Patomäki 2021). Warnings about history repeating itself (recession and conflict) raised over the years by many followers of Keynes, and perhaps especially the Brandt Commission, seem, currently at least, to be on the mark. In the 2010s and 2020s, right-wing populists became a major political force, winning elections and entering government. Many have argued that uneven growth, economic oscillations, concentration of resources and power, and related political developments, have been accompanied by declining support for democracy and rising authoritarianism (e.g. Patomäki 2018, 2021; Berberoglu 2021; Levitsky and Ziblatt 2018). While US tariff policy had already violated the basic principles of the WTO during Trump's first administration, his re-election in 2024 and second presidential term that began in 2025 have deepened and intensified the underlying tendencies expressed during that first term.[30]

Trump's tariff strategy in early 2025, for example, has been widely interpreted as ill-conceived and has created high levels of uncertainty in financial markets. The current system allows for the accumulation of surpluses and deficits. To describe trade deficits, irrespective of context, as indicative of exploitation of the United States is odd. The United States played a key role in the creation of, and has had a significant say over, the trajectory of the main international trade and finance institutions that set the rules of the system – the IMF, World Bank and WTO. US geopolitical strategy, with some reservations, encouraged the opening of China, and US corporations led the transfer of production (offshoring) from the United States to elsewhere, including China. Many countries listed for tariffs have a GDP that is far smaller than the United States. They are exporters of commodities and a restricted line of goods, while simultaneously lacking the capacity to import much from a far richer United States. In any case, the United States runs surpluses with many countries on services, including finance. As such, trade deficits are by no means indicative of insidious activity of others and the US's domestic problems are far more a consequence of investment decisions and wealth and income distribution over a long period in which successive administrations have lacked an effective industrial strategy or sufficient infrastructure development. This, however, by no means suggests there is not an evolved geopolitical, trade and financial relations problem with some countries, especially China.

In any case, the erratic approach of the Trump administration to international trade and financial management has underscored a long-term vulnerability of a global financial system that places a national currency at its centre. The credibility of the US government and its institutions matter. While it is unlikely to occur due to isolated actions, the reserve currency status of the United States could face threats if there is sufficient scale and duration of reckless actions.[31] This is especially so because the finance system itself has become an ever more complex ecosystem and this has forced central banks into more complicated and wide-ranging interventions, while also looking to maintain the financial functioning of the state (see Konings 2025).[32] With this in mind, the Trump administration's conduct in early 2025 was profoundly counterproductive. It led immediately to sharp falls in equity markets and fears of inflation and recession. This kind of situation typically leads to a 'flight to safety effect', which essentially means capital shifts into US securities, and if the situation is considered sufficiently dire, this can result in an 'inversion of the yield curve'. At the time of writing, however, yields were rising across the board rather than falling, indicating a sell-off of US securities. Given the context, this was widely received as a danger signal regarding the status of the $ and may have played some role in the pressure placed on Trump to pause his tariffs at that time (though, at the time of writing, the pause is limited temporally and substantially).

Two notable candidates for the effect on US Treasury securities in early April 2025 have been other countries such as China dumping American assets and hedge funds forced to unwind massive positions in US securities. The former speaks to geopolitics and trust, while the latter is indicative of how complex the financial ecosystem has become. The hedge fund 'basis trade' is conducted using repos to build massive 'long positions' combined with short selling futures contracts (IMF 2024: 37–8; Bank of England 2024: 86–8). This is an arbitrage trade with small margins for profitability that requires huge volumes. Just a few hedge funds, perhaps ten, dominate the trade and the positions are highly leveraged and vulnerable to shifting costs of repos, failure to rollover the repo to maintain the long position and changes in margin conditions for futures contracts. If any of these happen, hedge funds are forced to sell into falling markets, amplifying the effect of such falls. Central banks are then forced to act as 'dealer of last resort' and this is indicative of the new functions they have taken on. One might add that repos and derivatives markets have changed the context in which issues such as an ICU might be debated (e.g. some central banks now make widespread use of Forex swaps between themselves for currency operations – and for $ operations this creates an option for a select group of central banks with the Fed that are not available to smaller and poorer nations, see Dafermos et al. 2022). Changes to context, however, have not changed the attractions of an ICU because, at base, dependency on a dominant country and its national currency is deeply problematic for global trade and finance. Self-induced turmoil in markets, moreover, is yet another distraction from major global problems such as the climate crisis.

In late 2025, matters remain open regarding the eventual consequences of the Trump administration. Still, over the last few years, confrontations and conflicts between states have increased and deepened. The world is increasingly divided into camps, which reflect previous world divisions (East-West, North-South etc.), and in the process economic interdependence has become more and more weaponized.

Against this background, the contributions to this edited collection collectively explore several main themes:

- clarifications of the economic-theoretical and normative rationale of and for an ICU
- how the ICU idea could help to put the governance of the world economy on a more rational basis and how it might contribute to overcoming prevailing contradictions and how it might help resolve conflicts
- the possibility that new technologies of money and innovations of finance might facilitate a contemporary clearing system
- the degree to which urgent global problems and risks, such as climate change and ecological breakdown, provide arguments in favour of an ICU
- whether the overall world-historical context is currently favourable to transition to an ICU and whether there is any significant – actual or potential – political support for such a transition, and what this might entail

This last point is one on which a great deal hinges insofar as it brings together elements of all of the others. The underlying question it evokes is, 'are proposals *feasible* and, if so, are proposals *viable*?'. It is worth keeping in mind here as one reads through the contributions that framings of the question can be more or less institutionally conservative and more or less radically transformative, they can demand more of us as a species in our capacity to rationally work towards better or they can deny the very possibility of better. Whatever one decides in relation to this matter, the more ambitious proposals are, then the more acute the problems of political feasibility and justification of the proposed institutional design appear to become.

Following this introduction, in the second chapter 'Keynes versus the Globalists' Jan Kregel initially explores a theme focused on clarifications of the economic-theoretical rationale for the ICU concept. Kregel relies largely on Quinn Slobodian's (2018) history of neoliberalism, according to which neoliberals from the 1920s onwards were primarily concerned with insulating capitalism from democratic control. This involved a strategy of placing global economic governance beyond the reach of national governments and popular sovereignty, using international institutions and legal frameworks to protect the market from political interference. According to Kregel, when Keynes returned to the idea of monetary system reform in the early 1940s, the problem he faced 'was to find a mechanism which allows for diversity of national policy objectives within an institution providing international coordination of domestic policies, without gold as the standard'. In making sense of clearing Kregel pays particular attention to Keynes's 'banking principle'. Thereafter, he discusses the various modifications proposed by Schumacher and Kalecki and Schumacher, stressing the role of national currencies in this alternative plan. The focus on national currencies is brought up to date with a final discussion of the scope for central bank digital currency (CBDC) to enable 'complete bank disintermediation' and Kregel notes that 'The International Monetary Fund could close all country quota accounts and convert to an ICO [International Clearing Office]', a transition that could be combined with the establishment of an instrument to provide additional funding for development.[33]

While Kregel mainly positions an ICU as a technical device (even if this proposal presupposes far-reaching changes in the banking systems of all countries) that can be used to oppose neoliberal globalism, many others see Keynes's mature liberal internationalism (Markwell 2006) or his activities as a planner of the world system (Hirai 2024) as an alternative form of globalism. The possibility and feasibility of a global ICU, of course, forms one of the other main themes in the collection and this is taken up in chapter two. In a contribution entitled 'Regional Clearing Systems: from the European Payments Union to Current Initiatives Confronting Dollar Dominance' Massimo Amato, Luca Fantacci, and Lucio Gobbi explore how the theoretical and political underpinnings of Keynes's ICU proposal were applied at a regional scale in the European Payments Union in the 1950s and then analyse various regional payments systems that are currently being proposed or implemented, and this includes CBDC. They argue that the twin objectives of supporting regional trade growth and reducing exchange rate risk against the dollar are driving solutions based on multilateral payment technologies, both within monetary unions and in the absence of a common currency. They make the point that 'the spirit if not the letter of the ICU can be taken up in the present context through the proliferation of regional compensation schemes, which for the time being develop in a disorganized manner, but which at a later stage might be unified at a higher level'. From this perspective, perhaps the various clearing schemes in Africa, Asia, and Latin America can be viewed as building the kind of infrastructure (know-how, institutions and mechanisms) that can in time contribute to the construction of a global system. While this may not be the intent of those implementing the schemes we might add here that perhaps the interests, ambitions, and actions of actors might result in a broader, unforeseen, and 'rational' outcome in history – a Hegelian 'cunning of history'.[34]

In Chapter 4, 'Towards a New Global Financial Architecture: The Role of Multipolarity, Expanded BRICS and the Global South', Haider A. Khan takes a different but perhaps complementary approach to the theme of feasibility and viability in the context of localized schemes. Drawing on (while leaving the technical and model detail aside) his extensive scenario work on dynamic complex adaptive economic systems Khan argues that as conflicts escalate and the world system moves towards multipolarity, an opportunity exists for the Global South to partially delink from the post-1973 financial architecture and US hegemony. The possibility, he argues, raises the question of how to achieve a synchronized sustainable growth and development regime that is perceived to be fair by all and this invites debate regarding an international clearing union (ICU), and more broadly about a new global financial architecture. For Khan, while the creation of an alternative less asymmetric non-IMF-based architecture for global financial governance has in some ways become a more realistic institutional possibility, the path towards this is unlikely to be rapid. To reiterate, Khan's chief point is that the construction of an expanded BRICS-led supra-regional financial architecture along with regional financial architectures can be a strategic step forward. A new non-aligned movement and construction of pro-people development programmes can thereby become a reality, facilitating the gradual emergence of hybrid regional and new global financial architectures.

Of course, the division of the world into different regional or otherwise partial systems does not guarantee that parties to those systems will have progressive agendas regarding their own citizens or that the relations between the different groupings formed will be cooperative. As such, it does not follow necessarily that regional alternatives will gradually lead to the birth and rise of a new (or re-emergence of an old) global alternative, this time including an ICU. In Chapter 5, 'Resolving the BOP problematic: feasible reforms in the 21st century', Niina Kari and Lauri Holappa adopt a minimal approach to politically feasible global reforms in the contemporary geopolitical context. Their starting point is that current restrictions on policy space induced by the current world monetary system, especially in the form of balance of payments processes, are a strong argument in favour of the continued relevance of Keynes's ICU plan. However, for Kari and Holappa, the power politics of international monetary order make it next to impossible to realize anything like the plans proposed by Keynes, or Kalecki and Schumacher – at least in the foreseeable future. Kari and Holappa see macroeconomic policy autonomy and the space for democratic politics as closely connected and argue that US governments are likely to remain hostile to direct challenges to dollar hegemony (though it remains possible that the United States might itself create conditions for a loss of dollar hegemony). Given this situation they propose making access to dollars easier for less powerful countries victimized by trading asymmetries. They propose doubling (or more) the SDR quotas for low- and middle-income countries and sanctioning excessive surpluses and deficits above a certain income threshold. This framing falls into the category of more or less institutionally conservative in terms of its determinations regarding current feasibility.

The important issue that Kari and Holappa's contribution raises, of course, is that seeking to work within current constraints in terms of the power dynamics of those constraints cedes power over institutional change precisely to those organizational interests liable to resist or subvert even these small changes (in this case mainly at the IMF). As such, Kari and Holoppa's contribution provides a useful companion to Chapter 6, which also raises important questions of power. In this chapter entitled 'International Monetary Adjustment with and without a Global Fiscal Authority', Mathías Vernengo, Nathaniel Cline, and David Fields approach the concept of an ICU with a focus on the differences between the adjustment process in centre and periphery countries, highlighting that the process is asymmetric. They argue that central to the current adjustment process is the ability of the hegemon, which retains the key currency, to act as a global fiscal authority. The cases of the United States and the Eurozone in the aftermath of the Global Financial Crisis are used to illustrate the argument. The main conclusion drawn is that in a crisis period, a supranational fiscal authority with the ability to transfer resources is necessary for promoting a smooth adjustment of the balance of payments. However, something more is needed than just the redistribution of resources between deficit and surplus areas in conditions of spiralling contraction and deflation. Here it must be possible for the system as a whole to go into deficit through institutions that assume some state-like functions. With this in mind, they pursue an economic-theoretical theme and stress that for Keynes, the ICU should be paired with additional international institutions that could regulate global effective demand and organise substantial interregional redistribution. While they discuss throughout the chapter whether a state hegemon (currently the United States) might provide at least some of these functions, in however deficient form, they suggest, following Keynes, that new institutions 'might become the pivot of the future economic government of the world', although they are also quick to question any 'simple analogy between national states and a supranational entity'.

In Chapter 7 'An Analysis of Conflicts and the World Monetary System' Heikki Patomäki argues that despite the obvious need to reform the world monetary and trading system, it appears unreformable and that this involves a vicious circle. However, he takes a different approach to the previous chapters. Using counterfactual analysis, Patomäki makes the case that with the help of appropriate global reforms, contradictions and related negative tendencies could have been mitigated and in some cases absented or overcome. This is used to demonstrate the political possibility of an ICU despite recent history. He then turns to the future in the final section and explores three world monetary system scenarios. The first concerns the expansion of SDRs through the IMF, while the second explores how a global clearing union (GCU) might be achieved through a coalition of willing states. The third scenario focuses on the broader context and its changes – including through severe crises or disasters – that may enable or contribute to the realization of the second scenario. This provides a counterpoint to Kari and Holappa's thinking, a complement to Vernengo, Cline and Field's approach and a somewhat more optimistic take on the prospects of development than Khan.

For Patomäki, new international law and thus new governance systems offer less resistance and thus greater potential than working directly through reform of existing international organizations prone to institutional inertia such as the IMF. Also, Patomäki argues that the Trump II administration's framing of the dollar's reserve status as a burden accelerates concerns about the current monetary order's sustainability. Policies involving tariffs and controls against other countries escalate tensions and weaken multilateral institutions. Yet they are likely to instigate new rounds of discussions and encourage other countries to seek alternative mechanisms. The prevailing rhetoric, the erosion of US monetary hegemony, and the instability caused by trade wars inadvertently strengthen momentum for alternatives, potentially leading to a coalition of willing states establishing a global clearing union.

The difference of emphasis between the contributions so far illustrates that framing and normative commitments affect how an ICU is conceived and contextualized. This is taken up more explicitly in Chapter 8, 'Beyond Monetary Hegemony: Normative Underpinnings of a Global Clearing Union'. In this chapter, Konsta Kotilainen provides a thorough and systematic analysis of the economic-theoretical, ethical and political assumptions behind different ICU proposals. He begins with Keynes's proposal and then explores the assumptions of the Brandt Commission, Davidson and Stiglitz (and Greenwald) and much of this is presaged in our previous discussion, though Kotilainen's contribution is more detailed and comparative and its decomposition of the positions taken bears careful reading. Kotilainen eventually makes a case for a global currency union, but he too finds himself asking whether possibility currently translates into feasibility.

Chapter 9 'Designing the Rules and Principles of the International Clearing Union' by Adrien Faudot takes as its point of departure the claim that 'although the ICU would solve several structural problems of the current USD-dominated international monetary system, the new institutional architecture underlying the ICU induces several major questions'. These questions concern the autonomy of member states, control of cross-border financial flows, the role of the state and economic planning, and whether exchange rates should be fixed. For Faudot, different answers are possible and uncertainty persists regarding developments and consequences. As such an ICU is no panacea and much remains open. More generally, Faudot's chapter forces us to think about the extent to which a functional and viable ICU requires public regulation, control and restrictions.

As editors we would add here that given the uncertainties that might surround any particular ICU, it seems reasonable to advocate experimentation concerning different combinations of institutional arrangements and mechanisms (cf. Honneth 2007: 59, 100, etc.). What will and won't work will depend not just on design but on the appropriateness of design in the context of particular and perhaps changed and changing circumstances. However, there are important existential issues that demand attention. From this perspective, the tenth and final chapter of the book can be read as an important thought experiment, given the rapidly deepening global crises caused by climate change and ecological breakdown.

In 'The Ecor as Global Special Purpose Money: Toward a Green International Monetary System to Finance Sustainable and Just Transition', Nicolás Aguila, Paula Haufe and Joscha Wullweber propose a green version of the ICU. The problem they address is specific: the financial means to pursue a sustainable transformation are very unevenly distributed and proposals to provide finance to the Global South will continue to fall short in ambition unless a new, non-hierarchical international monetary system is created. Their answer to the feasibility problem is that the escalating climate crisis could create a 'critical conjuncture' where the creation of a new type of financing mechanism would become possible. The proposal focuses on a Green World Central Bank (GWCB), creating its own unit of account, the 'ecor'. Its purpose is to provide a source of funding needed to combat the climate crisis and advance the process of mitigation, adaptation and 'just transition' that is not limited by constraints in the existing trade system or by limitations of and dependence on private finance. According to the proposal, the ecor constitutes a global special purpose money similar to Keynes's bancor. Ecors would be created by the GWCB in the act of lending and credited to the GWCB accounts of countries to finance relevant imports. Creation, transfer and crediting would allow for expansionary adjustment of international imbalances and the amount of ecors would adjust elastically to the real requirements of urgent effective responses to climate change and ecological breakdown. Ecors transferred between deficit countries and surplus countries would only be able to be used within the system.

While Aguila, Haufe and Wullweber's proposal is intended to supplement rather than replace the current international monetary system, it is also conceived as a means to take the 'first step in setting up the infrastructure required to completely overcome the current hierarchy'. As such it seems reasonable to ask in closing whether the ecor could be incorporated into other ICU proposals and whether it might play some part in creating acceptance for a broader-based global ICU (back to coalitions of the willing perhaps?). For ecors to function effectively, they must have some meaningful use to both the main exporters of next generation 'green' technologies (capital equipment, etc.) and not just those importing it. There are a whole set of issues that then arise that speak once again to possibility and feasibility of an ICU. There is much to contemplate and further debates to be had, including in the context of possible future institutional experimentation. We hope this edited collection helps to reignite debate and that you find the following contributions thought provoking.

Notes

1 See especially Triffin (1960, 1968); Brandt Commission (1980); Davidson (1992–1993, 2002, 2004); Stiglitz (2006: 245–68); Greenwald and Stiglitz (2010). In this introduction, we outline the basics of these proposals and their contexts, although it should be said that especially Triffin would deserve a more thorough discussion.

2 A long series of policy-institutional and theoretical debates occurred before and after Hume. For example, for domestic discussion in Britain see the Bullionist and Anti-Bullionist debate, and the Banking School and the Currency School debate. For classic critique of the trading system see Bloomfield (1963).

3 And later a dollar hegemony.

4 These plans coincide with the emergence of 'world'-talk evident in terms such as world politics, world economy, world communications, and world order and phenomena such as world exhibitions and world conferences. 'World'-talk provided the basis of world-making projects. The ground for such projects was prepared by conceptual changes based on the Copernican revolution of science and concrete experiences about areas and others outside of Europe. After the industrial-mechanical revolution of the nineteenth century, the new infrastructures of communication and transportation turned the eighteenth- and early nineteenth-century ideas into a practical reality. They facilitated not only the final phase of European imperial expansion in the last decades of the nineteenth century and the first decades of the twentieth century but also enabled the spread of liberal and socialist criticism of Eurocentric imperialism around the world (typically, these ideas took on new context-bound forms in different local or glocal contexts; Helleiner 2023). Visions of common global institutions and talk of a 'new world order' also began to emerge at this time, culminating in Woodrow Wilson's fourteen points in 1918 and the establishment of the League of Nations and the International Labour Organisation (ILO) in 1919.

5 There are a whole set of further issues here regarding the history and philosophy of money that conventionally divide into commodity versus credit theories of money. These may not be especially relevant to the discussion here, but we note – as Keynes and many others did nearly a century ago – a general historical movement away from commodity theories and related practices and institutions towards more generic and abstract theories. In 1971, the United States delinked the dollar and

gold, and since then the world monetary system has relied on fiat money. In terms of theory, the recently developed positioning theory of money by Tony Lawson (2016, 2019: chapter 5; 2022) is in effect a generalization of the credit theory, although it involves criticisms of it as well (see Morgan 2025).

6 Discussion of a return to some form of gold standard was an important constituent in a series of post-war reconstruction conferences (Brussels in 1920, Genoa in 1922 etc.). A new gold exchange standard (whose chief difference was that it was a bullion convertibility system rather than a gold coinage-based system) was in operation by 1925 and eventually broke down in 1931. See Eichengreen (1996: 153–86).

7 For details and a comparison to Keynes's plans, see Faudot and Nenovsky (2023). The initial purpose of the BIS was to oversee the settlement of the First World War reparations.

8 He also wrote for other newspapers and was a contributor to *The Economic Journal* (edited by Keynes) and other academic reviews.

9 Polanyi (2001: 144) emphasizes that the nineteenth-century doctrine of economic liberalism formed a single interdependent whole: 'The utopian springs of the dogma of laissez-faire are but incompletely understood as long as they are viewed separately. The three tenets – competitive labor market, automatic gold standard, and international free trade – formed one whole. The sacrifices involved in achieving any one of them were useless, if not worse, unless the other two were equally secured. It was everything or nothing.'

10 Especially the process of establishing ICU looks similar in both accounts. As Walther Funk states in his July 1940 speech: 'Starting from the methods of bilateral trading already applied there will be a further development in the direction of multilateral trading and of the adjustment of the trade balances of individual countries, so that the various countries can engage in regulated trade relations among themselves through the medium of a clearing house.'

11 For the original proposal see Funk (1940); for brief discussions, Skidelsky (2001: 194–6); Patalano (2023: 307).

12 For a brief but systematic summary of the evolution of their main contents see, Skidelsky (2001: 231–2) and for a full list of all changes see, Keynes (2013: 449–68). See also Toporowksi (2022).

13 For a detailed discussion of their contribution and the context see, Faudot (2021). See also Osityński and Toporowski's (2022) edited collection *International Equilibrium & Bretton Woods*, which examines not only the history of ICU ideas but also the current world economy. It takes a Kaleckian perspective, and brigns together discussion of Keynes and Harry Dexter White (see the next section).

14 Faudot states, 'In subsequent letters to Keynes, Schumacher alluded to the possibility of publishing his proposal in the *Economic Journal*, but Keynes

repeatedly asked him to wait for the release of the official British proposal' (Faudot 2021: 755). Schumacher was German in origin and the first draft of his proposal was written between sessions working in the fields at an internment camp. In the first footnote of the *Economica* version, Schumacher explains the subsequent history of his proposal: 'This study was carried out for the joint Committee of the Nuffield College Reconstruction Survey and the Institute of Statistics, Oxford. It has been in private circulation since November, 1942. An earlier version, entitled Free Access to Trade, was circulated by the Royal Institute of International Affairs in March, 1942.'

15 The latter was originally the International Bank for Reconstruction and Development (IBRD), which is now a part of the World Bank Group, together with the International Development Association (IDA).

16 Many ambiguities and intrigues accompanied the progress of the Bretton Woods meeting. The US dollar was equated with gold and recognized officially as the key currency without the knowledge of Keynes and against the principles of the US-UK Joint Statement of Principles (agreed in April 1944). Although Keynes seems to have accepted the basics of the White Plan months before the BW conference (Hirai 2024: 146–8), it is significant that at the conference White and his staff had complete control over the organization of meetings, scheduling of subjects, rules of procedure, and drafting of all official documentation including daily minutes and the Final Act (Ruggie 1982: 406). As a result, many of the provisions included in the Final Act were not discussed in the meeting. It is also worth noting that in terms of the role of the US dollar, the White Plan was similar to the Funk 1940 plan, in which one national currency – the German mark – serves as the international unit of account (Funk was opposed to anchoring the German mark to gold, although throughout the 1930s and in 1940 there was a clear link between the two).

17 This was a compromise between the White and Keynes plans.

18 He continues, 'Indeed, the United States would come to use its influence abroad in the immediate postwar years, through the Marshall Plan, the Occupation Authorities in Germany and Japan, and its access to transnational labor organizations, for example, to shape outcomes much more directly, by seeking to moderate the structure and political direction of labor movements, to encourage the exclusion of Communist Parties from participation in governments, and generally to discourage collectivist arrangements where possible or at least contain them within acceptable Center-Left bounds' (Ruggie 1982: 394).

19 Little for example, is made of the Kalecki-Schumacher paper. Helleiner (2014: 242) mentions it only briefly but without substantial discussion under the subheading 'Eastern European Perspectives'.

20 See Triffin (1960); the book builds on two earlier articles.

21 In providing context for the Brandt Commission one should also note the role played by the Declaration on the Establishment of a New International Economic Order (UN 1974). This was a culmination of the long process of decolonization, which in turn was interwoven with the world-making project of collective self-reliance inspired or led by figures such as Mahatma Gandhi, Julius Nyerere and Mao Zedong. For what remains an excellent analysis of the ideologies behind the NIEO see Cox (1979). For discussion of the world-making project of collective self-reliance, the heyday of which was between 1955–79, see Alker (1981); Getachew (2019). For a recent exposition of the world-historical context of the Brandt Commission see Lees (2021: 85–7).

22 The idea was also that this system could connect existing regional arrangements, such as the European Monetary System. The European Monetary System was a system of fixed but variable exchange rates between several EU member states. It operated from 1979 to 1999, when it was replaced by the European Monetary Union.

23 Prior to 1981, the SDR was a mandatory bond of sorts, of which the central banks of IMF member states each held a specific amount. Since then the requirement to maintain SDRs has been relaxed, and the unit has consequently become less important, despite rounds of issues of new SDRs.

24 The report proposes that if the IMF demands deflationary structural adjustments from a state in exchange for loans, the onus is on the organization itself to show that these are justified. It must assume responsibility for the effects of these measures on solvency, income distribution, employment and social services. Furthermore, irrespective of the content of the conditions, the time allowed for implementing the adjustments must be sufficiently long (the use of a year as the basic time-unit of economic processes is arbitrary and highly problematic).

25 As a British 1980 Overseas Development Institute Briefing Paper (ODI 1980) states (and likely overstates): 'Very few of the [Brandt's Commission's] proposals are new and in fact most have been suggested in earlier international fora. For example, the influence of UNCTAD IV is evident in the proposals covering international trade in commodities and manufactures or the issue of the transfer of technology. Equally, the UN declaration on the New International Economic Order (NIEO) has clearly provided a rich source for many of the BC's proposals. The BC's recommendations also reflect the central theme of NIEO which was the need for a restructuring of existing international institutions toward greater participation by the LDCs in management and decision-making processes. The BC suggests institutional reforms to existing world organizations such as the IBRD and the IMF as well as new arrangements to meet the central objective of a transfer of greater power to the South. The uniqueness of the BC report therefore lies in its central theme of "mutuality of interest" which is claimed to be a concept capable of revitalizing the flagging North-South negotiations.'

26 Visit: https://www.nobelprize.org/prizes/economic-sciences/2001/summary/

27 The idea of global civil society emerged in the 1980s on par with the internet, and the term came into use in the early 1990s. The rise of the anti- and alter-globalization movement was also preceded by a proliferation of local and national protests against neoliberal policies. New campaigns, networks, and organizations were formed, and many were subsequently involved in the World Social Forum, which first met in Porto Alegre, Brazil, in 2001, and has organized subsequent meetings in the Global South in most years into the mid-2020s. See Pleyers (2011) and for a summary, Pleyers (2013). For a discussion on the difference between anti- and alter-globalization, and for an argument that a quick shift occurred in the early 2000s toward the latter, Pinsky (2010). The first moment of the movement turned out to be fleeting as its peak was during the late 1990s and early 2000s (it continues to exist). As we have summarized elsewhere (Patomäki and Morgan 2023: 591–2), there was a neoconservative turn in world history. George W. Bush took office in January 2001 and 9–11 happened eight months later. Both started to dominate the agenda of world politics from 2002 onwards. The global war on terror and neo-imperial tendencies captured the attention of the global media and many politicians instead of globalization struggles. The economic summits were taken to places where the protesters could not reach, such as Doha, Qatar. Several key NGOs active in global civil society came from Western Europe and often they were at least partly dependent on funding from public and private sources. Neoliberalism began to affect this too: funding criteria became increasingly about standard metrics, value for money and establishing simple goals, often involving identifying what would be achieved before anything had really been done. Big charities such as the Ford Foundation followed suit adopting a short-term project format, strict and laborious reporting, public-private 'partnerships', and the like. Many states downsized funding to civil society organizations. After a delay of a few years, these changes began to affect the movement and contributed to its decline, while the movement was also encumbered by internal conflicts and contradictions, especially the lack of agency in the WSF.

28 For example, the BRICS organization convened its first formal meeting in 2009 and in that year, the governor of China's central bank, Zhou Xiaochuan (2009), put forth a high-level proposal to replace the US dollar as the primary global reserve currency with a supranational reserve currency. However, the United States ignored the proposal, and it was eventually dropped. This encouraged China to pursue more targeted alternatives with trading partners in order to bypass dependence on the dollar.

29 For the English version published in the *BIS Review* visit: https://www.bis.org/review/r090402c.pdf

30 Donald Trump's tariff policies during his first presidency (2017–21) were widely seen as conflicting with several World Trade Organization (WTO)

rules and the spirit of international trade treaties. These rules and principles include multilateralism, the most-favoured-nation (MFN), and commitment to 'bound' tariffs (maximum rates). In his first term, the Trump administration also overstretched the national security exception and undermined the dispute settlement system of the WTO. During Donald Trump's second term, the United States has continued and intensified the trade war. With an ever more aggressive stance, there are now, in 2025, several ongoing and intensified violations of WTO rules and international trade principles.

31 A point made long ago by Susan Strange, among others.

32 The argument is shared by many who have taken an interest in financialization, hedge funds, private equity and the changing role of central banks.

33 See also Kazi and Haglund (2024).

34 This is not meant to be taken literally. G. W. F. Hegel developed the idea of the cunning of reason ('List der Vernunft') in his *Lectures on the Philosophy of History* (of which only the introduction and one part have been published in English). On the one hand, Hegel believed that some kind of divine spirit guides history, but on the other hand, his dialectic also develops a particular account of the logic of collective learning and its institutional counterparts. Systems and history are open, but world history is indeed based also on learning. For comments on Hegel from this perspective see Patomäki, (2022: 103–9; 2023: 90, 107–8).

References

Alker, Hayward R. (1981), 'Dialectical Foundations of Global Disparities', *International Studies Quarterly*, 25 (1): 69–98, available at https://www.jstor.org/stable/2600211.

Baker, P. Andrew, and Jamie Morgan. (2021), 'From the Political Economy of Financial Regulation and Economic Governance to Climate Change: An interview with Andrew P. Baker', *Real-World Economics Review*, 98: 170–203. http://www.paecon.net/PAEReview/issue98/BakerMorgan98.pdf.

Bank of England. (2024), *Financial Stability Report*, London: Bank of England, Financial Policy Committee, November. https://www.bankofengland.co.uk/financial-stability-report/2024/november-2024.

Berberoglu, Berch, ed. (2021), *The Global Rise of Authoritarianism in the 21st Century. Crisis of Neoliberal Globalization and the Nationalist Response*, London and New York: Routledge.

Bloomfield, Arthur. (1963), *Short-Term Capital Movements Under the Pre-1914 Gold Standard*, Princeton: Princeton University.

Bollard, Alan. (2020), *Economists at War. How a Handful of Economists Helped Win and Lose the World Wars*, Oxford: Oxford University Press.

Brandt Commission. (1980), *Report of the Independent Commission on International Development Issues. North-South: A Programme for Survival*, London: Pan Books.

Cox, Robert. (1979), 'Ideologies and the New International Economic Order: Reflections on Some Recent Literature', *International Organization*, 33 (2): 257–302, available at https://www.jstor.org/stable/2706612.

Dafermos, Yannis, Daniela Gabor, and Jo Michell. (2022), 'FX Swaps, Shadow Banks and the Global Dollar Footprint', *Economy and Space*, 55 (4): 949–68.

Davidson, Paul. (1992–3), 'Reforming the World's Money', *Journal of Post Keynesian Economics*, 15 (2): 153–79.

Davidson, Paul. (2002), *Financial Markets, Money and the Real World*, Cheltenham: Edward Elgar.

Davidson, Paul. (2004), 'The Future of the International Financial System', *Journal of Post Keynesian Economics*, 26 (4): 591–605.

Eichengreen, Barry. (1996), *Golden Fetters: The Gold Standard and the Great Depression, 1919–1939*, Oxford: Oxford University Press.

Elmer, Keegan. (2025), 'Supranational Currencies: Chinese Solutions to the Problem of Dollar Dominance. The Rise and Fall of Chinese Global Currency Reform Discussions after the Great Financial Crisis', Helsinki Centre for Global Political Economy Working Paper, 07/2025. Helsinki: University of Helsinki, available at https://www.helsinki.fi/en/networks/global-political-economy/working-papers.

Faudot, Adrien. (2021), 'The Keynes Plan and Bretton Woods Debates: The Early Radical Criticisms by Balogh, Schumacher and Kalecki', *Cambridge Journal of Economics*, 45 (4): 751–69, DOI: 10.1093/cje/beab018.

Faudot, Adrien, and Nikolay Nenovsky. (2023), 'Edgard Milhaud and the Case for Establishing an International Clearing Union in the 1930s: A Forgotten Forerunner of Keynes?', *Journal of the History of Economic Thought*, DOI: 10.1017/S1053837223000391.

Fine, Ben. (2024), *Economics Imperialism and Interdisciplinarity: Before the Watershed. Critical Reconstructions of Political Economy Volume 1*, Leiden: Brill (Studies in Critical Social Sciences).

Funk, Walther. (1940), 'The Economic Reorganization of Europe'. A speech given on July 25, 1940, available at https://web.archive.org/web/20180118071947/http://www4.dr-rath-foundation.org/brussels_eu/roots/06_economic_reorganization_europe.html.

Gerstle, Gary. (2022), *The Rise and Fall of the Neoliberal Order. America and the World in the Free Market Era*, Oxford: Oxford University Press.

Getachew, Adom. (2019), *Worldmaking After Empire. The Rise and Fall of Self-Determination*, Princeton, NJ: Princeton University Press.

Greenwald, Bruce, and E. Stiglitz Joseph. (2010), 'Towards A New Global Reserve System', *Journal of Globalization and Development*, 1 (2): 1–24.

Helleiner, Eric. (2014), *Foundations of Bretton Woods. International Development and the Making of the Postwar Order*, Ithaca, NY: Cornell University Press.

Helleiner, Eric. (2023), *The Contested World Economy. The Deep and Global Roots of International Political Economy*, Cambridge: Cambridge University Press.

Hirai, Toshiaki. (2024), *Keynes as an Economist, World System Planner and Social Philosopher. Economic Theory and Policy*, Cham: Palgrave Macmillan.

Hofmann, Reto. (2017), 'The Fascist New–Old Order', *Journal of Global History*, 12 (2): 166–83, DOI: 10.1017/S1740022817000031.

Honneth, Axel. (2017) *The Idea of Socialism: Toward a Renewal*. New York: Wiley

IMF. (2024), *Global Financial Stability Report, The Last Mile: Financial Vulnerabilities and Risks*, Washington DC: IMF, April. https://www.imf.org/en/Publications/GFSR/Issues/2024/04/16/global-financial-stability-report-april-2024.

Independent Commission on International Developmental Issues. (1980), *Report of the Independent Commission on International Development Issues. North-South: A Programme for Survival*, London: Pan Books, A summary of the report is available at http://www.stwr.org/special-features/the-brandt-report.html (accessed 16 August 2024).

Kalecki, Michał, and E. F. Schumacher. (1943), 'International Clearing and Long-Term Lending', *Bulletin of the Oxford Institute of Statistics*, 5(Supplement), August: 29–33.

Kazi, Dani, and Alec Haglund. (2024), *Beyond Dollar Dominance: New Money and Payment Systems for a Multipolar World*, London: Positive Money, December.

Keynes, J. M. (1930), *Treatise on Money. Volume 2: The Applied Theory of Money*, London: Macmillan, available at https://archive.org/details/in.ernet.dli.2015.150075.

Keynes, J. M. (1969/1942), 'Proposals for an International Currency (or Clearing) Union [February 11, 1942]', 9–18 in J. Horsefield (ed), (1969) *The International Monetary Fund 1945 1965. Twenty Years of International Monetary Cooperation, Volume III: Documents*, Washington DC: IMF.

Keynes, J. M. (2013), *The Collected Writings of John Maynard Keynes. Activities 1940–1944. Shaping the Post-War World: The Clearing Union, XXV*, ed. Donald Moggridge, Cambridge: Cambridge University Press.

Kindleberger, Charles. (1973), *The World in Depression, 1929–1939*, London: Allen Lane.

Kindleberger, Charles. (1984), *A Financial History of Western Europe*, London: Routledge.

Kohr, Leopold. (1980), 'Tribute to E. F. Schumacher', The Internet Archive (Wayback Machine, entry 'About E. F. Schumacher'), available at https://web.archive.org/web/20071011020125/http://www.schumacher.org.uk/about_efschumacher.htm.

Konings, Martijn. (2025), *The Bailout State; Why Governments Rescue Banks, Not People*, Cambridge: Polity.

Lawson, Tony. (2016), 'Social Positioning and the Nature of Money', *Cambridge Journal of Economics*, 40 (4): 961–96, DOI: https://doi.org/10.1093/cje/bew006.

Lawson, Tony. (2019), *The Nature of Social Reality: Issues in Social Ontology*, London: Routledge.

Lawson, Tony. (2022), 'Two Conceptions of the Nature of Money: Clarifying Differences Between MMT and Money Theories Sponsored by Social Positioning Theory', *Real-World Economics Review* 15 September 2022: 2–19, available at https://www.paecon.net/PAEReview/issue101/Lawson101.pdf.

Lees, Nicholas. (2021), 'The Brandt Line After Forty Years: The More North–South Relations Change, the More They Stay the Same?', *Review of International Studies*, 47 (1): 85–106, DOI: 10.1017/S026021052000039X.

Levitsky, Steven, and Daniel Ziblatt. (2018), *How Democracies Die. What History Reveals about our Future*, London: Penguin.

Markwell, Donald. (2006), *John Maynard Keynes and International Relations. Economic Paths to War and Peace*, Oxford: Oxford University Press.

Mead, W. R. (1989), 'American Economic Policy in the Antemillenial Era', *World Policy Journal*, 6 (3): 385–468.

Morgan, Jamie. (2022), 'Macroprudential Institutionalism: The Bank of England's Financial Policy Committee and the Contemporary Limits of Central Bank Policy', in P. Hawkins and I. Negru (eds), *Monetary Economics, Banking and Policy: Expanding Economic thought to Meet Contemporary Challenges*, 9–25, London: Routledge.

Morgan, Jamie. (2024), 'Economics Imperialism Then and Now: Ben Fine on the Changing Relationship Between Economics and the Other Social Sciences', *Contributions to Political Economy*, 43 (1): 215–48.

Morgan, Jamie. (2025, forthcoming), 'The Historical Context of the Experience of Money and the Road less travelled: the History of Economic Thought, Dennis Robertson's Money, the Thing Positioned and the Positioned Thing.' *Cambridge Journal of Economics*.

ODI. (1980), Overseas Development Institute Briefing Paper No:2 March 1980, available at https://alor.org/Storage/Library/PDF/Brandt_Commission.pdf (accessed 16 August 2024).

Osityński, Jerzy, and Jan Toporowski, eds. (2022), *International Equilibrium & Bretton Woods. Kalecki's Alternative to Keynes & White and Its Consequences*, Oxford: Oxford University Press.

Patalano, Rosario. (2023), 'International Clearing System as Alternative Monetary Order', *The European Journal of the History of Economic Thought*, 30 (2): 299–331, DOI: 10.1080/09672567.2023.2178477.

Patomäki, Heikki. (2001), *Democratising Globalisation. The Leverage of the Tobin Tax*, London and New York: Zed Books.

Patomäki, Heikki. (2008), *The Political Economy of Global Security. War, Future Crises and Changes in Global Governance*, London and New York: Routledge.

Patomäki, Heikki. (2009), 'Neoliberalism and the Global Financial Crisis', *New Political Science*, 31 (4): 431–42.

Patomäki, Heikki. (2018), *Disintegrative Tendencies in Global Political Economy: Exits and Conflicts*, London and New York: Routledge.

Patomäki, Heikki. (2021), 'Neoliberalism and Nationalist-Authoritarian Populism: Explaining Their Constitutive and Causal Connections', *Protosociology. An International Journal of Interdisciplinary Research*, 37: 101–51, DOI: https://doi.org /10.5840/protosociology2020376.

Patomäki, Heikki. (2022), *The Three Fields of Global Political Economy*, Abingdon and New York: Routledge.

Patomäki, Heikki. (2023), *World Statehood. The Future of World Politics*, Cham: Springer.

Patomäki, Heikki, and Jamie Morgan. (2023), 'World Politics, Critical Realism and the Future of Humanity: An Interview with Heikki Patomäki, Part 1', *Journal of Critical Realism*, 22 (3): 562–603, DOI: 10.1080/14767430.2023.2188527.

Pinsky, Marian. (2010), 'From Reactive to Proactive: The World Social Forum and the Anti-/Alter-Globalization Movement', *McGill Sociological Review*, 1: 3–28, available at https://www.mcgill.ca/msr/volume1/article1.

Pleyers, Geoffrey. (2011), *Alter-Globalization: Becoming Actors in a Global Age*, Cambridge: Polity.

Pleyers, Geoffrey. (2013), 'A Brief History of the Alter-Globalization Movement', trans. J. Zvesper, *booksandideas.net*, 20 June 2013, https://booksandideas.net/A-Brief-History -of-the-Alter.

Polanyi, Karl. (2001), *The Great Transformation. The Political and Economic Origins of Our Time*, Foreword by J. Stiglitz and a new introduction by F. Block, Boston, MA: Beacon Press. (Originally published in 1944)

Ruggie, G. John. (1982), 'International Regimes, Transactions, and Change: Embedded Liberalism in the Postwar Economic Order', *International Organization*, 36 (2): 379–415.

Schumacher, E. F. (1943), 'Multilateral Clearing', *Economica*, 10 (38): 150–16.

Skidelsky, Robert. (2001), *John Maynard Keynes. Fighting for Britain 1937–1946*, London: Papermac (Macmillan).

Slobodian, Quinn. (2018), *Globalists: The End of Empire and the Birth of Neoliberalism*, Cambridge, MA: Harvard University Press.

Steil, Benn. (2013), *The Battle of Bretton Woods. John Maynard Keynes, Harry Dexter White, and the Making of a New World Order*, Princeton, NJ: Princeton University Press.

Stiglitz, E. Joseph. (2003), 'Dealing with Debt. How to Reform the Global Financial System', *Harvard International Review*, 25 (1): 54–9, available at https://business .columbia.edu/sites/default/files-efs/pubfiles/1435/1435.2.pdf.

Stiglitz, E. Joseph. (2006), *Making Globalization Work. The Next Steps to Global Justice*, London: Allen Lane.

Toporowski, Jan. (2022), 'Kalecki and the Problem of International Money', in J. Osityński and J. Toporowski (eds), *International Equilibrium & Bretton Woods*.

Kalecki's Alternative to Keynes & White and Its Consequences, 58–71, Oxford: Oxford University Press.

Triffin, Robert. (1960), *Gold and the Dollar Crisis*, New Haven, CT: Yale University Press.

Triffin, Robert. (1968), *Our International Monetary System: Yesterday, Today, and Tomorrow*, New York: Random House.

UN. (1974), Declaration on the Establishment of a New International Economic Order, UN. General Assembly (6th special sess. 1974), Resolution No: 3201 (S. VI), available at file:///C:/Users/heikk/Downloads/A_RES_3201(S-VI)-EN-1.pdf.

Wionczek, Miguel. (1981), 'The Brandt Report', *Third World Quarterly*, 3 (1): 104–18, DOI: 10.1080/01436598108419547.

Xiaochuan, Zhou. (2009), 'Reform the International Monetary System', *BIS Review* 41/2009, available at https://www.bis.org/review/r090402c.pdf (retrieved 18 August 2024).

2

Keynes versus the globalists

From the gold standard to currency clearing to stabilization funds to digital currency clearing

Jan Kregel

Introduction: Keynes versus the globalists

From the beginning of his career, Keynes analysed and proposed reforms of the international financial system. In his early and most popular book, the 1919 *Economic Consequences of the Peace*, he noted that

> the principle of accumulation based on inequality was a vital part of the pre-war order of society and of progress as we then understood it . . . which it may be impossible to re-create. . . . The war has disclosed the possibility of consumption to all and the vanity of abstinence to many . . . the labouring classes may be no longer willing to forgo so largely, and the capitalist classes, no longer confident of the future, may seek to enjoy more fully their liberties of consumption so long as they last, and thus precipitate the hour of their confiscation. (Keynes 1971a: 11–13)

Keynes identified the characteristics of the 'principle of accumulation' as

> interference of frontiers and of tariffs was reduced to a minimum . . . The various currencies . . . all maintained on a stable basis in relation to gold and to one another, facilitated the easy flow of capital and of trade to an extent the full value of which we only realise now, when we are deprived of its advantages. Over this great area there was an almost absolute security of property and of person. (1971a: 9)

While Keynes predicted that it might be 'impossible to re-create' this system, the recent work of Quinn Slobodian (2018: 9–10) notes that a group of economists which he calls the 'Geneva School' Globalists moved quickly to retain these economic policies despite the change in the political landscape designed in Versailles. This movement, which was active well before the better-known Mount Pelerin initiative promoting neoliberal free market policies after the Second World War considered that the commitments in the Treaty 'to national sovereignty and autonomy were dangerous if taken seriously'. These neoliberal Globalists 'were stalwart critics of national sovereignty, believing that after empire, nations must remain embedded in an international institutional order that safeguarded capital and protected its right to move throughout the world. The cardinal sin of the twentieth century was the belief in unfettered national independence, and the neoliberal world order required enforceable isonomy – or 'same law', as Hayek would later call it – against the illusion of autonomy, or 'own law'. They envisaged the global political economy as 'partitioned into bounded, territorial states where governments ruled over human beings . . . and the world of property, where people owned things, money, and land scattered across the earth'. 'In this latter world the ubiquity of foreign investment had made it routine for people to own all or part of enterprises in countries where they were not citizens and had never even set foot. Money worked almost anywhere and could be exchanged into and out of major currencies at the fixed rates of the gold standard. Contracts were enforced universally by written and unwritten codes of business conduct'. It was not the role of nation-states to democratically attempt to formulate economic policy that would rewrite the laws of free market global capitalism.

Keynes, on the other hand, doubted the possible resurrection of the gold standard and global free trade and capital flows, based on his analysis of the economic impossibility of Germany satisfying the reparations enshrined in the Treaty and the problems created by the resolution of inter-Allied war indebtedness. It is not necessary to refer to the inconsistent national objectives of the French, British, Italian and Chinese governments concerning reparations to appreciate Keynes's assessment that they were politically incompatible with the restoration of the pre-war 'principle of accumulation' that the Geneva School sought to reestablish.

Indeed the use of monetary policy in support of restoration of the gold standard in the presence of free global international capital flows in the 1920s produced the financial instability in Austria and Germany and the New York Stock market crash which ushered in the 1930s Great Depression, the emergence of the Axis national-socialist governments who offered national policy autonomy and escape from the consequences of the 'non-state sphere' of economic governance promoted by the Globalists (Slobodian 2018: 10).

For Keynes, the debt and reparations problems generated what came to be called the 'transfer problem' and recognition of the deflationary impact of the adjustment process for international imbalances under the prevailing global financial system. Keynes continued to work on these issues in his *Tract of Monetary Reform*, which supported implementation of a system of nationally managed money in the absence of adherence to gold, and in the *Treatise on Money* (1971b) that outlined a process of global coordination under a system of supranational coordination of central banks' monetary policy.

Keynes versus Funk's new economic order

Keynes's *General Theory* had largely ignored these international financial issues, but in the 1940s his attention was drawn to discussions of the reform of the international financial system, provoked by the need to provide a public alternative to the ideas that were being broadcast by the German Minister of Foreign Affairs and President of the Reichsbank, Walther Funk, outlining the Nazi plan for a 'New Order'. The propaganda message of the German proposal was one of providing the income and employment growth that had been absent in the 1930s Depression and in which 'gold will have no place in the New World Order'.

When charged by the British Minister of Information to provide the Allies alternative to the German proposal, Keynes paradoxically replied that 'If Funk's plan is taken at its face value, it is excellent and just what we ourselves ought to be doing' (Keynes 1971c: 2).

On the basis of his analysis in the *Economic Consequences of the Peace*, Keynes had become a well-known critic of the Globalists return to liberal global trade and finance under the pre-war gold standard and had publicly opposed Britain's return to the gold standard in 1925. In simple terms, Keynes's argument was that the gold standard in the presence of free global capital flows required a monetary policy that was aligned with global standards since any attempt by national governments to use economic policy to support domestic policy objectives such as full employment would lead to capital inflows and outflows that would put pressure on gold reserves and policy reversal. Keynes thought the Geneva School evaluation of the benefits of such a system to be politically untenable.

The German New Order was clearly inspired by Hjalmar Schacht who resigned as president of the Reichsbank in 1939 to be replaced by Funk but maintained a position as minister without portfolio until 1943. Indeed, Keynes shared Schacht's views on international finance as a result of his analysis of the difficulties facing the German government in making reparations after the Treaty of Versailles. Thus, in 1940, Keynes was clearly opposed to any official propaganda response to the German proposals that might counter the German proposal by promising a return to the pre-war financial system based on gold.

His eventual response was to envisage an alternative international financial system without gold and a mechanism for international trade and payments adjustment that provided national autonomy over domestic policy. In one of the first publications on the issue, Keynes (1971c: 3) refers to the bilateral 'clearing' agreement between Spain and the United Kingdom,[1] noting that in addition to a traditional clearing in which 'everything which Spain sold to England would have to be spent in England' the existence of the sterling area as a counterpart 'provides advantages since Spain can use its claims for imports in any country using Sterling and to acquire imports from third countries who have acquired goods from the sterling area'. Thus, Keynes provides the embryo of a system without gold based on limited multilateral clearing between Spain and the Sterling Area.

Keynes identifies the 'underlying idea' taken from Schacht and Funk's interwar trading controls that imposed bilateral clearing of trade balances in the proposition that 'free trade depends on international trade being carried on by means of what is, in effect, barter' (Keynes 1971c: 8). But, he noted that the problem that has to be solved in such a system is 'maintaining equilibrium in the balance of payments between countries [which] has never been solved, since methods of barter gave way to the use of money and bills of exchange'. And he goes on to note that there is no reason to believe that the operation of currency 'laissez faire' would provide an 'automatic mechanism' of adjustment to equilibrium. 'The clue to the nature of any alternative which is to be successful is to recognize that a freely convertible international standard' 'throws the main burden of adjustment on the country which is in the debtor position on the international balance of payments – that is on the country which is by hypothesis the weaker and above all the smaller in comparison with the other side of the scales which . . . is the rest of the world' (1971c: 27).

Keynes not only questioned whether the mechanism would be automatic but suggested that it would be disequilibrating since, in the period 'preceding the present war, complete degeneration set in and capital funds flowed from countries of which the balance of trade was adverse into countries where it was favourable. This became, in the end, the major cause of instability'. Since this is just the opposite of what would be required to restore equilibrium

Keynes (1971c: 31) concludes: 'Nothing is more certain than the movements of capital funds must be regulated – which in itself will involve far-reaching departures from *laissez-faire* arrangements.' Thus, Keynes considered that what has been called 'asymmetric adjustment' in the presence of laissez-faire global capital markets under the gold standard as the main explanation of the failure of the system to maintain or automatically restore external equilibrium.

Since imbalance involves positions by both debtors and creditors, adjustment will require compatible action from both; the successful system should provide for action to adjust from both. This would involve deficit countries introducing policies to expand exports or reduce imports and surplus countries to increase imports or reduce exports. The asymmetry occurs if deficit countries cannot expand exports because surplus countries are unwilling to increase imports, they cannot meet existing service or repayment of debts incurred to the surplus countries. In the absence of the ability to roll over or default on the debt representing the external deficit, only policy to reduce national income is available, while the surplus countries need to take no action and indeed often take actions to prevent return to balance such as protection of domestic markets. Exactly the problem of German reparations: if Germany were to pay France indemnities, it would have to earn francs by selling exports to France, but this could not occur if France's national policy objective was protection of its domestic producers from competition from German imports. In such conditions, the alternative for Germany would be to import less, which required a reduction in domestic demand and employment for an already destitute population. Further, as Keynes had argued in the 1919 book, Germany required imports to support the domestic population and to provide the materials for export production. Imports and exports are complements not substitutes.

The problem could be partially alleviated by viewing adjustments globally, within a multilateral payments system, avoiding the bilateral reparations that caused political problems in Versailles. Clearly, Keynes's analysis of the operation of the pre-war system was in direct opposition to that of the Geneva School Globalists. From this point of view the problem Keynes faced was to find a mechanism which allows for diversity of national policy objectives within an institution providing international coordination of domestic policies, without gold as the standard. The management of external balances would also require management of international capital flows. Something similar to what is currently presented as 'subsidiarity' in the European Union without the ECU.

Keynes's banking principle approach to currency clearing

The key to Keynes's solution has generally been overlooked in public and academic discussions of the clearing proposal: it is Keynes's modest claim for his proposal as simply the application of an already common banking practice on the national level to the international level, what Keynes called the 'banking principle'. 'The idea underlying such a Currency Union is simple, namely, to generalise the essential principle of banking, as it is exhibited within any closed system.' This principle is the necessary equality of credits and debits, of assets and liabilities. If no credits can be removed outside the clearing system but only transferred within it, the Union itself can never be in difficulties. It can with safety make what advances it wishes to any of its members with the assurance that the proceeds can only be transferred to the clearing account of another member. Its problem is solely to see to it that its members keep the rules and that the advances made to each of them are prudent and advisable for the Union as a whole.

> In short, the analogy with a national banking system is complete. No depositor in a local bank suffers because the balances, which he leaves idle, are employed to finance the business of someone else. Just as the development of national banking systems served to offset a deflationary pressure which would have prevented otherwise the development of modern industry, so by extending the same principle into the international field we may hope to offset the contractionist pressure which might otherwise overwhelm in social disorder and disappointment the good hopes of our modern world. (Keynes 1969: 4)

The elaboration of this view is reflected in the opening sentences of the first chapter of Keynes's *Treatise on Money*,

> Money-of-Account, namely that in which Debts and Prices and General Purchasing Power are expressed, is the primary concept of a Theory of Money. A money of account comes into existence along with debts, which are contracts for deferred payment, and price lists, which are offers of contracts for sale or purchase. . . . Money itself, namely that by delivery of which debt contracts and price contracts are discharged, and in the shape of which a store of general purchasing power is held, derives its character from its relationship to the money of account, since the debts and prices must first have been expressed in terms of the latter. (Keynes 1971b: 3)

The 'introduction of a money of account gives rise to two derived categories – offers of contracts, contracts and acknowledgments of debt, which are in terms of it, and money proper, answering to it, delivery of which will discharge the contract or the debt'. This leads to

> [. . .] the discovery that for many purposes the acknowledgments of debt are themselves a serviceable substitute for money proper in the settlement of transactions. When acknowledgments of debt are used in this way, we may call them bank money – not forgetting, however, that they are not money proper. Bank money is simply an acknowledgment of a private debt, expressed in the money of account, which is used by passing from one hand to another, alternatively with money proper, to settle a transaction. (1971b: 5)

This bank money of account is liberated from any physical or commodity form and reflects what Luigi Einaudi (2006) has called 'imaginary money'. This bank money of account may serve as money proper when it is the object of action of bankers 'entering debits and credits in their clients' accounts'. Bankers managing clients' accounts denominated in money of account thus replace gold or bank notes as the 'primary concepts' of monetary theory and substitute for the quantity theory of prices.

This representation of the financial system thus evokes bankers' clients' balance sheets showing debts and credits denominated in a common money of account and a system of transactions based on the banker employing multilateral netting across client accounts. These operations were straightforward when transactions were between clients with accounts in the same bank. With a financial system comprised of multiple banks, transactions between clients with accounts in different banks required an arrangement allowing multiple bankers to settle their clients' net transactions across banks. The problem was resolved by the creation of bankers' clearing houses that grew up in all major financial centres. Keynes's post-war clearing proposal based on the banking principle thus posits a global clearing house in the form of a Currency Union, with individual member-nations' accounts represented by their current account debit and credit balances denominated in a common, notional, unit of account – bancor. No physical or physical commodity currency was required, neither were bank capital or bank reserves required in such a system. Only a consistent common recording of member-countries' external account transactions.

Such a system clearly satisfied the condition of eliminating gold from the system. All that was required was fixing the ratios of the member states national currencies in terms of the single unit of account – bancor. It was also symmetric since every debit entry in bancor gave rise to an automatic credit entry in terms of unit of account. Instead of a surplus country hoarding their balance in gold causing a reduction in deficit country exports, there was a credit balance that financed the deficit countries level of activity. In the absence of autonomous changes in domestic policies to support adjustment Keynes added a process of encouragement in the form of penalties the be applied when members exceeded preagreed limits on the size of individual surpluses and deficits.

A radical system or just scaling up: response to clearing

Despite Keynes's argument that this was simply a global application of principles already applicable in every banking system, most considered it radical because of the use of the single notional unit of account to evaluate the net balances which were converted from national currency values at fixed rates. But this was not the most important point. As Paul Einzig (1944) pointed out, bancor could not be traded in private financial markets and only represented the metric of inter-country indebtedness. National money could only be traded domestically, and Keynes's system would have eliminated one of the major activities of international banks – foreign exchange trading.[2]

J. W. Beyen (1951: 145) also pointed out that in the conditions of post-war reconstruction, '[t]he United States under the Clearing Union system might have found itself, under an unfavourable development, the owner of all the bancor issued by the Union and therefore would theoretically have entered into a commitment equal to the total sum of all the quotas. The Clearing Union was declared, for that reason, unacceptable to the United States'.

It was also viewed as presenting the risk of inflation again in the event of an unfavourable development, due to a large increase in the creation of global bancor credit. The problem is the distribution of the imbalances in the system. The system may be in global balance with debits equal to credits, but this does not mean all countries are in balance. If all countries are individually in balance, there is no net bancor creation. If one country is in deficit, the net bancor created is equal to that country's deficit (within its permitted maximum limit). However, if n-1 of the countries are in deficit with the nth country in surplus, the net bancor creation will be n-1 times the permitted limits of each country, representing the entire credit to the nth country. This is the condition referred to by Beyen and represents conditions of dollar scarcity which were thought to be a permanent condition of the post-war economy. The US Congress would clearly be hostile to a system of financing the entire European reconstruction. However, note that this is more or less what, in the event, did occur after Churchill's 'Iron Curtain' speech generated the Marshall Plan!

Bankers and orthodox economists had similar reactions. Criticisms from these sources reflected more than a doctrinaire commitment to laissez-faire and hostility to the latest economic theories. They also marked a renewal of the friction that characterized relations between the New Deal and Wall Street during the 1930s. Bankers, many of whom were Republicans, had not forgotten that Roosevelt vigorously attacked the 'malefactors of great wealth' and the 'privileged princes' to consolidate his political majority and then employed his legislative majority to regulate and reform the financial community – separating commercial from investment banking, invalidating gold payment clauses in private contracts, and devaluing the dollar. Harry C. Carr, president of the First National Bank of Philadelphia, offered a typical comment. Both schemes seemed (as explained and quoted by Eckes 2014: 86–7):

> [. . .] to be based upon the same idealistic, but totally impractical collectivism that has characterized so much of the New Deal thinking of the last twelve years. . . . Others saw the proposals as a thinly veiled design to transfer monetary sovereignty to a new 'super-government' that would then lend funds in competition with private sources. The Economic Policy Commission of the American Bankers Association concluded, after studying the recommendations, that 'excessive government lending will drive out the private enterprise which is the best hope for continuing progress'.

Nonetheless, Keynes's proposal did have public support:

> liberal editorial writers who found Keynesian logic compelling, the British plan had more appeal than the American draft. The New Republic and the Nation both applauded Keynes for according full employment higher priority than stable exchange rates. New Republic writer George Soule dismissed White's proposal as 'legalistic, pedestrian, and unimaginative.' Even Time and Fortune, the principal vehicles for Henry Luce's viewpoint, said that the clearing union held more promise than the stabilization fund for coping with acute problems of stabilizing currencies, averting depressions, and promoting investments. Keynes, said Time, had merely extended 'internationally the practice of domestic banking system as exemplified by the U.S. Federal Reserve System.' And Life editorial writer Russell Davenport, another Luce employee, privately told skeptical Republican congressmen that the American plan – the creation of Morgenthau's 'self-styled experts' – was hopeless, while the British plan was a least workable. (quoted in Eckes 2014: 85, for sources 295)

Paradoxically, the boom-bust cycle that had followed the Treaty in the 1920s was used as a counter against excessive credit creation presumed to be implicit in the proposal and thus to be avoided in preference to Globalist retention of the gold standard controls on global lending. Paradoxically, because it was the errors of reparations expectation which had produced the excessive international lending that had fueled inflation, the Treaty had virtually nothing by way of changes in the international financial system.

Extensions of Keynes's clearing proposal

An amendment to Keynes's proposal by E. F. Schumacher (1943) sought to confront this problem. The system replicates the payment system of trade bills under the Gold standard in which gold seldom ever moved in settlement of imbalances, it was always domestic netting of exporters selling their claims on foreigners at a discount to domestic bankers who sold them to importers who used them to discharge their payments to foreigners, paid by a foreign correspondent of the domestic bank. The system worked on the basis of these short-term movements of trade bills, not gold flows. It was interest rate differentials, not international price differentials, that produced stability under the gold standard (see Keynes Tract on IRPT). The details of Schumacher's proposal involve the creation of a system of National Clearing Funds in which importers make payments in domestic currency which are used to compensate domestic exporters. The Fund notifies the National Clearing Fund of the foreign exporter that payment has been received from the importer, and the exporter's claim is met by the foreign National Clearing Fund out of funds from importers in the foreign country. Each National Clearing Fund thus receives and disburses domestic currency: it receives currency from the home importers and disburses it to the home exporters. Clearing Funds of deficit countries will have a positive domestic cash balance, which it uses to buy domestic Treasury bills to neutralize the impact on internal monetary policy. Clearing Funds of surplus countries would be short domestic cash and would sell Treasury bills in the open market to make the domestic account balance. In this way National Clearing Funds would operate in a manner analogous to that of an Exchange Equalisation Account.

The system would also have an 'International Clearing Office – ICO' that acts as Trustee for the aggregate cash balances accumulated by National Clearing Funds in the form of national Treasury Bills. The assets of the ICO are 'owned' as investments by the National Clearing Funds of the surplus countries on a pro rata basis given by relative surpluses. Sort of a national international equity hedge fund. Automatic global capital flows finance global deficits. The ICO requires no finance of its own – no country quotas, no capital contribution, does not create a new international currency – not even bancor or unitas. It removes the US dollar and gold from the international settlement system.

Since it is impossible to disentangle the mass of individual transactions which give rise, during the course of business, to the various uncleared balances in the deficit countries and to ascribe any one particular balance, or part of it, to any one particular surplus country, all the surplus countries the joint owners of the balances in all the deficit countries. In this way, every national currency is made into a world currency; nor does the ICO require any special powers; it is not an agency for control, but a purely administrative body; it is just the central clearing office for the different National Clearing Funds. As a result of its (purely formal) operations, we get the following position: The Clearing Funds of surplus countries become indebted to their internal money markets and acquire an equivalent share in the ICO Pool; both their debt and their share in the Pool being equal to their trade surplus. The Clearing Funds of the deficit countries are left with balances of cash in hand (equal to their trade deficits) which belong to the International Clearing Pool. The National Clearing Funds, finally, of countries in external balance hold neither cash nor a share in the Pool.

In difference from Keynes's original proposal of interest penalties on excessive imbalance, ICO Clearing places quantitative limits on the size of a country's global credit or debit balance. Schumacher (1943: 150–65) recommended setting a limit on a country's debit balance, which leaves the potential credit balance variable – that is, it depends on the overall distribution of creditor and debtor countries and the limits placed on the latter countries. The main force limiting the size of the net creditor position is the fact that the holding of surpluses becomes unprofitable and risky. The surplus, instead of being convertible into gold or interest-earning investments, is tied up in the Pool: it is a share in the Pool. And the Pool's assets are always the weakest currencies of the world: the currencies of the countries that have been unable to earn as much as they have spent (for recent discussions concerning also Kalecki's contributions, see Faudot 2021; Osiatyński and Toporowski 2022).

In another amendment to extend the clearing union to accommodate international capital investment flows, Michał Kalecki and Schumacher (1943: 29) noted that: 'There is no merit in a general policy aiming at current account equilibrium for all countries, because different countries are at different stages of economic development, and a regular flow of investment from the more highly developed to the more backward regions of the world may redound to the benefit of all.' 'In order to achieve and maintain a truly international system in the post-war world the International Clearing Union must also assume the function of long-term lending to underdeveloped countries and wield certain additional powers', such as directed purchase and lending. The authors go on to recommend that the Board may direct countries to direct their purchases to particular countries to ensure limits on bilateral imbalances, noting that if investment decisions have to be taken by an international authority, there arises, of course, a political problem of the first magnitude. The mainly administrative functions to be discharged by the Board of the International Clearing Union are, relatively speaking, politically neutral. But investment decisions, and decisions directing a borrower to make his purchases in one particular country, involve a higher degree of political responsibility (for further discussions, see Kregel 2021).

Digital clearing

Current technological capabilities, however, suggest that these difficulties may be overcome. The development of cryptocurrencies has been based on a paradoxical combination of restoration of democratic individual control via the introduction of an ersatz gold standard system based on inviolable computer code. The creation of these systems as competitors for national or central banks' payment systems has created pressure on governments and central banks to create national digital currency systems. These proposals currently come in two forms. As I have noted elsewhere, there is already a private formulation of Keynes's system, which is a mirror of the Schumacher-Kalecki amended clearing system. Given the application of the technological base, it exerts clear competitive pressure in both the private and public sectors to either acquire or develop such systems.

The 'wholesale' system would simply provide existing private banks with digital reserve accounts at central banks and provide private banks the opportunity to offer their clients accounts in, or backed by, central bank digital reserves. This would produce minimal change from current systems. On the other hand, the 'retail system', would be the equivalent of allowing individuals direct deposit accounts in the central bank in digital form; it is presumed that clients would prefer to hold digital credits with the central bank rather than risky private banks with the result that the system would replace traditional paper currency and private bank deposits. The implication is that this would eliminate the need for a clearing system for private banking institutions and provide the basis of a national Clearing system within the central bank. If Central banks were to offer digital accounts to private clients, then there would no longer be any need for private bank provision of means of payment. Complete bank disintermediation would be one possible result. Indeed, the risk of bank runs and bank failures would also be eliminated, which would make bank regulation and deposit insurance redundant.

For example, central banks could be converted into national Clearing Offices to register and net the cross-border transactions as suggested in the amendments to Keynes's Clearing system by Oxford economists Schumacher and Kalecki mentioned above. The International Monetary Fund could close all country quota accounts and convert to an ICO. While this would technically challenge the position of private institutions and create incentives for them to implement a national clearing independently of national governments. This would also fulfil the technological requirements of a global clearing. The remaining impediment would then be the coordination of the different national central banks' digital currency systems. The final step would be the creation of the International Investment and Development Board such as originally suggested by Alvin Hansen (1944) or as discussed above in the Kalecki and Schumacher amendment to the Schumacher amendment of Keynes's original Currency Clearing proposal, but never formally instituted, although it was widely discussed in the formulation of both the British and US proposals at Bretton Woods. What eventually emerged was the World Bank, which ended up as a simple intermediary rather than an instrument to provide additional funding for development within an International Clearing Union.

Notes

1 Schacht had used bilateral clearing arrangements to support access of the German Reich to imports required for rearmament during the Nazi rearmament and after the outbreak of war most of the Allied governments had agreed bilateral trading arrangements in the absence of functioning international financial markets.

2 However, Keynes (1969: 11) had assured bankers that 'the fabric of international banking organisation, built up by long experience to satisfy practical needs, should be left as undisturbed as possible. Except as regards a provision, explained below, concerning the balances of Central Banks themselves, there should be no obstacle in the way of the existing practices of international banking except those which necessarily arise through measures which individual Central Banks may choose to

adopt for the control of movements of capital'. This was far more conciliatory than the threat of Secretary Morgenthau to drive them from the temple of international finance.

Bibliography

Beyen, Johan W. (1951), *Money in Maelstrom*, London: Macmillan.

Eckes, Alfred E. (2014), *A Search for Solvency: Bretton Woods and the International Monetary System, 1941–1971*, Austin: University of Texas Press.

Einaudi, Luigi (2006 [1936]), 'The Theory of Imaginary Money from Charlemagne to the French Revolution', in L. Einaudi, R. Faucci and R. Marchionatti (eds), *Luigi Eunaudi. Selected Economic Essays*, 153–81, Cham: Springer.

Einzig, Paul (1944), *Currency After the War – The British and American Plans*, London: Nicholson and Watson.

Faudot, Adrien. (2021), 'The Keynes Plan and Bretton Woods Debates. The Early Radical Criticisms by Balogh, Schumacher and Kalecki', *Cambridge Journal of Economics*, 45 (4): 751–69.

Hansen, Alvin (1944), 'World Institutions for Stability and Expansion', *Foreign Affairs*, 22 (January): 148–55.

Kalecki, Michał and E. F. Schumacher (1943), 'International Clearing and Long-Term Lending', *Supplement to the Bulletin of the Oxford Institute of Statistics*, 5 (August): 1943.

Keynes, J. M. (1969), 'Proposals for an International Currency (or Clearing) Union, February 11, 1942', in J. Horsefield (ed.), *The International Monetary Fund, 1945–1965, Vol. III: Documents*, 3–18, Washington: International Monetary Fund.

Keynes, J. M. (1971a), "Economic Consequences of the Peace", in *Collected Writings of John Maynard Keynes, Volume II*, ed. Donald Moggridge, London: Macmillan for the Royal Economic Society.

Keynes, J. M. (1971b), "A Treatise on Money", in *The Collected Writings of John Maynard Keynes, Volume V*, ed. Donald Moggridge, London: Macmillan for the Royal Economic Society.

Keynes, J. M. (1971c), "The Clearing Union", in *The Collected Writings of John Maynard Keynes, Activities 1940–1944 Shaping the Post-war World, Volume XXV*, ed. Donald Moggridge, Cambridge: Cambridge University Press.

Kregel, Jan (2021), "Another Bretton Woods Reform Moment: Let us Look Seriously at the Clearing Union", *a mimeo*. Available online: https://jankregel.org/wp-content/uploads/2022/11/Another-Bretton-Woods-Reform-Moment2021.pdf.

Osiatyński, Jerzy and Jan Toporowski, eds (2022), *International Equilibrium & Bretton Woods. Kalecki's Alternative to Keynes & White and Its Consequences*, Oxford: Oxford University Press.

Schumacher, E. F. (1943), 'Multilateral Clearing', *Economica*, 10 (38): 150–65.

Slobodian, Quinn (2018), *Globalists: The End of Empire and the Birth of Neoliberalism*, Cambridge, MA: Harvard University Press.

3

Regional clearing systems

From the European Payments Union to current initiatives confronting dollar dominance

Massimo Amato, Luca Fantacci and Lucio Gobbi

Introduction

The International Clearing Union proposed by Keynes at Bretton Woods was designed not only to avoid using a national currency as an international means of payment and reserve asset, but also to provide a source of funding for temporary balance of trade disequilibria. Moreover, the proposal for collective commodity management would have provided liquidity to the international currency by ensuring its convertibility in a basket of foodstuffs and raw materials. The ICU proposal was unsuccessful but experienced a successful regional application in Europe in the 1950s with the European Payments Union. Since the early 1960s, the regional EPU solution has attracted interest outside Europe.

Today, as emerging economies show a growing political interest in reducing their dependence on the US dollar, the issue of regional clearing regains attention. The twin objectives of supporting regional trade growth and reducing exchange rate risk against the dollar are driving solutions based on multilateral payment technologies.

This chapter starts by analysing the structural features of Keynes's Clearing Union proposal and discussing their relevance for rethinking and reshaping the international monetary system today (section 1) and it then illustrates the regional application of those features in the EPU (section 2). Finally, it analyses various regional payment systems that are currently being proposed or implemented, investigating how they may reduce reliance on the US dollar as a means for international settlement and how they may be understood (and perhaps further enhanced) in the light of the principles of multilateral clearing (section 3).

The structural features of the International Clearing Union and their relevance today

The International Clearing Union proposed by Keynes at Bretton Woods was designed not only to avoid using a national currency as an international means of payment and reserve asset, but also to provide a source of funding for temporary balance of trade disequilibria.

As we know, the plan was fully based on what we can call 'the principle of clearing' (Amato and Fantacci 2016): multilateral clearing, coupled with overdraft facilities based on the commercial capacity of each country and a symmetrical treatment of debtor and creditor positions, would have allowed minimizing the amount of international liquidity needed to oil the machine of international payments. Leveraging on the circuit velocity instead of on the quantity of money, the ICU would have allowed full financing of temporary international trade imbalances without the need for short-term capital movements. A system of adjustable pegs of national currencies to the international unit of account, the bancor, was designed to resolve any structural imbalance. Moreover, the proposal for collective commodity management would have given liquidity to the international currency by providing certain stability to its prospective value (Hayes 2018; Amato 2020), and by ensuring its convertibility in a basket of foodstuffs and raw materials (Fantacci 2024).

Eighty years have elapsed since the formulation of Keynes's proposal, fifty-three since the end of the Bretton Woods system, and above all seventeen since the outbreak of the GFC, which could possibly be interpreted as an initial weakening of US hegemony and the beginning of the end of a unilateralist model of international relations, both political and economic, as the reactions to the crisis suggest, since they did not happen under a common and recognized leadership.

The increasing signs of weakening of the present global monetary order are, we think, a sufficient reason to go back to Keynes's original project precisely today, not so much with a view to historiographical reconstruction (which, moreover, has already been extensively and excellently carried out, by Steil 2014), but with the aim of seeing whether and how the principles and aims that inspired that project can be reinterpreted and taken up again in a radically different context from that of 1944.

Indeed, the ICU proposal was unsuccessful at a global level, but it nonetheless experienced a successful regional application in Europe in the 1950s with the

European Payments Union; and, since the early 1960s, the regional EPU solution has attracted interest outside Europe.

Today, as emerging economies show a growing political interest in reducing their dependence on the US dollar, the issue of regional clearing regains attention. The twin objectives of supporting regional trade growth and reducing exchange rate risk against the dollar are driving solutions based on multilateral payment technologies.

If we want to assess the legacy of Keynes's ICU today, it is then necessary to separate the contingent elements of the Keynes plan from what we can call its structural components. The latter are essentially three, mutually interrelated and ultimately based on the third.

1. The first is the irenic trait of the proposal. It is well known how Keynes describes the nature of his plan and the conditions for it to be implemented, already in 1941 and then in the version of 11 February 1942:

> a greater readiness to accept super-national arrangements must be required in the post-war world than has been accepted hitherto. The arrangements proposed could be described as a measure of Financial Disarmament. They are very mild in comparison with the measures of Military Disarmament, which it is to be hoped the world may be asked to accept [version of 11 February 1942, CWK 25].

This was, from a political perspective, and with hindsight, the least realistic feature of the whole plan, given the way in which the relationships between former allies would quickly have evolved towards a Cold War needing to be heavily financed.

The Bretton Woods conference was convened in 1944 by the signatories of the Atlantic Charter, one of which was trying to save a colonial empire, while the other was gearing up to exercise hegemony in a global context on the verge of becoming fully bipolar. The post-war phase inaugurated at Bretton Woods, essentially marked by the hegemony of the dollar in a context of relative world political stability, is now coming to an end. The context is now that of an unstable world, characterized by potential fracture or recomposition of a global monetary order and by 'asymmetrical multipolarism' (Ashford and Cooper 2023), in which trade is very often weaponized, and in which the redefinition of value chains is accompanied by the redefinition of the payment and trade finance systems to which they give rise.

But in a time of potential deglobalization and trade wars, the issues raised by Keynes's plan are relevant, both in principle and in practice. Indeed, as Keynes emphasized when commenting on American intentions as expressed in the

Atlantic Charter, international trade can only become the trigger for balanced world development only if the starting conditions have been decided in such a way as to ensure substantial equal treatment for all participants (Fantacci 2017: 167). And the exigence of a fair rebalancing of the trade conditions is exactly what is at stake now for those emerging/emerged economies that often reposition themselves within the BRICS, and that, in any case, do not accept anymore their inherited position in the hierarchies of the postcolonial world.

2. The second crucial component of Keynes's project was its implicit adherence to the principle of comparative advantages. Obviously, as De Cecco (1975) had already shown when discussing the Ricardian foundations of the theoretical gold standard as opposed to List's 'National System of Political Economy', this aspect rests, not only on assumptions of political irenicism, but also on the assumption that capital investments remained preferably domestic. However, while classical liberalists simply assumed the absence of international capital movements, Keynes's ICU project was intended to provide liquidity to trade without the need of capital movements. In this case, the theoretical conditions for comparative advantage would have applied also in practice.

What we are witnessing at present is the need of a redefinition of specialization within changing global value chains, based at the same time on free trade and massive investments. The case of the African Continental Free Trade Area (AfCFTA) is by all means exemplar in this sense, as it goes along, not only (as we will see) with settlement and payment schemes, but also with the emergence of continental development banks (see following sections).[1]

While Keynes's ICU proposal aimed at setting all participants on an equal footing at a global level, based on fair quotas and on the symmetrical treatment of debtor and creditor positions in clearing mechanisms, the historical gold standard, gold exchange standard and Bretton Woods 'dollar standard' are to be interpreted as profoundly hierarchical and West-centred monetary systems, which manage to last as long as the force of the hegemon is able to hold together the overall framework of relations between centre, semi-periphery and periphery. This feature fully applies to the bipolar world in which Bretton Woods was launched, characterized by a firmly US-led 'benign multilateralism' [James 2012]. In short, as Marcello De Cecco argued in the 1970s, and as Perry Mehrling (2022) has recently reiterated, the relevant theme is here 'money and empire': a system based on an established hegemony can only last if a not-too-asymmetrical distribution of advantages and disadvantages arising from the participation in the system is guaranteed by the hegemon. To the extent that the project of American unilateralism is encountering ever-increasing difficulties, showing itself less and less multilateral and benign, the emerging asymmetrical multipolarism increasingly bears the features of a competition between regional poles in key leading sectors, with a focus on hegemonic control over strategic raw materials, but with much looser hierarchies and wider manoeuvring room for emerging economies.

Precisely in relation to the questioning of established hierarchies that characterizes the current phase of global relations, it is worth remembering that in Keynes's intentions, the ICU was only one of the three legs on which he aimed to ground the stability of the international negotiating table. The other two were an International Investment Fund, literally a development bank aimed at bridging technology gaps through international investments, and a Commod Control, i.e. a global buffer stock programme, aimed at reducing commodity price volatility through coordinated commodity management (in order to balance the interests of both commodity producers and consumers).

As we shall see, if there is a chance to return, if not to the project, then at least to the principles of the ICU, then these two issues (banks and regional development agencies and fairer management of commodity markets) are absolutely crucial.

3. The third essential component of the ICU project, which is even more relevant when it comes to re-evaluating the ICU's political message today, is the increasingly anti-hegemonic and multipolar feature of the proposed ICU operation. Whereas in Keynes's first drafts the hegemonic role of the United States and the United Kingdom is strongly emphasized, his later drafts envisage decidedly more open governance perspectives. This non-hegemonic and 'horizontal' trait relies not only on the provision of symmetrical rebalancing mechanisms but also on the necessary interplay between rules and discretion that Keynes put into the hands of a markedly supranational board (Draft of 11 February 1942, CWK 25: 117). Not only is the functioning of the ICU conceived as strictly multilateral and symmetrical, but governance itself is potentially multipolar and obedient to supranational logics.

Keynes was perfectly aware of the enormous ambition of his plan (CWK 25: 33), but, while he may have been over-optimistic on the maximum goal, he was strictly correct on the minimum point: no international monetary system can truly last without some form of cooperation among the actors involved. In fact, no system, from the classic gold-sterling-standard to the Bretton Woods gold-dollar-standard survived the collapse of the political conditions that underpinned it. The same would seem to apply, prospectively, to the current 'Post-Bretton Woods non-system' (Eichengreen 2008).

This is an even more crucial issue now, at a time in which international political and economic institutional settings and organizations are subject to increasingly marked centrifugal and disintegrative pushes. For some time now, particularly in the BRICS+ area, we have been witnessing an increasingly decisive strategy aimed at subtracting large areas of the globe from the dominance of the 'Washington Consensus', through the formation of regional monetary funds, and in general regional investment agencies. At the same time, the enlargement of the BRICS to vast African regions, starting with South Africa, which joined in 2010, up to the recent admissions, and above all the applications for admission that are still pending, risks leading to a substantial redefinition of the balances on the continent, jeopardizing the survival of organizations that arose with decolonization, for example, ECOWAS.

In this sense, the only way for the ICU spirit to be reappraised now, is to go even more decidedly in the direction of the fundamental anti-unilateralist character of the ICU project. This aspect is gaining greater momentum today, in the context of a potential redefinition of balances between blocs, one has to wonder whether there will be 'persistence in the structure of the system, which remains dollar-based and US-led to a remarkable extent', or whether 'the system is evolving away from the United States and the dollar, towards a multipolar world in which several consequential international and reserve currencies will coexist, other countries will no longer rely exclusively or even mainly on the US for international liquidity and governance will be a collective endeavour' (Eichengreen 2019).

The markedly optimistic, not to say utopian, trait of the three crucial components of the ICU plan explains why a diametrically opposite path was taken at Bretton Woods. But it is also the reason why it is perfectly reasonable, if not necessary, to reappraise them in the present context of an often strongly advocated redefinition of global equilibria.

Indeed, the question that is keeping political analysts, economists and historians busy is precisely whether the current tensions associated with an emerging multipolarism will give rise to an internal transformation of the inherited hegemonic order or a more radical change. But this is not the only question: the other, related question is whether the current asymmetrical multipolarism can give rise to stable alternative configurations. Conversely, the research question concerns constructing plausible scenarios about whether current trends are to be read as confirmations or denials of one's own hypotheses.

The two extreme scenarios are

(a) a continuation of the current monetary hegemony of the dollar due to a sheer lack of alternatives (argued with different arguments, for example, by Vernengo 2021 and Bordo 2017)

(b) an orderly transition to a new multipolar collaborative framework (cf. Carney 2019).

In between lies the much more potentially unstable and opaque scenario of an uncoordinated and potentially conflictual shift in economic, geopolitical and monetary power relations.

In all cases, a reconsideration of the potential and limits of the clearing scheme proposed by Keynes can help to better delineate the current picture. The variants to the scheme found in the different preparatory drafts drawn up by Keynes between 1941 and 1944 can also help in this sense.

In particular, one variant is of interest to us here: in the second version of the 'Proposals for an International Currency Union', drafted in November 1941, Keynes envisaged the construction of the multilateral and non-hegemonic order of the ICU starting from the adhesion not of individual nations but of homogeneous geographic-economic areas represented by a single currency, in the form of an actual means of exchange or of a pure unit of account:

> One view of the post-war world which I find sympathetic and attractive and fruitful of good consequences is that we should encourage small political and cultural units, combined into larger, and more or less closely knit, economic units. [. . .] Thus it would be preferable, if it were possible, that the members should, in some cases at least, be groups of countries rather than separate units. (CWK 25: 55–6)

The basic ICU rationale is the extension 'banking principle' already operating at the national level, to the international level. The effect Keynes expects from such an extension is by no means irrelevant, as he is well aware that the adoption of a multilateral payment system implies, ipso facto, the adoption of a scheme for financing international trade. The same applies to the EPU, the analysis of which constitutes one of the crucial points of the next section.

Even now, in many regional emerging economies, the crucial question is how to promote the establishment of a lively interregional trade without compromising the possibility of an opening to global trade. And now, as then, monetary (payment) and financial (clearing) conditions play an essential role.

From the considerations made so far, on the ICU and its historical fate, but also on the vicissitudes of the system that took its place at Bretton Woods, we now make our hypothesis for the second part of our discourse. The hypothesis is the following: the spirit if not the letter of the ICU can be taken up in the present context through the proliferation of regional compensation schemes, which for the time being develop in a disorganized manner, but which at a later stage might be unified at a higher level.

This is a hypothesis that deserves to be tested both in terms of its historical precedents (EPU as a model) and in terms of emerging practices, while being absolutely clear on one point: for the time being we are witnessing spontaneous phenomena and processes and not the unfolding and elaboration of a deliberate plan. We will leave the conclusions on possible scenarios and plausible dynamics to the end of the chapter.

The European Payments Union as a form of regional clearing

The European Payments Union, established in 1950 and functioning until 1958, was intended to serve both as a *payments system*, avoiding the need to rely on foreign exchange markets or on correspondent banking, and as a *financial system*, more specifically as a source of funding for temporary current account disequilibria, avoiding the need to rely on international capital markets. In technical terms, the dual function may be described as the combination of multilateral and intertemporal clearing.

This dual function of the EPU was clear from its genesis. After the Second World War, European economies needed to finance a chronic trade deficit, particularly with the United States. The European Recovery Program was originally designed and implemented with the purpose of financing the dollar gap. However, absent an actual recovery of European productive capacity, the gap persisted year after year: chronic European trade deficits acted as a bottomless sink for US aid. In fact, despite the ERP, recovery in production was dramatically hampered by restrictions to trade within Europe, due to the reluctance of individual countries to settle their reciprocal obligations with hard currency that could be used to purchase essential commodities in the United States, and in general in the Western Hemisphere.

It soon became clear to contemporary observers that 'the ultimate success of the European Recovery Program depends in large measure upon the nature and size of intra-European trade' (Mikesell 1948: 516). Even the United Nations

Economic Commission for Europe recognized that 'one of the preconditions for the cure of Europe's acute external disequilibrium is the restoration of intra-European trade' (1948: 88 quoted in Bean 1948: 403).

Already in the logic of the European Recovery Program, intra-European cooperation was considered as a condition for assistance. In a speech before the OEEC Council in Paris, on 31 October 1949, the head of the Economic Cooperation Administration, Paul Hoffman, went further, calling upon Europeans to demonstrate by early next year that they intended to move towards 'nothing less than an integration of the Western European economy' (Hoffman 1949, quoted in Berend 2016: 31).

This was achieved not in the form of a European Monetary Union, but of a European Payments Union: the records of the EPU, held by the Bank for International Settlements in the name of the member States' central banks, allowed to:

- keep track of mutual obligations arising from international trade at fixed (but adjustable) exchange rates
- calculate the net position of each Member State vis-à-vis the EPU, according to the principles of multilateral clearing
- perform a net settlement of outstanding positions on a monthly basis
- provide funding in the form of overdraft facilities to deficit countries up to a certain portion of their deficit (according to the size of the latter in relation to a predetermined quota)

The functioning of the system required a certain degree of coordination in the monetary policies of member states 'in exchange for an expanded level of trade and industrial production' (Lees 1962: 515). However, unlike other international monetary systems, such as the gold standard or a full-fledged monetary union, the EPU did not entail a conflict between domestic and international objectives (Lees 1962: 515).

The original plan envisaged the establishment of a supervisory board with ECA representation 'to maintain a kind of surveillance over the internal financial policies of the member countries' (quoted in Flexner 1957: 243–4). The idea, however, was eventually abandoned because European countries were reluctant to surrender part of their sovereignty to an international organization, especially where the United States were involved (Flexner 1957: 244).

Despite the fact that, in traditional accounts, the Marshall Plan gets all the credit for the recovery of Europe, it would not have achieved its goals without the EPU. The EPU finances trade, but also reconstruction and development and economic miracles, providing an alternative to financial markets as a source of funding for current account deficits, within the area of application, but without closing it off to trade with the rest of the world. That the EPU clearing system represented an alternative to private capital flows as a funding mechanism for current account disequilibria is perhaps confirmed by the fact that the EPU was eventually shut down precisely in the same year in which the Eurodollar market was developed.

The liberalization of international capital movements on the Eurodollar market was not the automatic consequence of technological progress, but the result of deliberate decisions, on the part of the governments of the United States and United Kingdom, to promote the development of such market as a source of funding for their respective current account deficits (Schenk 2010: 149).

Since the early 1960s, the regional EPU solution has attracted interest outside Europe. In particular, the EPU is at the origin of Robert Triffin's regional approach towards international monetary integration (Maes and Pasotti 2018). In the 1960s Triffin proposed similar schemes for other regions, in Latin America, Asia and Africa (Ibid. p. 185; see also Amato and Nubukpo 2020). None of these, however, lead to the establishment of regional clearing systems comparable to the EPU.

Variety of payment mechanisms and applications in three regional monetary areas

Since a payment system of the type of ICU is also, inextricably, a financing instrument, as argued above, it is worthwhile to explore the relationships between different payment systems and their financial aspect, in order both to investigate what we can call the trade-off between liquidity and risk, and to provide a typology according to which the emerging regional monetary projects can be evaluated.

Whenever two economic agents need to exchange goods or services with each other they put in place a financial contract, which determines the value in monetary terms of the exchange, the currency or commodity used in the transaction as well as the date of payment. Table 1 shows the basic characteristics regarding the principles governing real and financial payment contracts within the economic system.

The rows in Table 1 depict the settlement and termination modes of contracts and their main characteristics. In terms of payment modes, we indicate real time gross settlement (RTGS), gross settlement (GS), bilateral netting (BN) and multilateral netting (MN).

Table 1 Main Features of a Payment System

	Settlement Modes	Timing	Trade off	Regional System
A	Real Time Gross Settlement	Continuous	High liquidity cost and null counterparty risk	Target 2 (T2)
B	Gross Settlement	Deferred	Moderate liquidity cost and high counterparty risk	-
C	Bilateral Netting	Deferred	Low liquidity cost and low counterparty risk	Sistema de Pagamentos em Moeda Local (SML)
D	Multilateral Netting	Deferred	Lowest liquidity cost and moderate counterparty risk (but possibly with a change in counterparty)	Asian Clearing Union (ACU); Common Market for Eastern and Southern Africa (COMESA); PAPSS Sistema Único de Compensación Regional (SUCRE); European Payments Union (EPU); Keynes plan

Source: Gobbi (2018) and our elaborations

In RTGS, financial obligations between two economic entities are settled as they arise. For example, the sale of a good in a real market can ideally be split into two moments. The first, in which the asset is chosen by the potential buyer and in which the buyer accepts the terms of the financial contract (emergence of the debtor-creditor relationship), and the second, which coincides with a transfer of monetary means from the debtor to the creditor that extinguishes the relationship between the two counterparties. Since the financial contract is settled as soon as it comes into existence (Real Time), no credit risk arises. Nevertheless, this payment mode is the most onerous: the debtor must transfer to the creditor an amount of means of payment equal to the face value of the financial contract (Gross Settlement).

As for GS, in this type of contract the two counterparties indicate a specific date on which the debtor must settle its debt through the transfer of means of payment equal to the agreed nominal value. The difference from the real time case is that the debtor is given time in order to collect the amount due. This time extension of payment implies however a credit risk for the creditor. The liquidity outflow for debt payment, *ceteris paribus*, is the same as for RTGS. Nevertheless, since the debtor takes a longer time to close the financial contract, in terms of the financial burden for the debtor, GS is preferable to RTGS.

Netting systems are bilateral or multilateral. Bilateral netting occurs when two economic agents agree to offset their net financial position. In the case where economic agent A is a creditor of 10 euros to economic agent B and, at the same time, economic agent B is a creditor to agent A of 6 euros, the two agents may decide to originate a new contract in which A is a creditor of B for 4 euros. This makes it possible to reduce the liquidity required to settle the two original financial contracts. Usually, the netting procedure does not take place in real time but on a date defined by the counterparties. For this reason, bilateral netting results in the emergence of credit risk for the net creditor.

Multilateral netting, on the other hand, is the case where more than two agents want to offset their total net financial position. Assume that A, B, and C need to calculate their overall net financial position and that A is creditor to B and C respectively for 5 euros, and at the same time B is creditor to A for 5 euros. Therefore, A's total net creditor position is 5 euros, B's is 0 while C is net debtor for 5 euros. The multilateral netting procedure reduces systemic net financial exposure, but also in this case, netting increases credit risk compared to RTGS systems. Moreover, as the number of agents grows, it will not be straightforward for each agent to calculate their overall net financial position. In more realistic settings, the net financial position between agents is usually calculated by a clearinghouse. Often, financial contracts between agents are novated by contracts between each agent and the clearinghouse.

When analysing payment systems and the financial contracts subject to them, it is necessary to keep in mind that financial contracts put in place between counterparties (households, firms, states, other private actors) are one thing while financial contracts entered into between actors in the payment system are another. It is perfectly usual that the payment of a gross settlement contract entered into between two enterprises may be settled in bilateral netting between two banks.

After this general overview we can now turn to regional cross-border monetary agreements. To date, there are several regional systems that use the clearing principle (bilateral or multilateral) to settle transactions among participants. This section presents six cases and it focuses on the main features of each of them. As we shall see, with the Eurozone's exception, the main reason why public or private actors join these systems is to reduce the need for liquidity. This need takes the form of demand for the most important currencies traded in international money markets, principally dollars and euros.

1. Sistema de Pagamentos em Moeda Local (SML)

SML has been designed by the Brazilian central bank and operates jointly with the central banks of Argentina, Uruguay, and Paraguay (Fritz et al. 2023; Shvandar and Khomyakova 2022). Its main purpose is to conduct international transactions of goods without using third-party international currencies, reducing liquidity costs and, more importantly, without the need to enter into foreign exchange contracts. The system processes bilateral payments between Brazil and other components of the system in net settlement. As well described by Fritz et al. (2023).

> The SML has been designed as a simple payment system that allows the use of the national currency for bilateral trade denomination and settlement between an importer, an exporter, and commercial banks. Consequently, there is no need to exchange, for example, the Brazilian Real for US dollar and then Argentinian Peso (or vice versa). Payments are made in local currencies through local banks previously authorised to transfer the operations from private agents to the central banks and vice versa. Although the trading parties and their respective banks only settle payments in local currency, the net settlement of all operations is cleared, usually in US dollars, directly between the two regional central banks involved in this operation. The use of a central currency for the net settlement of operations is explained by the fact that neither central banks are willing to hold the other's currency in their foreign exchange reserves. Therefore, the reliance on the US dollar is reduced, but the use of this currency cannot be completely discarded. The maximum period for this clearing is three days, but it usually takes just 24 h.

2. Sistema Único de Compensación Regional (SUCRE)

SUCRE was established in 2009 by the Bolivarian Alliance for the Peoples of Our America, an international organization founded in 2004 by Cuba and Venezuela and now including ten full members among Latin American and Caribbean countries. SUCRE is the unit of account for the multilateral clearing system. Its main objective was to reduce the use of foreign currency by member countries netting payments and by granting payment deferrals in commercial transactions. SUCRE also offers the possibility of a bilateral netting of trade deficits between countries (Shvandar and Khomyakova 2022).

3. Regional Payment and Settlement System (REPSS)

As for Africa the first significant case was that of the Common Market for Eastern and Southern Africa (COMESA), established in 1994 by Djibouti, Egypt, Kenya,

Madagascar, Malawi, Mauritius, Sudan and Zimbabwe, in order to strengthen trade interaction among countries in the area, the REPSS was introduced.

REPSS is managed by the COMESA Clearing House, based in Harare, Zimbabwe. It is a multilateral clearing system with end-of-day settlement. Banking intermediaries access the system through their respective national central banks. Hence, central banks can avoid the complex payment chains that sometimes occur in correspondent bank arrangements. The currencies in which central banks settle their net payments are the dollar and the euro. The special feature of the COMESA clearing house is that the clearing of payments made in international currencies is not centralized, but is carried out by each member central bank at its own rates (Shchegoleva 2017).

4. PAPSS

On 13 January 2022, the Pan-African Payment and Settlement System (PAPSS) has been launched, operated by Afreximbank, established as a continent-wide multilateral financial institution in 1993 and gradually recapitalized to cope with growing institutional commitments. When read together and in perspective, both these dynamics hint at a shared long-term strategy aimed at

(i)   increasing inter-African trade by amending the terms of trade with the ROW

(ii) decreasing the adhering states' dependence on the dollar as a currency for trade and its financing

From the perspective of what interests us here, attention must first converge on the PAPSS platform, which is not mentioned except in passing by Fritz et al. (2023), but which seems to fit very well into the typology of local monetary union sketched in the article on the basis of Latin American experiences in particular.

The declared goal is to rationalize local initiatives already in place on the continent, such as REPSS, which we discussed above: the strategic aim is to integrate REPPSs into PAPPS, thereby emancipating the payment system from the use of dominant currencies

We could hierarchize as follows the operations that PAPSS should take charge of, on the basis of *not* adopting a common unit of account, and thus certainly on the basis of the accumulation of suitable monetary reserves. In any case, the design of the PAPPS is consistent with the criteria set forth by Chang (2000), quoted by Fritz et al. 2023:

a reduction of foreign currency flows and associated transaction costs can be obtained mainly in two ways. First, the number of transactions is reduced to net final settlement at the end of the period, while transactions of equal value cancel out. Second, temporary liquidity is provided to the deficit countries' central banks by the surplus countries' counterparts, as they allow each other to cancel mutual obligations not immediately, but only at the end of a clearing period. In effect, an efficiently run regional payment system in this simple version may slightly improve the terms of trade for intra-regional trade transactions.

Under this framework, PAPPS could provide essentially three facilities:

(a) payment (real time gross settlement, like TARGET)
(b) netting (liquidity saving mechanism, like EPU)
(c) financing (overdraft facilities, like ICU)

5. Asia

Central banks of India, Iran, Nepal, Pakistan and Sri Lanka since 1974 have agreed to settle their regional payments using a multilateral clearing system called Asian Clearing Union. Subsequently, the system expanded by incorporating Bhutan, Myanmar and Maldives. As with other regional clearing systems, the main objectives are to reduce transaction costs and the need for liquidity to finance international transactions. Settlement of net payments takes place primarily in dollars or euros (Shvandar and Khomyakova 2022). The United States has recently imposed a number of restrictions on the use of the system (Financial Express 2023), another case of what is called a 'weaponization' process of the payments system (Fantacci and Gobbi 2024, 2023).

The payment systems analysed generally pertain to countries where saving international currency reserves and reducing liquidity costs is vital to the stability of their economic and financial systems. The use of clearing, bilateral or multilateral, perfectly meets this need.

6. Target 2

A typical example of a regional monetary system using a real time gross settlement system is T2, the payment system of the twenty countries that make up the Eurozone. Payment orders from commercial banks and central banks holding an account with the ECB are settled in T2. T2 is used for both transactions pertaining to monetary policy operations and interbank payments, is participated by more than 1,000 banks and transacts an amount of payments close to the entire euro area GDP value every five days. As with all payment systems operating in real time, a process very cash-intensive, the main variables for assessing their efficiency relate to the ability to be able to conduct predefined time transactions, liquidity reservation facility, payments priorities and liquidity pooling (ECB 2024).

The recent evolution of T2 proves that even a RTGS system can acquire a financial dimension, by offering a source of funding for balance of payments disequilibria of member countries. Since the outbreak of the GFC in 2007–8, T2 balances of national central banks have diverged, with the accumulation of substantial debtor positions (most notably Italy and Spain) and creditor positions (mostly Germany) with overall outstanding credits and debts exceeding €1,000 billion (Figure 3.1). T2 remains a RTGS system, which allows cross-border payments between any two entities within the Eurozone to be settled in real time. However, to the extent that after the GFC the inflows and outflows for each member country are no longer balanced, these very settlements cause the respective central banks to accumulate net debtor or creditor positions vis-à-vis the clearing system as a whole. While T2 continues to function as a RTGS for public and private actors within the Eurozone, for the central banks of member countries it acts as a clearing system that fails to clear: the financial function

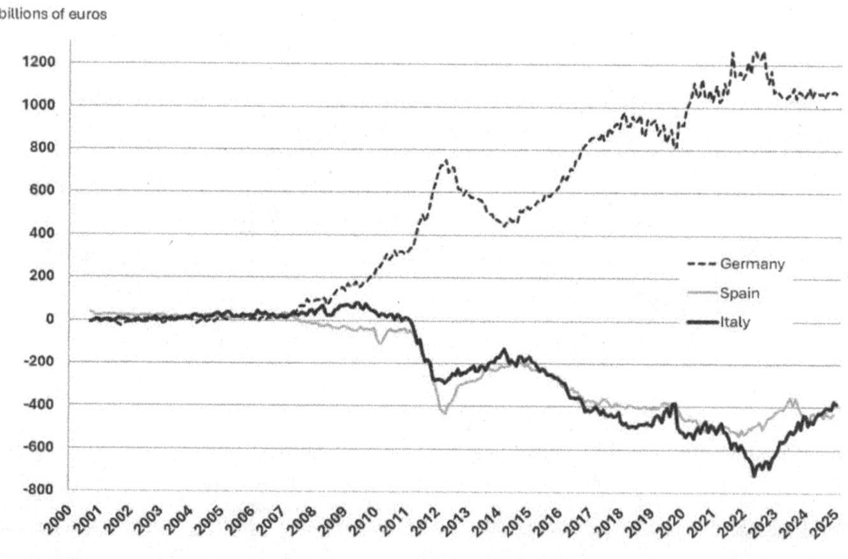

Figure 3.1 T2 balances. Source: https://www.eurocrisismonitor.com/.

dominates over the payment function (for a proposal to reform T2, see Amato, Fantacci, Papadimitriou, Zezza 2016). The case of T2 raises the question of whether it could represent a precedent for other regional payments systems, which in principle could follow similar trajectories, morphing from (real-time) settlement systems into full-fledged international clearing systems with a substantial financial function.

This section clearly shows how a payment system can be designed to meet the needs of its members. Moreover, it highlights how these needs are different between the different regions considered. Furthermore, all the systems presented focus on a geographically defined economic area where ICU has a planetary horizon. Nowadays, the historical and geopolitical conditions seem to indicate that the regional scale is the maximum attainable.

The BRICS community and multilateral development banks

The process of globalization, from the fall of the Berlin Wall to GFC, was characterized by the widening of the trade network between countries, the growth of China's role as a major global creditor as well as a strengthening of US hegemony in the international financial system. From that point on, abetted by the loss of importance of Europe's role, the process of 'friendshoring' initiated by the United States, combined with the growing leadership of non-G7 economies in the production of a range of goods and services, as well as in the supply of raw materials, seems to have reversed the direction of globalization.

More precisely, it is not that the world is de-globalizing; on the contrary, there are pushes that are taking entire production chains out of G7 countries without witnessing a re-nationalization of supply chains. Nonetheless, this does not imply that this process is necessarily efficient, as it is often dictated by political relations between states rather than economic reasons.

Leading this metamorphosis of globalization is the BRICS+ group. The original bloc of BRIC countries (Brazil, Russia, India and China) was born in 2009 as a reaction to the GFC that erupted in 2007 and, following South Africa's accession in 2010, updated its acronym to BRICS. As of this year (2024), the community expanded to include five more countries (Iran, Egypt, Saudi Arabia, the United Arab Emirates and Ethiopia), thus redefining itself into the expanded BRICS+ group (Second Joint Declaration of BRICS Country Leaders.[2])

Looking at the BRICS+ community, albeit for different reasons, the decrease in the use of the dollar seems to be a shared goal. This theme emerges explicitly, as the Second BRICS Joint Declaration (Article 12) clearly states:[3]

> In the interest of promoting international economic stability, we have asked our Finance Ministers and Central Bank Governors to look into regional monetary arrangements and discuss modalities of cooperation between our countries in this area. In order to facilitate trade and investment, we will study feasibilities of monetary cooperation, including local currency trade settlement arrangement between our countries.

We gather here some relevant information with respect to the potential role played by the implementation of cross-border payment systems, and the diffusion of bilateral trade agreements in the process of dedollarization among BRICS+ countries.

Considering trade relations, China has been the main trading partner of Brazil for fourteen years and bilateral trade reached a record $171.5 billion in 2022, up 4.9 per cent year on year (Global Times 2024). At the BRICS summit in Johannesburg in 2023, South Africa and China announced that Chinese companies had signed agreements to purchase South African products worth about $2.2 billion. At that same gathering, plans were announced for China to import more South African agri-food products, as well as donate $8.9 million worth of Chinese energy equipment to South Africa, in addition to an irredeemable loan worth $26.9 million to enable the country to cope with the energy crisis (Virusha 2023). The value of trade between India and China has also increased between 2012 and 2022 by 83 per cent (Pravakar and Ashwani 2023; Gobbi 2023). India's Ministry of Commerce claimed that India's total exports to Russia increased 46.2 per cent year-on-year to $2.7 billion in the first eight months of fiscal year 2023/4 ended March, while imports increased 54.8 per cent to $40.5 billion in the same period (Reuters 2024).

Focusing on payment systems, in February 2023, the central banks of China and Brazil signed an MOU to establish yuan clearing arrangements in Brazil (Yeping and Jingyi 2023). Since 2014 the Russian Federation, due to the conflict in Crimea and Donbass as well as the violation of Ukraine's territorial integrity, has been the target of financial sanctions by NATO member countries and their allies. Since the beginning of the conflict, Russia's central bank has tried to respond to sanctions by creating its own credit card payment system called Mir. In 2021 the Mir system processed about 25 per cent of payments within the Russian financial system. In order to reduce dependence on the SWIFT system of payments, the Russian government developed a replica called SPFS (System for Transfer of Financial Messages). The following year China also launched its own system called CIPS (Cross Border Interbank Payment System). Unlike SPFS, CIPS is not only a messaging system to transmit payment orders, but also a settlement and clearing system to enable the execution of payments (Fantacci and Gobbi 2024, 2023). Considering the Russian case, we note how over the decade between 2012 and 2022 dollar-denominated exports declined by 30 per cent.

A further thrust to the dedollarization process may come from the enlargement of the BRICS community into BRICS+, with the joining of several commodity and oil producing countries. An emblematic example of the potential internationalization of the yuan is the fact that China and Saudi Arabia have reached an agreement on a currency swap worth about $7 billion. The three-year agreement provides for a maximum of 50 billion yuan or 26 billion riyals (Reuters 2023b).

The BRICS community has equipped itself with a new multilateral development bank (MDB) in 2014. The establishment of the New Development Bank (NDB) and the Contingent Reserve Arrangement (CRA) (Hooijmaaijers 2022) was announced at the sixth summit of BRICS countries. The main objective of this institution is to raise and mobilize resources for financing development projects of community countries. The NDB's subscribed capital is $50 billion immediately available, with an authorized capital of $100 billion. Considering governance, the governing body consists of the board of governors and finance ministers of the five BRICS countries, and the voting power is proportional to the capital shares held by each country. Capitalization allows the NDB to do its borrowing at low cost with a benefit to all members (Hooijmaaijers 2022) and to take advantage of the benefits of diversification of lending. When it comes to the CRA, it consists of a financial safety net that allows the provision of liquidity should actual or potential pressures arise on the balance of payments in the short term.

In the same year, twenty-one countries located in Asia, including China and India, created the Asian Infrastructure Investment Bank (AIIB). The AIIB was formed by fifty-seven countries joined by others in the following years with US$ 100 billion in authorized capital. Considering governance, the maximum share held by non-regional members cannot be more than 25 per cent (Wang 2019). To date, the percentage of Asian shareholders is 76 per cent, and China is the largest shareholder with a 26.5 per cent share (AIIB 2023)

As argued by Ye (2017) the Asian Infrastructure Investment Bank has adopted a more internationalist approach than the New Development Bank. The first

Table 2 Comparison of GDP of Countries Belonging to the G7 and BRICS +

Countries BRICS	GDP ($ billions)	Global GDP Share	Countries G7	GDP ($ billions)	Global GDP Share
China	$19.374	18%	US	$26.855	25%
India	$ 3.734	4 %	Japan	$4.410	4%
Brazil	$ 2.081	2 %	Germany	$4.309	4%
Russia	$ 2.063	2 %	UK	$3.159	3%
South Africa	$ 399	0.4 %	France	$2.923	3%
Saudi Arabia	$ 1.062	1 %	Italy	$2.170	2%
Argentina	$ 641	0.6 %	Canada	$2.090	2%
United Arab Emirates	$ 499	0.5 %			
Egypt	$ 387	0.4 %			
Iran	$ 386	0.4 %			
Ethiopia	$ 156	0.2 %			
Brics+ total	**$ 38.767**	**29%**	**G7 total**	**$45.916**	**43%**

Source: World Bank

goal of the AIIB is to implement a sustainable one through cooperation between countries belonging to the region and other multilateral banks. The AIIB is concerned with enhancing infrastructure connectivity in Asia by investing in infrastructure and other productive sectors (AIIB 2023).

As with the NDB, the establishment of an MDB managed by the member countries of the regional community has a strong political impact. This is clear from the words of US Treasury Secretary Lawrence Summers, who in early April 2015, following an avalanche of countries asking to join the AIIB, said, 'This past month may be remembered as the moment when the United States lost its role as guarantor of the global economic system' (Summers 2015).

Figure 3.2 shows the value of loans disbursed by major Multilateral Development Banks (African Development Bank (AfDB); Development Bank of Latin America (CAF); Asian Infrastructure Investment Bank (AIIB);New Development Bank (NewDB); Asian Development Bank (AsDB); Inter-American Development Bank (IADB); International Bank for Reconstruction and Development (IBRD); International Development Association (IDA); International Finance Corporation (IFC); European Bank for Reconstruction and Development (EBRD); European Investment Bank (EIB)). The light grey line indicates institutions where the majority of voting rights belong to lender countries while the dark grey line represents institutions where the majority of voting rights belong to borrower countries.

It can be clearly seen that the majority of disbursed funds mainly pertain to foreign countries, typically members of the G7. Over the years 2014–19,

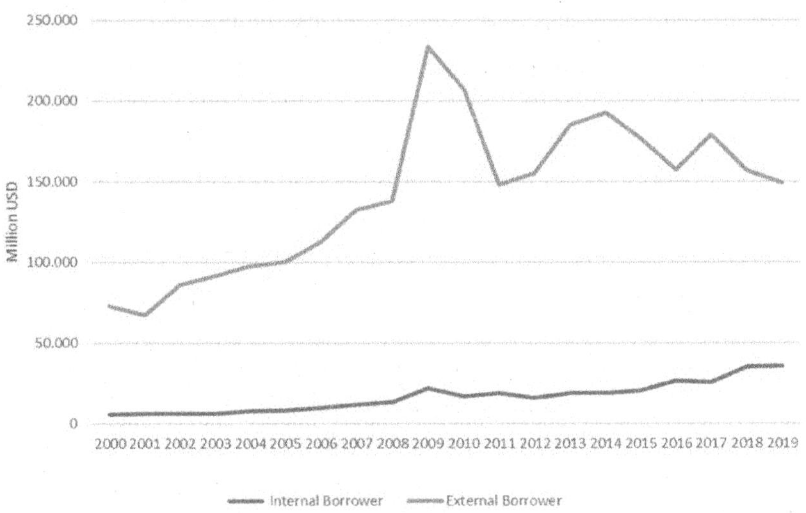

Figure 3.2 Funds allocated by MDB borrowers or lenders. Source: Annual reports of each institution.

however, the funds disbursed by resource-receiving countries has grown by 88 per cent while that of disbursing countries has dropped by 22 per cent.

Multi-currency CBDCs as a form of regional clearing[4]

If there were an international clearing system, such as the ICU designed by Keynes, cross-border settlements could rely ultimately on the possibility of settling (net) balances through the accounts of member central banks with the clearing centre. Instead, the current international payments system is based on correspondent banking: a network of agreements between private banks, located in different jurisdictions, on the basis of which one maintains an account with the other in local currency (Brandl and Dieterich 2023; Robinson, Dörry, and Derudder 2023). This private infrastructure, to date mainly centred on the 'offshore dollar' or 'eurodollar' system, plays a key role in making possible those cross-border payments that underpin international trade, finance and foreign remittances (Murau, Rini, and Haas 2020).

This current configuration has been the subject of much criticism from monetary authorities, such as Fabio Panetta (2023), governor of the Bank of Italy and former member of the board of the ECB, and international bodies, such as the IMF (Adrian and Mancini Griffoli 2023) and the WEF (2023). On the one hand, the system is judged to be inefficient due to excessive slowness, high costs and lack of transparency. On the other hand, since 2011 there has been a major reduction in the number of correspondent banking relationships. The trend towards oligopolistic concentration could be further reinforced by digitization. The outcome would be particularly inauspicious for the most vulnerable countries which, due to a reduction in the number of 'corridors' available to them, would have increasingly limited access to the international financial system.

To address these problems, a number of initiatives have been launched internationally to improve the functioning of cross-border payments. This is where wholesale CBDCs appear. The G20 roadmap, established by the Saudi Arabian presidency in 2020, is currently being developed by the Financial Stability Board (FSB), in collaboration with the Committee on Payments and Market Infrastructure (CPMI) of the Bank for International Settlements (BIS) and other leading international organizations and standards setting bodies. The 2020 CPMI report, in particular, emphasized the importance of exploring the international dimension of CBDCs to improve cross-border payments. To this end, since the joint work published in 2021, CPMI has been working closely with the Innovation Hub of the BIS, the International Monetary Fund and the World Bank. The catalytic role has undoubtedly been played by the BIS. Indeed, the latter has initiated, in collaboration with some national central banks and in parallel with other types of experiments, several projects aimed at testing the potential of wholesale CBDCs in cross-border payments (Table 3).

There are several options on the ground. It is worth noting, however, that this is not merely a technical issue, but a deeply political one. As Tobias Adrian, head of the IMF's Monetary and Capital Markets Department, has pointed out, the payments system is one of the fundamental pillars of the international monetary system along with exchange rate agreements and capital controls. No wonder, then, that in a recent speech, Banque de France Deputy Director Denis Beau said that 'with the ongoing work on wholesale CBDCs, central banks are laying the groundwork for a new global and multilateral monetary system'.

Indeed, as emerging economies show a growing political interest in reducing their dependence on the US dollar, the issue of regional clearing regains attention. The twin objectives of supporting regional trade growth and reducing exchange rate risk against the dollar are driving solutions based on multilateral payment technologies, both within monetary unions and in the absence of a common currency.

Table 3 Cross-border CBDCs Promoted by BISIH

		Jura	Dunbar	mBridge	Icebreaker	Mariana
Experiment design	BISIH centres	CH	SG	HK	SE	EU, SG, CH
	Central banks	Bdf, SNB	MAS, SARB, RBA, BNM	HKMA, BoT, PBoC, CBUAE	CBs of SE, NO and IS	BdF, MAS, SNB
	Output	Prototype	Prototype	Pilot	PoC	PoC
	Type of CBDC	Wholesale, Intraday	Wholesale, O/N w/o interest	Wholesale, Intraday & O/N	Retail	Wholesale
	Currencies	EUR, CHF	AUD, MYR, SGD, SAR	HKD, CNY, THB, AED	ILS, NOK, SEK	EUR, SGD, CHF
	Transaction type	Retail value	Simulated	Retail value	Simulated	Simulated
	Interoperability model	Common plat. w subnetworks	Common platform	Common platform	Hub and spoke	Common platform for FX
	DLT	Corda	Corda, Quorum	mBridge Ledger	Corda, Hyperledger Besu, Ethereum Quorum	Ethereum
	Operator	Private	Central banks	Central banks	Central banks	Central banks
	Extra use cases	PvP,[1] DVP,[2] offshore	PvP,[1] offshore	PvP	PvPvP	FX trading PvP

[1] A settlement mechanism that ensures that the final transfer of a payment in one currency occurs if and only if the final transfer of a payment in another currency or currencies takes place.

[2] A securities settlement mechanism that links a securities transfer and a funds transfer in such a way as to ensure that delivery occurs if and only if the corresponding payment occurs.

Source: BIS 2023

A significant initiative of the latter type is mBridge, a prototype of multi-currency central bank digital currency jointly developed by the BIS Innovation Hub Hong Kong Centre, the Hong Kong Monetary Authority, the Bank of Thailand, the Digital Currency Institute of the People's Bank of China and the Central Bank of the United Arab Emirates.

As other similar initiatives, mBridge is usually presented merely as a technical device to provide 'faster, cheaper and more transparent payments across borders' (BISIH 2022: 5). However, upon closer inspection, such experiments prove to offer also a distinctly financial service. For instance, Inthanon LionRock2, a project developed by BIS together with the Hong Kong Monetary Authority and the Bank of Thailand, builds on smart contracts to develop an 'algorithmic liquidity saving mechanism to reduce the nostro-vostro liquidity' (ibid.). In other terms, this platform based on DLT helps reduce the reliance on correspondent banking as a source of funding for international payments.

The establishment of wholesale CBDCs for use in payments could impact two of the fundamental pillars of the current system. On the one hand, they would call into question the coordinates governing public-private relations in global currency governance. On the other, as feared by the Atlantic Council, their spread could even pose a possible threat to the hegemony of the dollar (Tran and Matthews 2023). Indeed, wholesale CBDCs are designed precisely to facilitate cross-border payments without having to resort to currency markets, where the dollar has so far retained an 85 per cent share. In turn, the reduction in the use of the dollar as a medium of exchange in international payments would inevitably lead to a further decline in its holding as a reserve instrument by central banks (accentuating a descent that has already been going on for a couple of decades).

Moreover, one need not even imagine that, in its hegemonic position at the centre of the international monetary system, the dollar would be replaced by another currency. Already in official reserves what the dollar has lost has been gained not by a single rival currency (and certainly not by the euro), but by a plurality of smaller currencies. *A fortiori*, in the system of international settlements, interoperable digital technologies, such as wholesale CBDCs, could make it possible to reduce dependence on the dollar without necessarily requiring its replacement by another single currency. The scenario could be one of progressive fragmentation.

A more desirable alternative might involve the establishment of a global central bank. This role could be assumed by an international body such as the BIS, which could aspire to become fully, according to the original design of its creators, a central bank of central banks. The International Monetary Fund also seems to be moving in this direction with the creation of the XC platform, aimed at creating a single, globally unified ledger: could this be a first step towards transforming the Fund into a Clearing Union on the model designed by Keynes?

Conclusions

We started from an analysis of the reasons for Keynes's failure at Bretton Woods but also from the acknowledgement that the hegemonic balance of the dollar can no longer be taken for granted. We then tried to analyse the *lato sensu* anti-hegemonic tendencies that are now emerging. It would be excessive, however, to consider the emerging phenomena in the current framework as elements of an alternative order in the process of being composed. We are in an intermediate phase, in which an old order is beginning to show its limits and a new order is far from appearing on the horizon. Indeed, we can read the phenomena analysed as both elements of response to the potential disintegration of the old order and as active factors in that disintegration, but certainly not as elements of a new order with already defined features. However, precisely for this reason, it is worthwhile not only to closely follow these attempts as ambiguous indications of a potentially 'productive incoherence', but also to read Keynes's project at Bretton Woods as a framework that could be, with some care, adapted to the new situation.

On the one hand, the ICU is for Keynes compatible with the adherence not of individual states but of cohesive monetary economic blocs; on the other hand, it is an expression of the need for an overarching principle of order, which, as Eichengreen (2019) rightly points out, becomes even more necessary in a framework of greater horizontal articulation of relations between economic blocs than in a framework dominated by an undisputed hegemon.

As emerging economies show a growing political interest in reducing their dependence on the US dollar, the issue of regional clearing regains attention. The twin objectives of supporting regional trade growth and reducing exchange rate risk against the dollar are driving solutions based on multilateral payment technologies. It is perhaps too soon to say whether these will develop into full-blown applications of the clearing principle at a regional scale, such as in the case of the European Payments Union. There is, however, the possibility that they will increasingly acquire the function not just of facilitating cross-border settlements, but also of providing a source of international liquidity to fund balance of payments disequilibria.

This chapter is a first step and a first attempt at framing, which will obviously require both theoretical refinement and careful monitoring of the lines of evolution of a global world at risk of fragmentation.

Acknowledgement

This work was supported by the Italian Ministry for Universities and Research, grant PRIN PNRR 2022 n. P2022EZBTE, CUP: G53D23006790001, financed by the European Union – Next Generation EU.

Notes

1 For Keynes, the specialization implied by comparative advantage could be seen as an efficient solution because no industry is strictly strategic, and therefore the only constraint is given by productive efficiency, which is then reflected in the relative prices of technically reproducible goods, while for raw materials and commodities in general Keynes envisages a regime of controlled prices, also thanks to a third pillar of his post-war plan, an international institutions for the management of commodity buffer stocks, which in turn would strengthen the smooth functioning of the ICU.

2 https://brics2023.gov.za/wp-content/uploads/2023/08/Jhb-II-Declaration-24-August-2023-1.pdf

3 http://www.brics.utoronto.ca/docs/100415-leaders.html#:~:text=We%20call%20upon%20all%20states,our%20own%20countries%20and%20worldwide.

4 This section builds largely on Fantacci and Magurno (2023).

Bibliography

Adrian, T., and T. Mancini Griffoli. (2023), The Rise of Payment and Contracting Platforms, Fintech Notes No 2023/005, IMF, retrievable online at: https://www.imf.org/en/Publications/fintech-notes/Issues/2023/06/16/The-Rise-of-Payment-and-Contracting-Platforms-534794.

Amato, M. (2020), 'The Nature of Money in a Clearing System. From Liquidity to Liquidness', *PACO* (PArtecipazione e COnflitto, * The Open Journal of Sociopolitical Studies), 13 (1): 409–37.

Amato, M., and K. Nubukpo. (2020), 'A New Currency for West African States: The Theoretical and Political Conditions of its Feasibility', *PSL Quarterly Review*, 73 (292): 3–26.

Amato, M., L. Fantacci, D. Papadimitriou, and G. Zezza. (2016), 'Going Forward From B to A? Proposals for the Eurozone Crisis', Economics Working Paper Archive wp_866, Levy Economics Institute.

Ashford and Cooper. (2023), 'Yes, the World Is Multipolar And that isn't Bad News for the United States', *Foreign Policy*, 5 October, retrievable online at: https://foreignpolicy.com/2023/10/05/usa-china-multipolar-bipolar-unipolar/.

Asian Infrastructure Investment Bank AIIB. (2023), AIIB Annual Reports and Financials. https://www.aiim.org/en/news-events/annual-report/overview/index.html.

Bean, R. W. (1948), 'European Multilateral Clearing', *The Journal of Political Economy*, 56 (5): 403–15.

Beau, D. (2023), Unveiling the Potential of Wholesale CBDC: What Insights and Prospects?, Concluding Remarks by Denis Beau, First Deputy-Governor of the Banque de France. Conference Banque de France, 3 October, retrievable online at: https://www.banque-france.fr/en/governors-interventions/unveiling-potential-wholesale-cbdc-what-insights-and-prospects.

Benn, Steil. (2014), *The Battle of Bretton Woods John Maynard Keynes, Harry Dexter, and the Making of a New World Order*. ISBN 978-0-691-16237-9. OCLC 876136552.

Berend, T. I. (2016), *The History of European Integration – A New Perspective*, New York: Routledge.

BIS Innovation Hub. (2022), Using CBDCs Across Borders: Lessons From Practical Experiments, Bank for International Settlements, June.

BIS Innovation Hub. (2023), Lessons Learnt on CBDCs. Report Submitted to the G20 Finance Ministers and Central Bank Governors, Bank for International Settlements, July.

Bordo, M. D. (2017), 'The Operation and Demise of the Bretton Woods System; 1958 to 1971', Working Paper 23189, http://www.nber.org/papers/w23189 National Bureau of Economic Research.

Brandl, B., and L. Dieterich. (2023), 'The Exclusive Nature of Global Payments Infrastructures: The Significance of Major Banks and the Role of Tech-driven Companies', *Review of International Political Economy*, 30 (2): 535–57, DOI: 10.1080/09692290.2021.2016470.

Carney, M. (2019), The Growing Challenges for Monetary Policy in the Current International Monetary and Financial System, Speech given by Mark Carney, Governor of the Bank of England, Jackson Hole Symposium 2019, 23 August 2019.

Chang, R., 2000. Regional Monetary Arrangements for Developing Countries. (Working Paper). https://www.g24.org/wp-content/uploads/2014/03/210.pdf(open in a new window)

De Cecco, M. (1975), *Money and Empire: International Gold Standard, 1890–1914*, Oxford: Blackwell Publishers.

Economic Commission for Europe. (1948), *A Survey of the Economic Situation and Prospects of Europe*, Geneva: United Nations Department of Economic Affairs.

Eichengreen, Barry. (2008), *Globalizing Capital: A History of the International Monetary System*, Princeton: Princeton University Press.

Eichengreen, B. (2019), 'Two Views of the International Monetary System', *Intereconomics*, 54 (4): 233–6.

European Central Bank. (2024), What is T2, available at: https://www.ecb.europa.eu/paym/target/t2/html/index.en.html.

Fantacci, L. (2017), 'Reconciling money and goods: Keynes's commodity and currency plans for the postwar worlds.' *Annali della Fondazione Luigi Einaudi*, 51 (1): 149–76.

Fantacci, L. (2024), 'Shifting Liquidity Preference from Money to Goods: Hayek and Keynes on a Commodity Reserve Currency', in Maria Cristina Marcuzzo, Annalisa Rosselli, and Arie Arnon (eds), *Money in Times of Crisis: Pre-Classical, Classical and Contemporary Theories*, Roma: Bardi.

Fantacci, L., and L. Gobbi. (2023), 'The Future of the International Monetary System: Geopolitics and Technology', in N. Bilotta e F. Botti (eds), *Digitalization and Geopolitics: Catalytic Forces in the Future International Monetary System*: 19–47, Roma: Edizioni Nuova Cultura, Istituto Affari Internazionali.

Fantacci, L., and L. Gobbi. (2024), 'Stablecoins, Central Bank Digital Currencies and US Dollar Hegemony: The Geopolitical Stake of Innovations in Money and Payments', *Accounting, Economics, and Law: A Convivium* 14 (2): 173–200. https://doi.org/10.1515/ael-2020-0053.

Fantacci, L. and Magurno, J. (2023), 'Monete digitali: ritorno a Keynes?', ISPI Global Watch, 22 dec. https://www.ispionline.it/it/pubblicazione/monete-digitali-ritorno-a-keynes-157839

Financial Express. (The) (2023), US Imposes Restrictions on ACU Payment, available at: https://thefinancialexpress.com.b.

Flexner, K. F. (1957), 'The Creation of the European Payments Union: An Example in International Compromise', *Political Science Quarterly*, 72 (2): 241–60.

Fritz, B., A. Kaltenbrunner, L. Mühlich, and B. Orsi. (2023), 'South-South Monetary Regionalism: A Case of Productive Incoherence?', *New Political Economy*, 28(5): 818–31, DOI: 10.1080/13563467.2023.2184471.

Global Times. (2024), China, Brazil Foreign Ministers Vow to Bring Partnership to New Heights, available at: https://www.globaltimes.cn/page/202401/1305725.shtml.

Gobbi, L. (2018), 'Clearing Mechanism in Real and Financial Markets', PhD thesis, University of Trento.

Gobbi, L. (2023), 'De-Dollarizzazione: La Sfida Dei Paesi BRICS', *Moneta e Credito*, 76 (304).

Hayes, M. (2018), 'The Liquidity of Money', *Cambridge Journal of Economics*, 42 (5): 1205–18.

Hoffman, P. (1949), Statement by the E.C.A. Administrator at the 75th Council Meeting, Organisation for European Economic Co-Operation, Paris, 31 October, retrievable online at www.let.leidenuniv.nl/pdf/geschiedenis/eu-history/EU_03.doc.

Hooijmaaijers, B. (2022), 'The Internal and External Institutionalization of the BRICS Countries: The Case of the New Development Bank', *International Political Science Review*, 43 (4): 481–94.

James, H. (2012), 'The Multiple Contexts of Bretton Woods', *Oxford Review of Economic Policy*, 28 (3): 411–30.

Lees, F. A. (1962), 'A Critical Analysis of the European Payments Union', *The Journal of Finance*, 17 (3): 514–5.

Maes, I., and I. Pasotti. (2018), 'The European Payments Union and the Origins of Triffin's Regional Approach Toward International Monetary Integration', *History of Political Economy*, 50 (1): 155–90.

Mehrling, P. (2022), *Money and Empire: Charles P. Kindleberger and the Dollar System*, Cambridge: CUP.

Mikesell, R. F. (1948), 'Regional Multilateral Payments Arrangements', *The Quarterly Journal of Economics*, 62 (4): 500–18.

Murau, S., J. Rini, and A. Haas. (2020), 'The Evolution of the Offshore US-Dollar System: Past, Present and Four Possible Futures', *Journal of Institutional Economics*, 16 (6): 767–83. doi: 10.1017/S1744137420000168.

Panetta, F. (2023), 'The World Needs a Better Cross-Border Payments Network', *Financial Times*, 31 October, retrievable online at: https://www.bancaditalia.it/media /notizie/2023/Panetta-The-world-needs-FT.pdf.

Pravakar S. e Ashwani, B. (2023), 'Rising India–China Trade Deficit: Policy for Bridging the Gap', *Economic and Political Weekly*, 9 settembre, 58 (36), https://www.epw.in/ journal/2023/36/discussion/rising-india%E2%80%93china-trade-deficit.html.

Reuters (2023), "Exclusive: India, Russia Suspend Negotiations to Settle Trade in Rupees", disponibile al link: https://www.reuters.com/markets/currencies/india -russia-suspend-negotiations-settle-trade-rupees-sources-2023-05-04/

Reuters. (2023a), Rupee Payments Double Value of India's Engineering Exports to Russia, available at: https://www.reuters.com/world/india/rupee-payments-double -value-indias-engineering-exports-russia-2024-01-31/.

Reuters. (2023b), China, Saudi Arabia Sign Currency Swap Agreement, avaialble at: https://www.reuters.com/markets/currencies/china-saudi-arabia-central-banks-sign -local-currency-swap-agreement-2023-11-20/.

Robinson, G., S. Dörry, and B. Derudder. (2023), 'Global Networks of Money and Information at the Crossroads: Correspondent Banking and SWIFT', *Global Networks*, 23: 478–93. https://doi.org/10.1111/glob.12408.

Schenk. (2010), 'The Regulation of International Financial Markets from the 1950s to the 1990s', in Battilossi, S., and J. Reis (eds). *State and Financial Systems in Europe and the USA*. Farnham: Ashgate.

Shchegoleva, N. G. (2017), Retrospective of Payment Systems of Regional Unions of African and Latin American Countries: Experience for the EAEU. In Russia: Trends and Development Prospects. Yearbook. Resp. ed. V.I. Gerasimov. Moscow (In Russ.).

Shvandar, K., and L. Khomyakova. (2022), 'Regional Payment Systems of Asia, Africa, Latin America as a Tool for Regional Integration. Prospects for the Eurasian Economic Union', Finansovyj žhurnal – *Financial Journal*, Financial Research Institute, Moscow 125375, Russia, 14 (2): 43–54, April.

Summers, L. (2015), 'A Global Wake-up Call for the US?', *Washington Post*, 5 April. www.washingtonpost.com/opinions/a-global-wake-up-call-for-the-us/2015/04/05/6f847ca4-da34-11e4-b3f2-607bd612aeac_story.html (accessed 10 June 2016).

Tran, H., and B. C. Matthews. (2023), CBDCs will Further Fragment the Global Economy – and Could Threaten the Dollar, *Atlantic Council*, November 16, retrievable online at: https://www.atlanticcouncil.org/blogs/econographics/cbdcs-will-further-fragment-the-global-economy-and-could-threaten-the-dollar/.

Vernengo, M. (2021), 'The Consolidation of Dollar Hegemony After the Collapse of Bretton Woods: Bringing Power Back in', *Review of Political Economy*, 33 (4): 529–51.

Virusha, S. (2023), South Africa and China: Trade Relations Grow Stronger, available at: https://www.globalcompliancenews.com/2023/09/09/south-africa-and-china-trade-relations-grow-stronger/#:~:text=Trade%20between%20China%20and%20South,markets%20for%20South%20African%20products.

Wang, H. (2019), 'The New Development Bank and the Asian Infrastructure Investment Bank: China's Ambiguous Approach to Global Financial Governance', *Development and Change, International Institute of Social Studies*, 50 (1): 221–44.

World Economic Forum. (2023), Unlocking Interoperability: Overcoming Regulatory Frictions in Cross-Border Payments, White Paper, September, retrievable online at: https://www.weforum.org/publications/unlocking-interoperability-overcoming-regulatory-frictions-in-cross-border-payments/.

Ye, Y. (2017), 'Jinzhuan Yinhang de Bentuhua Fazhan Jiqi Chuangxin Yiyi' ['The Localization of BRICS Bank and Its Significance for Innovation'], Shanghai: Shanghai Institute of International Studies.

Yeping and Jingyi. (2023). https://www.globaltimes.cn/page/202303/1288326.shtml

4

Towards a new global financial architecture

The role of multipolarity, expanded BRICS and the Global South

Haider A. Khan

Introduction

The world has been through repeated financial and economic crises as neoliberal policies for liberalization that served mainly the perceived interests of the elites in the Global North – the United States in particular – unravelled. A quick retrospective look at the 2008 crisis is instructive. Despite the initial bafflement as the world economy was hit by the biggest financial crisis since the Great Depression, by now there is broad agreement on the underlying causes of the crisis: banks and financial institutions indulged in excessive leverage and excessive risk-taking while regulators did not provide an adequate regulatory framework. In the United States, the proximate causes also included the Fed policy under Alan Greenspan of supporting an artificial housing boom, after the bursting of a stock market bubble, through low interest rates and lax regulations in the housing and financial sectors in particular. Through various channels, the crisis was transmitted to other sectors of the economy, and to nations across the world, leading to significant human development impacts on the poor and vulnerable, particularly in the Global South. The Stiglitz report for the UN, among other sources, emphasizes that the deeper causes relate to a historic reversal of post-depression national and global economic governance checks and balances.

As the Stiglitz commission report put it:

> the standard policy nostrums – that countries should have sound macroeconomic policies strong governance, transparency, and good institutions – may be less

than helpful. Countries that held themselves out as models of best practices have been shown to have had deeply flawed macroeconomic policies and institutions and to have suffered from major shortfalls in transparency. (Stiglitz et al. 2010: 14–5)

Against this backdrop, there have been many calls for changes in the global financial and economic governance architecture that would lead to a more stable and less risky international financial system.[1]

Among the thinkers of the Global South as well as responsible economists from the Global North, if not the earlier Mexican crisis, then certainly the Asian Financial Crisis and the contagion it created unleashed a process of questioning the wisdom of the standard recipe of the Washington Consensus. This process of questioning intensified after the 2008 global crisis and is still continuing. Furthermore, assessment of the real costs of crises has forced onto the policy agenda the question of what kinds of national and international policies and institutions – particularly for global financial governance – are appropriate during the current period and in the foreseeable future. For policymakers from the Global South, finding an approximately right institutional structure for a new global financial architecture has become even more urgent. Recently, several leaders from Africa have directly called for creating a new global financial architecture. What advice can economists from the Global South give to their policymakers at this juncture?

As Morgan and Patomäki argue in the introduction to this edited collection, there are multiple reasons why debate regarding an International Clearing Union (ICU) remains of contemporary concern. Among these, they also emphasize the practical need for the creation of appropriate institutions and agency. In previous writings (Khan 2004a, 2004b, 2006) I have explored how a bridge between the concept of an (ICU) – notably associated with J. M. Keynes and with debates initiated in the 1940s – and the realities of the twenty-first century might be built.[2] In this contribution, I focus on the scope for transitions in the context of uneven development and some twenty-first-century nodal points in historical development. The current polarized system exhibits intensifying turmoil and conflict and with this in mind I argue that implementation of a global ICU and transition to a more cosmopolitan order will likely first require regional organizations in the Global South, and it is the scope for this that I focus on in particular. An expanded BRICS and the Global South will need to think carefully and pragmatically about the best dynamic trajectory within a transitional 'hybrid global financial architecture' (HGFA).

It should be noted that in the main body of the discussion I have attempted to minimize the use of technical jargon drawn from international economics and have relegated the more arcane points to endnotes. These also include extensive reference to my own technical works on the subject at hand, many of which provide supporting detail. I hope this strategy will make the substance of my analysis more accessible across disciplinary barriers while preserving the clarity of the main theme. I now turn to some crucial aspects of uneven economic development that will play important explanatory roles.

Uneven development and the role of historical contingencies

A convenient and wide-ranging guide for recent uneven development literature is the 2023 book, *A Modern Guide to Uneven Economic Development* edited by Reinart and Kvangraven. However, historically, uneven development as a concept, after the initial formulation by Marx, Lenin, Hilferding, Trotsky and others earlier, had been taken up and developed further by political economists such as Lowy (1981), Harris (2008) and by geographers such as Smith (2008) and Harvey (2011). In this chapter, the role of international economic and financial unevenness is stressed in particular.[3]

The role of structural unevenness in the global economy is particularly important to recognize within the proposed framework of analysis. The range of economies, the types of polities, the institutional capacities and resource endowments including technological progress and capacities for innovation all vary widely. A simple system of gold standard or adjustable peg or free and flexible exchange rate together with free multilateral trade under, say, the World Trade Organization arrangement may therefore be simplistic. It may serve the needs of one group of actors, for example, the advanced economies with well-developed financial services sectors. How best to achieve a synchronized growth and development regime that is perceived to be fair by all is indeed a challenging problem.

It is worthwhile to point out that a unique set of historical circumstances led to the Bretton Woods system that initially was second best to Keynes's more comprehensive plan for post-war international financial settlements. The White Plan from Washington made US dollar the main currency for global financial settlements under US hegemony implemented through the IMF. As the US balance of payments started to show ever larger deficits, partly because of wars but also because of increased US consumption of imported goods, the United

States suspended the gold window in the early 1970s. Here a second set of unique historical circumstances favouring US financial supremacy came into play.

After the energy – in particular oil – crisis that followed the war in the Middle East in 1973, the US deficit increased even more. The question arose as to how to recycle these 'petro-dollars'. Ultimately, Saudi Arabia and other OPEC nations agreed to buy US Treasury bills. Essentially this meant financing US deficits by recycling the surplus abroad by lending money to the US Treasury. Thus, the exorbitant privilege of the US dollar that De Gaulle had complained about earlier became even more so. The United States could merrily get real goods and services by non-gold-backed US dollars. This system plus ancillary financial messaging system such as SWIFT (Society for Worldwide Interbank Financial Telecommunications), has meant that unlike other debtor countries, the United States can freely spend more than its domestic national income without the kind of painful adjustments resulting in austerity and low growth performance for almost all of the countries in the Global South. But now that period of exorbitant privilege enjoyed by the United States may be coming to an end.

Specificities and vulnerabilities of the Global South: How to overcome the vulnerabilities?

The methodological approach adopted here is a type of constructivist and evolutionary analysis of our complex international economic system and political economy.[4] The evolutionary approach has been followed implicitly by authors such as Akyuz (2002), Eichengreen (1999), Greenwald and Stiglitz (2010a, 2010b), Ocampo (2010). In my formulations of the evolutionary approach to global financial architecture, I follow the more explicit approach – particularly as found in the history of technological innovations and the evolution of institutions more generally. In the area of technological innovations, the key references are Nelson (2006), Nelson and Winter (1982), and David (1985, 1990). Nelson (2006) also attempts to generalize Darwin's approach by applying it to technological evolution. But the credit for doing so in a more generalized Darwinian way to institutional evolution in general really belongs to Hodgson. More specifically, in Hodgson (1993, 2001, 2006, 2013, 2015) and Hodgson and Knudsen (2010), we find an explicit modern interpretation of Darwin's theory much like Gould's essays, particularly in Gould (1980). My own evolutionary approach to (hybrid) global financial architecture is indebted to this literature.

Two key characteristics of institutional evolution including the evolution of global financial architecture from the gold standard up to now are:

1. Institutions evolve depending on selection that are non-neoclassical. Ideal optimization is not the rule. Much makeshift experimentation over time can be observed.
2. In line with this proposition, rationality of institutions more bounded and functionally adequate for a time but changes in a non-deterministic and sometimes turbulent way during periods of crisis.

In analysing the problems of payments across borders in the context of the developing countries in the Global South, from the perspective of the Global South in particular, the following features of these countries can be highlighted, among others:

1. Developing countries in the Global South have fewer resources for coping with financial crises, particularly one that is global in its scope;
2. Most developing countries in the Global South lack automatic stabilizers due to the embryonic nature of their fiscal and social protection systems;
3. They have limited ability to borrow in international financial markets and this limits their ability to pursue countercyclical policies;
4. These threats are often exacerbated by global financial market integration and Free Trade Agreements and bilateral investment treaties. Many World Trade Organization commitments also affect the developing countries in the Global South countries adversely.

IMF pro-cyclical Structural Adjustment Policies can also restrict the policy space. The social and political construction of global and regional financial arrangements also depends critically on a supporting structure of *complementary institutional network*, norms, ideas and practices.[5] For example, both the gold standard and the Bretton Woods (BW) systems were based on complementary economic and political institutions that became unstable during crisis periods. A transition from the gold standard that was destroyed through instabilities in both economic and political institutions, required historically a new set of complementary economic and political institutions formalized in Bretton Woods and subsequent arrangements. Arguably, now in the post-BW world of turbulence, a new complementary set of political and economic institutions needs to be built. *Global financial architecture* (GFA) and *Regional financial architecture* (RFA) both depend on their respective locations within a complementary institutional network in a global system of nation-states and international organizations. Given the real interdependencies in the international system, the social and political construction of global and regional financial arrangements also depends critically on a supporting structure of a complementary institutional network, norms, ideas and practices.

Clearly, all actors have some stake in sustained growth and stability with equity. At the same time, part of the complexity of the global financial system arises from various contradictions and asymmetries in the system itself. Thus, the central argument of this paper is that sustainable policies at the national level require a supporting network of *global and regional financial architectures* that go some distance towards resolving the key issues arising from such contradictions and asymmetries, particularly between the Global North and the Global South. Appropriate national policies, in turn, can contribute to the sustainability of given financial architectures. It can be shown that following an evolutionary theory of international financial institutions, two broad types of possible GFA can be identified.

Previous work by Barry Eichengreen and others[6] show that it is possible to move beyond the post-Bretton Woods situation. In contrast with the conservative Meltzer report, all of these authors emphasize the need to strengthen the IMF in certain dimensions. However, not all of them recognize the crucial need also for the RFAs and the role they can play in creating an enabling environment for the state to implement beneficial economic policies. A completely evolutionary theory of GFA recognizes the need for transitional regional financial architectures from both an *evolutionary* and a *structural* perspective. However, as Eichengreen notes, given the lack of political resolve, there is little chance of creating *institutional structures* in the manner of the 1944 Bretton Woods agreement. The recent path of the world economy likely does not lead there. At the same time, the recent path does not lead to only neoliberalism. It is possible to both reform the IMF, as Eichengreen suggests, and to create new RFAs to complement such reforms. With this in mind, one important task is to identify a spectrum of GFAs. Most important among these are those that combine GFAs according to reform of the IMF with appropriate RFAs to achieve more constructive outcomes in terms of sustainability and equity.[7]

Fortunately, barring such events as wars, revolutions, complete meltdowns of financial systems, and so on, there is not at present an unmanageably large number of outcomes that are possible for the GFA. In fact, if we are willing to assume a continuum with nothing but an overarching *global* architecture for international finance with regional impurities added as another type, we have just two types of possible evolutionary outcomes for the institutional history of GFAs from a theoretical point of view.

The first type, which can be created at special evolutionary moments, can be called *Overarching Global Financial Architecture*. The gold standard under the UK hegemony and Bretton Woods under the threats of a post-war depression provide two examples. Recent history does not support the hope that something like the nineteenth-century gold standard system or a nodal site of organizational agreement like Bretton Woods is about to happen again. Therefore, a second type of evolutionary path resulting in a hybrid form should be recognized. This is the hybrid coexistence of a GFA together with one or many RFAs. We can call this type a *hybrid GFA* for shorthand reference. Once again, Asia after the Asian Financial Crisis is a good place to begin the analysis.

In the Asian case, as many have observed, the financial sector liberalization followed the pre-Asian Financial Crisis architecture by default. There were some short-term gains from the policy, but ultimately it resulted in severe instability. More generally, as Kaminsky and Reinhart (1999) show, based on the episodes of seventy-six currency crises, of which twenty-six are also characterized by banking crises, financial sector liberalization can result in a boom-bust cycle by providing easy access to short-term financing. Proponents of liberalization suggest some sort of micro sequencing in order to prevent such adverse consequences. With some variations, the most commonly suggested sequence is: improve the quality of regulation, make sure they are enforced, and then improve the supervisory mechanisms. As Azis (1999) nevertheless points out (albeit not using the same terminology as developed here), there is a contradiction in this type of GFA arrangement.

When the Asian crisis countries liberalized the financial sector in the 1980s, the preconditions (assumptions) for stability were not in place. Yet, they were rushed to liberalize by the International Financial Institutions. Ironically, when at the early stage the policy showed favourable impacts, for example, higher economic growth, and greater access to financial services, the International Financial Institutions applauded these Asian countries. But when the crisis hit, the very same countries previously praised were swiftly placed into the category of those with misplaced development strategies. All of a sudden, nothing was right with these countries. When confronted with such an embarrassing contradiction, the international institutions are quick to claim that they actually *saw* the faults and had *already reminded* the governments about the existing flaws, such as weak banking systems, unsustainable exchange rate systems, and widespread corruption (see Azis 1999). This illustrates the problems of the current GFA.

While a sudden move from the current GFA to an ICU-type system does not seem realistic, various processes involving hybrid forms *are* possible. The tentative steps taken towards regional cooperation in Asia since the Asian Financial Crisis illustrate the opportunities and challenges posed by the need to evolve towards a *hybrid* GFA, or if the acronym is extended *HGFA*. The opportunities and challenges arising from the current global crisis and the role an expanded BRICS can play, can be analysed in this context.

New historical conjuncture: An evolutionary institutional theory perspective

The overarching historical reason for new openings is the shift away from unipolarity. Even when the USSR existed, we had two bounded regional systems in the world led by the two great powers, the United States and the USSR. They were bounded politically through being hegemonic in their own geographically bounded areas, although proxy wars and other contestations over the Global South would continue until the fall of the USSR. Most importantly, since trade and investments were also bounded, especially in the Soviet bloc, the United States could exercise hegemony over the Global South by relationships of asymmetric dependencies dominated by the United States and the institutions it had set up after the Second World War.

After the fall of the USSR, there was a presumption of growing US hegemony and, to some significant degree, the United States enjoyed dominance in a system with unipolar tendencies. This situation helps to explain why the Global South, including Russia and even China, accepted, albeit never without variation, neoliberal doctrine and practices. In China, there was, however, always opposition within governing circles. Moreover, there is considerable debate regarding the original goals and subsequent extent of transitions and transformations that have occurred in China (see, e.g., Weber 2021). Speaking personally, I have experienced these contestations during my many visits and conversations with influential policymakers in China from 1991 until now. In particular, when I was at UNCTAD during the Global Financial Crisis, I witnessed some open and angry debates between Chinese neoliberals and their opponents. Now since 2018 at least, the US ruling class seemingly is bent on confrontation with China. Together with the tragic proxy war in Ukraine and the indiscriminate use of economic sanctions against Russia, China, and other countries by the United States and its junior partners, including the EU and Japan, this aggressive stance against China has pushed China and Russia closer. Now, these two countries are more willing than before to set up alternative payment mechanisms and a new modified type of global financial architecture. Will this succeed, and how fast can dedollarization and the US hegemonic decline proceed?

In my earlier works including the chapter in my 2004 book on *Global Markets and Financial Crises*, using a theory of evolution of institutions in a complex system, I outlined a plan for the formation of a regional financial architecture in Asia and other regions, and reform of the IMF by making its treatment of surplus and deficit countries symmetric. However, I have in the past been more optimistic regarding the prospects for change at the IMF. It has been evident recently that there is a lack of political will at the IMF and the US Treasury – despite some pious or perhaps even sincere rhetoric at times – and it does not seem that the United States or the IMF will take the path of significant reform. As I suggested earlier, drawing on Eichengreen, though, this is not an unequivocal point. While it is becoming increasingly clear that even in a multipolar system, older institutions like the IMF and World Bank and their European counterparts are likely to largely bow to US command there is a more complicated set of considerations here. Since the Global South cannot withdraw from the T-bills based US dollar hegemony all at once, if the current manifestation of political will in the BRICS and the Global South strengthens, a gradual delinking over the next two decades will be politically and economically feasible. What is achievable more quickly will be the strengthening of bilateral and regional *swap arrangements* and formation of both general *regional payments mechanisms with 'currency-equivalents' like Asian Drawing Rights* (ADR) – and even a Global South monetary unit such as an *Asian Currency Unit* (ACU) in the future – along with *specialized Global South financial institutions* like AIIB and Latin American and African regional banks run by experts from the Global South who have both technical expertise and a vision for alternative pro-people development in the Global South.

Recall that one of the major purposes of an ICU is to reduce tensions and provide for a payments system across national borders for mutual benefit. However, from the policy perspective, it is important to know if the existence of a Global South based regional financial architecture would help transition to an ICU and what their role might be in regard to future crises. This is perhaps a counterfactual question, but even so, it is vitally important one from the point of view of possible progress and thus well-being on a global scale.

In contrast with the behaviour of the IMF, within the proposed HGFA with regional financial architectures, at least the following aspects will be possible on the basis of applying an evolutionary theory of financial instabilities under globalization in a multipolar system:

1. Through constant regional monitoring the Global South will sense the danger of financial and other crises ahead of time. Even a regional monitoring unit alone would have been able to do better than the IMF team in Asia before and during the Asian Financial Crisis.
2. Through constant formal and informal contact with the officials in member governments and the private sector, the proposed HGFA will be able to size up the possible extent of the problem earlier and better than the IMF's record so far.
3. Through prompt and early action, the proposed HGFA will provide liquidity to the system, and punish bad management in coordinated measures with the national governments.
4. The proposed HGFA will be able to start regional discussions about bankruptcy and work out procedures by keeping in close touch with the history and legal issues facing particular countries.
5. The proposed HGFA will be in a position to use both moral suasion and credible toughness to keep both creditors and debtors in line.

Gradual dedollarization and multiple clearing systems under a new transitional hybrid global financial architecture in the multipolar world

The replacement of the gold standard – and British hegemony – by the dollar-based system was the result of two world wars and two decades of interwar crises. The breakdown of the system in 1971 was followed by the 1973 Arab-Israeli war and the agreement by Saudi Arabia in particular to accept a dollar-US T-bills bases international payments system. The current account surpluses of the resource-rich Global South countries were generally converted to T-bills in the capital account. The US dollar thus became the currency of account for all the parts of the balance of payments including the reserve account.

The United States from 1973 onwards has had the luxury to run both budget deficit and trade deficit without having to follow expenditure-reducing policies. When other currencies, such as the Japanese yen, were deemed to be undervalued by US policymakers, United States exercised hegemonic privilege to pressure the offending countries to revalue. In case of Japan during the 1980s, the Plaza

Accord revalued the yen. The bursting of Japan's bubble economy and subsequent decades-long stagnation forestalled the claim that the yen might replace the US dollar. What we have now, however, is a world of multiple currency transactions that is gaining momentum with the increased use of United States and EU sanctions as weapons of power. Ironically, the exercise of such hegemonic power by the United States is serving as a spur for the BRICS plus and the Global South to break away from the US dollar-based order.

At present, currency diversification is playing an important role in this accelerated stage of dedollarization. Such currency diversification could and most likely would play a strategic role in reducing dependence on the US dollar. At minimum, such a strategy would mitigate market and other risks associated with exclusive reliance on the US dollar by vulnerable countries. But to be successful, the alternative currencies and payment mechanisms must be viable.

The BRICS plus central banks have begun to act to make various dedollarization moves viable. It is well known that those CBs that can act with sovereignty (witness China, India and Russia among others) can formulate monetary policy in the national interest, manage currency reserves, plan the promotion of alternative payment systems etc. central banks are well placed in such sovereign countries to build institutional international collaboration. One of the most important aspects of such central banks is to promote regional (and for BRICS plus, cross-regional) financial architectures. Clearly the expanded BRICS and the Global South countries are headed in this direction.

It is important to note particularly that central banks of sovereign countries with monetary sovereignty are vital to the project of dedollarization. Through proper and timely adjustment of real interest rates, central banks can smooth out business cycles except when there is a liquidity trap. Managing liquidity becomes important particularly at such times and the government has to use fiscal instruments for stimulating investment and consumption as well. Exchange rate policy is another vital area for central banks. Likewise, the central banks are playing important roles in arranging currency swap agreements. Both bilateral and multilateral arrangements in swaps and other payment mechanisms are important in reducing dollar dependence.

Will the advent of Central Bank Digital Currencies play a role in dedollarization? Here there are both early mover and network aspects. BRICS-plus countries can play a pioneering role and reap network advantages by setting up swap arrangements and so on. But by themselves Central Bank Digital Currencies are not panaceas. They have to form a strategic part of a set of coherent and coordinated policies among the BRICS-plus group and more generally the Global South. BRICS-plus central banks are also playing an increasingly important role in fighting for reforms in international financial institutions. Generally, these have been geared towards making these institutions fairer.

Promoting a fairer multipolar system will require treating the US dollar as one important currency but not the dominant one. The United States will continue to be a great economic power but not the only one. A symmetric payments system will increasingly move towards the use of Special Drawing and Asian Drawing Rights like currencies of settlement. Most importantly, the United States will no longer be able to live beyond its means by issuing more debt by whatever amounts it wishes because that will require increasing the rate of interest which is tantamount to decreasing the price of T-bonds of various maturities.

Changes in the world financial and economic order have consequences for developing countries in the Global South directly, through banking regulations and global/regional policies, and also indirectly through the impact on developed countries themselves, which can affect lending, foreign investments as well as international aid. In this context, it is possible to find motivations for undertaking a study that will examine the principal changes that have taken place (or are likely to do so) as a result of the financial and economic crisis. These changes can also include alterations in financial and economic governance mechanisms and policies given the general economic context in which countries, in particular developing countries, are operating.

Particularly in this changing context in a complex global economic system, it is significant that the leaders of the BRICS countries (i.e. Brazil, the Russian Federation, India, China and South Africa) approved as early as March 2013, during their meeting in Durban, the creation of a New Development Bank to finance investment in infrastructure and more sustainable development in BRICS and other emerging and developing countries. As the March 2013 Durban Summit Declaration and Action Plan states:

> In March 2012 we directed our Finance Ministers to examine the feasibility and viability of setting up a New Development Bank for mobilising resources for infrastructure and sustainable development projects in BRICS and other emerging economies and developing countries, to supplement the existing efforts of multilateral and regional financial institutions for global growth and development. . . . We have agreed to establish the New Development Bank. The initial contribution to the Bank should be substantial and sufficient for the Bank to be effective in financing infrastructure.[8]

On the part of the expanded BRICS and the Global South strengthening financial stability through prudent reserves management and institutional development nationally and internationally in the Global South will be crucial. For this reason, robust risk management, international policy coordination, development of world-class financial standards, and capacity building along with technical assistance as forms of South-South cooperation must be accelerated. Through contingency planning and timely interventions, crisis management will become more feasible. Ultimately, a gradual move towards a genuinely symmetric international payment mechanism where no single currency is dominant will be necessary. A necessary condition for this to happen is the end of US hegemony. The world is indeed moving in this direction. The real question is: Will the United States agree to a non-violent end to its dominance? The answer is not clear at this point.[9] It is absolutely fundamental to recognize the importance of a peaceful transition. In the nuclear age, direct great power violent confrontation could easily escalate into a nuclear war where all will be losers. Therefore, difficult as it might be for the US policymakers to give up adventurism[10] in a desperate bid to recover from declining hegemony through attempts at dominance, they are unwise moves in the extreme. In fact, these forever wars are already depriving US citizens of real economic and military security. Negotiations in good faith with full recognition of reality are an urgent necessity under such circumstances.

The argument so far has rightly emphasized the long-standing grievances of the Global South under US hegemony and the rise of multipolarity together with the expanded BRICS as the key deep causal factors in creating a bifurcated payments system and monetary order on the way, eventually, to a fair cosmopolitan symmetric order. Although not the main causal factor by any means, the increasing use of sanctions[11] by the United States and EU have accelerated the trend towards bifurcation. Consequently, the incentives for dedollarization have been strengthened leading towards the increasing use of Alternative Payments and Messaging Systems replacing SWIFT.

The upshot is that other things being equal, the massive-sanctions-using US financial hegemony was not going to be seriously threatened for at least another decade. But seizing Russia's assets and current sanctions against PRC has made China in particular anxious. Alternative payment systems and dedollarization have accelerated. But further institutionalization of these trends will require at least another decade. We will see a fully bifurcated hybrid global financial architecture by 2040 at the latest. One might argue that this is taking shape in front of our eyes right now.

Thus, spurred by sanctions and hybrid wars, we can already discern a move away from the risks of appropriation by the United States, United Kingdom and EU states under the emerging multipolar system. The formation of a trading currency – but not a unique reserve currency – by the expanded BRICS is on the agenda now. It will most likely not be a Bretton Woods-like system – but nevertheless will be a clear alternative to the Washington Consensus and respond effectively to the payment necessities of the Global South at this juncture. This prospect has already sharply accelerated the ongoing dismantling of the dollar-based economic world order.

Given that the proposed new synthetic BRICS-plus trading currency can be based on an index of currencies of participating countries it is possible that these arrangements can be further strengthened through proposals that expand the underlying currency basket, adding a number of exchange-traded commodities. While models are never entirely realistic a model of this design can be shown to have a high degree of resilience and stability, and this speaks to its use as a transitional strategy.

Currently, the United States is clearly struggling to maintain its global dominance. If history is any guide, just as Britain previously was unable to keep its empire and its central position in the world due to the obsolescence of its colonial economic system, the probability of US failure to dominate under new historical conditions is increasing. US empire is given cohesion and is undergirded by NATO and other security treaties, by more than 800 bases abroad and by the forward placement of US military in many bases. In a multipolar world of nuclear powers where the United States no longer has hegemonic status but is still unwilling to reach new realistic accommodations peacefully through multilateral negotiations, the current arrangements will increasingly become more precarious. The British decline led to two post–Second World War bounded orders until the fall of the USSR. Will the US decline lead to two bounded but also interacting mixed economic systems?

Conclusion

The world system is at a point of bifurcation. So far, the US hegemony is ending in a disorderly manner. For our purposes the world system does not need a new hegemon. It needs a gradual working out of a new and fair cosmopolitan order achieved without violence. As a pragmatically conceived intermediate step, a Hybrid Global Financial Architecture has been proposed here as a bridge that can be fairer to the Global South than the US dominated system has been. Breaking away from the US hegemony in global financial governance requires, among other things, a partial or incremental move away from the use of the US dollar and other Northern currencies on the part of the expanded BRICS and the Global South. Ultimately, however, the emerging multipolar international system will require a new, more balanced and fair international monetary order. This has been the main thesis of this paper.

The fundamental requirement for financial stability and independence of the Global South at this juncture would seem to be the creation of an expanded BRICS, including many energy producers that can lead to both supra-regional financial architecture for the Global South along with specific Regional Financial Architectures in Asia, Africa and Latin America, each with sufficient liquidity and technical expertise. (The Asian Development Bank provided quite a bit of liquidity to Korea in particular during the Asian Financial Crisis but did not even have a monitoring unit when the crisis broke out). Furthermore, the autonomy and integrity of Global South future regional financial architectures in Asia and elsewhere are issues that need discussion. The relationship between the new RFAs and the IMF also needs to be further specified. These are evolutionary matters.

Over the past decade or so, developing countries in the Global South have been able in varying degrees to resist relying upon the IMF through measures such as:

- The over-accumulation of reserves;
- International capital flows, mainly from the PRC, and other East Asian economies;
- Bilateral swap arrangements;
- Regional banks and financial arrangements;
- South-South developing countries financial assistance.

Going down this list, one goes from more costly to more cost-effective measures. A hybrid GFA will be a further movement in the direction of cost-effectiveness for the Global South. In international politics, as I have discussed in my recent papers, in a multipolar world, there will also be an opportunity to launch a new non-aligned movement from the Global South and reduce global political tensions. What is needed is a combination of bold vision and practical realism supported by relevant expertise for the benefit of the great majority of the people on our planet.

In times of crisis, there are well-meaning suggestions targeted at radical institutional restructuring that fade away when the immediate crisis is over. Only a few farsighted or worrying types may still voice lingering concerns. Following this literature, but more importantly, the recent twenty-first-century global crisis and the history of the Asian Financial Crisis motivate my proposals for moving away from an overarching type of GFA – to use the terminology developed here. Given the features of the real economic world, an evolutionary approach admits of multiple evolutionary equilibria and a need for realistic institutional design that recognizes path dependence and the role of alternative theories and interpretations without the disabling and in most cases incorrect slogan that there is no alternative.

Although social and political construction of new institutions and arrangements are difficult, except for rare circumstances, there is usually more than just one possibility. Real struggles among competing ideas, norms and politics at different levels are necessary aspects of the process of choosing among possibilities. Such an approach to constructing a new and better global order applied to the recent international financial and economic history leads to the identification of two broad categories of global financial architectures. The hybrid variety advocated here on the basis of both realism and systemic efficacy and equity will nevertheless involve much institution building that is always fraught with the dangers of politics gone awry. Therefore, from the point of view of the Global South, a gradual step-by-step approach is likely preferable, and great care is necessary. The alternative may well be violent great power conflict in an age of widespread nuclear capability. That way lies disaster, and this may well be the most important reason to put the question of the international payments system within the broader critical realist framework of an emergent multipolar order. Keynes may be long gone but the issues he and others brought to the fore are more than ever relevant.

Notes

1 See among others, Eichengreen (1999), Greenwald and Stiglitz (2010a, 2010b), Ocampo (2010), BRICS (2023), Khan (2004a,2004b; 2006; 2013a, 2013b), Khan and Patomäki (2013) and the references therein. For the evolution of Keynes's own ideas on the post–Second World War monetary system during the war, see the references to his work in the bibliography at the end of this chapter. See also Helleiner (2014).

2 See Keynes (1969[1942]) and for various subsequent interventions and discussions see Triffin (1961, 1968); Brandt Commission (1980); Davidson (1992–3, 2002, 2004); Stiglitz (2006); Greenwald and Stiglitz (2010a) and the papers cited in the

references section here that were presented at the ICU conference in Helsinki, March 2024.

3 Khan (2004a, 2004b, 2012, 2013a, 2013b, 2021a, 2021b, 2023a-f, 2024a-f) places the issue of unevenness and institutional change in evolutionary theoretical and historical context. Specific issues ranging from macro instabilities to micro corporate governance, sanctions and critiques of the current system are also covered.

4 Technically, this belongs to analysis of *dynamic complex adaptive economic systems*. The technical work on aspects of this *dynamic complex adaptive economic systems* in international finance has been done in Khan (2004a, 2021a, 2021b), Khan, Ghorbani, Shabani and Band (2023) and Lin et al. (2008) among other sources. The institutions I discuss and the alternatives I propose here are all path dependent, but in a non-deterministic manner. Social practices based on collectively held ideas by both elite and non-elite groups can matter in crucial ways. However, given the structural aspects of global financial and economic system and the conflicting ideas and norms, there are serious contradictions at all levels of the system. Recognition of such contradictions and conflicts at both ideational and material levels dialectically forms the 'critical' part of my constructivist adaptive complex systems approach (Khan 2004a, 2006, 2011).

5 Aoki (2001) presents a formal theory of complementary institutional network. Earlier Amable (2000) had presented a broader version of institutional complementarity in an informal manner.

6 See in addition to Eichengreen (1999) cited earlier, Tobin and Ranis (1998); Azis (1999); Khan (2004a, 2004b; 2006, 2013a, 2013b).

7 Formally, the heuristic argument presented above can be established via a careful consideration of *path dependence* during evolution of the GFA. In order to do this in a conceptually rigorous manner, the concept of *path dependence* itself has to be refined and formalized in a specific way. I have developed this idea elsewhere and will only sketch the conceptual path to be followed. Eschewing the formal apparatus of graph theory and neural network dynamics which can be used to describe these rigorously, we can simply say that in deterministic path dependence there is only one choice of path. Everything is as it should be, since there are no bifurcations at any point in history. In fact, we can make a stronger statement. At *no* point in history is there even a *possibility* of even a bifurcation. Most people will see this as an extreme, and in case of human institutional design, perhaps as an unrealistic case. The purely stochastic case is all *random mutation*. Again, there is no way that conscious choice can play a role here either. Blind chance determines the outcome. The last type of path dependence, that is, the PD variety leaves some room for evolution to be a result of at least some kind of boundedly rational human activities. In this case, a complex set of human activities including learning and improving

policy-making capabilities can influence which network of paths are followed over time. While the number of available paths at any point in history may be large, they are never infinite. Therefore, combinatorial mathematics will in most cases show the existence of the most likely evolutionary outcome. However, the caveat that large, seemingly random fluctuations (e.g. a war) can throw these calculations off is always a (rare) possibility.

8 See also Conway-Smith (2013); Griffith-Jones (2011).

9 See Khan (2023f) for a discussion of the various nuances from a geopolitical perspective.

10 As thoughtful realists like Mearsheimer, Walt, Layne and others have pointed out, the United States is a rich country that is vulnerable only to nuclear (and now hypersonic and other types of missiles with conventional warheads) attacks. Therefore, it has been tempted to go abroad and engage in proxy wars and direct wars against weaker nations. Continuing on this path where great powers like PRC or Russia are involved is a recipe for catastrophe.

11 For technical details and modelling strategies, see Khan (2023d) and the references therein. Modelling issues for dedollarization and alternative payments systems are discussed in Khan (2021a-d; 2023 a-f; 2024a-f). Relevant twenty-first-century issues such as energy and ecological crises are also addressed in both global and local contexts.

References

Akyuz, Yilmaz. (2002), *Reforming the Global Financial Architecture*, Geneva: UNCTAD.

Amable, B. (2000), 'Institutional Complementarity and Diversity of Social Systems of Innovation and Production', *Review of International Political Economy*, 7 (4): 645–87, Winter.

Aoki, M. (2001), *Toward a Comparative Institutional Analysis*, Cambridge, MA: MIT Press.

Azis, Iwan. J (1999) *Do We Know the Real Causes of the Asian Crisis? Global Financial Turmoil and Reform: A United Nations Perspective*, Tokyo: The United Nations University Press.

Brandt Commission. (1980), *Report of the Independent Commission on International Development Issues. North-South: A Programme for Survival*, London: Pan Books.

BRICS. (2023), Johannesburg II Declaration, Sandton, Gauteng, South Africa, 23rd August 2023.

Conway-Smith, E. (2013), 'Developing Nations to Meet at the BRIC Beach Party in South Africa', Global Post, available at: http://www.globalpost.com/dispatch/news/regions/africa/south-africa/130323/developing-nations-meet-bric-summit-durban.

David, P. A. (1985), 'Clio and the Economics of QWERTY', *American Economic Review*, 75 (2): 332–7.

David, P. A. (1990), 'The Dynamo and the Computer: An Historical Perspective on the Modern Productivity Paradox', *American Economic Review*, (2): 355–61.

Davidson, Paul. (1992–3), 'Reforming the World's Money', *Journal of Post Keynesian Economics*, 15 (2): 153–79.

Davidson, Paul. (2002), *Financial Markets, Money and the Real World*, Cheltenham: Edward Elgar.

Davidson, Paul. (2004), 'The Future of the International Financial System', *Journal of Post Keynesian Economics*, 26 (4): 591–605.

Eichengreen, Barry. (1999), *Toward a New International Financial Architecture: A Practical Post-Asia Agenda*, Washington, DC: Institute for International Economics.

Gould, Stephen Jay. (1980), *The Panda's Thumb*, New York: W.W. Norton.

Greenwald, Bruce, and Joseph E. Stiglitz. (2010a), 'Towards A New Global Reserve System', *Journal of Globalization and Development*, 1 (2): 1–24.

Greenwald, Bruce, and Joseph E. Stiglitz (2010b), 'A Modest Proposal for International Monetary Reform', in S. Griffith-Jones, J. A. Ocampo, and J. E. Stiglitz (eds), *Time for a Visible Hand: Lessons from the 2008 World Financial Crisis*, 314–44, Initiative for Policy Dialogue Series, Oxford: Oxford University Press.

Griffith-Jones, S. (2011), South-South Financial Cooperation. Background Paper No 2 to UNCTAD's *Least Developed Countries Report, 2011*, available at: http://www .stephanygj.net/papers/SOUTHSOUTHFINANCIALCOOPERATION2012.pdf.

Harris, Donald. (2008), 'Uneven Development', in Steven N. Durlauf and E. Blume Lawrence (eds), *The New Palgrave Dictionary of Economics*, 2nd edn, Houndmills: Palgrave Macmillan.

Harvey, D. (2011), 'Roepke Lecture in Economic Geography – Crises, Geographic Disruptions and the Uneven Development of Political Responses', *Economic Geography*, 87 (1): 1–22.

Helleiner, Eric. (2014), *Forgotten Foundations of Bretton Woods: International Development and the Making of the Postwar Order*, Ithaca, NY: Cornell University Press.

Hodgson, G. M. (1993), Economics and Evolution: Bringing Life Back into Economics, Cambridge and Ann Arbor: Polity Press and University of Michigan Press.

Hodgson, G. M. (2001), *How Economics Forgot History: The Problem of Historical Specificity in Social Science*, London and New York: Routledge.

Hodgson, G. M. (2006), 'What Are Institutions?', *Journal of Economic Issues*, 40: 1–25.

Hodgson, G. M. (2013), *From Pleasure Machines to Moral Communities: An Evolutionary Economics without Homo Economicus*, Chicago: University of Chicago Press.

Hodgson, G. M. (2015), *Conceptualizing Capitalism: Institutions, Evolution, Future*, Chicago: University of Chicago Press.

Hodgson, G. M., and T. Knudsen. (2010), *Darwin's Conjecture: The Search for General Principles of Social and Economic Evolution*, Chicago: University of Chicago Press.

Kaminsky, Graciela L., and Carmen M. Reinhart. (1999), 'The Twin Crises: The Causes of Banking and Balance-of-Payments Problems', *American Economic Review*, 89 (3): 473–500.

Khan, Haider A. (2004a), *Global Markets and Financial Crisis*, New York: Macmillan and Springers.

Khan, Haider A. (2004b), *Innovation and Growth in East Asia: The Future of Miracles*, New York: Macmillan and Springers.

Khan, Haider A. (2006), 'Managing Global Risks and Creating Prosperity: The Role of the IMF and Regional Financial Architectures', in Junji Nakagawa (ed), *Managing Development: Globalization, Economic Restructuring and Social Policy*, London: Routledge.

Khan, Haider A. (2012), Constructing Global Governance of Global Finance: Towards a Hybrid Global Financial Architecture. Econpapers. https://econpapers.repec.org/paper/pramprapa/40249.htm

Khan, Haider A. (2013a), Global Financial Governance: Towards a New Global Financial Architecture for Averting Deep Financial Crises. EconPapers. https://econpapers.repec.org/paper/pramprapa/49275.htm

Khan, Haider A. (2013b), 'Basel III, BIS and Global Financial Governance', *Journal of Advanced Studies in Finance*, IV (2(8)): 121–44.

Khan, Haider A. (2021a), Governing a Complex Global Financial System in the Age of Global Instabilities and BRICS: Promoting Human Capabilities through Global Financial Stability and Growth with Equity, Chapter 37 in P.B. Anand, Shailaja Fennell and Flavio Comim (eds).

Khan, Haider A. (2021b), 'AI, Deep Machine Learning via Neuro-Fuzzy Models: Complexities of International Financial Economics of Crises', *International Journal of Computation and Neural Engineering* 7 (3): 122–34. DOI: 10.19070/2572-7389-2100016.

Khan, Haider A. (2023a), Geoeconomics, China, Fourth Industrial Revolution and the Future. EconPapers. https://econpapers.repec.org/paper/pramprapa/117362.htm

Khan, Haider A. (2023b), The Economic and Geopolitical Consequences of Belt and Road Initiative (BRI) for China: A Preliminary Model-based Analysis. EconPapers. https://econpapers.repec.org/paper/pramprapa/117005.htm

Khan, Haider A. (2023c), Geoeconomics, Structural Change and Energy Use in Iran: A SAM-Based CGE Analysis with Some Geoeconomic and Geopolitical Considerations. EconPapers. https://econpapers.repec.org/paper/pramprapa/117155.htm

Khan, Haider A. (2023d), Towards a General Complex Systems Model of Economic Sanctions with Some Results Outlining Consequences of Sanctions on the Russian Economy and the World. EconPapers. https://econpapers.repec.org/paper/pramprapa/116806.htm

Khan, Haider A. (2023e), Towards a New Non-Aligned Movement(NNAM) and a New International Economic Order: A Strategy for Comprehensive Non-Capitalist Development in the 21st Century. EconPapers. https://econpapers.repec.org/paper/pramprapa/117143.htm

Khan, Haider A. (2023f), War and Peace in East Asia: Avoiding Thucydides's Trap with China as a Rising Power. Econpapers. https://econpapers.repec.org/paper/pramprapa/117089.htm

Khan, Haider A. (2024a), 21st Century Accelerated Dedollarization, Multipolarity and The Global South Beyond Modern Money Theory: Governance of a Complex Global Financial System in the Age of Global Instabilities. Econpapers. https://econpapers.repec.org/paper/pramprapa/119650.htm

Khan, Haider A. (2024b), Development Orders and Disorders: Real Competition in Complex Global Capitalist System, China's Ambiguous Case, and the Need for Democratic Socialism in the 21st Century. Econpapers. https://econpapers.repec.org/paper/pramprapa/119640.htm

Khan, Haider A. (2024c), Dialectics of Emergy in a Social Accounting Matrix. Econpapers. https://econpapers.repec.org/paper/pramprapa/119651.htm

Khan, Haider A. (2024d), Ecological Crisis and the Global South Internationalist Ecosocialism: A Strategy for Comprehensive Sustainable Non-Capitalist Development in the Global South. Econpapers. https://econpapers.repec.org/paper/pramprapa/119639.htm

Khan, Haider A. (2024e), Ecological Thinking of Tagore and Ecological Equity: A 21st Century Perspective. Econpapers. https://econpapers.repec.org/paper/pramprapa/119665.htm

Khan, Haider A. (2024f), Geoeconomics of a New Eurasia During the Fourth Industrial Revolution: The Role of China's Innovation System, BRI and Sanctions from the Global North. Econpapers. https://econpapers.repec.org/paper/pramprapa/119637.htm

Khan, Haider A., Shahryar Ghorbani, Elham Shabani, and Shahab S. Band. (2023), 'Enhancement of Neural Networks Model's Predictions of Currencies Exchange Rates by Phase Space Reconstruction and Harris Hawks' Optimization', *Computational Economics*. February. DOI: 10.1007/s10614-023-10361-y.

Khan, Haider A., and Heikki Patomäki. (2013), A Reconstructive Critique of IPE and GPE From a Critical Scientific Realist Perspective: An Alternative Keynesian-Kaleckian Approach. EconPapers. https://econpapers.repec.org/paper/pramprapa/49517.htm.

Lowy, Michael. (1981), *The Politics of Uneven and Combined Development*, London: Verso.

Nelson, R. R. (2006), 'Evolutionary Social Science and Universal Darwinism', *Journal of Evolutionary Economics*, 16: 491–510.

Nelson, R. R., and S. G. Winter. (1982), *An Evolutionary Theory of Economic Change*, Cambridge, MA: Harvard University Press.

Ocampo, J. A. (2010), 'Reforming the Global Reserve System', in S. Griffith-Jones, J. A. Ocampo, and J. E. Stiglitz (eds), *Time for a Visible Hand: Lessons from the 2008 World Financial Crisis*, New York: Oxford University Press, Chapter 16.

Smith, Neil. (2008), *Uneven Development: Nature, Capital and the Production of Space*, Athens: University of Georgia Press.

Stiglitz, Joseph E. (2006), *Making Globalization Work. The Next Steps to Global Justice*, London: Allen Lane.

Stiglitz, Joseph E., and members of the UN Commission of Financial Experts. (2010), *The Stiglitz Report: Reforming the International Monetary and Financial Systems in the Wake of the Global Financial Crisis*, New York: The New Press.

Tobin, James, and Gustav Ranis. (1998), *The IMF's Misplaced Priorities: Flawed Funds, The New Republic*, available online at the following address: http://www .thenewrepublic.com/archive/0398/030998/tobin030998.html.

Triffin, R. (1961), *Gold and the Dollar Crisis*, New Haven, CT: Yale University Press.

Triffin, R. (1968), *Our International Monetary System: Yesterday, Today, and Tomorrow*, New York: Random House.

Weber, I. (2021), *How China Escaped Shock Therapy: The Market Reform Debate*, London: Routledge.

5

Resolving the balance of payments problematic

Feasible reforms for the twenty-first century

Niina Kari and Lauri Holappa

Introduction

A looming climate catastrophe, deflationary bias, severe debt distress and outright debt crises in poorer economies, as well as persistent underdevelopment, all plague the global economy. Contrary to the common optimistic narrative, inequality between the Global North and the Global South has increased since the 1960s (Hickel 2017: 2216–7). Although multiple factors and tendencies contribute to these problems, the international monetary system often plays a significant role. In this chapter, we focus on the problem of delimitation on economic policy autonomy which arises from the balance of payments constraint. As already recognized by John Maynard Keynes, balance of payments issues can create obstacles to the pursuit of otherwise prudent economic policies (Keynes 1936/2003: 213–4). Today, balance of payments concerns hinder, among others, policies to promote full employment, economic development and ecological transitions. Hence, Keynes's proposal for an International Clearing Union deserves renewed consideration. Addressing the balance of payments constraint requires at least some alterations to how the international monetary system operates.

Unfortunately, despite the recent resurgence in interest towards the international monetary order in general and dollar dominance in particular, many of the discussions appear quite disparate, even within academia. We focus here on two prominent distinct scholarly traditions concerned with the architecture of the international monetary system. The first is the mainstream International Political Economy (IPE) scholarship concerned with the geopolitics of international monetary hegemony. The second is the more normatively oriented post-Keynesian scholarship on the international monetary system, which includes numerous proposals to reform it. In addressing the balance of payments problematic in the current geopolitical context, we combine these two theoretical traditions. Namely, we assess and combine viable components of different reform proposals while also addressing the question of political feasibility and the underlying geopolitics of any reform to the prevailing international monetary order.

Our focus is on the limitation on economic policy space that arises from the balance of payments constraint. Our normative concern is to expand macroeconomic policy autonomy and thus the space for democratic politics. Firstly, we review IPE scholarship on the international monetary system and describe the prevalent approaches to the dollar system and global balance of payments imbalances. Secondly, we turn to the post-Keynesian scholarship discussing the international monetary system. We then contextualize the balance of payments problematic and thus illustrate the continued relevance of Keynes's proposal for an International Clearing Union (ICU). We also revisit a contemporary critique of the Keynes plan by Michał Kalecki and Ernst F. Schumacher, who argued that the ICU system would be too stringent towards developing countries. By contrast, we demonstrate that a revised ICU plan by the late post-Keynesian Paul Davidson offers a solution to the Kalecki-Schumacher critique. Next, to fully grasp the balance of payments problematic in the contemporary context we complement these older contributions with an analysis of the global dollar system in its current form. In so doing we seek to illuminate the asymmetries and hierarchies underpinning balance of payments concerns in the current international monetary system. In the remaining sections, we synthesize minimal and politically feasible reforms that would address the balance of payments constraint in the contemporary geopolitical context.

IPE scholarship and the international monetary system

International Political Economy as a distinctive discipline and scholarly tradition began to develop in the 1970s with the publication of key contributions by Susan Strange (1971) and Robert Keohane and Joseph S. Nye (1971, 1977) but the groundwork was already laid by some more historically oriented economists in the previous decades. The earliest IPE work on the global dollar system and international monetary hierarchy can be traced back to the works of John H.

Williams (1943), Robert Z. Aliber (1966) and Charles P. Kindleberger (1967). The early contributors largely assumed that there was space only for one dominant international currency at a time as international clearing cannot be efficiently organized on a multilateral system. Thus, international monetary politics was initially described and conceived as a continuous struggle for the status of the global monetary hegemon.

However, the mainstream position has become more nuanced and flexible over the years. Contemporary mainstream research has questioned the old key currency approach and argued that historically there have been instances of multiple important international currencies, especially during the interwar period. Hence, it is now often suggested that the US dollar might be 'displaced gradually by multiple international currencies'. This view is frequently complemented by assumptions that the dollar is on the verge of transforming into a 'negotiated currency' instead of being an undeniable top currency. In practical terms, a negotiated currency differs from top currency by the actions that are required from the issuing government to uphold the international position of its currency: a dominant top currency is in such demand that the issuer can largely bypass any foreign requests or wishes while the issuer of a negotiated currency must try to lure other countries to use its currency by carefully tailoring its monetary policy to satisfy also foreign needs (Oatley 2014: 60). In addition to using carrots, the issuer of a negotiated currency may also resort to sticks, such as sanctioning countries that try to exit the purview of the monetary hegemony.

IPE scholarship provides numerous explanations of how and why currencies can obtain a powerful position in the international monetary hierarchy. Some scholars emphasize the path-dependencies arising from the position of a leading currency: businesses want to use the top currency in their transactions and invoicing simply because it is so liquid and switching to a competing currency might be financially risky (ibid. 61). Other scholars highlight the importance of geopolitics. For instance, many governments are dependent on the US security guarantees and are thus forced to respect the vital economic interests of the United States which means using the US dollar as a reserve and trade currency (see e.g. Kirshner 2008, 2009).

What is lacking from the mainstream of IPE scholarship is, however, any analysis of the potential for systemic changes in the international monetary system. Most debates are about the fate of the dollar, the rise of the Chinese renminbi or the prospective number of leading international currencies. There seems to be very limited space for more imaginative and profound changes in the traditional IPE analysis of the global monetary system. This is not surprising as mainstream IPE is heavily influenced by the state-centric tradition of International Relations theory and suffers from the same limitations as its parent discipline.

Nevertheless, more open-minded discussions have been prevalent in post-Keynesian and old Keynesian economics as one of the most radical reforms to transform the international monetary system was originally proposed by Keynes himself. We now turn to the classical Keynes plan and the balance of payments constraint which it was originally developed to manage and regulate.

The balance of payments constraint and continued relevance of the Keynes plan

In this section, we articulate what we mean by the balance of payments constraint and how it constrains economic policy space. We argue that the persistence of this problem in the current international monetary system justifies revisiting Keynes's plan for an International Clearing Union.

The balance of payments constraint may arise from persistent current account deficits. Simple accounting identities can at times obscure real processes: while a current account deficit is always balanced by a capital surplus in terms of accounting, the underlying dynamic of running a persistent current account deficit while borrowing from abroad may be unsustainable (Vernengo and Caldentey 2020: 335–6). In specific contexts, the balance of payments constraint creates limits on the sustainability of fiscal expansion and large-scale investments. In particular, problems arise when fiscal expansion increases demand for imported goods but does not increase exports to the same extent. The country runs a current account deficit, which is financed through using foreign currency reserves or by borrowing externally. Once the reserves are depleted, the country becomes dependent on capital inflows. Without these inflows, it cannot finance the current account deficit. Thus, it will be forced to reduce imports. A more likely outcome, however, is that the country is still able to borrow but that this will create downward pressure on its currency. Investors will demand more of the domestic currency in exchange for hard currency, such as dollars, which feeds pass-through inflation (Holappa 2020: 153–4).

While neoclassical economists focus on quantitative thresholds, such as 50 per cent or more monthly inflation, post-Keynesian emphasize the qualitatively distinctive features of hyperinflation. The problem is not moderate or even high inflation as such, rather a hyperinflationary spiral, a process which is characterized by a vicious cycle dynamic that is difficult to control. One important component in an open economy is the self-fulfilling prophecy where economic actors exchange national currency into foreign currency as they anticipate the inflation to accelerate, thus contributing to depreciation and inflation through higher import prices. In turn, workers are incentivized to demand wage rises to maintain their living standards while firms tend to raise prices to maintain profit rates (Kulesza 2017: 2–4).

This dynamic can be particularly detrimental for a country whose currency has unstable or relatively low global demand and that needs to import critically important goods such as food, medication, raw materials, energy and intermediary or capital goods. While all countries import some of these resources, the degrees of dependence vary, also over time. For instance, with population growth and climate change, more countries will depend on food imports in the coming decades (Ravilious 2013). Furthermore, abrupt changes in the price of food or energy can trigger a balance of payments crisis in any country that needs foreign currency to import them (Bonizzi et al. 56). Degree of development also matters since poorer economies lack a diversified productive capacity and rely more on exporting primary commodities. One avenue to develop would be to upgrade the country's productive capacity towards more refined manufactured goods, which usually necessitates importing capital and intermediary goods. Hence, the balance of payments constraint is a particularly formidable hindrance to development via industrialization.

In terms of causality, the balance of payments constraint arises from a combination of different factors and tendencies in the international monetary system. One critical component is relatively unregulated currency speculation and capital flows. Although the balance of payments constraint takes a particular form in the context of flexible exchange rates, a similar dynamic can emerge in the context of fixed exchange rates as well. Flooding the international market with one's domestic currency creates downward pressure on its price, which makes it more difficult to maintain a peg. Another factor, already touched upon, is the degree of dependence on vital imports, which conditions the severity of the impact of currency depreciation on the economy. Many other contributing factors arise from the operation of dollar hegemony, such as the selling of key resources in dollars, the international hierarchy between different currencies and the arbitrary standards by which international liquidity is distributed. We will elaborate on these dimensions in the third section of this chapter.

The balance of payments problematic could be depicted in simplistic terms by arguing that whenever a country runs a persistent current account deficit, its currency depreciates and the price of its imports rises, which leads to an inflationary spiral, which in turn undermines long-term growth. Such a mechanical depiction, however, would fail to represent the indeterminacy and human agency involved. The process is not automatic, and key actors can choose between various strategies. For instance, there are numerous components that shape decision-making in foreign exchange markets beyond just quantitative data on current account deficits. More qualitative factors include economic events both globally and nationally as well as the domestic political situation. There are also more arbitrary components such the interpretations and expectations of the traders themselves. However, the increased use of artificial intelligence in foreign exchange trading has reduced the role of human agency in this process. Given that artificial intelligence is based on algorithms, there is indeed a mechanical component in this process (Azimova 2020: 91–3).

Nonetheless, governments and central banks can pursue various strategies to better shelter themselves from the balance of payments constraint or at least mitigate its effects. Central banks can, for example, raise interest rates to attract capital thus facilitating the pursuit of otherwise expansionary fiscal policies (although the fiscal expansion would need to compensate for the monetary tightening). Capital controls can also be used to make capital flows less volatile and encourage more long-term investment. Indeed, there has been an increase in the use of capital controls since the Global Financial Crisis especially in emerging economies (Das and Ordal 2022: 5–6). In particular, controls on capital outflow can inhibit dollar drainage from the economy (Asuyn et al. 2024: 1). However, capital controls cannot be used to guarantee access to sufficient liquidity, which is at the heart of balance of payments crises. While capital controls can manage the type of flows, they cannot increase their overall magnitude (indeed inflow controls have the opposite effect). The governments may also try to lure foreign direct investment to accrue more foreign currency. However, while FDI flows are more secure than portfolio flows, they too involve considerable risks, most notably of exchange rate volatility (Bonizzi et al. 2019: 55). The latter, in turn, can exacerbate the balance of payments constraint. On the other hand, there are avenues to access dollars ranging from swap lines and repurchase agreements provided by the Federal Reserve to Special Drawing Rights from the IMF. But as we will elaborate on in the third section of this chapter, access dollars is hierarchical with most Global South countries belonging to the bottom tier.

The limitation on economic policy space that arises from the balance of payments constraint can be elucidated in terms of a trichotomy articulated by Konsta Kotilainen. Kotilainen conceptualizes macroeconomic policy autonomy in terms of three temporal junctures. Whether the government can implement the policy without immediately running into external constraints, whether it is able to achieve its policy objectives, and whether it is able to maintain its achievements, are all measures of its autonomy, but in different time horizons (Kotilainen 2024: 115–6). In terms of this temporal trichotomy, balance of payments problems do not prevent the implementation of fiscal stimulus or large-scale investments in the first instance. Rather, they tend to hinder the achievement of the intended policy goals either directly (by undermining local production and economic growth) or indirectly (by discouraging the government from the pursuit of the policies to avoid other unwanted consequences).

In contrast to this nuanced approach, certain influential formulations of the balance of payments constraint are unduly deterministic. This includes the influential articulation of the balance of payments constrained growth by Anthony Thirlwall:

> if balance of payments equilibrium must be maintained, a country's long run growth rate will be determined by the ratio of its rate of growth of exports to its income elasticity of demand for imports. (Thirlwall 2011: 430–1)

Given the myriad factors that impact economic growth, such a simplistic hypothesis obscures the complex causality involved. Nonetheless, a better balance of payments position does grant greater macroeconomic autonomy. This, in turn, means that the government has more policy tools available to it to support and maintain economic growth.

Due to these considerations, we use the term the balance of payments constraint here with reservations. In terms of limiting economic policy space, the constraint is better conceptualized as a slippery slope than a brick wall. This threshold is not immutable and depends heavily on context. As we argue in the third section, the position of the country in the international currency hierarchy augments its susceptibility to balance of payments crises.

Notwithstanding these caveats, we maintain that the balance of payments constraint is a persistent problem in the international monetary system. For instance, the hyperinflationary period in Venezuela in the 2010s illustrates its potentially destructive consequences. As oil prices plummeted in 2014, Venezuela's current account position deteriorated quickly from a surplus to a deficit by 2015. It lacked foreign exchange to pay for key imports, such as capital, intermediary and basic consumer goods. In turn, imports were reduced by almost a fifth with a devastating impact on national production. In 2014, the economy contracted almost 4 per cent while inflation rose close to 70 per cent (Kulesza

2017: 26). The government resorted to rationing foreign exchange, which led to severe shortages in production inputs and basic goods, further accelerating inflation. An inflationary spiral emerged from a combination of price increases of key imports and distributive struggles between capital and labour to maintain profit rates and living standards respectively. Expectations of depreciation also fed the inflationary spiral as increasing numbers of firms and households exchanged their bolivars into dollars. Only exchange controls mitigated the dumping of the local currency, thus preventing full-scale dollarization of the economy (Kulesza 2017: 24–31). In the case of Venezuela, the balance of payments constraint was made tighter by its heavy reliance on oil export revenue for foreign exchange and its dependence on importing essential goods, partly due to the lack of diversification of its economy. However, these issues – reliance on exporting a raw material or primary commodity, dependence on key imports and lack of diversified productive capacity – are not exclusive to Venezuela but characterize many poorer economies.

Although we outlined some manoeuvres available to individual governments to loosen the balance of payments constraint, many of these strategies can also generate contradictions when pursued by a critical mass of countries simultaneously. For example, problems arise when many countries try to achieve current account surpluses at once. Since current account surpluses and deficits balance out globally, also net importers are needed. A generalized race to generate current account surpluses only results in a deflationary bias and makes it more difficult for any individual country to generate a surplus. Competition to attract foreign direct investment through raising interest rates or offering tax benefits involves similar contradictions (Bonizzi et al. 2019: 55). Given that the balance of payments problematic involves this type of interdependence and global dynamics, it can only be fully resolved through international cooperation.

The balance of payments problem was recognized by Keynes already in the 1940s in his plan for an International Clearing Union (ICU). Ever since the *General Theory* (1936), Keynes had been pushing for the institutionalization of demand management measures that could guarantee constantly high levels of effective demand and full employment. The problem with such a policy agenda, as outlined above, is that growing domestic demand goes always at least partially to the consumption of imports. Hence, significant international differences in domestic demand growth are likely to be translated into current account imbalances if the exchange rate mechanism cannot guarantee balanced trade.[1] The conclusion is, thus, obvious: possibilities to implement Keynesian policies which stimulate aggregate demand are hampered by the potential beggar-thy-neighbour policies of other countries.

The main problem is that current account deficits must be offset by capital flows if constant depreciation of the exchange rate cannot be maintained. However, strategies aiming at attracting enough capital inflows to compensate for the current account deficit have usually ended badly as speculative short-term capital inflows have ultimately reversed leading to the collapse in the exchange rate and the consequent inflation spiral (McCombie 2003; Vernengo and Pérez Caldentey 2020). Keynes's solution was to eliminate the possibilities for extreme profit-led growth strategies by establishing an international clearing union with mechanisms to disincentivize and sanction excessive current account surpluses. For instance, states with excessive surpluses would be encouraged to boost domestic demand and provide credit, appreciate their currency vis-à-vis the global currency bancor or raise wages (i.e. internal revaluation), reduce impediments to imports, or provide loans to less developed states (Horsefield 1969: 6–8). The risk of losing a significant share of the external surplus would incentivize governments to shift away from the strictest low-cost growth models and let the domestic demand grow at least moderately. It would ensure that all countries contributed their share to global demand growth and, thus, enable high-pressure demand strategies for all countries.

Instead of ICU, what emerged out of the Bretton Woods negotiations was an international monetary system centred on the US dollar. While the global dollar system has mutated in critical ways over the past decades, the balance of payments constraint persists. Although the Keynes proposal appears progressive in hindsight, it also suffered from certain weaknesses, which need to be fully addressed to devise viable reforms for the twenty-first century. It is to these weaknesses that we now turn.

More policy space for developing economies: The Kalecki-Schumacher critique and the Davidson plan

In this section, we first revisit a contemporary critique by Ernst Schumacher and Michał Kalecki, who argued that the Keynes plan failed to fully consider the predicament of developing countries. Although this critique has continued relevance, we argue that at least a partial solution is provided by the Davidson plan which creates more scope for development strategies in the Global South.

A system along the lines of the ICU plan which sanctions both excessive current account deficits and surpluses may pose specific problems for countries lacking in productive capacity and thus valuable exports. Even Keynes himself argued that if a state has insufficient productive capacity to finance its standard of living, this standard must be reduced (Horsefield 1969: 5). This issue was explicitly raised by Michał Kalecki and Ernst Schumacher in their contemporary critique of the Keynes plan. Kalecki and Schumacher argued that in a global economy with countries in different phases of development, it is not only to be expected that some countries will be net importers and others net exporters, but that this is indeed desirable. In terms of balance of payments, the current account deficits of poorer economies should be mirrored by net borrowing from richer economies (Kalecki and Schumacher 1943: 29–30). In essence, poorer economies should be able to import capital and intermediary goods to industrialize and develop their export sectors.

Based on this critique, Schumacher and Kalecki advanced their own compromise proposal which retained some of the most fundamental aspects of the Keynes plan, such as international clearing and bancor, but discarded others. Most importantly, Kalecki's and Schumacher's intention was to ensure sufficient international liquidity by different means than Keynes, who saw penalization of surplus hoarding as an indispensable component of the plan. Kalecki and Schumacher proposed that there would be no sanctioning of excessive surpluses. Rather, long-term bancor loans would be provided by an International Investment Board for economies in transition, that is undergoing major readjustments. This category of countries would include developing countries aiming to industrialize as well as those industrialized countries that required post-war reconstruction. Additionally, there would be another category of countries whose deficits could not be attributed to these types of transitions. Kalecki and Schumacher advanced a unique (and somewhat controversial) solution to help them achieve a balanced current account: the International Investment Board would *compel* its borrowers to buy more imports specifically from these countries (Kalecki and Schumacher 1943: 30–2).

Some of the central components of the Kalecki-Schumacher critique are still relevant today. There are indeed valid reasons to advise against sanctioning current account imbalances of developing economies. Firstly, in order to develop, poorer economies need to diversify and upgrade their production, and thus import capital, technology and intermediary goods. To do this, they may need to run current account deficits. Conversely, and secondly, it makes as little sense to sanction excessive current account surpluses of developing economies. To import said capital goods, developing economies also need to accrue hard currency. Thus, there is an incentive to export dollar-denominated goods. Indeed, most late developers, most notably China, have been successful in industrializing through a strategy of accumulating current account surpluses. This strategy entails suppression of domestic demand and investments in advanced production capacity, which benefit from large economies of scale. The combination of high output and weak domestic demand have, in turn, translated into massive current account surpluses (Schwartz 2019: 499). This avenue to development, which has proved so successful in China, should not be precluded by draconian sanctioning of current account surpluses of poorer economies. However, in the current ecological context, industrialization cannot assume the same form it did in the nineteenth or twentieth century. There are immense challenges related to combining development with planetary boundaries. Economic structures need to be substantially altered to ensure that human needs – both more basic and qualitative ones – are met without depleting finite resources or transgressing critical planetary boundaries (O'Neill et al. 2018: 1–6). Processes of development in the twenty-first century should be combined with ecological transformation where the cultivated industries and production would be based on renewable energy and be as sustainable and low carbon as possible.

Nonetheless, given that there are still developing economies which also lack valuable exports, the universal application of the sanctioning mechanisms suggested by the Keynes plan is not advisable. It is also worth noting that adjusting their exchange rates downwards would not resolve the problem. If a country genuinely lacks exports with sufficient demand, lowering prices does not automatically resolve the issue. Instead, what is required is increase in productive capacity, which could be financed by investment loans by the international investment bureau, as proposed by Kalecki and Schumacher. Moreover, developing economies should not be forced to balance their current accounts prematurely. In fact, one can find this type of solution in an updated ICU plan by the post-Keynesian economist Paul Davidson.

Among others, Davidson has kept the Keynesian tradition of reform proposals to the international monetary system alive. Like the original Keynes plan, the Davidson plan would include a global reserve currency, ensure sufficient global demand by precluding reserve hoarding, shift more responsibility for adjustment onto surplus states, enable states to oversee and control capital movements and increase the provision of global liquidity (Davidson 1992: 158–9). Notwithstanding the similar mechanisms to deal with excessive surpluses as the Keynes plan, however, the Davidson plan distinguishes between richer and poorer deficit countries. While a rich deficit country would be required to reduce its trade deficit, poorer economies would be provided with direct transfers of liquidity instead (Davidson 1992: 163–4). Thus, there could be different rules of adjustment based on the level of development.

However, before presenting a viable synthesis appropriate for our time, the discussion on reforming the international monetary system needs to be updated with an understanding of the global dollar system in its current form. In today's context, the balance of payments constraint is related to an international currency hierarchy and dollar hegemony in specific ways which will be elaborated on in the next section.

The BOP constraint in the hierarchical and asymmetric global dollar system

The international monetary system has evolved in profound ways since the aforementioned debates in the 1940s. Due to these changes, the balance of payments constraint looks slightly different in today's context. In this section, we elucidate how the balance of payments constraint is related to the hierarchical and asymmetric global dollar system in its current form. We also explain the relative endurance of dollar hegemony despite its problems, which informs our discussion of feasible reforms to the international monetary system in the next section.

Although the Bretton Woods system ended in the 1970s, the US dollar is still the predominant global reserve currency. A significant portion of global trade (around 40 per cent) and many key resources are still invoiced in dollars (Brüggen at. al. 2025). It is the most important currency in trade invoicing and financing (Bonizzi et al. 2019: 52). Dollars are also the most common currency to be used as a vehicle currency in currency exchanges (Maronoti 2022). The various components of dollar hegemony are intertwined: actors tend to accumulate reserves in a currency that can easily be used to access key resources, make debt payments or buy other currencies. Hence, US dollars and dollar-based assets are the most liquid in the world. There also tends to be a retreat to dollar-based assets in times of uncertainty, reflecting a common perception of their relative safety (House Financial Services 2023).

Due to this dollar dominance, there is a structural tendency in the current international monetary and financial system for many countries – especially developing ones – to grow indebted in dollars. Since most key resources are sold in dollars, importing them requires either dollar reserves or dollar credit. Thus, sustained current account deficits tend to contribute to dollar-denominated external debt as currency reserves are depleted. There is an inherent risk of insolvency and a balance of payments crisis associated with this indebtedness. Hence, the balance of payments constraint takes a particular form under dollar hegemony. Many developing economies are between a rock and a hard place. To reduce their dependence on various imports, including capital goods, they need to diversify and upgrade their production, which often necessitates importing said capital goods. Fundamentally transforming the economy – which in today's context would need to include an ecological transformation – is a process that takes years, potentially even a decade. For the most part, dependence on hard currency during this process is unavoidable (Bonizzi et al. 2019: 52–4). This is the case even if the global economy shifts away from fossil fuels (which are mainly invoiced in dollars), since many key resources related to the green transition, such as certain minerals, are also sold in dollars.

This predicament faced by peripheral economies is further exacerbated by the inherent asymmetry of the dollar system. Namely, the US monetary policy tends to shape financing conditions globally. For instance, interest rate hikes by the Federal Reserve since March 2022 significantly contributed to debt distress in developing economies. The increase in interest rates in the US motivated a reversal of capital flows away from the Global South and increased their borrowing costs. (Financial Times 2023). In 2023 it was reported that lower-income countries would face the highest debt servicing costs since 1998, reaching 16.3 per cent of government revenue in ninety-one countries (Debt Justice 2023). High borrowing costs and debt crises are now seriously impeding economic development and climate action. Indeed, it is estimated that forty-seven emerging and developing economies cannot make the necessary investments towards these goals without facing issues of solvency (Debt Relief for Green and Inclusive Recovery 2024).

A further problem for many developing economies is that the currencies and debt they issue are in the lower tier in the global hierarchy. As emphasized by Daniela Prates, the degree of economic policy space is significantly shaped by the position of the country in the international currency hierarchy. The dollar is at the pinnacle of the hierarchy as the unrivalled key currency and is the most liquid form of money in the international arena. Certain currencies, such as the euro, the pound and the yen, are also highly liquid. Currencies issued by emerging and poorer economies, by contrast, are less liquid. The balance of payments constraint is tighter for these issuers of 'peripheral currencies' (Prates 2020: 503–7). Although these currencies may at times experience booms, demand for them is less stable, and hence the issuing countries are more vulnerable to balance of payments crises. Developing economies also tend to have thinner markets for foreign exchange. Overall, core economies have more avenues and better prospects to secure access to US dollars than those in the periphery (Bonizzi et al. 2019: 56).

Nonetheless, while issuing a hard currency loosens the balance of payments constraint, even large economic areas, such as the Eurozone, can become critically reliant on dollars. For instance, in the leadup to the Global Financial Crisis, many European banks and financial institutions were heavily involved in borrowing and lending in dollars through the offshore dollar system (Tooze 2018: 83–92). When wholesale funding markets froze at the start of the crisis, these institutions became dependent on the Federal Reserve for dollars. Although the ECB provided almost 100 billion euros in liquidity, it could not supply the dollars that the European financial system desperately needed. Even the ample dollar reserves of the German car export champions were grossly insufficient to fill the dollar shortage, which exceeded 2 trillion dollars. This experience illustrates that current account surpluses alone do not guarantee sufficient dollar liquidity if the financial system is deeply integrated with the global dollar system. Although the Eurozone was a net exporter to the United States at the time, it did not have nearly enough dollars to support its financial institutions and banks (Tooze 2018: 205–7). While non-US central banks can provide unlimited liquidity in their own currency, they cannot do so in dollars. This creates a structural dependence on the Federal Reserve as a lender of last resort (Murau et al. 2023: 497–501).

Although the Federal Reserve has served as a lender of last resort to *some* institutions since the Global Financial Crisis, provision of emergency dollar liquidity overlaps with and reinforces existing hierarchies in the international monetary system. Today, there are three mechanisms to access emergency dollar liquidity. The first and the best is swap lines with the Federal Reserve. In a swap arrangement, each central bank creates a deposit account for the other in its own currency. For example, the Federal Reserve lends dollars to the ECB and vice versa ECB lends euros to the Federal Reserve. In turn, they agree to reverse the operations at a specific date with an agreed-upon exchange rate (Tooze 2018: 215). Although the counterparty central bank is supposed to pay back the dollars as part of the arrangement, some of these swap lines have been made permanent. When lending is automatically renewed in this manner, it is akin to an endless stream of dollar liquidity. Only a few central banks in advanced economies with close ties to the United States have access to permanent and unlimited swap lines with the Fed: the ECB, Bank of Japan, Bank of England, the Swiss National Bank and the Bank of Canada. In addition, there are fourteen national central banks, including those of Brazil and Mexico, that have access to temporary swap lines (Murau et al. 2023: 502–4).

The second-tier mechanism is the FIMA (Foreign and International Monetary Authorities) repo facility of the Federal Reserve. This is a facility for repurchase agreements where actors sell an asset, such as a Treasury bond, to gain dollars and promise to repurchase the asset later. To access this facility, the central banks of course need to have treasury bonds to sell. Like the swap lines, the FIMA repo facility was created in the context of economic turmoil, namely during the Covid pandemic, but was eventually continued. While this mechanism is more burdensome than the swap lines, it provides an avenue for accessing dollars for those countries that are not geopolitically close with the United States, but do own dollar assets, such as China (Murau et al. 2023: 504–5). Note, however, that this second tier involves somewhat circular logic: to access dollars, you already need to have dollar assets. It thus provides little relief to those who have difficulty accruing dollars in the first place.

The third-tier mechanisms to access dollars are governed by the IMF. One is the special drawing rights (SDR) system, created already in 1969 by the IMF. Through the SDR system, central banks can borrow dollars from other IMF members. Creation of new SDRs is governed by the Executive Board of the IMF and their allocation corresponds to the IMF member quota shares – with the member with the largest quota share, the United States, receiving the most SDRs. Due to idiosyncratic features of the SDR system, the buyer of SDRs needs to pay interest on the amount of SDRs holdings used to purchase the currency. Access to dollars through the SDRs is limited as it depends on how much SDRs holdings the member has at its disposal. It also bears costs due to interest rates paid on the differential between holdings and allocations. There are also other third-tier avenues to access dollars, such as directly borrowing from the IMF. However, IMF loans tend to come with rather stringent conditionality (Murau et al. 2023: 506–9). Indeed, structural adjustment programmes mandated by the IMF and the World Bank in exchange for their lending only recreate the problem of limited economic policy space to pursue fiscal expansion or large-scale investments that the BOP constraint initially generates.

In the context of today's international monetary system, access to sufficient international liquidity does not depend as much on current account balances as it did in Keynes's times, but more so on the position of the country in the international monetary hierarchy. Nowadays, the balance of payments constraint is fundamentally shaped by the hierarchical structure of the global dollar system. While the constraint does not apply to the United States, it is also significantly relaxed for economic areas that have access to the Fed's swap lines (Schwartz 2019: 512). The US dollar is the predominant unit of account which grants the United States maximal economic policy space whereas the shape of the hierarchy below the top is determined by differential access to dollars. Emphasis on monetary sovereignty alone tends to obscure this reality of the international monetary hierarchy (see e.g. Bonizzi et al. 2019: 54–7; Prates 2020: 505–8). Earlier we compared the balance of payments constraint to a slippery slope rather than an outright barrier. The hierarchy of the international monetary system impacts the likelihood of slipping over the edge, with those at the bottom facing the greatest risk.

Despite these issues of hierarchy, asymmetry and outright inequity, there are tendencies in the global political economy that continue to perpetuate dollar hegemony. Firstly, global current account imbalances are closely tied to the operations of the dollar system. The United States tends to run persistent current account deficits with chronic exporters, including many oil exporters and late developers. Through their current account surpluses, net exporters accumulate dollars in their banking systems and they become increasingly intertwined with the global dollar system. Net importers are also pulled into the use of the dollar through the supply of dollar lending from net exporters. This contributes to another important path dependency: actors indebted in dollars want to be paid in dollars, which further embeds them in the dollar system (Schwartz 2019: 491–2). Secondly, the value of dollar assets is underpinned by the ability of US firms to capture profits in global supply chains. These disproportionate profit shares are achieved particularly through stringent intellectual property protections (Schwartz 2019: 506–8). These tendencies explain the extensive entanglement of most countries in the global dollar system, especially through their financial systems. Thus, although there has been a discernible decline in the importance of the United States in global trade, its position as the central hub of the global financial system is still unrivalled.

Dollar hegemony is also a critical component of the geopolitical power of the United States. Yet, the interconnections between dollar hegemony and American dominance remain largely underexplored. As Herman Schwartz points out, recurrent predictions of the demise of the dollar (already by Triffin in 1960s) arise from this gap: there is a paucity of understanding of how dollar dominance is sustained by American structural power. One banal analysis is that the current account deficit and foreign indebtedness of the United States will inevitably lead to the collapse of the dollar. In fact, these deficits underpin mechanisms that perpetuate dollar dominance. They also enable the United States to extract real resources from the rest of the world in exchange for its own currency without the associated risk of a balance of payments crisis – an example of real power par excellence (Schwartz 2019: 49–493). Unsurprisingly, the US political elite seem committed to maintain dollar dominance (House Financial Services 2023). Even the Trump administration, despite its desire to achieve a trade surplus and openness to a weaker dollar, wants to retain its role as the dominant reserve currency.

US governments are likely to be hostile to direct challenges of dollar hegemony, such as the institution of a new global currency, in the foreseeable future. Nonetheless, it is noteworthy that the United States has been open to increases in provision of international liquidity, whether in the form of swap lines or SDRs, in times of crisis. Depending on the orientation of the government, it is not inconceivable that it could do so again.

In the next section, we first outline the premises of our own version of the ICU plan. We then draw on the various contributions covered thus far to synthesize reforms which would resolve the balance of payments constraint before more comprehensive reforms or revolutions (such as instituting a new global currency) of the international monetary system can be achieved.

A feasible synthesis for the twenty-first century

Although we are sympathetic to the aspiration towards a genuinely global currency, the goal of expanding economic policy space, especially to enable full-scale ecological transformations, is too urgent to wait for the end of dollar hegemony. In the next section, we briefly consider why various ICU proposals have not gained wider purchase in the past eighty years. We then synthesize the most politically feasible aspects of the various proposals. In particular, we outline minimal reforms that could resolve the balance of payments constraint in the foreseeable future *without locking dollar hegemony in*. We thus aim at transitional reforms, which eliminate some of the contradictions of the current system while creating space for its eventual transformation.

We argue that despite the limitations of the established IPE approaches to the international monetary system, a combination of post-Keynesian ICU research and IPE could be especially fruitful. It is not, after all, particularly difficult to envisage well-functioning global monetary arrangements but the social-scientific merits of such blueprints are quite insignificant if no analysis concerning the mechanisms and processes that can lead to the realization of such plans is provided. Hence, we need to combine a realistic analysis of the geopolitics of the international monetary system with any plans aiming at its radical reformation.

Our attempt to outline a minimalistic version of the ICU is, thus, based on an analysis of the main political obstacles standing in the way of such reforms. We aim at presenting a version of the ICU plan which maintains the most crucial components of the original plan and its later formulations but is moderated in some aspects in order to improve its feasibility.[2]

The most radical element of the Keynes plan was the idea to sanction excessive current account surpluses symmetrically with deficits. This shifted the adjustment burden from the debtor countries to *both* debtor and creditor countries. Such a contractual clause would have also significantly limited the international spread of deflationary economic policies as too strict export-led growth strategies aiming at drastically restricting domestic demand growth would have become impossible. Thus, limiting excessive current account surpluses is one of the key components that we want to maintain in our plan. The other one is the provision of sufficient international liquidity to low-income countries. Here, our proposal follows the aims of the Kalecki and Schumacher plans of the 1940s but reformulates their proposals to be suitable in the current political-economic context.

Multiple versions of the ICU plan have been drafted since Bretton Woods, but no serious political process around any of the plans has taken place after the 1940s.[3] This can be explained by two types of reasons. Firstly, the eventual solution in the Bretton Woods negotiations laid the foundation for a dollar-based international monetary system which has created deep path dependencies. Dollar hegemony has also served the interests of particularly financial capital and American consumers. The commitment of previous US administrations to dollar hegemony can be partly explained in terms of political alignment with these interests. Although there has been a dramatic shift in terms of these class alignments with the Trump administration, that is more concerned with onshoring manufacturing to the United States, it too is committed to maintaining dollar dominance. Thus, reforming the current system faces many practical and political obstacles.

The original ICU plan included the idea that all international transactions would be conducted in bancor. Overall, it is difficult to see why the United

States would be willing to give up the dollar's special status. Historically dollar dominance has allowed the United States to run constant fiscal and current account deficits as the global trade in strategically important commodities is mostly US dollar denominated. Dollar hegemony also contributes to the price stability of the dollar since its role as the leading reserve and vehicle currency creates additional demand for dollars. This makes any deep currency crisis unlikely, even in the context of Trump's erratic trade policies. As noted, dollar hegemony shelters the United States from the balance of payments constraint. Although the Trump's second term administration seems to be rather concerned over the excessive strength of the dollar and its consequences for the US manufacturing sector, it nonetheless wants to uphold a privileged status for the United States in the global financial system.[4]

It is also unlikely that bancor-based international monetary order could be created without the participation of the United States in the current geopolitical context. Establishing such a system would be in direct conflict with the geoeconomic interests of the United States. Hence, countries relying on the US military assistance or security guarantees would be unlikely to join such a venture. This would exclude almost all European countries from any potential future bancor coalition and render the whole attempt unrealistic. Consequently, all the proposed ICU blueprints suffer from a severe lack of political feasibility.

Secondly, as outline above, the original Keynes plan had also some Eurocentric deficiencies, which may explain why it has not gained more political traction. Most notably, the Keynes plan lacked any major elements fostering industrialization of developing countries, as Kalecki and Schumacher so forcefully argued. Next, we turn to the details of our plan.

A modest clearing union with radical effects

To develop viable versions of the Keynes plan, we need to address its original shortcomings. Thus, we formulate modest adaptations of the Keynes plan which include the most vital elements of the original plan but also address the specific needs of the Global South. Our proposals here are based on two possible scenarios in terms of US governments.

The first proposal is based on a scenario where there is some form of return to the pre-2025 status quo in how the United States relates to the rest of the world. That is, it is assumed that the next administration is more concerned with US soft power and influence than the current one. Firstly, the plan would not involve the creation of a global currency in the short term. Given the infeasibility of immediately replacing the dollar with a global currency, we propose instead more extensive use of SDRs. Since SDRs provide access to a basket of currencies, whose composition evolves over time, it allows for the gradual decline of the dollar hegemony.

Secondly and relatedly, to resolve the balance of payments problem, we propose increased provision of international liquidity along the lines of the Kalecki and Schumacher plan. However, contra Kalecki and Schumacher, who suggested that this increased liquidity be provided in the form of *bancor loans*, we propose *SDR grants* instead. The problem with loans would be that the interest and debt payments related to them would necessitate developing economies to accrue hard currency. However, as Kalecki and Schumacher recognized, the provision of international liquidity cannot be completely unlimited either (Kalecki and Schumacher 1943: 30). Therefore, the SDR grants would be meant for a specific purpose, namely to avoid balance of payments problems due to *economically and ecologically necessary transitions*. To avoid any potential misuse of the aid, there would be disciplinary procedures involving its repayment with sanctions if it were used for wrong purposes.

The amount of available SDR grants should be open for negotiations but it is obvious that significant increases are needed already because the amount of available SDRs have not grown as fast as the global GDP or trade in recent years (Kring et al. 2024: 3). Simply correcting such deviations would require doubling the SDR quotas for low- and middle-income countries (ibid.). However, even larger increases are needed as SDRs have not been able to function as an effective alternative for US dollar loans even previously.

Thirdly, our plan would include sanctioning excessive surpluses and deficits *above a certain income threshold*. Specifically, low-income and low-middle-income countries with gross national incomes per capita below $4,465 would not face the disciplining measures related to excessive current account deficits or surpluses (World Bank 2024b). This would create more space for them to transform their economies and upgrade their production, also through current account surpluses, which was so successful in China. However, given that China has now clearly surpassed this threshold with its gross national income per capita of almost $13,000, its current account surpluses, if excessive, would be sanctioned in this system (World Bank 2024a).

By sanctioning excessive current account surpluses of more advanced economies, the new system would dramatically reduce the deflationary bias in the global economy and thus contribute to global aggregate demand. This increase in exogenous demand would greatly facilitate and support to implementation of more Keynesian demand-led policies domestically in both advanced and developing countries alike.

Penalization of excessive surpluses of richer economies would be particularly beneficial to advanced economies wishing to pursue more high demand expansionary policies. While they would not be able to access SDR grants for development, they could receive them in cases where ecological transformations would otherwise lead to balance of payments crises. This system of sanctions would also correct a fundamental asymmetry in the international monetary system where there are mechanisms to discipline persistent current account deficits – most notably through the BOP constraint – but no mechanism to discipline excessive current account surpluses.

It is important to acknowledge that even these minimal reforms would face formidable political challenges. Even a more progressive government in the United States could object to the increased use of SDRs as it is a subtle form of undermining long-term dollar hegemony. However, several US administrations have agreed to additional SDR allocations in the context of crises, such as the Global Financial Crisis and the Covid pandemic (Murau et al. 2023: 507). Indeed, provision of international liquidity through this channel would reduce the pressure for the United States to run current account deficits, which have contributed to its de-industrialization and fostered significant political resistance, manifesting itself most notably in the elections of Trump. The next administration will likely feel pressured to address these concerns.

Elsewhere there may be significant opposition to sanctioning excessive surpluses from governments such as Germany and China that perceive them (wrongly or rightly) to be behind their countries' economic success. Certain chronic surplus countries – namely the Netherlands and Germany – have not agreed to reduce their surpluses even in the context of a monetary union in Europe – why would they agree to it writ large? One persuading argument would be to emphasize the global scope of the sanctioning mechanisms. This could increase support for the system as different parties would be assuaged by the knowledge that the same rules apply to everyone. Indeed, emphasis on universal rules could find resonance in the heartland of ordoliberalism. Moreover, through increased access to international liquidity, there would also be less incentives to accumulate current account surpluses in the first place.

From the perspective of the Global South, the change would be far more dramatic. Provision of liquidity for necessary transitions would allow developing countries to transform their economies in a way that suited them.

Late development would no longer be dependent on suppression of domestic demand and accumulation of current account surpluses. Indeed, given that resolving the balance of payments constraint and deflationary bias in the global economy feature so large in our proposal, it would likely find widespread support in the Global South, who has suffered the most from these pernicious problems in the international monetary system.

Our second scenario focuses on the implications of the Trump era. Here we formulate a version of the plan that could be feasible even in the context of a US administration that is openly hostile to multilateralism. Despite its erraticism, the Trump administration has been consistent in its concern with reversing the US current account balance into a surplus and promoting its manufacturing base. Sanctioning excessive current account surpluses of other countries would obviously serve this goal. Given that Trump's tariff plans are unlikely to be enough to reverse the long-standing US current account deficits as they also strengthen the international value of the dollar, this proposal could be offered as a superior alternative. However, in this scenario the sanctioning of excessive deficits would also need to be discarded to convince the United States to join the system (since it would otherwise face immediate sanctions for its deficit).

Thus, this version of the sanctioning system could be sold to an administration that is exclusively focused on the trade balance and its narrow interpretation of US national interest. Nonetheless, the underlying normative goal of these reforms would remain the same – to reduce the deflationary bias in the global economy and expand economic policy space, especially for the Global South. From the perspective of Europe, such a rule-based system would be preferable to a chaotic trade war, even though it would also challenge its export-oriented growth model. However, this model is being undermined anyway by the US-led trade war. Given that even Germany has now shown a willingness to deviate from strict fiscal discipline, it is conceivable that the EU could turn to more demand-led growth in the future.

The other key component of our plan – the addition of international liquidity – would face more serious challenges. It is highly unlikely that the Trump administration would be willing to supply more liquidity to other countries in any form. Hence, in this scenario we propose that a coalition of the willing could supply other hard currencies, such as euros, renminbi and pounds, as additional international liquidity. A country facing a balance of payments constraint could easily trade these hard currencies for dollars in the international market. From a geopolitical perspective, this exercise of soft power could win the respective powers – be it the EU, China or the UK – new political allies from the Global

South. Especially for the EU, this could prove to be vital now as the US administration has largely turned its back.

Given that many factors contribute to the balance of payments constraint in its current form, there of course would be various ways to address it. We have focused here on the provision of international liquidity and sanctioning excessive current account surpluses. Nonetheless, there are multiple measures that could be pursued individually or combined with our proposed reforms. For instance, capital controls can reduce destabilizing capital flows which often play a central role in balance of payments crises. However, as noted, capital controls alone do not increase access to hard currency and may even have the opposite effect. On the other hand, as Amato, Fantacci and Gobbi argue in this book, regional payments systems (depending on their configuration) could facilitate the flow of key resources as well as economize the use of hard currency, thus reducing dependence on dollars (Amato et al. in this contribution). Similarly, debt restructurings could reduce the amount of money going towards debt repayments and thus release more money for investments. However, while this would alleviate the situation in the short-term, indebtedness in dollars is a structural feature of the current international monetary and financial system. Hence, issues related to dollar-denominated debt would resurface over time unless the problem is treated at its source. This is what we aim to do with the provision of liquidity for necessary investments and transitions.

Even though our focus has been on drafting a version of the ICU plan that could also be attractive to future US administrations, it is not entirely impossible that ICU could be created without the participation of the United States. The historically high tariffs of the Trump administration and its attempts to weaken the dollar might bring about a gradual process of international decoupling from excessive dollar usage. This, again, could open the possibility to form a multilateral trading system based on the control of imbalances instead of a system built around a monetary hegemon running constant current account deficits. At the time of writing it is, however, still too early to predict how radical transformations the second Trump term will produce.

In addition to the aforementioned policy options and reforms related to the monetary and financial system, there are also other dimensions that contribute to persistent underdevelopment and reduced economic policy space in the Global South. Most notably, international trade regulations and agreements as well as tendencies of unequal exchange between richer and poorer economies all play a significant role in global inequality (Hickel et al. 2021: 1042). Furthermore, unstable commodity, raw material and energy prices can all interfere with and impede development processes. Heavy dependence on exporting primary commodities on the one hand, and importing food, raw materials and energy on the other, renders developing economies very vulnerable to price fluctuations of these goods. Thus, some form of commodity control, as originally suggested by Keynes in some versions of his ICU plan, would certainly facilitate development in addition to contributing to global price stability (Keynes 1980: 39). Although these issues are obviously important, we have chosen to focus here on minimal reforms to the international monetary system with maximal impact.

The first step towards reform would be a recognition by a critical mass of countries of the advantages of alternative systems. For those committed to free trade, the reforms would create greater prospects for consensual multilateralism as there would be safeguards against beggar-thy-neighbour policies and less reason to fear unemployment due to trade. As noted, penalization of excessive current account surpluses could very well be supported by the United States. Already since Obama's presidency, several US administrations have expressed concern over China's trade surplus (BBC 2012). Indeed, universal sanctioning of excessive current account surpluses and deficits could peacefully achieve the same objective that successive US governments, including this one, have pursued through trade wars.

Conclusions

This chapter is intended as a modest contribution to the tradition of devising progressive reforms to the international monetary system. At the heart of this endeavour is the normative goal of expanding economic policy space and possibilities for democratic alternatives in terms of economic strategies. While expanding the scope for democratic politics is valuable in and of itself, the expansion of policy space also improves the prospects for development and ecological transitions. In this chapter, we have identified the balance of payments constraint as a critical impediment to these goals, especially at the bottom of the hierarchical global dollar system.

To solve the balance of payments issue, we formulated minimal reforms which would increase the provision of international liquidity and sanction excessive current account surpluses, while paying special attention to the challenges of less developed economies. Most importantly, our proposals aim to alter the basis on which international liquidity is provided. Instead of being based on geopolitical access to the United States, arbitrary distribution of natural resources such as oil, or a growth strategy focused on maximizing exports to accumulate hard currency, we proposed provision of liquidity for economically or ecologically necessary transitions. At the same time, we formulated reforms which would allow space for the international monetary system to evolve over time.

Notes

1 Post-Keynesian theory has always been critical towards such mechanisms but also empirically oriented mainstream economists have come to the same conclusion (see e.g. Harvey 2009; IMF 2006).

2 Our approach can be criticized by arguing that we equate what is possible to what is currently existing. Such an interpretation would, however, be misguided as our attempt is to draft a reform plan that brings about significant structural changes in the world economy. Hence, the transformative potential of our plan should be judged by its potential social consequences – not by comparing it to more radical ICU blueprints as the mere existence of more ambitious blueprints tells nothing about the potential of our plan.

3 Different versions of the ICU plan are presented in Konsta Kotilainen's working paper (2022).

4 Trump administration's views on the international monetary system have been most thoroughly elaborated by Trump's key economic policy adviser Stephen Miran in his November 2024 policy memorandum where he laid out his so-called 'Mar-a-Lago Accord' proposal. Miran seems to suggest that the major owners of US dollar reserves should reduce their dollar holdings while major holders of US treasuries should convert their previous market-rate bonds to zero-rate 100-year 'century bonds'. This would help the manufacturing sector of the United States by weakening the dollar while at the same time providing essentially free financing for the US government. However, if the dollar's international role is severely undermined, the United States can no longer run continuous current account deficits which would also reduce its ability to run constant public sector deficits. It is unclear whether all these aspects and interconnections are understood by Miran and other key policymakers in the Trump administration.

References

Aliber, Robert Z. (1966), *The Future of the Dollar as an International Currency*, New York: Praeger.

Aysun, U., C. Karlia, and S. Oronde. (2024), 'Capital outflow restrictions and dollar drainage', *Economic Systems* 48 (2): 101176.

Azimova, T. (2020), 'Artificial Intelligence (Ai) in the Foreign Exchange Market', in C. Koutra and H. I. Ahmad (ed), *Emerging Human and Techno-Human Business Management Dynamics in a Globalized Environment*, Nova Science Publishers, Incorporated.

Balogh, T. (1943), 'New Plans for International Trade: The Foreign Balance and Full Employment', *Bulletin Of The Oxford University Institute Of Economics & Statistics*, 5 (S5): 33–40.

BBC. (2012), 'US President Asks China to Follow "Same Rules" in Trade'. Available at: https://www.bbc.com/news/business-17036837 (Accessed 1 June 2024).

Bonizzi, B., A. Kaltenbrunner, and J. Michell. (2019), 'Monetary Sovereignty is a Spectrum: Modern Monetary Theory and Developing Countries', *Real-World Economics Review*, 89: 46–61.

Brüggen, A. G. Georgiadis and A. Mehl. (2025), 'Global Trade Invoicing Patterns: New Insights and the Influence of Geopolitics', *The International Role of the Euro*, June 2025, The European Central Bank.

Das, M., and H. Ordal. (2022), 'Macroeconomic Stability or Financial Stability: How are Capital Controls Used? Insights from a New Database', *Journal of Financial Stability*, 63: 101067.

Davidson, P. (1992), 'Reforming the World's Money', *Journal of Post Keynesian Economics*, 15 (2): 153–79.

Debt Justice. (2023), 'Lower Income Country Debt Payments to Hit Highest Level in 25 Years'. Available at: https://debtjustice.org.uk/press-release/lower-income-country -debt-payments-set-to-hit-highest-level-in-25-years (Accessed 1 June 2024).

Debt Relief for Green and Inclusive Recovery. (2024), 'Report: Defaulting on Development and Climate – Debt Sustainability and the Race for the 2030 Agenda and Paris Agreement'. Available at: https://drgr.org/research/report-defaulting-on -development-and-climate-debt-sustainability-and-the-race-for-the-2030-agenda -and-paris-agreement/ (Accessed 1 June 2024).

Financial Times Editorial Board. (2023), 'How to Avoid a Developing World Debt Crisis', *Financial Times*, Available at: https://www.ft.com/content/1bbce83b-aebe -4fd2-afd2-02e45ed5338d (Accessed 1 June 2024).

Harvey, J. T. (2009), *Currencies, Capital Flows and Crises: A Post Keynesian Analysis of Exchange Rate Determination*, Abingdon: Routledge.

Hickel, J. (2017), 'Is Global Inequality Getting Better or Worse? A Critique of the World Bank's Convergence Narrative', *Third World Quarterly*, 38 (10): 2208–22.

Hickel, J., D. Sullivan, and H. Zoomkawala. (2021), 'Plunder in the Post-Colonial Era: Quantifying Drain from the Global South Through Unequal Exchange, 1960–2018', *New Political Economy*, 26 (6): 1030–47.

Holappa, Lauri R. A. (2020), 'The Bond-Market-Power Fallacy, Academic Dissertation, University of Helsinki.

Horsefield, J. K. (1969), The International Monetary Fund, Washington: IMF.

House Financial Services Subcommittee on National Security, Illicit Finance, and International Financial Institutions. (2023), 'Dollar Dominance: Preserving the U.S. Dollar's Status as the Global Reserve Currency', Available at: https://www.congress .gov/event/118th-congress/house-event/116068/text (Accessed 1 June 2024).

IMF. (2006), 'Exchange Rates and Trade Balance Adjustment in Emerging Market Economies'. Available at https://www.imf.org/external/np/pp/eng/2006/101006.pdf (Accessed 1 June 2024).

Kalecki, M., and E. F. Schumacher. (1943), 'New Plans for International Trade: International Clearing and Long-Term Lending', *Bulletin of the Oxford University Institute of Economics & Statistics*, 5 (S5): 29–32.

Keohane, R. O., and J. S. Nye. (1971), 'Transnational Relations and World Politics: An Introduction', *International Organization*, 25 (3): 329–49.

Keohane, R. O., and J. S. Nye. (1977), *Power and Interdependence. World Politics in Transition*, Boston: Little, Brown and Company.

Keynes, J. M. (1936 [2003]), *The General Theory of Employment, Interest, and Money*. A Project Gutenberg of Australia eBook.

Keynes, J. M., and D. E. Moggridge. (1980), *The Collected Writings of John Maynard Keynes. 25, Activities 1940–1944 : Shaping the Post-War World: The Clearing Union / John Maynard Keynes*; ed. Donald Moggridge, London: Macmillan.

Kindleberger, C. P. (1967), 'The Politics of International Money and World Language', Essays in international finance, no. 1. International finance section. Department of economics. Princeton University.

Kirshner, J. (2008), 'Dollar Primacy and American Power: What's at Stake?', *Review of International Political Economy*, 15 (3): 418–38.

Kirshner, J. (2009), 'After the (Relative) Fall: Dollar Diminution and the Consequences for American Power', in E. Helleiner and J. Kirshner (eds), *The Future of the Dollar*, Ithaca: Cornell University Press.

Kotilainen, K. (2024), From Monetary Sovereignty to Macroeconomic Policy Autonomy?: Examining Promises, Limitations, and Reform Possibilities of a Nation-State-Centric Macroeconomic Governance Architecture.

Kring, W. N., R. R. Bhandary, R. Thrasher, M. Zucker-Marques, and T. Hirschel-Burns. (2024), 'The Bretton Woods Institutions at 80: Towards a Bigger, Better and More Inclusive Global Economic Governance Architecture', Boston University Global Development Policy Center.

Kulesza, M. (2017), *Inflation and Hyperinflation in Venezuela (1970s–2016): A Post-Keynesian Interpretation* (No. 93/2017). Working paper.

Maronoti, B. (2022), 'Revisiting the International Role of the US Dollar', *BIS Quarterly Review*, 5.

McCombie, J. S. L. (2003), 'Balance-of-Payments Constrained Economic Growth', in J. E. King (ed), *Elgar Companion to Post Keynesian Economics*, 15–20, Cheltenham: Edward Elgar.

Miran, Stephen. (2024), 'A User's Guide to Restructuring the Global Trading System', Hudson Bay Capital working paper. https://www.hudsonbaycapital.com/documents/FG/hudsonbay/research/638199_A_Users_Guide_to_Restructuring_the_Global_Trading_System.pdf (Accessed 13 April 2025).

Murau, S., F. Pape, and T. Pforr. (2023), 'International Monetary Hierarchy Through Emergency US-Dollar Liquidity: A Key Currency Approach', *Competition & Change*, 27 (3–4): 495–515.

Oatley, T. (2014), 'The Political Economy of the Contemporary Dollar Standard', in T. Oatley and W. K. Winecoff (eds), *Handbook of the International Political Economy of Monetary Relations*, 54–68, Cheltenham: Edward Elgar.

O'Neill, D. W., A. L. Fanning, W. F. Lamb, and J. K. Steinberger. (2018), 'A Good Life for All Within Planetary Boundaries', *Nature Sustainability*, 1 (2): 88–95.

Prates, D. (2020), 'Beyond Modern Money Theory: A Post-Keynesian Approach to the Currency Hierarchy, Monetary Sovereignty, and Policy Space', *Review of Keynesian Economics*, 8 (4): 494–511.

Ravilious, K. (2013), 'Over Half the World's Population Could Rely on Food Imports by 2050 – Study'. *The Guardian*, Available at: https://www.theguardian.com/environment/2013/may/07/half-population-food-imports-2050 (Accessed 1 June 2024).

Schwartz, H. M. (2019), 'American Hegemony: Intellectual Property Rights, Dollar Centrality, and Infrastructural Power', *Review of International Political Economy*, 26 (3): 490–519.

Strange, S. (1971), *Sterling and British Policy: A Political Study of an International Currency in Decline*, London: Oxford University Press.

Thirlwall, A. P. (2011), 'The Balance of Payments Constraint as an Explanation of International Growth Rate Differences', *PSL Quarterly Review*, 64 (259): 429–38.

Tooze, A. (2018), *Crashed: How a Decade of Financial Crises Changed the World*, London: Penguin.

Vernengo, M., and E. Pérez Caldentey. (2020), 'Modern Money Theory (MMT) in the Tropics: Functional Finance in Developing Countries', *Challenge*, 63 (6): 332–48.

Williams, J. H. (1943), 'Currency Stabilization: The Keynes and White Plans in Foreign Affairs', *American Economic Review*, 21 (4): 645–58.

World Bank. (2024a), 'GNI per capita, Atlas Method (current US$)'. Available at: https://genderdata.worldbank.org/en/indicator/ny-gnp-pcap-cd (Accessed 1 June 2024).

World Bank. (2024b), 'World Bank Country and Lending Groups'. Available at: https://datahelpdesk.worldbank.org/knowledgebase/chapters/906519-world-bank-country-and-lending-groups (Accessed 1 June 2024).

6

International monetary adjustment with and without a global fiscal authority

Nathaniel Cline, David Fields and Matías Vernengo

Introduction

This paper explores the limits of the International Clearing Union (ICU) proposal in resolving balance of payments crises, recognizing the asymmetric adjustment mechanisms of core and peripheral countries. Keynes's proposal for an ICU aimed to address payments imbalances by creating a supranational institution to manage international transactions, issue a global currency, and, importantly, to encourage equitable adjustment between surplus and deficit countries. The ICU would act as a closed payment system that allows for units to overdraft and imposes penalties for persistent imbalances. The ICU, however, works towards this equitable payments balance at any level of global effective demand.

During a crisis, the need for a central fiscal authority becomes critical. Redistribution alone is insufficient; there must be an authority with the power and willingness to actively deficit spend. As Kindleberger (1973) suggested, the global financial hegemon has the power to coordinate macroeconomic policies and provide markets for distress goods. We argue this need is illustrated in the divergent experiences of the Eurozone and the United States in response to crisis.

Comparing the United States and the Eurozone reveals an important difference. In fiscal federal unions like the United States, there is a federal fiscal authority that can not only transfer between surplus and deficit units within the union but can issue debt in its own currency and thus engage in transfers to sub-units as a whole. In the case of the United States, transfers between surplus and deficit states can be large. It would be misleading, though, to assume from these large transfers that simple fiscal transfers between states would resolve persistent external imbalances. In fact, it can be shown that during major crises, the United States does not respond with interstate transfers, but instead transfers federal funds to states as a whole. The relevant transfer in the crisis was then not among states, but between states and the federal government acting as a fiscal authority. At the global scale, this suggests that stable adjustment process between countries with persistent external imbalances would require some form of global financial authority in the face of a crisis.

The rest of this chapter is divided into three sections. The following section discusses the history and history of thought on balance of payments adjustment, emphasizing the asymmetric nature of all hitherto existing systems. A third section lays out the need for a fiscal authority in any currency union, using the contrasting examples of the Eurozone and the United States. The conclusion then reflects on the potential for the hegemon to supply the global economy with sufficient effective demand through its fiscal powers.

A brief history of balance of payments adjustment[1]

Historically, the development of ideas concerning adjustment of international monetary imbalances is relatively recent. Long-distance trade, of course, has existed for a long while, but it only rose to prominence with global finance during the European global expansion of the sixteenth century. Early political advice from that loosely defined and disparate Mercantilist or Cameralist School suggested that countries should avoid trade deficits and accumulate metallic reserves to preclude external problems. This advice stemmed in general from a concern with a desire to combine economic growth with the construction of state capacity. This was to be achieved by a diverse set of policies (dependent on the particular author) ranging from import prohibitions to legalized monopolies, to early capital controls in the form of limits on precious metal exports.

Among the early responses to mercantilist thinking, David Hume famously argued against intervention to produce a favourable balance of trade. He purported to show, with his ingenious price-specie-flow mechanism, that the balance of payments was self-adjusting (Hume 1752). In Hume's argument, money is the primary determinant of the price level, and thus inflows of precious metals (he assumed trade was settled in specie) would simply raise domestic prices. He went on to claim that the balance of trade is a consequence of relative prices; thus, a temporary surplus in the balance of trade would result in gold inflows, rising domestic prices and eventually falling exports and rising imports. Intervention, it was assumed, was unnecessary and it would be detrimental.

Although Hume overstated the role of specie in settling trade balances, it is true that international financial integration lagged significantly. In fact, the lack of capital mobility was one of the assumptions required by David Ricardo for his notion of comparative advantage. Before the early part of the nineteenth century, there was not a significant international market for sovereign debt, and international lending was limited.[2]

It was the British who demonetized silver, which had been the essential metallic currency for centuries, if not millennia, and then imposed a Pound standard under the guise of a gold standard in the last quarter of the nineteenth century.[3] This period is sometimes referred to as the 'first' globalization. Following the integration of world trade with railroads and steamboats, and the improvement in telecommunications with the development of the telegraph, there was a boom of cross-country financial flows (Obstfeld and Taylor 2004).

The modern conventional view on the functioning of the gold standard is, in its fundamentals, not very different from Hume's specie-flow mechanism, as pointed out by Eichengreen (1996). In this view, flows of capital move in the right direction, eliminating imbalances and stabilizing the international economy. The modern conventional view has modified Hume's mechanism, replacing physical gold flows with the notion of the gold standard as a 'credible commitment' device for central banks and national governments. The stability of the system is then still maintained by private capital flows. De Cecco (1984) has forcefully argued that the automatic stability of the gold standard system was a myth. The evidence presented in Bloomfield (1963) suggested that even in the classical gold standard flows of capital were in fact destabilizing. Against the nostalgic references to the 'good old days of the international gold standard' he argues that 'disequilibrating movements of short term capital, destabilizing exchange speculation, capital flight, threats to the continued maintenance of convertibility, concern as to the adequacy of international reserves and the volume of floating international indebtedness – all these at times were in evidence in the pre-1914 system and in some cases necessitated measures going well beyond routine application of discount-rate policy' (Bloomfield 1963: 2). By the time of Bretton Woods, the consensus had shifted, and the view was that capital flows were destabilizing, and capital controls had to be imposed (Nurkse 1944).

An alternative view to the one based on Hume and conventional wisdom can be derived from Kindleberger (1973), based on his theory of hegemonic stability.[4] In this view, the stability of the gold standard system resulted from the effective management by the leading hegemonic member, that is, the United Kingdom (UK). According to Kindleberger (1973: 289–90) the Bank of England stabilized the system by acting as the lender of last resort, ensuring the coordination of macroeconomic policies, and providing countercyclical long-term lending.

This suggests that it was the relevance of the UK's position in world trade and finance that allowed for the stability of the system. De Cecco (1984: 20) argues that 'the system was really based on sterling rather than gold'. In this view, neither credibility nor cooperation was at the centre of the working of the international gold standard. Hegemonic power was instead. The role of the City of London, as the financial centre of the world, allowed the Bank of England to manage the international monetary system, as the conductor of an orchestra, as Maynard Keynes had suggested. The City of London could lend long and borrow short, functioning as the banker of the world. Whenever the exchange rate fell to the gold export point, an increase in the Bank rate would avoid the outflow of gold. The command over gold flows was asymmetric, since changes in the interest rates of other countries had less effect than the Bank of England's discount rate.

Furthermore, in the case of peripheral countries, adjustment tended to be in the quantities rather than in prices. Hence, outflows of capital caused by a crisis in the centre led to a severe contraction of the domestic economy. Stagnation was the only instrument to avoid deficits in the current account of the balance of payments. Also, most countries in the periphery of the system were regularly forced to suspend payments in gold. As Ford (1962: 189) noted, 'automatic income adjustment forces . . . provided the main adjustment mechanism, whilst the gold standard "medicine" of higher interest rates in the face of gold losses played a subsidiary role in promoting long term adjustment'.[5] Note that this adjustment goes beyond simply introducing Keynesian elements into the process of balance of payments adjustment as done by James Meade in his classic work (Meade 1951). In Meade's work, the economies have a tendency in the long run to full employment, and persistent imbalances would be dealt with by changes in the exchange rate. In some ways, the policies of the International Monetary Fund (IMF), allowing, or even promoting, devaluation in the case of fundamental imbalances is based on a similar theoretical construct.

This classical gold standard was relatively short-lived, roughly dating from the 1870s until the First World War. The collapse of the hegemonic position of the United Kingdom (UK) during the interwar crisis proved fatal (De Cecco 1984). The failures of the interwar gold standard created serious doubts about the self-adjusting nature of external imbalances, and of the capitalist world economy itself, since monetary instability was seen as central to explain the Great Depression (Nurkse 1944; Kindleberger 1973).

The Keynes and White Plans at Bretton Woods were alternative methods of dealing with the issue. In Keynes's proposal, no one country's currency would serve as the international currency, as in the classical gold standard. Instead, a new international currency would be created (bancor) which would anchor all nations' currencies and be used to settle international payments. This would be bank money and issued by the International Clearing Union. Nations with temporary balance of payments disequilibria would be allowed overdrafts on their ICU accounts. This would avoid the immediate need to adjust. It would also, in principle, mean that countries would have little incentive to accumulate large reserves. This overdraft policy would also be combined with controls on speculative flows of capital. Longer-term imbalances would be disincentivized by applying a penalty to surplus countries and revaluation or other adjustments for deficit countries. In this way, Keynes envisioned a more symmetric system of international adjustment in contrast to the asymmetric system of the classical gold standard. The Clearing Union would allocate reserves such that the long-run sum of worldwide balance of payments would be zero, that is, the sum of all balance of payments surpluses would equal the sum of all deficits within any given period (Richardson 1985).

Although Keynes's plan would in principle make adjustment more symmetric, he also argued that the ICU, on its own, would be insufficient to deal with global fluctuations in effective demand. On this point, it is worth quoting from his first draft of the plan:

> There are various methods by which the Clearing Union could use its influence and its powers to maintain stability of prices and to control the Trade Cycle. If an International Economic Board is established, this Board and the Clearing Union might be expected to work in close collaboration to their mutual advantage. If an International Investment or Development Corporation is also set up together with a scheme of Commodity Controls for the control of stocks of the staple primary products, we might come to possess in these three Institutions a powerful means of combating the evils of the Trade Cycle, by exercising contractionist or expansionist influence on the system as a whole or on particular sections. (CWJMK, vol. XXV: 133)

The ICU would be paired with additional international institutions that could regulate global effective demand, and perhaps eventually, and in somewhat utopian fashion it 'might become the pivot of the future economic government of the world' (CWJMK, vol. XXV: 189). It is on this point that the current paper wishes to focus. In the next section we will lay out the case that is the complementary institution of a fiscal authority that distinguishes the currency unions of the Eurozone and the United States, and that the fundamental role of such a supranational authority would have been fiscal in nature.

Alas, Keynes's plan lost out to Harry Dexter White's initiative, an international monetary system resting on US dollar dominance (Helleiner 2014; Faudot 2021). Rather than being anchored by bancor, the system of exchange rates would be anchored by the US dollar, which in turn was tied to gold in the beginning. Notably, White also emphasized the need for capital controls and exchange rate management. The system worked, albeit imperfectly, but was seen as doomed relatively early on, with both friends, like Robert Triffin, and foes, more prominently Milton Friedman, criticizing it (Friedman 1953; Triffin 1960).

During the Bretton Woods era, peripheral economies were able to insulate themselves from international financial markets by introducing capital controls, which were not only allowed, but in many ways promoted. Balance of payments adjustments still depended on a painful combination of contractionary depreciation, and contractionary macroeconomic policies.[6] However, foreign exchange controls reduced the risks of runs on the domestic currency and allowed governments to set the interest rate for domestic purposes as Keynes had suggested during the negotiations of Bretton Woods. However, for authors in the periphery, like Prebisch, it was clear that the system imposed additional constraints on peripheral economies that precluded catching up with the centre (Pérez Caldentey and Vernengo 2022).

The most important consequence of low rates of interest was that they allowed financing public spending at low costs. In other words, capital controls enabled not just the use of monetary policy to achieve full employment, but also the expansion of the role of the state. Monetary sovereignty is not just about monetary policy, but fundamentally about the ability of the state to promote social policies in a sustainable way.

The collapse of Bretton Woods in part reflected the limitations of the adjustment mechanism and represented an intellectual victory for Milton Friedman and others that believed in the automatic adjustment process, with flexible exchange rates. Persistent disequilibria between deficit and surplus countries ever since, however, has cast a long shadow over the idea of the sustainability of the flexible dollar standard. The notion that the collapse of Bretton Woods represented the beginning of the end of dollar hegemony is still widespread, even if incorrect (Vernengo 2021).

The demise of Bretton Woods and increasing challenges to national monetary sovereignty led eventually to a more complete dominance of the dollar. Like the demonetization of silver during the height of British Hegemony, the demonetization of gold after 1971 is in many ways a return to the pre-Bretton Woods era. Capital mobility was reinstated, and the US dollar took the place of gold. Nostalgia about gold may lead some peripheral countries to dollarize formally, but in many ways the system has been more dollarized. However, the lesson for peripheral countries today is that balance of payments problems will not disappear with flexible rates and free capital mobility. Understanding that the costs of balance of payments adjustments were quite high in the pre-Bretton Woods era should be a stern warning.

Current account deficits, in the absence of the devaluation alternative, are corrected by contraction of domestic demand. The post-Bretton Woods or flexible dollar standard has been one of persistent imbalances, and recurrent cycles of debt and default for peripheral countries.[7] After the series of financial crises that started with the Tequila 1995 and ended with the Argentine default in 2002, most developing countries have accumulated large amounts of dollar reserves as an insurance mechanism to preclude currency crises, and sovereign defaults.[8] For the most part, the system has been able to function because of pervasive financial crisis in the United States, along with the very low interest rates there, which altogether have created the conditions for lifting financial constraints on most peripheral countries. The pandemic, in particular the acceleration of inflation towards the end of it, and the higher rates of the Federal Reserve (Fed), however, reverted the tendency, setting in motion a new debt crisis for the periphery.

In other words, the global monetary system is highly dependent on the domestic policy decisions of the hegemonic country. The United States can in general ease pressures with lower interest rates, and facilitate a non-contractionary adjustment in the periphery, but also the Fed can provide direct swap lines to facilitate the adjustment in selected countries, for strategic and geopolitical reasons. In this sense, the Fed's network of direct swap lines shapes global financial flows and, thus, constitutes a US engineered international monetary hierarchy (Carré and Le Maux 2020; Pape 2022; Murau et al. 2023). The IMF, in spite of some noticeable changes, remains essentially an instrument of the United States and other creditor countries to promote contractionary adjustment in the periphery (Ford and Vernengo 2014). The ability to directly or indirectly provide funds on a global basis in the key currency resembles, to a great extent, the power that a fiscal authority has in providing funds on a domestic basis. In the next section the role of the fiscal authority is discussed in the context of the 2008–9 Global Financial Crisis and the subsequent European Union (EU) debt crisis of 2010.

The role of a fiscal authority in the external adjustment

The 2008–9 crisis had its epicentre in the United States, in the aftermath of the housing bubble, which in turn had followed the dot-com bubble of the 1990s, and the rapid recovery that ensued. The US economy has been driven to some extent, consumption-led, fuelled by private debt accumulation, which tends to be considerably more volatile than public debt (Schularick 2014). The ability of the United States to repeatedly recover from the crisis was related to the ability of the government to borrow at very low rates in its own currency, without any significant constraint other than the political ones, which are not minor. Nevertheless, even if a common currency exists, and public debt is in the country's own currency, the existence of a supranational central bank and interstate transfer mechanisms might not be sufficient to promote recovery. The contrast between the Eurozone and the United States' national or subnational units suggests that fiscal federalism is essential.

The Eurozone is characterized by not only a common currency, but by the Target2 settlement system between member states, that is, in theory, a highly integrated financial market infrastructure for frictionless settlement of financial transactions across national borders (Cesaratto 2013). As Lavoie (2015) argues, this system bears resemblances to Keynes's International Clearing Bank in that it allows advances to deficit countries to avoid adjustment for a time. Given this framework, it is widely recognized among many economists that the fiscal crisis faced by some Eurozone countries was the result, not of internal fiscal excess, but of fundamental imbalances made worse by the adoption of a common currency. Indeed, as Wynne Godley pointed out long ago, European structural payment imbalances would not be automatically corrected by market forces (Godley 1992).[9] In this case, a common currency arrangement without a centralized fiscal authority able to spend in its own currency will potentially exacerbate the balance of payments problems of member countries or sub-regional units. Some countries will be permanently outsold, and under the current arrangements, if capital flows are not accommodating, will be forced to make large income adjustments to resolve their balance of payments. In other words, they are forced as noted by Ford/Kindleberger to adjust by reducing the level of activity and imports.

Arguably, more substantial interregional redistribution would resolve the problems these countries face. The United States, whose states enjoy a common currency within a substantial federal fiscal system that redistributes funds among the states, is the obvious choice for comparison.[10] However, it is important to note that this is not the equivalent to the Hobbesian defence of a strong sovereign state, supranational in this case, as the solution to conflict, and a simple analogy between national states and a supranational entity. The US ability to promote a domestic recovery on the basis of federal transfers rests on a fiscal pact, and it is not dissimilar to that of other countries that do have a sovereign currency, including peripheral ones. On the other hand, the US international role stands on the peculiar position of the dollar, which, in turn, depends on military power. The Euro Area provides an interesting contrast, since it does have a common sovereign currency, but no fiscal pact.

Residents of states pay taxes to the federal government and states receive government expenditures through federal programmes, grants, salaries and other means. However, the payments states receive are decided upon different grounds than the taxes they pay. Thus, a state like Mississippi pays very little in taxes but receives a substantial amount of government spending. In contrast, states like Minnesota pay into the system much more than they receive. In normal times this prevents large balance of payments crises from emerging between states. Mississippi is, thus, permitted a higher average growth rate than would otherwise be implied by their balance of payments. These transfers are several times larger than the convergence funds within the Eurozone, being of the order 10 per cent of GDP in the case of Mississippi (D'Apice 2016). The Eurozone, given its institutional architecture, does not readily possess the regional fiscal apparatus necessary to counterpoise divergent growth trajectories (Blyth 2016; Kirshner 2016; Gräbner et al. 2020).

It would be misleading to assume from these large transfers that simple fiscal transfers between states would resolve Europe's fiscal problems. The United States did not respond to the crisis by transferring large amounts of money between states as it does in normal times. The key point was that the US federal government went into deficit to transfer money to states as a whole. The relevant transfer in the crisis was then, not among states, but between states and the federal government. What would be needed then for the Eurozone would be a similar fiscal union, which would finance all member states, and not necessarily just transfers between say Germany and Greece in the middle of a crisis.[11]

The degree of interstate transfers in the United States is shown in Figure 6.1. Note that between 2004 and 2007 it appears that the federal government is actually a net drag on the states. This is likely not quite correct because the expenditures in the chart do not count expenditures which cannot easily be allocated among states, like for instance federal interest payments.

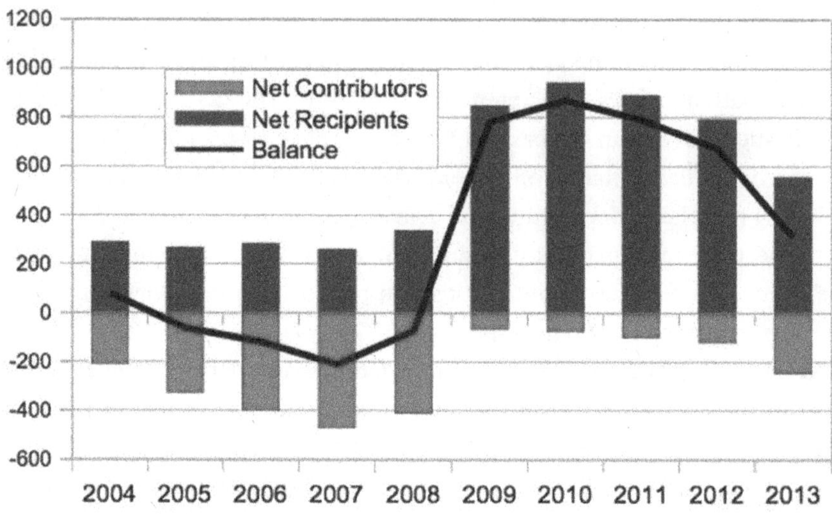

Figure 6.1 The degree of interstate transfers 2004–2013. Source: Expenditures provided by the Pew Fiscal Federalism Initiative, tax data from the IRS, author's calculations.

The issue can be seen clearly too if the transfers are broken down by state as is done in Figure 6.2. One can see that by 2009, only a few states remained net contributors to the system while the others all became net recipients. In other words, the crisis forced the US federal government to intervene and promote a direct transfer from the federal government to almost all the states. It is not a simple interstate transfer from surplus to deficit states, as would have been in the Keynes plan in Bretton Woods, but the existence of a fiscal authority with the ability to spend not just the resources from the states, but to create resources out of thin air, so to speak.[12] Note that causality goes from spending to revenue, and that the spending by the federal authority would create the tax revenue, not just at the federal level, but at the state level too.

Both views would agree that the crisis was not the result of fiscal problems, even in Greece, that had higher fiscal deficits than others, and where the numbers had been fudged with, the levels were not particularly high, at least from the perspective of the EU. Lavoie (2015) argues that, in the absence of fiscal transfers from a federal EU, if the ECB had the ability to buy euro-denominated bonds of peripheral countries and keep their borrowing costs low, fiscal policy could be used by member countries, without risk of default. At heart the problem there was a monetary sovereignty problem, in this view. Basically, the ECB could transform what was effectively a foreign currency problem, since peripheral

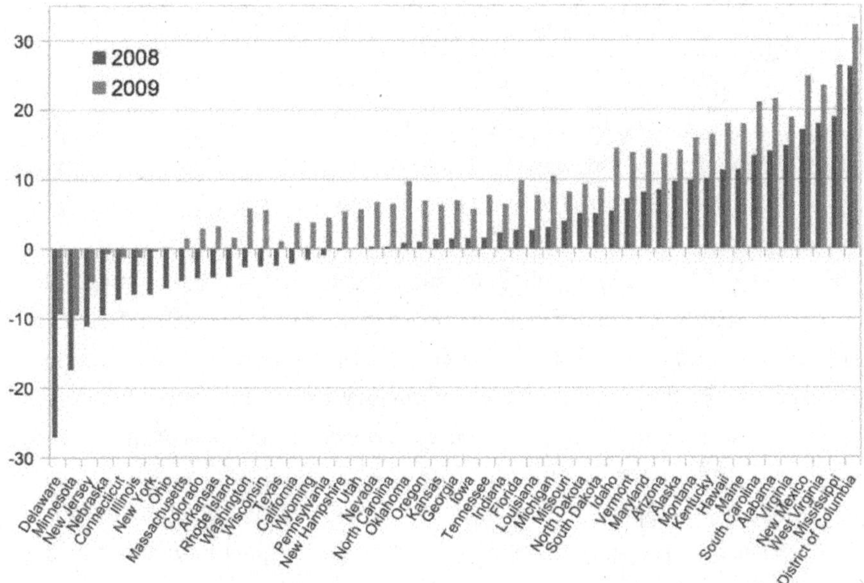

Figure 6.2 Fiscal transfers between the states 2008–9. Source: Expenditures provided by the Pew Fiscal Federalism Initiative, tax data from the IRS, author's calculations.

countries had a constraint in euros, into an essentially domestic problem, eliminating the risk of default. However, the rules of the euro do not allow the ECB to purchase sovereign debt from the member countries. The creation of the risk-free asset is the essential function of the central bank as a fiscal agent of the state to promote financial stability.[13]

On the other hand, it is also true that the manifestation of the euro crisis is in the form of a regular balance of payments problem, with countries in the periphery displaying current account deficits, as noted by Cesaratto (2015). In a sense, both views are correct. The imbalances in the current account, becomes relevant because, in the absence of fiscal transfers, and of a monetary authority providing a zero-risk asset for governments to borrow in times of crisis, the adjustment is done by variations of the level of income. Just to illustrate the dimension of the adjustment in quantities, it suffices to say that Greek real Gross Domestic Product (GDP) remains about 22.5 per cent below its previous peak in 2007, as of 2023.

Note that, in the European crisis, even if the ECB bought the bonds of peripheral countries, following the unconventional policies of the Fed, and kept their rates low, that would be equivalent to suggest that there are no differences between the debt of peripheral countries, like Greece, and core countries, like Germany. In other words, a broader fiscal unity than exists presently, and some sense that Greeks and Germans are essentially citizens with the same standing. Fiscal unions often require a greater degree of social solidarity. Alas, this fiscal union does not exist in the Eurozone, and therefore, the relationship between countries like Germany and Greece is that of regional supremacy and subordination.

The country with the key global currency, the United States, has the ability to do on a global basis what it does for its own states domestically. Countries can essentially do the same for their own subnational units, but supranational organizations, like the EU, that have a monetary union, but not a fiscal one, are constrained in their ability to promote a smooth adjustment of the balance of payments. The United States does, in a selective and limited way, provide what Kindleberger suggested in his classic work on the subject, global effective demand. Keynes's plan at Bretton Woods envisaged a global currency, and a centralized clearing system, but without a fiscal authority, which was, at any rate, politically unfeasible. It was the Marshall Plan and the Cold War that forced the United States to act as the provider of global demand. The global economy needs a supranational system if American hegemony is to be substituted for a more rational and equitable system.

Conclusion

Balance of payments adjustments are seen within the economics profession as essentially automatic. Some more realistic views suggest that, at least in the short run, the adjustment might be costly, in particular as a result of imperfections in the capital markets, and access to credit is limited. But even then, in general, the main imperfection causing crises is associated with government excesses and, in particular, with fiscal deficits. In fact, currency crises, the most dramatic event in case of persistent external imbalances, are often modelled as the result of monetization of the fiscal deficit. Alternative views on currency crises invert the causality between fiscal and balance of payments problems in a currency crisis. Currency crises are not caused by excessive fiscal spending financed by monetary emissions, which would lead to inflation, and eventually after a run on the currency and depletion of reserves to a devaluation, but on external problems, be that an interest rate or a terms of trade shock.

There two key problems with the conventional view, are, on the one hand the notion that increases in money supply have direct impact on prices, and no effect on quantities, and on the other that these models presume that fiscal deficits and debt denominated in domestic currency are the problem in currency crises, when the relevant debt is the foreign one, denominated in foreign currency. In other words, whereas default in the former is not possible, in the latter it clearly is. The mismatch between government receipts in domestic currency and foreign debt obligations in foreign currency is the key problem in currency crises. Fiscal deficits might play a role in a currency crisis, but it is ultimately an indirect one. If the fiscal deficit, by leading to an increase in the level of activity, and not prices, leads to a current account deficit, then it does exacerbate the external constraint of the economy, and might contribute to the eventual depreciation of the domestic currency. Note that this suggests that the variations of the level of income are more relevant for the adjustment of the balance of payments, than changes in the exchange rate, something noted for the case of peripheral economies, in particular Argentina during the gold standard, by A. G. Ford. In other words, the balance of payments adjustment is asymmetric and not automatic, since contractionary policies must be enforced, which has ultimately been the role of the IMF.

The hegemon plays a crucial role, since in the global economy, it has the ability to promote a smooth, or less costly adjustment, for countries in the periphery. The power extends to the ability to arbitrate, to some extent, which economies can grow without hitting the proverbial external constraint. In the last two decades, most peripheral countries have increased significantly their external reserves in the key currency, to preclude the need for costly external adjustment.

Notes

1 For a short review of the history of international monetary arrangements see Cline et al. (2023).

2 So much so that the first significant debt crisis is often associated with the Latin American post-independence defaults in the mid-1820s. See Dawson (1990). It is also worth noting, in the context of this paper, that in the 1840s several states in the newly formed United States defaulted as well. In this period, the United States lacked not only substantial transfers between states, but also a Federal Government willing to engage in substantial transfers to subnational units. See Greenberg (2020) Of course, within Europe, where public debt first originated in the late medieval period in the Northern Italian City States, there was a longer history of financial integration and debt defaults (Fratianni and Spinelli 2006; Stasavage 2015). For a long discussion of sovereign debt-defaults see Reinhart and Rogoff (2009).

3 On the pre-gold standard era see Flynn and Giráldez (1995, 2002). They propose a view of the integration of the global economy based on monetary factors, in which silver is central. Note that their views have been criticized by revisionists authors. For a discussion of the limits to the revisionist views regarding the literature on the rise of the global economy, particularly the persistence of conventional Monetarist views on the functioning of the international monetary system, despite the important critique of the Eurocentric nature of the conventional literature see Fields and Vernengo (2016).

4 For a discussion of the origins of Kindleberger's ideas and the views on key currencies of John Williams, see Mehrling (2022). The work of both Susan Strange and Maria da Conceição Tavares is also relevant in this context. For their views see Vernengo (2021).

5 It is worth noticing that in the first edition of his history of the international monetary system, Eichengreen did not include the work of Ford, and the asymmetries in the adjustment between centre and periphery, but he included it in the second edition. See Eichengreen (1996).

6 Currency crises occurred with some regularity, often associated with increases in the interest rate of the hegemonic country, and negative shocks to the terms of trade. Contrary to the dominant view that implied that crises resulted from fiscal excesses (e.g. Krugman 1979), the fiscal problems were often the result of an external shock (Cline and Vernengo 2016).

7 The hegemony of the dollar has little to do with a revived Bretton Woods system, in which a relatively fixed exchange rate in China and exporting to the US market reestablished the centrality of the dollar (Dooley et al. 2003; Dooley et al. 2014). The notion here is that the end of Bretton Woods itself implied an even more clear dominance of the dollar, the currency in which the key energy commodities are denominated in international markets (Fields and Vernengo 2013).

8 On the long waves of debt-default see Suter (1989).

9 For example, Jordá et al. (2016: 45) find that 'in advanced economies financial crises are not preceded by public debt build-ups nor are they more likely when public debt is high'. They do suggest that high public debt limits the ability of the government to rescue the private sector in case of a crisis, but there is little discussion of the reasons for that, which in many cases, when it comes to austerity policies, are related to political rather than sustainability issues.

10 Indeed, several papers make the comparison between Eurozone countries and US states, e.g. Eichengreen (1990) or Dreyer and Schmid (2015).

11 Alternatively, the European Central Bank (ECB) could act as a true lender of last resort, and it could have made sure that Greek debt was effectively equal to German bonds, reducing the costs of financing deficits in Greece, as noted by Lavoie (2015). Economic policy asymmetry, however, constitutes the modus operandi of the Eurozone, which ensues regional segmentation.

12 Note that in Keynes plan there would be an international currency, the bancor, but not a supranational fiscal authority. The White Plan, in turn, dispensed the idea of an alternative currency, and promoted the use of the dollar. For a discussion of both plans see Steil (2013).

13 For the monetary sovereignty view see Lavoie (2015), for the balance of payments crisis view see Cesaratto (2015).

References

Bloomfield, A. (1963), 'Short-Term Capital Movements Under the Pre-1914 Gold Standard', *Princeton Studies in International Finance*, 11.

Blyth, M. (2016), 'Policies to Overcome Stagnation: The Crisis, and the Possible Futures, of All Things Euro', *European Journal of Economics and Economic Policies: Intervention*, 13 (2): 215–28.

Carré, E., and l. Le Maux. (2020), 'The Federal Reserve's Dollar Swap Lines and the European Central Bank During the Global Financial Crisis of 2007–09', *Cambridge Journal of Economics*, 44 (4): 723–47.

Cesaratto, S. (2013), 'The Implications of TARGET2 in the European Balance of Payment Crisis and Beyond', *European Journal of Economics and Economic Policies: Intervention*, 10 : 359–82.

Cesaratto, S. (2015), 'Balance of Payments or Monetary Sovereignty? In Search of the EMU's Original Sin: Comments on Marc Lavoie's "The Eurozone: Similarities to and Differences from Keynes's Plan"', *International Journal of Political Economy*, 44 (2): 142–56.

Cline, N., and M. Vernengo. (2016), 'Interest Rates, Terms of Trade and Currency Crises: Are We on the Verge of a New Crisis in the Periphery?' in O. Canuto and A Gevorkyan (eds), *Financial Deepening and Post-Crisis Development in Emerging Markets*, London: Palgrave-Macmillan.

Cline, N., C. Schönerwald da Silva, and M. Vernengo. (2023), 'Exchange Rate Arrangements: Fix, Float, or Manage?' Political Economy Research Institute (PERI-UMass), Working Paper No 586.

D'Apice, P. (2016), 'Budget-Related Cross-Border Flows: EU Versus US', available at https://cepr.org/voxeu/columns/budget-related-cross-border-flows-eu-versus-us.

Dawson, F. G. (1990), *The First Latin American Debt Crisis: The City of London and the 1822-25 Loan Bubble*, New Haven: Yale University Press.

De Cecco, M. (1984), *The International Gold Standard: Money and Empire*, New York: St. Martin's Press.

Dooley, M., D. Folkerts-Landau, and P. Garber. (2003), 'An Essay on the Revived Bretton Woods System', NBER, Working Paper No 9971.

Dooley, M., D. Folkerts-Landau, and P. Garber. (2014), 'The Revived Bretton Woods System's First Decade', NBER, Working Paper No 20454.

Dreyer, J. K., and P. A. Schmid. (2015), 'Fiscal Federalism in Monetary Unions: Hypothetical Iscal Transfers Within the Euro-Zone', *International Review of Applied Economics*, 29 (4): 506–32.

Eichengreen, B. (1990), 'One Money for Europe? Lessons from the US Currency Union', *Economic Policy*, 5 (10): 117–87.

Eichengreen, B. (1996), *Globalizing Capital a History of the International Monetary System*, Princeton: Princeton University Press.

Faudot, A. (2021), 'The Keynes Plan and Bretton Woods Debates: The Early Radical Criticisms by Balogh, Schumacher and Kalecki', *Cambridge Journal of Economics*, 45 (4): 751–70.

Fields, D., and M. Vernengo. (2013) 'Hegemonic Currencies During the Crisis: The Dollar Versus the Euro in a Cartalist Perspective', *Review of International Political Economy*, 20 (4): 740–59.

Fields, D., and M. Vernengo. (2016), 'Dis-Orient: Money, Technological Development and the Rise of the West', *Review of Radical Political Economics*, 48 (4): 562–8.

Flynn, D., and A. Giráldez. (1995), 'Born with a "Silver Spoon": The Origin of World Trade in 1571', *Journal of World History*, 6 (2): 201–21.

Flynn, D., and A. Giráldez. (2002), 'Cycles of Silver: Global Economic Unity Through the Mid-Eighteenth Century', *Journal of World History*, 13 (2): 391–427.

Ford, A. G. (1962), *The Gold Standard, 1880–1914: Britain and Argentina*, Clarendon: Oxford University Press.

Ford, K., and M. Vernengo. (2014), 'Everything Must Change so that the IMF Can Remain the Same: The World Economic Outlook and the Global Financial Stability Report', *Development and Change*, 45 (5): 1193–204.

Fratianni, M., and F. Spinelli. (2006), 'Italian City-States and Financial Evolution', *European Review of Economic History*, 10 (3): 257–78.

Friedman, M. (1953), 'The Case for Flexible Exchange Rates', in M. Friedman (ed), *Essays in Positive Economics*, Chicago: University of Chicago Press.

Gräbner, C., P. Heimberger, J. Kapeller, and B. Schütz. (2020), 'Is the Eurozone Disintegrating? Macroeconomic Divergence, Structural Polarisation, Trade and Fragility', *Cambridge Journal of Economics*, 44 (3): 647–69.

Greenberg, J. R. (2020), *Bank Notes and Shinplasters: The Rage for Paper Money in the Early Republic*, Philadelphia: University of Pennsylvania Press.

Godley, W. (1992), 'Maastricht and All That', London Review of Books, 14(19), 8 October, available at https://www.lrb.co.uk/the-paper/v14/n19/wynne-godley/maastricht-and-all-that.

Helleiner, E. (2014), *Forgotten Foundations of Bretton Woods: International Development and the Making of the Postwar Order*, Ithaca: Cornell University Press.

Hume, D. (1752), 'Of the Balance of Trade', in E. Rotwein (ed), *David Hume: Writings on Economics*, Madison: University of Wisconsin Press, 1970.

Jordá, O., M. Schularick, and A. Taylor. (2016), 'Sovereigns Versus Banks: Credit, Crises and Consequences', *Journal of the European Economic Association*, 14 (1): 45–79.

Keynes, J. M. ([1941] 1980), 'The Origins of the Clearing Union, 1940–1942', in D. Moggridge (ed), *The Collected Writings of John Maynard Keynes*, XXV, Cambridge: Cambridge University Press.

Kindleberger, C. P. (1973), *The World in Depression, 1929–1939*, London: Allen Lane.

Kirshner, J. (2016), 'The International Consequences of Financial Fragility', *Current History*, 115: 23–8.

Krugman, P. (1979), 'A Model of Balance of Payments Crises', *Journal of Money Credit and Banking*, 11 (3): 311–25.

Lavoie, M. (2015), 'The Eurozone: Similarities to and Differences from Keynes's Plan', *International Journal of Political Economy*, 44 (2): 3–17.

Meade, J. (1951), *The Balance of Payments*, Oxford: Oxford University Press.

Mehrling, P. (2022), *Money and Empire: Charles P. Kindleberger and the Dollar System*, Cambridge: Cambridge University Press.

Murau, S., F. Pape, and T. Pforr. (2023), 'International Monetary Hierarchy Through Emergency US-Dollar Liquidity: A Key Currency Approach', *Competition & Change*, 27 (3–4): 495–515.

Nurkse, R. (1944), *International Currency Experience*, Geneva: League of Nations.

Obstfeld, M., and A. Taylor. (2004), *Global Capital Markets: Integration, Crisis, and Growth*, Cambridge: Cambridge University Press.

Pape, F. (2022), 'Governing Global Liquidity: Federal Reserve Swap Lines and the International Dimension of US Monetary Policy', *New Political Economy*, 27 (3): 455–72.

Pérez Caldentey, E., and M. Vernengo. (2022), 'Prebisch's Critique of Bretton Woods Plans Its Relation to Kalecki's and Williams' Ideas', in J. Osiatynski and J. Toporowski (eds), *Kalecki's Alternative to Keynes and White and its Consequences*, Oxford: Oxford university Press.

Reinhart, C., and K. Rogoff. (2009), *This Time is Different: Eight Centuries of Financial Folly*, Princeton: Princeton University Press.

Richardson, D. R. (1985), 'On Proposals for a Clearing Union', *Journal of Post Keynesian Economics*, 8 (1): 14–27.

Schularick, M. (2014), 'Public and Private Debt: The Historical Record (1870–2010)', *German Economic Review*, 15 (1): 191–207.

Stasavage, D. (2015), 'Why Did Public Debt Originate in Europe?', in A. Monson and W. Scheidel (eds), *The Political Economy of Premodern States*, Cambridge: Cambridge University Press.

Steil, B. (2013), *The Battle of Bretton Woods: John Maynard Keynes, Harry Dexter White, and the Making of a New World Order*, Princeton: Princeton university Press.

Suter, C. (1989), 'Long Waves in the International Financial System: Debt-Default Cycles of Sovereign Borrowers', *Review* (Fernand Braudel Center), 12 (1): 1–49.

Triffin, R. (1960), *Gold and the Dollar Crisis: The Future of Convertibility*, New Haven: Yale University Press.

Vernengo, M. (2021), 'The Consolidation of Dollar Hegemony After the Collapse of Bretton Woods: Bringing Power Back In', *Review of Political Economy*, 33 (4): 529–51.

7

An analysis of conflicts and the world monetary system

A case against unilateral responses and for a twenty-first-century global clearing union

Heikki Patomäki

Introduction

As a result of the birth of the Bretton Woods system in the 1940s and its transformation in the 1970s, the world economy is centred on the US dollar. Different ICU plans exemplify alternatives to using one or more national currencies as the basis of the world monetary system. On the one hand, this contrast between the current system and ICU provides opportunities to look at the functioning and effects of the current system from a fresh perspective. On the other hand, the same contrast also raises questions about the feasibility of the alternatives. Prevailing disintegration tendencies and confrontations seem to make the realization of a global clearing union unlikely. In what follows, I try to explain the current world political situation and the possibilities of implementing an ICU-style rational alternative from an integrative global political economy perspective, combining world politics, pluralist economics, and realist and pragmatist philosophical ideas (see Kotilainen and Patomäki 2022).

The role of the US dollar in the world economy and claims about US hegemony (leadership) as something good for the whole world are closely connected.[1] The common idea in these discussions has been that the US's benevolent leadership in the world economy creates the conditions for a liberal international order (LIO) that benefits everyone.[2] In International Political Economy (IPE), this idea has been articulated as the theory of hegemonic stability (HST), according to which leadership by a single hegemonic state is both a necessary and sufficient condition for an open, liberal world economy. Critics disagree. The position of the United States as the 'leader' grants it many privileges and liberties that are not shared and do not benefit the rest of the world.[3] A case in point is the role of the US dollar in the world economy. The US dollar's role as the world's key reserve currency has provided the United States with unearned privileges, resources and power while creating unwanted and unnecessary dependencies on US domestic economic policies, particularly in the Global South.

Critics have responded to this situation in various ways.[4] They may argue for replacing the US dollar with a more diversified system of national currencies and/or for replacing the US dollar with an alternative key currency such as the euro or, in particular, the renminbi (yuan). Some advocate regional solutions, which may involve clearing unions, though often in a rather technical sense of the term. Several international reformists have proposed expanding the role of Special Drawing Rights (SDRs) to reduce reliance on any single currency and to create a mechanism for redistributing resources in the world economy. A globalist alternative – professed in this paper – is a new kind of worldwide clearing union involving novel regulative components, such as the principle of an equal obligation of surplus and deficit countries to adjust. Institutional components include a global central bank.

Perceptions change and in the mid-2020s, the Trump administration's rhetoric and policies frame the dollar's reserve currency status more as a burden than a privilege. The US-China trade war and military confrontation demonstrate how conflict-ridden world politics can be. Many of the conflicts and confrontations stem, at least partially, from the way the world's monetary and trade relations remain organized around the US dollar. Since the 1960s, several rounds of global discussions on reforming the system have taken place in changing historical contexts. Many of these struggles have focused on SDRs. SDRs managed by the IMF were first created when the dollar-based monetary system went into crisis in the 1960s. The aim was to supplement the supply of gold and dollars as reserve assets. The delinking of the dollar from gold and the move to floating exchange rates in the first half of the 1970s rendered the existing SDRs largely irrelevant, although multiple actors have proposed the strengthening of this multilateral alternative. After 1969, SDRs have only been issued three times, and each time the context involved a major crisis (in 1978, mistrust in the dollar at the time when the 'great inflation' reached its peak; in 2009–11, the uncertainty generated by the Global Financial Crisis and the subsequent euro crisis; and in 2021, when the Covid-19 pandemic, impending financial crisis, and the large fall in global GDP and trade were seen to require exceptional measures).

The United States holds a veto over SDR allocations due to its significant voting share in the IMF.[5] The United States has opposed most proposals to expand SDRs – except on the three occasions mentioned – and has outright rejected the proposals to establish new global ICU-style arrangements. Discussions about ICU and related ideas have been sporadic and often limited to small and specialized academic circles. However, there are important exceptions to this. In particular, in 2009, the governor of China's central bank, Zhou Xiaochuan (2009), put forth a high-level proposal to replace the US dollar as the primary global reserve currency with a supranational reserve currency (for a summary of Chinese discussions, see the introduction). The United States ignored this, and the proposal went nowhere. Despite the latest round of SDR expansion, most of the SDRs rest in the central banks of the developed countries, which do not seem to find significant use for them. Based on these kinds of experiences over the past half-century, it may appear that the global monetary system is unreformable – at least as long as the world is not facing a crisis comparable to the two World Wars or the Great Depression between them.

In this chapter, I argue that this unreformability involves a vicious circle. An adequate global monetary system would reduce, mitigate and eliminate causes that co-generate conflicts between states, especially trade wars. The absence of an adequate global system and thus the apparent unreformability of the world monetary system is in a significant part responsible for the current world political situation.[6] The liberal end-of-history optimism of the 1990s has turned into the gloomy 2020s. The world economy continues to grow but is unstable, exhibiting uneven growth, economic imbalances, financial instabilities, deepening ecological crises and insufficient or contradictory responses to these. Territorial states seem incapable of governing the world economy adequately, and the outcome involves the securitization of commodity chains, weaponization of interdependence and the increasing division of the world into two mutually hostile camps.

To reiterate the point: the underlying contradictions and related negative tendencies could have been mitigated and in some cases overcome by means of appropriate reforms. For many, the difficulty of achieving global reforms indicates that the only way forward is through unilateral actions, whether by individual countries, regional blocs or alliances of some sort – in the 2020s, this stands especially for the BRICS countries. However, unilateral responses do not solve the global problem. Moreover, actions that can be perceived to go against the leadership of the United States evoke the fear of ever-growing disorder among those who rely on the ideas of a benevolent hegemon and hegemonic stability.

    Deweaponizing Interdependence

The responses of the hegemon to improve its position or counter its perceived relative decline – and the consequent responses by others who are constructed as rivals or enemies – tend to further intensify the prevailing geoeconomic and political competition and deepen the division of the world into hostile camps. It is possible to schematically visualize the vicious circle as follows:

In this chapter, I argue that while this cycle is indeed vicious, it can be broken. First, I discuss the HST and its conceptual basis and performative effects. To be sure, the United States (and Western) foreign policymakers do not rely only on the idea of hegemonic stability of the liberal order. HST overlaps for example with the perceived division of the world into democracies and authoritarian states. Second, I outline a contrastive storyline, which sets the postcolonial developmental states against Western neo-imperialism. From this point of view, the essential confrontation is between the supremacy of the West and the developing states struggling for equality in the world system and its governance. Third, I summarize some of the prevailing global political-economic developments in terms of uneven growth, economic imbalances, financial instabilities and contradictory responses to these developments. Actors make sense of the events and changes they experience and observe in terms of ideas and stories, which are entwined with their positioning and interests, and it is this complex that (co-)determines their responses. In the fourth section, I take a closer look at the contradictions of the current world monetary system and employ this analysis in my diagnosis of recent world historical events, episodes and trends. I also consider a related counterfactual question: how different would the world be if the ICU had been implemented in the 1940s or 1970s? I make a case for peaceful transformations and new ICU-style institutions. In the final section, I outline three scenarios about the future of the world monetary system, followed by a short conclusion.

The presumption that the United States is a benevolent hegemon

The theory of hegemonic stability emerged in the 1970s when the partial collapse of the Bretton Woods system was widely conceived as a sign of crisis in US global leadership. This perception was further reinforced by the Vietnam War and the rise of the New Left movement. The theory was first proposed by economic historian Charles P. Kindleberger (1973) in his book *The World in Depression 1929–1939*. In the last chapter of the book, 'An Explanation of the 1929 Depression', Kindleberger discussed four partly contrastive historical eras, suggesting a rough correlation between leadership and stability in the world economy[7] (the term 'stability' tends to be associated with peace, even if only tacitly).[8] The theory claims that the stability of the world economy is dependent on the benevolent leadership of the hegemonic state – before the First World War, Britain, and since the Second World War, the United States.

In its standard version (developed by Krasner 1976; Gilpin 1981; Kindleberger 1981), the theory assumes that maximum global welfare and Pareto optimality are achieved under free trade and that a hegemonic distribution of potential economic power is likely to result in an open trading structure and, more generally, in an open world economy. Indeed, the liberal international order is viewed as a global public good that only a hegemonic leader-state can provide. The global public good is supposed to include the definition and enforcement of property rights, resolution of disputes and the strengthening of stability and security. For many, the problem lies in free-riding by the lesser states in Europe, Asia and the Global South; the poor seek to exploit the rich. However, the emphases of the different versions of the theory vary in this regard, and some of them 'even' allow that the hegemon can sometimes be the sole benefiter.

Kindleberger (1981: 248) asks 'how should one distinguish exploitation from leadership?' and answers:

> Management of the gold-exchange standard by Britain from 1870 to 1913 and by the United States from 1945 to 1971 can be viewed as provision of either the public good of international money, or the private good for itself of seignorage, which is the profit that comes to the seigneur, or sovereign power, from the issuance of money. Of course it can be both. Public goods are sometimes competitive with private good [. . .] and sometimes complementary: maintenance of Pax Britannica or Pax Americana provides peace for the world as well as the status quo for the provider.

Whereas Kindleberger emphasizes ambiguities, moral responsibilities, and the need to counter business cycles,[9] IR theorists such as Gilpin (1981: 145) have put forward a more straightforwardly neo-imperial interpretation: premodern empires such as the Roman Empire and the modern hegemonic powers Britain and the United States are similar because they supply public goods (security and protection of property rights, enabling free trade) in exchange for revenue. The arrangement includes a monetary system revolving around the hegemon's currency. In the post–Second World War decades, the dollar was the basis of the world monetary system and the United States was the world's banker. According to Gilpin (1981: 174–5), the US finances its global military and political position not only by its trade surplus (which turned into a persistent deficit in the 1970s and has remained in red ever since)[10] but also by printing money. In the Cold War circumstances, this possibility of printing money meant that 'in effect, America's allies extended credit to the United States to finance its world position because it was in their economic and security interests to do so.'[11]

While theories such as the HST make truth claims, they also articulate certain practical knowledge and world understandings. They participate in justifying that practical knowledge by universalizing it into an international purpose that is supposed to be compelling to everyone (Ashley 1989). In the case of HST, this normative purpose is defined in terms of public good, a concept derived from neoclassical economics. Already in the 1970s and early 1980s, the concepts of neoclassical economics had spread and become part of popular consciousness in the US (increasingly defining the 'common sense', e.g. George 2013); and were doing more and more so elsewhere in the West and the world, especially through transnational social relations (including those of the academia), consensus building, and agreements (e.g. Carroll and Sapinski 2016). While the articulation of the theory was largely based on this economistic common sense and the standard concepts of neoclassical economics, the substance of the theory was derived from the day-to-day dilemmas of the US foreign policymakers mixed with American ethnocentrism, assumptions about the benevolence of the United States and claims that the 'small exploit the rich' (Grunberg 1990).[12] In a situation where the decline of the US hegemony begins to look real (first in 1970s and 1980s, and then again since the early 2000s), the theory encourages intensely self-regarding thinking: the 'only thing to do is to ignore everyone else and look after your own individual or national interests' (Strange 1987: 552). Trump's I and II administrations have radicalized these aspects of the theory in a way that amounts to violating the basic rules and principles of the world's multilateral trading system.

The theory of hegemonic stability is not the only sense-making storyline in the United States. First, although the developers of HST are considered neorealists, some US-based political realists have been sceptical of the idea of the United States as a benevolent liberal hegemon. They have been in the minority yet often prominent. For example, these realists have opposed NATO expansion, warning that if NATO expands to the East, a confrontation with Russia will arise and the result will be a serious conflict at some point.[13] Moreover, for many political realists, ethical evaluations – for example, 'the US is a benevolent hegemon' – are ideological by-products of the art of politics. Classical realist criticism is particularly aimed at those forms of liberalism which believe self-confidently in their own superiority and righteousness and in the moral baseness of the enemy who must be punished for its crimes. From a classical realist perspective, such liberalism tends to form a closure that is incapable of learning from history and its failures and mistakes (Morgenthau 1947: 36–41). Morgenthau and similarly minded contemporary political realists call for limits to self-centredness. It is essential to look at things also from the perspective of others and add breadth, colour, diversity and nuance to judgements about them.

Second, in practical politics, different structures of meaning tend to get mixed up. Such mixing can reinforce overlapping meanings and thus weaken the warnings of classical realists. In particular, the idea of a benevolent hegemon can also stem from the contrast between freedom/democracy and serfdom/authoritarianism. Many political theories defend and justify liberal freedoms and rights and democracy, while in discursive practices, their value can be taken as given, something that appears necessary, timeless and universal (cf. Ashley 1989: 258–60). Standard versions of economic modernization theory (for a discussion, Patomäki 1999); hypotheses such as liberal-capitalist peace and democratic peace (critical analysis, Patomäki 2018: 45–9); and philosophical interpretations of world history such as Francis Fukuyama's 'end of history' thesis, have further supported the idea that the United States, presumably located at the end-point of human development, is benevolent.[14] Many variations and combinations of these kinds of elements are possible, all of which can blend into the mythic ideas such as 'Western civilisation' or 'manifest destiny of the US', the latter exhibiting ethnocentrism at its purest (ultimately the United States is taken as God's chosen nation; for a discussion of relevance in the contemporary era, see e.g. Marsden 2011). The main point in this context is that the causal belief in the positive effect of US 'leadership' is widely shared in the United States and among its foreign policymakers and that various mixtures of meaning based on these kinds of elements constitute the mode of responsiveness of the United States in concrete situations such as when the expansion of SDRs is placed on the decision-making agenda at the IMF.

The economic developments in the 1980s and 1990s and the end of the Cold War seemed to engender a short 'unipolar moment', sidelining the hegemonic stability problem for a while. The declinist problematic returned in the 2000s and 2010s. The relevant political economy developments include trends such as the declining US share of world GDP (from 40 per cent in 1960 to 23–24 per cent in the early 2020s in nominal US dollar terms, and to 15–16 per cent in PPP terms); and the declining US share of world trade (14 per cent of exports in 1970 to 8 per cent in the early 2020s). US trade deficits have more than doubled since 2000 and US debt was about 125 per cent of GDP in 2024. In 2023, the US government spent more than $1 trillion on interest costs (net costs of $0.7 trillion are equivalent to 2/3 of military expenditure).[15] As a result, first Fitch in August 2023 and then Moody's in May 2025 downgraded the US credit rating. The US dollar continues to dominate trade and forex markets (e.g. 90 per cent of forex transactions involve the US dollar), but the US dollar share of foreign reserves has declined from 72 per cent in 2000 to less than 60 per cent in the early 2020s. None of these indicators means anything as such, but they can be perceived as problems by foreign policymakers, particularly in HST terms.

Perceived US problems have also included the multipolarization of the world, the failures of the US policy in the Middle East (especially the failure of the protracted war in Iraq and its consequences), and the Global Financial Crisis of 2007–9. In situations characterized by hegemonic decline, HST encourages increasingly self-regarding thinking and actions (for an analysis of the leadership styles of the US presidents since 2001, Mendes 2023). As the hegemon narrows the concept of the common good and identifies it with its short-term interests, various shifts occur – fewer restraints, more plainly double standards, and a deepening inability to see the collective consequences of one's actions. From this perspective, the Trump II administration can be interpreted as the next stage of development: instead of double standards, standards are largely abandoned and replaced by 'transactional politics', in which bilateral agreements are concluded on the terms of those who hold the 'best cards' (those with the most power resources to trade things or force others to their will). This also has consequences for the governance of the world economy. Depending on the responses of others, the subsequent process is likely to involve a spiral of tit-for-tat retaliations.

Alternative storyline: Postcolonial developmental states are opposed to Western neo-imperialism

During the last two centuries, many intellectuals and actors across the world have embraced variations of economic liberalism to promote free trade and free markets to foster prosperity, peace and individual freedom. However, many contenders have tried to restrict foreign influence or subordination to Western powers; create a national-statist, regional, or wider unity to create the conditions for development and industrialization; or overcome the underlying capitalist relations of production and exchange (Helleiner 2023; Patomäki 2023 chps 4 and 6). In the early twenty-first century, the most visible alternative set against the US-led liberal order can be labelled as 'postcolonial developmental states opposed to Western neo-imperialism'. This label expresses on an abstract and general level the ideals and structural constraints that the BRICS countries and a significant part of the Global South share. There are some commonalities but no single uniform identity or well-developed ideology. The positioning of each country and region in the world economy is unique – each has its history, and within each country, there are debates about what the nation's or state's ideal and material interests are (e.g. Nau and Ollapally 2012; reviewed in Patomäki 2014). The wider context of the debates about ideal and material interests includes the contemporary systems of regional and global governance, the institutional basis of which was created at the end of the Second World War, including the UN system, the Bretton Woods institutions, and the WTO (GATT).

The expression 'postcolonial developmental states opposed to Western neo-imperialism' has multiple components. 'Postcolonial' indicates (i) that formally the colonial and imperial era is over; (ii) that both one's self-understanding and positioning in the world economy and system have been shaped by experiences of Europe-originated industrial, colonial, and imperial expansion; and (iii) that various asymmetries and neo-imperial tendencies continue to characterize the world in the twenty-first century. The term 'developmental state' was initially coined to describe a specific late twentieth-century East Asian form of state ('the plan-rational capitalist developmental state, conjoining private ownership with state guidance'; Woo-Cumings 1999: 2), but the term can be used also in a deeper and wider historical sense, describing various state-forms from the sixteenth and eighteenth-century Holland and Britain to the twentieth-century Soviet Union and Japan (Bagchi 2004). Through changing geohistorical situations, especially since the nineteenth century, developmental states have been constructed as a response to the exigencies and requirements that emerged due to the expansion or dominance of the centres of growth and military power in the global political economy. What matters in this context is that the idea of a developmental state and related policies and institutions differ in some important ways from economic liberalism in its various historical guises.[16]

The third part of the expression is 'opposed to Western neo-imperialism'. In the early twentieth century, the term 'imperialism' was at times used also critically (just consider J. A. Hobson and V. I. Lenin), but after the Second World War, the term became almost universally negative in meaning. As the era of formal empires was ending, only a few wanted to use the term to describe their own activities or power. It is indicative that Hans Morgenthau (1948: 26) wrote that 'today "imperialism" and "imperialistic" are indiscriminately applied to any foreign policy, regardless of its actual character, to which the user happens to be opposed'.

Nonetheless, it took decades before the process of decolonization was concluded. While building formal empires through military conquest may no longer be considered desirable or acceptable (although a shift into that direction seems to be occurring in the mid-2020s), or has ceased to be feasible, various forms of economic and cultural neo-imperialism continue to be practised.[17] Economic imperialism employs asymmetric power relations to promote certain economic ideals and interests, while cultural imperialism pursues particular forms of popular consciousness (not least 'Americanisation'). The opposition to Western cultural and economic 'imperialism' can take forms such as reducing reliance on Western markets, creating alternative sources of funding, or creating a spatially wide economic whole to further self-guided industrialization and development.

What is particularly important is that the opposition to Western dominance also concerns power over the processes of global regulation and governance. In the early 2000s, it remained plausible to state that '[w]hen the US and the EU

Commission can agree on which direction global regulatory change should take, that is usually the direction it takes' (Braithwaite and Drahos 2000: 27). Since then, however, multilateral negotiations in various functional areas have either come to a factual standstill or have had only very limited success (the failure of the Doha round being a case in point). Multipolarization in the context of current institutional arrangements characterized by institutional 'inertia', and related attempts to balance global influence and prevent hegemony, are among the key causes of the gridlock and decline of global governance in the early twenty-first century (Hale et al. 2013: 34–48). The institutional inertia has two sides: first, the formal, treaty-based nature of many of the post-war institutions makes them cumbersome to change, and second, once power is formally vested in a certain institutional arrangement, that institution then has additional power to defend the status quo (e.g. voting powers in the IMF; veto powers in the UN Security Council). The problematic nature of the situation in the 2020s is evident even for some adamant supporters of economic liberalism. As the research and analysis division of The Economist Group, EUI, writes in their 2023 democracy report entitled 'The Age of Conflict':

> The position of the US as the global hegemon is increasingly contested by rising powers such as China, fuelling instability across the world. Though its predominance has waned, the US retains economic and military primacy and continues to dominate international political and economic decision-making. Meanwhile, the European powers, whose economic weight in the world is greatly diminished compared with the post-war period, continue to enjoy a privileged position in major world institutions. A failure on the part of the Western powers to reorganise the global, multilateral system in conformity with the increasing economic and political importance of emerging economies is generating resentment against the West. The preservation of an antiquated international political system that does not reflect the shift in the global balance of economic power, in particular to Asia, is increasing the risk of tensions spilling over into conflict. (EUI 2024: 23)

Resentment of the Western countries' domination of international institutions is not the only problem; there is also the criticism of perceived double standards, not least concerning military interventions, but also more generally about commitment to agreements and principles of multilateral cooperation (ibid., p. 31; cf. note 3). When there is no universal and legitimate principle of the rule of law, a selective application of law tends to mean the acceptance and legitimation of unilateral use of power. The idea that a particular actor is above the law, but demands that everyone else abides by it, is in essence an argument for a 'universal monarchy' (to use the European term that originates from the Middle Ages and later found its way into Immanuel Kant's writings, for example) or even 'universal dictatorship' (as an analogy for Carl Schmitt's justification of dictatorship). A king – or, in today's world, a 'leader' or 'hegemon' – is above the law but demands that their subjects follow the law and obey orders (for different viewpoints on this, Forsberg and Patomäki 2023: 41–2). A unilateral denial by others of this kind of selectivity may, in turn, be a step towards a Hobbesian 'anarchy', where the interpretation of the law is in effect left to all relevant actors themselves (in the case of international law to sovereign states; this tendency has been the problem of international law all along, cf. Koskenniemi 2005). Such tendencies have become increasingly stronger since the 2010s.

The dynamics of contradictions and antagonisms in the world political economy

Especially since BRICS was formed in 2009 and Xi Jinping assumed power in China in 2012, the critics of the hegemony of the US dollar have argued for replacing the US dollar with a more diversified system of national currencies and/or for replacing the US dollar with an alternative non-global reserve currency. While the BRICS have been pushing for IMF voting reforms, they have also established the BRICS Development Bank and a reserve currency pool ('contingent reserve arrangement'). They have made trade agreements based on the use of BRICS currencies instead of the US dollar and are developing an alternative payment system to SWIFT. In the early 2020s, at the time of the intensification of geopolitical conflicts and when the US interest rate hikes hit many countries especially in the Global South (revealing once again the structural power of the United States and US-based financial institutions in the world economy), the idea of a common BRICS currency has gained some momentum.[18]

Independently of how important the steps taken so far have been in an economic sense, these kinds of ethical-political aspirations are clearly in conflict with simultaneous attempts to retain or restore the hegemony of the United States and reinforce the position of the dollar as the key currency. Behind this visible contradiction lies political-economic processes that have been ongoing for decades, stemming from uneven growth[19] and significant imbalances in the world economy. In 1979, the US economy was eighteen times bigger than that of the Chinese, whereas in 2023 the two GDPs were nearly the same (18 trillion vs. 25 trillion in current US dollar terms, but 32 vs. 25 trillion in current international PPP terms).[20] Since 1993, the US trade deficit with China expanded (Xu 2012), and the gap was becoming ever larger until President Trump started a trade war against China. In 2018, the deficit was 418 billion US dollars; in 2022, 382 billion; in 2023, 280 billion; and in 2024, 295 billion.[21]

As a result of uneven growth, trade imbalances and the prevailing frameworks of interpretation, China has come to be seen as the main adversary and primary threat to the United States. US complaints have included unfair trade practices and currency manipulation or lack of transparency in exchange rate policy. While already the George W. Bush administration moved to perceive China as a threat, this perception has gained further strength since the Global Financial Crisis of 2007–9. In 2011, the Obama administration declared a 'pivot to Asia' and the twenty-first century as 'America's Pacific Century'. These were linked to military 'forward positioning' and US-led free trade efforts in the Pacific region. The Trump administration's economic and security policies made the existing US policy steeper and more unpredictable; the US self-regard started to exhibit protectionist tendencies, and there was a declaration of trade war. The Trump I foreign trade doctrine was known officially as the 'America First Trade Policy'. It included exploiting the leverage of interdependence for forced market opening or improved market access for American goods and services. Biden's government continued by and large similar policies under the rubric of 'invest, align, and compete', focusing on outcompeting China and preserving or developing a free and open Indo-Pacific region that excludes China. Trump II has intensified the trade war not only with China but with most countries, with highly uncertain consequences.

In the United States, a popular (including in foreign policy circles) though misleading way of understanding the consequences of this geoeconomic and political struggle is the concept of the 'Thucydides trap'. The 'trap' indicates a strong tendency towards a war between China and the United States. Paraphrasing Thucydides, the basic storyline is that 'because the Chinese have grown in power and alarmed the Americans, this is making a war between them nearly inevitable'. Even Graham T. Allison (2017), who coined the phrase, admits that the 'trap' is not a theoretical concept but rather a mere metaphor.[22] A worrying aspect of the 'Thucydides trap' conceptualization of the conflict is that these kinds of anticipations tend to be self-fulfilling, particularly since other antagonisms are pushing towards the same direction. Moreover, in China, the situation and US actions acquire meaning in a very different framework. For the

Chinese, the problem is a US imperial presence that mirrors Western interference in Chinese affairs during the so-called 'century of humiliation' (Maritan 2024).

The division of the world into democracies and autocracies affects the dynamics of the global political economy. The dividing lines correlate with how actors identify with the ideal of liberal democracy and/or with different stories of world history and politics; that is, ideological accord is part of the overall group dynamic. However, the 'great' or 'super' powers can and do support actors sympathetic or important to them, regardless of how autocratic or democratic these others are. Moreover, according to recent reports on the state of democracy in the world (EUI 2024; IDEA 2023; V-Dem 2023), BRICS countries are to varying degrees autocracies or flawed democracies, while the US allies vary from full and flawed democracies to hybrid regimes and autocracies. The United States itself is classified as a flawed democracy and is verging on becoming an autocracy (it is likely categorized as an autocracy in 2026).[23] Social reality is multifaceted, and complex, and involves ambiguities, conflicting interpretations and contradictions. The lack of critical self-reflection can easily contribute to conflicts and their development. Moreover, when conflicts escalate, the ability to see one's actions in a critical light or the different aspects of others disappears. If the world is not already seen as black and white, it becomes simplified, and in that kind of situation, overlapping antagonisms tend to reinforce each other.

The contestations and struggles over the position of the US dollar are part of the overall dynamics of global political economy and security. The United States has been able to take advantage of its special position in the world economy. It has maintained high levels of consumption – including military consumption – in part by creating more dollars for the needs of the world economy. This has cumulative consequences over time. The US mission of preserving 'hegemonic stability' by unilateral measures if needed, and perhaps 'to make America great again', intra- and interact with other tendencies and mechanisms in the global political economy, involving rising inequalities, existential insecurities and increasingly authoritarian and nationalist political systems within many countries. Because of such disintegrative tendencies, since the early 2010s, we have seen processes of securitization of value chains and the weaponization of interdependence.[24] The US tech-oriented geopolitics includes sanctions against China and attempts at tackling commodity- and value chains by decoupling and friendshoring.[25] Similarly, China tries to secure access to critical inputs and minimize exposure to the weaponization of trade, and it has responded to many moves by the United States either by precautionary measures (e.g. reducing trade through the Strait of Malacca) or by imposing similar restrictions and major attempts at friendshoring (in particular the Belt and Road Initiative). As a result of these and other processes, the world is being divided into two camps, increasing the probability of a military catastrophe.

The current world-historical conjuncture illustrates how unilateral efforts to build non-global alternatives to the current dollar-centric system can be intertwined with geopolitical conflicts. When postcolonial developmental states are opposed to the status quo-oriented Western powers and their narratives, this is in effect an instance of the recurring conflict between 'haves' and 'have-nots' that has occurred several times in modern world history.[26] When analysing similar international conflicts in the nineteenth and early twentieth centuries, famously, E. H. Carr (2016: 195) employed an analogy to capital vs. labour in domestic politics:

> In the latter part of the nineteenth century and the first part of the twentieth the 'have-nots' of most countries steadily improved their position through a series of strikes and negotiations, and the 'haves', whether through a sense of justice, or through fear of revolution in the event of refusal, yielded ground rather than put the issue to the test of force. This process eventually produced on both sides a willingness to submit disputes to various forms of conciliation and arbitration, and ended by creating something like a regular system of 'peaceful change'.

This indicates that what is needed is the establishment of an international procedure, however imperfect, of peaceful change. Although interests can be redefined, typically changes do not happen without (at least short-term) harm to the ideal or material interests of the dominant party in a given geohistorical context. Peaceful changes are not possible unless common global institutions make them possible; or unless the dominant actors become willing to allow for those institutions to be changed (peaceful changes of power relations). Although the dominant actors may, in principle, change and allow for other changes, the institutional inertia that stems from veto power is not compatible with the idea of peaceful change.

Carr (ibid., p. 196) continued his analysis by stressing that it is unlikely that 'the party at whose expense the change was to be effected would acquiesce in it without the existence of means of pressure to compel him'. In the international sphere, war or the threat of war, tacit or overt, or the aftermath of a massive war, has appeared as a condition of significant changes given the absence of adequate and legitimate common institutions.[27] Bearing in mind all the catastrophes of the twentieth century, and also considering weapons of mass destruction and the collective threat they pose, the dangerousness of such a connection should be obvious to all parties involved. A better common procedure on a global scale is needed.

The possibilities and limits of Keynes's ICU plans: A counterfactual analysis

When peaceful changes do not seem possible for a 'have-not', there are two non-exclusive possibilities in principle: either try to increase your independence from the larger entity (world economy, global institutions) or prepare to use force if the situation calls for it. In an intertwined world withdrawing from the activities of the world economy or global institutions is difficult, if not completely impossible, but one can try to build degrees of separateness together with other like-minded states. The ensuing intensification of conflict with the 'haves' can easily become securitized and weaponized – and self-reinforcing.

The central purpose of Keynes's original ICU plan was to prevent the recurrence of such tendencies (resulting in rounds of self-defeating devaluations, trade wars, etc.). What is characteristic of Keynes's plan is that it saw economic developments from the standpoint of all actors and countries simultaneously. Perspective-taking is the very basis of cognitive and moral learning, enabling actors to see the social world from an increasingly differentiated and generalizable perspective. In close interaction with other 'Cambridge apostles' (Donnini Macciò 2016), Keynes developed the capacity to see part-whole relationships in the international system (notably in *The Economic Consequence of Peace*) years before he developed the basic concepts of what is now known as Keynesian economic theory. In the context of the debates of the 1930s about exchange rates and payment practices, the Second World War, and Keynes's response to the German bilateral clearing agreements and 1940 proposal for a new economic order, he drafted a series of ICU proposals in 1941–3 (for detailed accounts, Skidelsky 2001: 179–228; Markwell 2006: 233–47). In spring 1944, however, Keynes accepted Harry Dexter White's plan, which became the basis of subsequent Bretton Woods negotiations.

In his draft proposals, Keynes aimed at facilitating full-employment policies in all countries simultaneously, trying to avoid fallacies of composition and maximize generalizability. The mutual dependency of the parts and whole works through effective demand and the multiplier effect. Countries are not isolated systems. Moreover, in the world as a whole, trade deficits and surpluses cancel out. Over time, countries with trade surpluses tend to have savings surpluses, whereas countries with trade deficits tend to accumulate debt. In Keynes's plans, the adjustment obligation would have applied to both surplus and deficit countries. Adjustments were meant to occur in a common multilateral system, which would have included a central bank for the whole world and a common central bank currency. In some versions, Keynes proposed mechanisms for confiscating resources from surplus countries in the name of the common good, but only if they were not willing to increase their domestic demand for imports to restore balance. The aim was to enable a 'new deal' everywhere, benefiting the surplus and deficit countries alike, while leaving room for the choice of rational policies within the states. In some versions, Keynes envisaged the use of the union's idle credit balances to finance international bodies concerned with relief and reconstruction, buffer stocks for commodities and international investment (Markwell 2006: 242).

The extent to which ICU would have been able to prevent or at least significantly mitigate the disintegration tendencies and conflicts of the first decades of the 2000s depends on which version would have been implemented, whether designed by Keynes or others.[28] Regardless of the version, however, the ICU would have created a context in which the HST or similar ideas are unlikely to have emerged as a plausible interpretive framework in the United States or its allied countries. Although no version of the ICU would have barred uneven growth in the world economy (which is a good thing for opportunities to develop and catch up), it would have affected, for example, the economic developments of China and the United States through the introduction of some adjustment measures within the framework of the ICU mechanisms. This is likely to have happened already at the end of the 1990s or the beginning of the 2000s. The basic premise is that China would have increased domestic demand or external investments more rapidly than what has happened, for example by raising the wage level of workers, while the United States would have limited its consumption while increasing its exports, especially to China. A likely effect would have been the evening out of growth differences at least to some extent and the slowing down of the deindustrialization process. This accords with Marie Duggan's (2013) counterfactual analysis based on balance of payments data, suggesting that for the United States and China since 1982, Keynesian ICU would have prevented or slowed down US deindustrialization, while yet permitting export-led growth in China.

For many countries in the Global South, the ICU would have improved prospects for economic growth quite markedly, probably already during the time of decolonization in the 1950s–1970s. Since the early 1980s, a large number of countries have run into debt problems and been forced to deflate their economies in a way that has led to mass unemployment (and/or contributed to the expansion of a large informal sector with very low levels of fragile income), low investment, and often also to the accumulation of phantom loans. The prescriptions of the actual IMF have tended to lower growth and increase inequalities. A Keynesian-Kaleckian ICU would have better enabled developmental state policies and, simultaneously, full and equitable participation in the world economy. Particularly those versions of ICU that involve taxation of surplus countries, finance for development and investment, and buffer stocks for commodities could have made a significant difference (of course, depending on the precise scale and functioning of these mechanisms).

Some ICU proposals of the 1940s went beyond Keynes's plans, often by emphasising the importance of investments. Michał Kalecki proposed an international investment organization with both short- and long-term financing facilities (Kalecki and Schumacher 1943; Kalecki 1946). The idea of Roy Harrod was to use the world's central bank as the world's 'investment machine' through money creation (see Skidelsky 2001: 220). By using money creation, the world's central bank could engage in financing development or eliminating poverty (or eliminating the causes of climate change and mitigating the effects of warming and their consequences; Stiglitz 2006: 260–8). If realised in the 1940s or later, for example in the 1970s, these kinds of ideas would have made a big impact on the development of the world economy.

Although, if implemented, the ICU and related plans would in all likelihood have produced a world less prone to conflict and nationalism than our actual world, all social formations are formed as a result of multiple causal processes. In a capitalist market society, there may be inherent tendencies towards free-market ideologies (Kalecki 1943) and financialization (Minsky 1982), although the power of all tendencies is context-dependent. Moreover, the social world is open-systemic, meaning that we cannot assess counterfactual histories as if they were controlled laboratory experiments. Many external factors and unexpected qualitative changes could have led to problematic developments or crises despite the ICU. Still, as argued above, there are good reasons to believe that an ICU would have prevented or at least mitigated the currently prevailing disintegrative tendencies and conflicts.

However, none of the ICU plans proposed in the 1940s or later involved a procedure for peaceful changes. The idea behind all the plans was to create a new institution that would have remained more or less the same from then on regardless of the problems it faced or how the world changed (although

Keynes considered some future possibilities). Thus, the ICU's learning ability and self-transformative capacity would have been poor, which is likely to have led to problems over time. For example, Keynes paid only a little attention to the problem of adjusting exchange rates and at least some versions of the plan envisaged a special role for the United States and United Kingdom in the system – both potential major problems. Even if the ICU had lasted much longer than the original Bretton Woods system, there is no sure guarantee that it would still exist or function as intended in the 2010s and 2020s. A twenty-first-century version of the ICU must include legitimate and sustainable procedures of change. As democracy is about resolving conflicts peacefully, the issue of conflicts and changes is intertwined with the question of democracy.

Three scenarios about changes of the world monetary system

My overall argument is that the absence of an adequate global monetary system is a significant cause of disintegrative tendencies in the world political economy and that many of the current antagonisms and conflicts in world politics are a visible manifestation of these tendencies. If we take the current world political situation as a sign of what is possible or 'realistic' in general, then we fall into a circular conclusion that can, through discursive practices, contribute to maintaining the prevailing vicious cycle. In this final section, I present three scenarios of how the world's monetary system may be reformed without a large-scale or total military catastrophe, that is, through peaceful changes.

Scenario 1: Perhaps the most popular and in any case the simplest alternative to the current system is to increase the number of SDRs and strengthen their role in the global economy. The IMF Articles of Agreement include a so-far unrealized obligation to make the SDR the principal reserve asset of the international monetary system. This scenario does not involve significant institutional changes or innovations and is therefore easy to see as the most 'realistic' option. Many major decisions such as an increase in SDRs require a supermajority of 85 per cent of the votes. The distribution of voting power is a function of member states' shares of total quotas; also changes in this regard require a supermajority. What this means is that SDR-based reform of the world monetary system is only possible if the United States or any country group with a total of more than 15 per cent of the votes does not oppose the reform. Given the narrowly defined interests of the United States,[29] this does not seem very likely in the 2020s. So far, the United States has agreed to the expansion of SDRs only during a crisis that (i) has directly affected the United States and (ii) during Democratic administrations (Carter, Obama and Biden). These conditions may reoccur during the 2020s or early 2030s, but it would still only be a matter of limited temporary expansion at best, taking place under the conditions of the current quotas and rules. Of course, all demi-regularities are context-bound, but even though the actors can act otherwise, usually such changes require structural changes in the context.

In terms of assessing the effects of such an IMF-reform, and their significance, it seems clear that SDRs can assume some of the functions of a Keynesian ICU. SDR additions to existing reserve assets allow member states to adjust more easily without resorting to harmful deflationary policies (a member's use of its SDR allocation is essentially without conditions, unlike IMF loans). There are many versions of an SDR-based reform. Edwin Truman (2022) proposes moderate, regular annual allocations of SDRs based on their quotas at the level of 150–200 billion USD per year. Most of the allocations would continue to go to the richest countries and biggest economies, including the United States, Japan, China, the United Kingdom and the biggest EU countries. The IMF pays interest on SDR holdings. If a country exchanges its SDRs for hard currency, it loses this modest source of income. Using SDRs is equivalent to borrowing directly from other member countries, while this kind of lending remains voluntary.

To make the rich countries more favourable to such a reform, Truman (ibid.) recommends raising the interest rate, which is currently calculated on the basis of a basket of currencies. While regular annual allocations may be a low-cost alternative to the costs of *ex ante* reserve accumulation via borrowing from global financial markets (or through generating current account surpluses at the expense of domestic investment), its real impact is mostly limited to mitigating short-term crises. It would not have any significant effect on development, processes of uneven growth or a gradual accumulation of surpluses and deficits – not to speak of the global distribution of income, wealth or power.

Moreover, the current scale of SDRs is minuscule. If the idea is simply to keep the relative number of SDRs roughly the same as it is now or increase that number only moderately, then the SDRs do not matter much in terms of the overall dynamics of the global political economy (the current stock of SDRs is less than 1 per cent of global GDP, and only a very small part of the stock is used in any given normal year). There are also more ambitious SDR reform proposals, but if the chances of approval of a Truman-like proposal in the IMF seem weak, it can be concluded that the more ambitious plans have hardly better chances of success. More equally divided quotas would democratize the IMF to a degree, and thus facilitate peaceful changes, but the basic principle would remain 'one dollar, one vote'.

Scenario 2: The process of establishing a global clearing union or bank (GCU from now on) can be started by a coalition of willing states with the support of global civil society movements and organizations. This idea of starting a new system is based on the observation that while 'institutional inertia' and related practices and power relations tend to prevent changes in many international organizations such as the IMF, new international law and thus new governance systems are relatively easy to create.[30] It only requires a grouping of interested countries that is of sufficient size for initiating such a system.

In scenario 2, such a coalition or club of the willing negotiates and concludes a GCU treaty, inviting and encouraging other states to join whenever they are ready and willing to do so. Unlike unilateral initiatives, which can be regional or transregional like BRICS, here the idea is from the start to create a comprehensive global system that expands and evolves over time. In terms of substance, the starting point for such a system is the idea that many harmful imbalances can be avoided if there is an impartial system of adjustments that treats deficit and surplus countries in an equal and symmetrical manner. Since in the current situation, the world is more and more divided (and further dividing) into geopolitical groups, it is important that in this matter, the club of the willing includes countries from different groupings.

Diverse ICU plans can be systematically evaluated in terms of their preconceptions, justification, potential political support, institutional transformation effects, functional efficiency, and feasibility (these criteria are from Patomäki and Teivainen 2004, ch 1; for a similar evaluation of different ICU designs see Kotilainen in this book). Regardless of which plan the relevant actors end up with as the basis of the ICU campaign and negotiations, in the twenty-first century it must include a procedure for peaceful changes. Not only are compromises necessary in a world characterized by different frameworks of interpretation and divergent senses of the ideal, but the system, once established, must be able to learn from criticism and its own mistakes. New problems and conflicts will arise and must be resolved. As the world-historical context is in a constant state of change, no institutional arrangement can be final or, in its designed form, even very long-term. Thus, the coalition of the willing should establish an ICU-style organization, including an accessible and equitable procedure for changes. This means that the organization must be democratic, combining different understandings, such as equality of states, representation of the population and active civil society participation.[31]

Creating new international law may be institutionally and legally easier than changing existing organizations such as the IMF, yet that does not mean that the plan is easily realizable. We know that the Global South has been trying to bring about changes in the world monetary system for a long time and that many (post) Keynesian (political) economists have made numerous proposals for the ICU or some such since the 1960s. In the introduction, I mentioned the Chinese 2009 proposal. In recent years, especially at the BRICS meetings, there have been discussions in this direction, although the starting point seems to be that only unilateral and non-inclusive progress in the matter is possible. Given the currently prevailing disintegrative tendencies, geopolitical conflicts and related processes of de-democratization, global civil society is weaker than it was a quarter of a century ago and few governments are interested in or even aware of opportunities like GCU. The immediate or relatively short-term possibilities of implementing GCU in the 2020s or early 2030s seem weak unless a strong impetus for changes emerges from somewhere.

Moreover, in the mid-2020s, the immediate impact of the Trump II administration is a significant disruption to global economic cooperation, making the establishment of an International Clearing Union (ICU) on a universal basis nearly impossible. The administration's unilateral approach to trade and monetary policy – characterized by protectionism, tariffs and potential capital controls – escalates tensions with key economic partners and weakens multilateral institutions. However, these disruptions create strong incentives for other nations to seek alternative financial and trade mechanisms. At the same time, Trump's arguments and actions change the discursive field. The US Republicans have become wary of the financial and political distortions created by countries running massive trade surpluses. This was also Keynes's starting point in the 1940s, when the United States was the main surplus country. While Trump's policies do not include advocating for a supranational monetary system akin to Keynesian ICU, they inadvertently strengthen political momentum for an alternative. The erosion of US monetary hegemony, coupled with trade wars and aggressive fiscal interventions, further highlights the instability of the current system. As the administration's actions undermine – whether intentionally or not – confidence in the dollar-based monetary system, the quest for alternatives becomes stronger.

Scenario 3: In this scenario, the threat of war; a small-scale catastrophe; a realization that a process will lead to a disaster, or a breakthrough in another area of global governance generates momentum for a GCU. We know that since their inception, SDRs have been issued three times, and to reiterate, each time the context has involved a major crisis. Crisis, in its most general sense, connotes a potential turning point in a process, which decides whether an existing identity or system will continue as it is, be transformed, or even cease to exist and be replaced by something else (although continuity is involved in every change). Very often in discussions of crisis, what is at issue is not prediction but the etymologically related practice of critique, which focuses on the causes of the crisis. Although causal claims will almost invariably be disputed, the crisis itself will often function as a clear indicator that previously influential theories have been faulty. A crisis also provides an opportunity to learn, as in the alleged Chinese saying that every crisis is both a threat and an opportunity.

Although there is no reason to exclude the possibility that the current gridlock in global governance could be broken in the economic area, or that the establishment of the GCU could be a key factor in the transformation of systems of global governance, the current context must become markedly different in some significant respects for such a change to become possible. A crisis is likely to be involved. In the 2020s or early 2030s, a widespread sense of crisis can emerge from a war or a rapid acceleration of climate change. Both can lead to a widely shared perception of an impending global disaster. The evidence of impending disaster can in turn prompt transformative efforts through social movements, the research community, international organizations and some governments. On the other hand, a global disaster, such as a full-scale war between the United States and China, could lead to such massive destruction that no positive change scenario can be based on its very uncertain consequences.

Evidence of an impending disaster is all the more convincing the more palpable it is, even though from a rational point of view it is in no way justified to wait until a reasonably predictable process will actually lead to catastrophic consequences (see Morgan and Patomäki 2023: 725–34, for a discussion on what is predicable or anticipatable in open systems). Consider the following sub-scenarios: (i) the annual human and economic costs of global warming-related extreme weather events will rapidly increase to ten or fifty times the current level; (ii) the Gulf Stream loses its strength and Europe's climate becomes radically colder than it is now; or (iii) there is a limited nuclear war over Ukraine, Taiwan or between India and Pakistan, with a long nuclear winter radically changing the circumstances on the planet for at least a decade. Several other similar sub-scenarios are plausible as well.

A breakthrough in global governance in the field of security or environment would involve a critique of the prevailing causal explanations, theories, ideas, and stories and this change will affect also the field of the economy – not least because recognising the role of political economy in security and environment is a likely part of this learning process.[32]

Conclusions

In this chapter, I have analysed the dangers of world monetary and trading systems (i) based on the central position of a single national currency and (ii) characterized by the absence of adequate common institutions. I started by depicting how, when the original Bretton Woods system was no longer sustainable, an interpretation arose in the United States that the cause of the then-current problems was a lack of adequate leadership. Without a hegemonic state, the world will drift into disorder and possibly a new world war. A doctrine which equates one national interest, involving its currency, with the good of the whole world, and which believes that national decline means problems for everyone, naturally begins to demand the re-strengthening of that nation-state and the special protection of its interests. 'Make America Great Again' can assume multiple meanings, not only those proposed by Donald Trump.

In the United States, in addition to some left-wing critics, many 'realists' have tried to curb or have rejected the normative idea of the superiority of the United States and its normative role as the leader of the (neoliberal) world. Because of different geohistorical experiences, but also due to the rise of authoritarian nationalist populism (see Patomäki 2021), similar discussions and debates occur across the world. The majority of people live in countries that align with a story that is critical of the US-led 'rule-based' liberalism, namely the story of postcolonial developmentalism opposed to Western neo-imperialism. The causes of the prevailing conflicts and confrontations are manifold, as each conflict is characterized by many historically specific conditions and features, but overall the world is more divided than ever since the so-called Cold War.

In this chapter, I have argued that the mechanisms and contradictions of the political economy have been co-generating these conflicts and confrontations and thus the current division. With adequate global institutions and mechanisms (including but not confined to ICU), these tendencies could and likely would have been absent or at least significantly mitigated. Various ICU plans have all aimed at a rational monetary and trade system (some of them also involve mechanisms for long-term investments for development), enabling sustainable growth and close to full employment within states. Keynes's and some others' goals have also included the prevention of politico-economic conflicts from escalating into the security field.

In this chapter, I have not compared or evaluated different ICU proposals, although I have suggested that what may seem 'realistic' may not be institutionally or politically so and may even be unrealistic from the perspective of overall dynamics. To concretize these claims, I briefly discussed a counterfactual world trajectory where an ICU-type plan would have been accomplished either in the 1940s or in the 1960s and 1970s when the original Bretton Woods system no longer worked adequately. Following this, I outlined three scenarios for the realization of a global clearing union or world central bank in the 2020s or 2030s. The point of these scenarios is not only to anticipate possible and likely futures but also to harness resources and activities for avoiding an undesirable possibility and realizing a desirable one.

My conclusion is that while the second scenario may not be enough in itself to produce change, the impetus for change can arise from a crisis or its anticipation. This can be interpreted optimistically or pessimistically. From a rational point of view, it would be much better if learning did not require further deterioration of the situation and crises but could take place based merely on rational deliberation and discussion (see also Patomäki 2023a). To this, I can only add that such learning would also be in the enlightened long-term interest of the United States. None of the foreseeable and impending crises or major global catastrophes will be good for 'America', and certainly will not make it 'great again'.

Notes

1 Concepts and ideas are constitutive of foreign and economic policies. Paraphrasing Keynes, '[p]ractical men, who believe themselves to be quite exempt from any intellectual influences, are usually the slaves of some defunct or contemporary theorist'. From another direction, theorists often articulate practical and material interest-based concerns into general claims about the world. The formation of concepts and ideas is a process, where actors with concept- and theory-laden pre-understandings try to solve problems in everyday situations, while they also reflect upon the meaning of situations in terms of human nature, world history, etc. It is an empirical question what the concepts and ideas prevailing in any given context are. For more systematic social-ontological discussions, also in the context of foreign policy analysis, see chapters 2–4 of Patomäki 2002.

2   The dominant way of looking at social reality in the US-based IR and IPE
    corresponds to the orthodox, quasi-official account of US foreign policy before
    Trump I and II. This account involves a normative belief in the principles of
    the liberal international order (LIO) and a causal belief in the positive effect of
    US 'leadership' (Hozic and Oren 2024). Whereas IPE focuses on public goods
    and the liberal world economy, the benevolence of the United States can also be
    justified in terms of democracy and human rights or modernization. Different
    emphases, definitions and theories converge on the assumption of US benevolence,
    resonating with US nationalism (more on this later). For the past two decades
    or so, especially after the Global Financial Crisis and following the rise of China,
    there has (again) been a growing concern about the erosion, decline, or collapse of
    the US-led liberal world order and a related concern about the decline of the US
    hegemony or 'greatness'. Many stress that the current neoliberal order has created
    losers also within the West and that these losers have turned against LIO. For a
    sample of recent discussions, Norrlof 2010; Gills and Patomäki 2017; Mearsheimer
    2019: Hathaway and Shapiro 2020; Barnett 2021; Adler-Nissen and Zarakol 2021;
    Flaherty and Rogowski 2021; Goldstein and Gulotty 2021; Lake et al. 2021; Weiss
    and Wallace 2021; Mendes 2023; and Larson 2024.

3   A report available at the site of the Ministry for Foreign Affairs of the People's
    Republic of China summarizes such complaints as follows: 'Since becoming
    the world's most powerful country after the two world wars and the Cold War,
    the United States has acted more boldly to interfere in the internal affairs of
    other countries, pursue, maintain and abuse hegemony, advance subversion
    and infiltration, and willfully wage wars, bringing harm to the international
    community. The United States has developed a hegemonic playbook to stage "color
    revolutions," instigate regional disputes, and even directly launch wars under
    the guise of promoting democracy, freedom and human rights. Clinging to the
    Cold War mentality, the United States has ramped up bloc politics and stoked
    conflict and confrontation. It has overstretched the concept of national security,
    abused export controls and forced unilateral sanctions upon others. It has taken a
    selective approach to international law and rules, utilizing or discarding them as it
    sees fit, and has sought to impose rules that serve its own interests in the name of
    upholding a "rules-based international order"' (CMFA 2023).

4   I examine the first two possibilities in the context of the aspirations of BRICS,
    while the three scenarios outlined at the end of this paper focus on the latter two.
    Regarding other papers in this book, Amato et al. and Kahn discuss regional
    solutions, Kari and Holappa argue for the reform of the IMF and expanding SDRs,
    while Faudot, Kotilainen and Aguila et al. explore the possibility, underpinnings
    and consequences of global ICU-type systems. For further possibilities and
    discussions, see references in these papers.

5 As of 2024, 85 per cent of the Fund's voting power is required for major decisions to take effect, and even after some voting reforms, the United States retains a share of more than 16 per cent of the votes.

6 Absences can be causes, even if they can never cause anything on their own. This can be analysed in terms of John L. Mackie's (1980) account of cause as an INUS condition (an insufficient but non-redundant part of an unnecessary but sufficient condition). Mackie's standard example concerns a fire that has partly destroyed a house. Experts conclude the fire was caused by an electrical short-circuit within the house. Many other INUS conditions were necessarily involved in generating the fire, such as the presence of flammable material and oxygen and the absence of sprinklers. However, sprinklers' absence differs from the absence of adequate common institutions, because institutions also mould elements of social reality, in particular identities, interests and positioning, shaping agency and conditions of cooperation.

7 Kindleberger discusses only two cases of stability and instability and his interpretations of history are contentious. For example, the claim that 1846/1860–1913 is an example of stability is questionable if not outright false. The claim to apparent stability in Europe hides uneven growth, the long downward wave from the beginning of the 1870s to the 1890s competitive neo-imperial expansion, constant warfaring outside Europe, formation and subsequent attempts to repress the working class, struggles over democratization and nationalism, alliance formations in the interstate field, an arms race, and multiple international crises. Together these processes formed the components of the causal complex that generated – in a non-deterministic way – the First World War in 1914 (see Patomäki 2008: 36–99; cf. Polanyi 1957).

8 'Stability' has often been conceived as the opposite of violent conflicts and war. Against this, Kenneth Waltz (1986, pp. 161–162) famously clarified his views by arguing that international stability means only two things, namely that 'anarchy' (= non-hierarchy) prevails and that the number of principle parties that constitute the 'system' remains unchanged. This move makes the Waltzian theory of international politics either trivial or absurd. Besides coalitions, Waltz's (1979) main explanandum is stability. Waltz's theory tries to predict the number of great powers by tautologically referring to the number of poles in a power-balancing system. I consider this to be the *reductio ad absurdum* of Waltzian neorealism (See Patomäki 2002: 74).

9 Exceptionally, Kindleberger (1973, p. 308) was open to the alternative of new 'international institutions with real authority and sovereignty' to govern the world economy (i.e. an evolutionary path towards a 'post-hegemonic' situation, with increased trans-nationalization of state authority, governing a trans-nationalized economic system). However, he too seems to have assumed that agenda-setting and

decision-making must always be hierarchical at least to a degree; i.e. one state must always lead and others must follow.

10   Macrotrends, US Trade Balance 1970–2024, available at https://www.macrotrends .net/countries/USA/united-states/trade-balance-deficit, retrieved 2024-02-13.

11   Gilpin's list (trade surplus and printing money) is not exhaustive. Moreover, the US *net income from abroad* has been positive simultaneously with its negative trade balance. This also indicates the changing position of the US multinational corporations in the world political economy. They have constructed global production chains and taken advantage of the tax and other opportunities of the re-emergent global financial system, thus building also wealth chains. The rise of the US net income has been especially rapid since 2007. Trading Economics, United States - Net Income From Abroad, available at https://tradingeconomics.com/ united-states/net-income-from-abroad-us-dollar-wb-data.html, retrieved 2024-02-13.

12   Further, the theory accepts uncritically the idea that free trade and security of property rights are public goods. Numerous nationalist, Keynesian, Marxian, and feminist critics have disagreed.

13   Perhaps most famously, in June 1997, fifty prominent foreign policy experts, including former senators, retired military officers, diplomats, and academicians, signed an open letter to President Clinton expressing their opposition to NATO expansion. They believed that the policy was a historic error. This letter, with explanations, is available at https://www.armscontrol.org/act/1997-06/arms -control-today/opposition-nato-expansion. Other well-known realists opposing NATO expansion have included William J. Burns (a long-term diplomat and the current CIA director), George F. Kennan (a renowned diplomat and architect of America's post–Second World War strategy of containing the Soviet Union), and John Mearsheimer (a self-labelled 'offensive realist' and one of the most famous and controversial IR scholars).

14   Different assumptions and concepts combine as part of the background of the prevailing social world. Democracy promotion during the so-called third wave of democratization resonated with the penetration of the (neo)liberal 'new world order' (declared at the end of the Cold War) into every region of the world, while layers of concepts drawn from neoclassical economics sedimented into the social background in many contexts across the world. One aspect of this resonance has been the explicit democracy promotion by the United States, the EU and several international organizations such as the OECD and various parts of the UN system. Mostly these Western or West-led actors have been promoting 'polyarchy', 'low-intensity democracy' or 'competitive elitist democracy', a form, which is compatible with neoliberal policies (see Patomäki 2021, for a detailed discussion on the ambiguous and ambivalent relationship between different forms of neoclassical

economics and variations of the ideology of neoliberalism, on the one hand, and democracy, on the other). It is indicative of the limits and contradictions of this kind of democracy promotion, and it is no coincidence that by the early 2020s, the third wave of democratization is over. According to V-Dem (2023), advances in global levels of democracy made over the last thirty-five years have been wiped out and the world is back to the situation of the mid-1980s. The United States itself is now classified as a 'flawed democracy'.

15　The Congressional Budget Office (CBO) has projected that interest costs will exceed their previous high relative to the size of the economy, reaching 3.2 per cent of GDP ($951 billion) in 2025 (the previous high was in 1991, a result of developments that started in the 1970s, interrupted by the 'roaming 1990s' and the 'unipolar moment'). (Source: https://www.pgpf.org/budget-basics/what-are-interest-costs-on -the-national-debt).

16　Postcolonial developmentalism represents historical continuity to the anti-colonial project of collective self-reliance. Ideologically this project was based on a form of dependency-avoiding radical political economy, involving attempts to catch up with the industrialized West (or the Soviet Union). In the 1970s, the leaders of collective self-reliance (Gandhi's followers, Mao, Nyerere, etc.) demanded a New International Economic Order (NIEO). The heyday of this project – closely connected to the movement of non-alignment – was in 1955–79. By the 1980s, the political failure of NIEO had become obvious. Key countries such as China began to turn outwards and participate in market-driven globalization, albeit cautiously at first.

17　From a political realist perspective, the current war in Ukraine – like some other post-Cold War wars – is subject to two possible interpretations, depending on whether it is seen as defending the status quo or exhibiting an imperial tendency to expand territorially. In the first interpretation, Russia is defending the status quo against the NATO and EU expansion into the territories of the former Soviet Union; in the second interpretation, Russia is expansive and tries to (re)build a territorial empire. See Forsberg and Patomäki 2023, for debates about this. Force can also be used to support the spread of economic and cultural imperialism, with no territorial claims.

18　The BRICS currency could be a basket-type reserve currency backed with precious metals (gold and silver). The BRICS' 2015 summit decided to explore creating a new reserve currency that these countries would use in preference to the dollar. At the 2023 summit, Brazilian President Luiz Inacio Lula da Silva called for the BRICS countries to create such a currency for trade and investment. Lula is quoted as arguing that 'developing countries should not be charged interest rates that are 8 times higher than those charged to richer countries'. This proposal found support, especially in Russia, which is under severe sanctions because of the invasion of Ukraine. 'BRICS summit: Leaders eye expansion, common currency',

DW (Deutsche Welle) 23.8.2023, available at https://www.dw.com/en/brics-summit
-leaders-eye-expansion-common-currency/live-66606155. According to some
sources, the 10 June 2024 BRICS meeting in Nizhny Novgorod, Russia, announced
new trade agreements involving non-BRICS countries based on the use of local
currencies, while these sources also mention the arrival of the bloc's independent
payment system. The formulations of the Joint Statement of the BRICS Ministers
are more cautious (see https://www.mea.gov.in/bilateral-documents.htm?dtl
/37860/joint+statement+of+the+brics+ministers+of+foreign+affairsinternational
+relations).

19   Processes of uneven growth in the world economy involve both vicious and
virtuous circles of cumulative causation (cf. Kaldor 1996). When particular
constraints and mechanisms tend to slow down economic growth or cause
stagnation and underdevelopment, feedback loops that often work through
political processes and changing power relations, can further strengthen such
developments. On the other hand, the Keynesian demand-led Kaldor-Verdoorn
effect can generate a virtuous circle between output and productivity growth
(Kaldor 1966). There are two main explanations for the Kaldor-Verdoorn effect:
(i) economies of scale prevail in manufacturing and (ii) learning by doing
increases skill levels and can lead to innovation. Output can only grow if there
is sufficient demand for the produced goods, so an increase in demand in world
markets can lead to investments and higher productivity. Hence the Kaldor-
Verdoorn effect resonates with the so-called new trade theory (e.g. Krugman
1980). World trade enables markets to grow, increases product diversity, brings
benefits from economies of scale and causes real wages to increase. Although
a sceptical post-Marxian economist may hold that the subsequent fall in
profitability will eventually undermine the effects of increased demand (Shaikh
2016, pp. 654–7), evidently China has sustained this effect continuously since
the early 1990s (for three decades). Entering the 2020s, China's growth rate has
slowed down, its financial sector has gone into crisis and the trade war with the
United States has negative effects, but still, China's growth remains significantly
faster (5.2 per cent in 2023 and expected 4.5 per cent in 2024) than growth in the
OECD world.

20   World Bank open data, the international PPP figures are from 2022.

21   'United States goods trade deficit with China from 2013 to 2023 (in billion U.S.
dollars)', *Statista Research Department*, 1.3.2024, https://www.statista.com/statistics
/939402/us-china-trade-deficit/.

22   Allison's interpretation of Thucydides is based on neorealism and fails to
understand Thucydides' dramatic reconstruction of the story of the Peloponnesian
war – or grasp the limits of Thucydides' imaginary. Given the evidence that
Thucydides in fact provides, the war was 'inevitable' only because of the insistence

of Pericles that Athens should keep the empire and make no concessions, although its actions were giving rise to widespread grievances (for a critical realism-based discussion of this point, see Patomäki 2002: 186–9).

23 See the most recent V-Dem Democracy Report 2025 (https://www.v-dem.net /publications/democracy-reports/). Here, I do not have the space to discuss different models of democracy or the prevailing de-democratization tendencies (democracy comes in different forms and shapes, Held 2006; cf. Held and Patomäki 2006). It should be mentioned, however, that behind these tendencies lie increased inequalities within most countries during the last decades. Although inequalities between countries have decreased, especially due to the rise of China (and Asia), socio-economic differences have increased and deepened in the world. Through multiple but varying mechanisms, this has fuelled polarization and political turmoil, not least in the United States. Increasing inequalities between social classes and regions, and underlying political economy processes such as deindustrialization, have generated a rise of anti-elite populism. The polarization of societies, often also feeding violent conflicts and wars, is harmful to democracy (e.g. Piketty 2014, 2020; Patomäki 2018).

24 Actors can bring about securitization by presenting something as an existential threat and by dramatizing an issue as having absolute or very strong priority, and this can justify exceptional – typically non-democratic military – measures. Weaponized interdependence in turn refers to a situation where states with political authority over central economic nodes 'can weaponize networks to gather information or choke off economic and information flows, discover and exploit vulnerabilities, compel policy change, and deter unwanted actions' (Farrell and Newman 2019: 45). It is revealing how the Trump administration quickly adopted the ideas of Farrell and Newman's 2019 article as a 'good playbook to implement' (2023, pp.101–102).

25 Decoupling implies increasing separation, disengagement, or dissociation of us (i.e. 'our' part of the world economy) from them. Friendshoring in turn means trading primarily with 'friendly' countries sharing 'similar values' to secure access to critical inputs and minimize exposure to the weaponization of trade.

26 It is worth noting though that when the conflict between 'haves' and 'have-nots' was discussed and debated in International Relations during the interwar era, the 'haves' were the established European empires (especially British and French), while the 'have-nots' were their imperialistic challengers (Italy, Japan, Germany). Following the process of decolonization, this distinction has been understood more democratically.

27 As Roberto Unger (2014) argues, the extent to which change depends on crisis or catastrophe is not an invariant element but susceptible to historical modification. Although in the twentieth and twenty-first centuries 'the main

impulse to significant change has been external especially in the form of war and of ruin' (consider the establishment of the League of Nations and the UN system, or the Bretton Woods institutions), social contexts can become more open to transformations without such an impulse. The key word here is significant: what changes are supposed to be significant? There are also implicit assumptions about the desired direction of changes in Unger's argument. In particular, the neoliberal transformations since the 1980s have occurred mostly peacefully, and they have also led to changes in the systems of regional and global governance (e.g. the establishment of the EU and WTO). Socially and democratically oriented changes have been more difficult to achieve and as I argue in this paper, the existing global institutions appear almost unreformable (see Hale et al. 2013, for an analysis of the current gridlock; extended and deepened in Patomäki 2023a, chp. 7). One of the aims of rational social science is to increase the likelihood of peaceful changes under 'normal' circumstances.

28 For the controlled use of counterfactuals, see Tetlock and Parker 2006; Forsberg and Patomäki 2023, ch 1.

29 An extreme case of such narrowness concerns the alleged cost of SDRs to the United States (and some other OECD countries) holding more SDRs than their allocations, thus facilitating the use of SDRs by other members. For more than twenty years, the US Congress has required the US Department of the Treasury to report on the cost to the United States of participation in the SDR regime. The total net interest cost to the United States has been 2.6 million USD a year on average, which is merely equivalent to the budget of a small research institute in human sciences. Over the same period, the United States reported a capital gain of $36.1 million per year. Both amounts are insignificant on the scale of the US federal budget or the global economy, and yet they are watched so pedantically (Truman 2022: 8).

30 Originally, this idea emerged from the successful 1990s campaigns (for the ban on landmines and ICC; see Patomäki 2001: 182; Patomäki and Teivainen 2004: 98–100). After the (neo)conservative turn in world history, following George W. Bush's taking office in January 2001, and the 9–11 eight months later, attempts to apply this idea in various campaigns for global taxes, world parliament, etc., have so far been unsuccessful.

31 I first proposed such a combination of principles for a currency transaction tax organization (Patomäki 2001: 199–205). Recently, I have modified this idea to make it applicable in the context of a global greenhouse gas tax proposal (Morgan, Patomäki, and Wahlsten 2023: 273–4). It is beyond to scope of this paper to discuss the precise ways in which the idea of combining these principles is applicable in the case of GCU.

32 Of course, these connections raise important new questions concerning the relationship between growth and ecological constraints. For an argument that

the immediate rational response to the currently prevailing contradictions and disintegrative tendencies in the global political economy would be global Keynesianism shorn of the 'growthist' and technocratic connotations Keynes's name sometimes conveys, see Patomäki 2023b. In a short piece discussing the macroeconomic implications of declining population (Patomäki 2022), I argue that 'it looks clear that in an ecologically sustainable economic system, aggregate demand, savings, and investments would have to be controlled or at least steered on a macroeconomic level. This would seem to imply intensive and extensive planning at different scales of organization, including globally'.

References

Adler-Nissen, R., and A. Zarakol. (2021), 'Struggles for Recognition: The Liberal International Order and the Merger of its Discontents', *International Organization*, 75 (SI2): 611–34. DOI: https://doi.org/10.1017/S0020818320000454.

Allison, G. (2017), *Destined for War: Can America and China Escape Thucydides' Trap?*, Boston: Houghton-Mifflin-Harcourt.

Ashley, R. (1989), 'Imposing International Purpose: Notes on a Problematic of Governance', in E.-O. Czempiel and J. Rosenau (eds), *Global Changes and Theoretical Challenges*, 251–90, Lexington, MA: Lexington Books.

Bagchi, A. K. (2004), *The Developmental State in History and in the Twentieth Century*, New Delhi: Regency Publications.

Barnett, M. (2021), 'International Progress, International Order, and the Liberal International Order', *The Chinese Journal of International Politics*, 14 (1), 1–22. DOI: https://doi.org/10.1093/cjip/poaa019.

Braithwaite, J., and P. Drahos. (2000), *Global Business Regulation,* Cambridge: Cambridge University Press.

Carr, E. H. (2016), *The Twenty Years' Crisis, 1919–1939*. Reissued with a New Preface from M. Cox, London: Palgrave Macmillan (Springer).

Carroll, W., and J. Sapinski. (2016), 'Neoliberalism and the Transnational Capitalist Class', in S. Springer, K. Birch, and J. MacLeavy (eds), *Handbook of Neoliberalism*, 39–49, London and New York: Routledge.

Chen Weiss, J., and J. Wallace. (2021), 'Domestic Politics, China's Rise, and the Future of the Liberal International Order', *International Organization*, 75 (SI2): 635–64. DOI: https://doi.org/ 10.1017/S002081832000048X.

CMFA. (2023), US Hegemony and its Perils, A February 2023 report available at the site of the Ministry for Foreign Affairs of the People's Republic of China, available at https://www.fmprc.gov.cn/mfa_eng/wjbxw/202302/t20230220_11027664.html.

Donnini Macciò, D. (2015), 'Ethics, Economics and Power in the Cambridge Apostles' Internationalism Between the Two World Wars', *European Journal of International Relations,* 22 (3): 696–721. DOI: https://doi.org/10.1177/1354066115600506.

Duggan, M. (2013), 'Taking Back Globalization: A China-United States Counterfactual Using Keynes's 1941 International Clearing Union', *Review of Radical Political Economics*, 45 (4): 508–16. DOI: https://doi.org/10.1177/0486613412475191.

EUI. (2024), *Democracy Index 2023. Age of Conflict,* London: The Economist Intelligence Unit, https://www.eiu.com/n/campaigns/democracy-index-2023/.

Farrell, H., and A. Newman. (2019), 'Weaponized Interdependence: How Global Economic Networks Shape State Coercion', *International Security*, 44 (1): 42–79.

Farrell, H., and A. Newman. (2023), *Underground Empire. How America Weaponized the World Economy,* London: Allen Lane.

Flaherty, T., and R. Rogowski. (2021), 'Rising Inequality as a Threat to the Liberal International Order', *International Organization*, 75 (SI2): 495–523. DOI: https://doi.org/10.1017/S0020818321000163.

Forsberg, T., and H. Patomäki. (2023), *Debating the War in Ukraine. Counterfactual Histories and Future Possibilities,* London and New York: Routledge.

George, D. (2013), *The Rhetoric of the Right. Language Change and the Spread of the Market,* London & New York: Routledge.

Gilpin, R. (1981), *War and Change in World Politics,* Cambridge: Cambridge University Press.

Goldstein and Gulotty. (2021), 'America and the Trade Regime: What Went Wrong?', *International Organization*, 75 (SI2): 524–57. DOI: https://doi.org/10.1017/S002081832000065X.

Grunberg, I. (1990), 'Exploring the "Myth" of Hegemonic Stability', *International Organization*, 44 (4): 431–77.

Hale, T., D. Held, and K. Young. (2013), *Gridlock: Why Global Cooperation Is Failing When We Need It Most,* Cambridge: Polity Press.

Hathaway, O., and S. Shapiro. (2020), 'The United States has Abdicated its Dominant Role. Here's How to Fill the Gap', *Foreign Policy*, 237, https://foreignpolicy.com/2020/07/04/after-hegemony/.

Held, D. (2006), *Models of Democracy,* 3rd edn, Cambridge: Polity Press.

Held, D., and H. Patomäki. (2006), 'Problems of Global Democracy: A Dialogue', *Theory, Culture & Society*, 23 (5): 115–33.

Helleiner, E. (2023), *The Contested World Economy. The Deep and Global Roots of International Political Economy,* Cambridge: Cambridge University Press.

Hozic, A., and I. Oren. (2024), IR Knowledge Production and the Crisis of the Liberal International Order. A paper prepared for the CEEISA–ISA Joint International Conference, Rijeka, Croatia, June 2024.

IDEA. (2023), *The Global State of Democracy 2023. The New Checks and Balances,* Stockholm: International Institute for Democracy and Electoral Assistance, available at https://www.idea.int/publications/catalogue/global-state-democracy-2023-new-checks-and-balances.

Kalecki, M. (1943), 'Political Aspects of Full Employment', *Political Quarterly*, 14 (4): 322–31. DOI: https://doi.org/10.1111/j.1467-923X.1943.tb01016.x.

Kalecki, M. (1946), 'Multilateralism and Full Employment', *Canadian Journal of Economics and Political Science*, 12 (3): 322–7.

Kalecki, M., and E. Schumacher. (1943), 'International Clearing and Long-Term Lending', *Bulletin of the Oxford Institute of Statistics*, 5 (Supplement August): 29–33.

Kaldor, N. (1966), *Causes of the Slow Growth in the United Kingdom*, Cambridge: Cambridge University Press.

Kaldor, N. (1996), *Causes of Growth and Stagnation in the World Economy*, Cambridge: Cambridge University Press.

Kindleberger, C. (1973), *The World in Depression 1929–1939*, London: Allen Lane Penguin Press.

Kindleberger, C. (1981), 'Dominance and Leadership in the International Economy: Exploitation, Public Goods and Free Riders', *International Studies Quarterly*, 25 (2): 242–54.

Koskenniemi, M. (2005), *From Apology to Utopia. The Structure of International Legal Argument*, Reissue with new epilogue, Cambridge: Cambridge University Press.

Kotilainen, K., and H. Patomäki. (2022), 'From Fragmentation to Integration: On the Role of Explicit Hypotheses and Economic Theory in Global Political Economy', *Global Political Economy*, 1 (1): 80–107. DOI: https://doi.org/10.1332/JIFQ7497.

Krasner, S. (1976), 'State Power and the Structure of International Trade', *World Politics*, 28 (3): 317–47.

Krugman, P. (1980), 'Scale Economies, Product Differentiation, and the Pattern of Trade', *The American Economic Review*, 70 (5): 950–9.

Lake, D., L. Martin, and T. Risse. (2021), 'Challenges to the Liberal Order: Reflections on International Organization', *International Organization*, 75 (SI2): 225–57. DOI: https://doi.org/10.1017/S0020818320000636.

Larson, D. W. (2024), 'Is the Liberal Order on the Way Out? China's Rise, Networks, and the Liberal Hegemon', *International Relations*, 38 (1): 113–33. DOI: https://doi.org/10.1177/00471178221109002.

Mackie, J. L. (1980), *The Cement of the Universe. A Study of Causation*, Oxford: Oxford University Press.

Maritan, M. (2024), 'US Imperialism and its legacies in East Asia: Thucydides trap or Thrasymachus paradox?', *Fudan Journal of the Humanities and Social Sciences*, 17: 417–36. DOI: https://doi.org/10.1007/s40647-024-00402-7.

Markwell, D. (2006), *John Maynard Keynes and International Relations. Economic Paths to Peace*, Oxford: Oxford University Press.

Marsden, L. (2011), 'Religion, Identity and American Power in the Age of Obama', *International Politics*, 48 (2/3): 326–43.

Mearsheimer, J. (2019), 'Bound to Fail. The Rise and Fall of the Liberal International Order', *International Security*, 43 (4): 7–50. DOI: https://doi.org/10.1162/ISEC_a_00342.

Mendes, P. (2023), 'The Dynamics of Change in United States Foreign Policy: Contexts, Leadership, and Hegemonic Legitimacy', *Social Sciences*, 12 (10): 560. DOI: https://doi.org/10.3390/socsci12100560.

Minsky, H. (1982), *Can "It" Happen Again? Essays on Instability and Finance,* Armonk, NY: M.E. Sharpe.

Morgan, J., H. Patomäki, and J. Wahlsten. (2023), 'The Transformative Potential of Responding to Climate Change: Towards a Dynamic Global Tax', in H. Patomäki (ed), *World Statehood. The Future of World Politics*, 255–79, Cham: Springer.

Morgenthau, H. (1947), *Scientific Man vs. Power Politics,* London: Latimer House.

Morgenthau, H. (1948), *Politics Among Nations. The Struggle for Power and Peace,* New York: Alfred A. Knopf.

Nau, H., and D. Ollapally (eds) (2012), *Worldviews of Aspiring Powers: Domestic Foreign Policy Debates in China, India, Iran, Japan and Russia,* Oxford: Oxford University Press.

Norrlof, C. (2010), *America's Global Advantage: US Hegemony and International Cooperation,* Cambridge: Cambridge University Press.

Patomäki, H. (1999), 'Good Governance of the World Economy?', *Alternatives*, 24 (1): 119–42.

Patomäki, H. (2001), *Democratising Globalisation. The Leverage of the Tobin Tax,* London: Zed Books.

Patomäki, H. (2002), *After International Relations. Critical Realism and the (Re) Construction of World Politics,* London and New York: Routledge.

Patomäki, H. (2008), *The Political Economy of Global Security. War, Future Crises and Changes in Global Governance,* London: Routledge.

Patomäki, H. (2014), 'Nousevien mahtien aatteita [Ideas of the Rising Powers]', A book review of H. Nau and M. Ollapally (eds), *Worldviews of Aspiring Powers. Domestic Foreign Policy Debates in China, India, Iran, Japan and Russia, Ulkopolitiikka,* 51 (3): 66–7.

Patomäki, H. (2018), *Disintegrative Tendencies in Global Political Economy. Exits and Conflicts,* London and New York: Routledge.

Patomäki, H. (2021), 'Neoliberalism and Nationalist-Authoritarian Populism: Explaining Their Constitutive and Causal Connections', *Protosociology. An International Journal of Interdisciplinary Research*, 37: 101–51.

Patomäki, H. (2022), Economic Impacts of Population Reduction. A Contribution to GTI Forum The Population Debate Revisited, Great Transition Initiative, available at https://greattransition.org/gti-forum/population-patomaki.

Patomäki, H. (2023a), *World Statehood. The Future of World Politics,* Cham: Springer.

Patomäki, H. (2023b), 'Economics Needs to Ditch Most of What it Does and Adopt a Realist Global Political Economy and Futures Approach', *Real-world Economics Review*, 106 December 2023: 149–57. Open access: http://www.paecon.net/PAEReview/issue106/Patomaki10.

Patomäki, H., and T. Teivainen. (2004), *A Possible World. Democratic Transformation of Global Institutions*, London: Zed Books.

Patomäki, H., and B. K. Gills. (2017), 'Trumponomics and the "Post-Hegemonic" World', *Real World Economics Review*, 78, 29 March 2017: 91–103. Open access: http://www.paecon.net/PAEReview/issue79/Patomaki79.pdf.

Patomäki, H., and J. Morgan. (2023), 'World Politics, Critical Realism and the Future of Humanity: An Interview With Heikki Patomäki, Part 2', By J. Morgan. *Journal of Critical Realism*, 22 (4): 720–66. Available at https://www.tandfonline.com/doi/full/10.1080/14767430.2023.2188541.

Piketty, T. (2014), *Capital in the Twenty-first Century*, Cambridge, MA: The Belknap Press of Harvard University Press.

Piketty, T. (2020), *Capital and Ideology*, Cambridge, MA: The Belknap Press of Harvard University Press.

Polanyi, K. (1957), *The Great Transformation. The Political and Economic Origins of Our Time*, Boston, MA: Beacon Press. (Original work published 1944)

Shaikh, A. (2016), *Capitalism: Competition, Conflict, Crisis*, Oxford: Oxford University Press.

Skidelsky, R. (2001), *John Maynard Keynes. Fighting for Britain 1937–1946*, London: MacMillan (Papermac).

Stiglitz, J. (2006), *Making Globalization Work. The Next Steps to Global Justice*, London: Allen Lane (Penguin Books).

Strange, S. (1987), 'The Persistent Myth of Lost Hegemony', *International Organization*, 41 (4): 551–74.

Tetlock, P., and G. Parker. (2006), 'Counterfactual Thought Experiments. Why We Can't Live Without Them & How We Must Learn to Live With Them', in P. Tetlock, R. Lebow, and G. Parker (eds), *Unmaking the West. "What-if" Scenarios that Rewrite World History*, 14–44, Ann Arbor, MI: The University of Michigan Press.

Truman, E. (2022), The IMF Should Enhance the Role of SDRs to Strengthen the International Monetary System. Working Paper 22–20, December 2022. Washington, DC: PIIE (Peterson Institute for International Economics). Available at https://www.piie.com/publications/working-papers/imf-should-enhance-role-sdrs-strengthen-international-monetary-system.

Unger, R. M. (2014), 'Roberto Unger on What is Wrong With the Social Sciences Today?', *Social Science Bites / SAGE*, 9 January 2014, available at https://www.socialsciencespace.com/2014/01/roberto-mangabeira-unger-what-is-wrong-with-the-social-sciences-today/.

V-Dem. (2023), *Democracy Report 2023. Defiance in the Face of Autocratization*, Gothenburg: University of Gothenburg, Varieties of Democracy Institute (V-Dem Institute), available at https://v-dem.net/documents/29/V-dem_democracyreport2023_lowres.pdf.

Waltz, K. (1979), *Theory of International Politics*. New York: Addison-Wesley.

Waltz, K. (1986), 'Reflections on "Theory of International Politics": A Response to My
  Critics', in R. Keohane (ed), *Neorealism and Its Critics*, 322–46, New York: Columbia
  University Press.
Woo-Cumings, M. (1999), 'Introduction: Chalmers Johnson and the Politics of
  Nationalism and Development', in M. Woo-Cumings (ed), *Developmental State*,
  1–31, Ithaca and London: Cornell University Press.
Xiaochuan, Z. (2009), 'Reform the International Monetary System', *BIS Review* 41/2009,
  available at https://www.bis.org/review/r090402c.pdf (retrieved 10 February 2024).
Xu, X. (2012), 'Rethinking the China-US Balance of Trade: 1990–2005', *iBusiness*, 4 (1):
  43–50. http://dx.doi.org/10.4236/ib.2012.41006.

8

Beyond monetary hegemony

Normative underpinnings of a global clearing union

Konsta Kotilainen

Introduction

During 2021–3, various supply shocks connected with the Covid-19 pandemic and the Russian war in Ukraine led to a worldwide upsurge in inflation. As a reaction to this development, the Fed started raising its interest rates first in March 2022, and most other central banks soon followed suit. Because most states had run deficits to recover from the contraction in economic activity caused by the pandemic and the lockdowns, especially the Fed's high interest rates in turn pushed many countries at least to the brink of a foreign currency debt crisis. Those developing countries unable to refinance their dollar-denominated debts suffered the gravest consequences, and many of them defaulted.[1] The new Trump administration's erratic actions, including the shutdown of USAID and global tariff attacks, have deepened their predicament. Moreover, it is no longer only the Global South or the BRICS that cannot count on the monetary hegemon, but even the G7 and the EU now face somewhat similar concerns.[2]

Such macroeconomic problems and broader geoeconomic conflicts, including the new trade wars and prior weaponization of economic and financial interdependencies for geopolitical purposes (see e.g. Drezner et al. 2021; Farrell and Newman 2019), have intensified long-standing debates about the role of the US dollar as the global reserve and trade currency. At the same time, the world is failing to finance efforts at tackling global catastrophic risks, ranging from climate change and mass biodiversity loss to threats posed nuclear weapons and artificial intelligence. Indeed, humanity has been spending more on ice cream than on addressing the gravest such risks (Ord 2020: 57–8). Worse still, the rapidly increasing total global military spending[3] is shifting resources to activities that directly *aggravate* some of these risks.[4] Moreover, the United States is now in the process of withdrawing from the Paris Climate Accords and the World Health Organization, and it remains unclear whether it will exit the WTO or even much of the UN system.

The geoeconomic confrontation and paralysis of multilateral cooperation, including in the G20, at a time when more, rather than less, global governance would urgently be needed, is a potent recipe for a global catastrophe. The Trump administration is making things worse, but we should not forget that there are various kinds of background causes for the present disintegration and gridlock (for some relevant analyses, see e.g. Hale et al. 2013; Patomäki 2018). Indeed, far-right administrations, including in the United States, Israel, and Russia, are as much a symptom as they are a cause of the problems. This paper will concentrate on one of the arguable drivers or enablers of the ongoing fragmentation, that is the inadequate global monetary governance arrangement, or more specifically, its allowance for 'monetary hegemony' – hegemony in monetary relations, or more broadly, within the monetary realm.

It is important to stress straightaway that at issue here is not *dollar* hegemony as such, but, indeed, *monetary* hegemony more generally.[5] We may define *monetary hegemony* as exceptional monetary (and related macroeconomic) power[6] of any single political entity (such as a state, region, or bloc) over other relevant entities. *Monetary hegemon* refers to an entity exercising such power. The relevant monetary (and macroeconomic) powers include, but need not be limited to, currency-related powers.[7] Relatedly, *hegemonic currency* might be employed as a shorthand expression for a currency issued by the monetary hegemon.[8] The United States is the current monetary hegemon and its dollar the present 'hegemonic currency'. Before the First World War, the monetary hegemon was the UK and its pound sterling the hegemonic currency.[9] Given these definitions, there are *at most* one (global[10]) monetary hegemon (and hegemonic currency) at a time. To be sure, future hegemons do not need to be nation-states.

Going forward, the Chinese renminbi, European euro, a future joint currency of the BRICS,[11] or the currency of some other nation, region or bloc – may well replace the dollar as the hegemonic currency. While this might benefit the new monetary hegemon in question (and harm the current one), very little, if anything, would have been gained *overall*. Potentially something might well even be lost. Even if actors have varying interests and values, the new monetary hegemon would hardly be any more 'benevolent' than the present one (we certainly should not count on that possibility). It is not even clear that the new hegemon itself would be a 'winner'. For what it is worth, the Trump administration appears increasingly convinced that the hegemonic status of the dollar is more of an 'exorbitant burden' than an 'exorbitant privilege' (relatedly, see Klein and Pettis 2020, Chapter 6). Such assessments are highly normative and contestable. Yet, ultimately, geopolitical and economic power games may well only have losers.

I question the idea that *any* monetary hegemon would be likely to remain benevolent or that a hegemon would necessarily be needed to serve some positive global function (whether conceptualized in terms of global public goods or in some other way). To be sure, monetary hegemony *can*, even in the light of some fairly cosmopolitan criteria, be better than a lack thereof. For instance the post–Second World War Bretton Woods era monetary hegemony of the United States probably provided more autonomy for most states to pursue progressive economic policies than the lack of monetary hegemony in the preceding interwar period. Yet, the absence of a monetary hegemon certainly does not *need* to imply a lack of such autonomy – or even some basic form of 'stability' (as in standard hegemonic stability theory). Everything depends on what, if anything, would replace monetary hegemony. Indeed, my argument is that a lack of monetary hegemony would be normatively desirable *provided* that it could be replaced by adequate global institutions of monetary and macroeconomic governance, or, more specifically, a Global Clearing Union (GCU). Furthermore, replacing monetary hegemony with some such common institution might well be the only viable alternative.[12]

As things stand, of course, the dollar remains the hegemonic currency. Since countries with dollar-denominated debts are highly vulnerable to dollar shortages and rate hikes, important questions about both the global effectiveness and legitimacy of the Fed's actions have recently returned with a vengeance. Could the Fed, the central bank of the present monetary hegemon and therefore a *de facto* global central bank, plausibly pursue policies that meet the needs and legitimate grievances of all countries?

Many in the West have argued that the Fed could achieve at least some relevant forms of cross-border effectiveness. By extending existing swap line arrangements, for instance, the Fed might gradually be able to satisfy global dollar demand. While the Fed's standing swap lines only cover the neighbours and geopolitical allies of the United States, as a technical matter they could be extended further. Indeed, occasionally swap lines have been offered to also countries such as Brazil, even if only temporarily.[13] To be sure, currently the worry is that even the Fed's 'standing' swap lines might not stand in a year or two.[14]

Extending swap lines is of course a partial answer even in terms of mere global effectiveness. These arrangements were created as a solution to the problems caused by the lack of dollar liquidity faced by financial institutions outside the United States. They could also help to ease the balance-of-payments constraints of the states to whose central bank they are extended (if the central banks were able or willing to channel the thereby acquired dollars to serve the dollar-denominated debts of these states). Even if in this way potentially important for the macroeconomic policy autonomy of states, the swap lines do not address all the relevant global repercussions of, for instance, the Fed's interest rate policies. If, say, the Fed raises its rates, other states may be forced or at least incentivized to follow it on pain of currency depreciation and 'pass-through' inflation even if they do not possess dollar-denominated debt. Tackling issues such as these would require changing the Fed's mandate to include concerns of other countries and perhaps even including international representation on the Fed's board (as Kindleberger 1981: 325–6 suggested). Moreover, because the US's fiscal trajectory is potentially even more important for the financial position of the rest of the world than the Fed's monetary policies and related arrangements, similar reforms might need to be applied to the Treasury, too! Such reforms are hardly more 'realistic' than establishing a GCU. For the sake of the argument of this paper on the normative underpinnings of such plans, we might take these scenarios to be equally realistic or feasible (even if my own suspicion is that establishing a GCU would probably be more feasible than reforming the Fed and the Treasury along the lines described here; I will examine this and related issues in a separate paper on the feasibility question).

What about global legitimacy? For better or worse, the growing geoeconomic tensions imply that several key actors – notably China, the expanding BRICS, and even the G7 and EU – are, in fact, increasingly uncomfortable with dollar hegemony. Against the backdrop of such grievances – whether justified or not – this paper argues that a GCU-type arrangement could allow for normatively more viable (and probably at least as effective) governance than the monetary hegemony of any single actor. While various kinds of national, regional and bloc-based responses to the ongoing conflicts and risks may appear unavoidable given the current circumstances – and some such responses can indeed be defended up to a point[15] – only arrangements based on genuinely cosmopolitan principles and procedures will ultimately be viable. Within economic governance, one such solution is to build on the idea of International Clearing Union (ICU) put forward by J. M. Keynes (1943/69) during the Second World War. Current and aspiring hegemons alike should acknowledge that only inclusive global monetary integration, instead of monetary hegemony, can adequately address geoeconomic conflicts and related risks.

This chapter seeks to substantiate this claim by pursuing normative research on existing clearing union proposals.[16] It also seeks to lay groundwork for subsequent normative research on monetary and clearing union designs. The key ethical and political underpinnings and related institutional elements of a few of the most prominent existing clearing union proposals (made by Keynes, the Brandt Commission, Paul Davidson, and Joseph Stiglitz and Bruce Greenwald) are outlined. The proposals are then assessed against a set of democratic, ethical-social and existential criteria that are argued to reflect key concerns humanity faces. Although each proposal is found to have its own merits, none of them turns out to be fully satisfactory in all relevant respects. More generally, the ICU's West-centric aspects must be rethought. Besides addressing geoeconomic conflicts, it is concluded that an appropriately updated *Global* Clearing Union could even play a helpful role in resolving other related and potentially fatal current and future issues.

Assessing the normative underpinnings of a few prominent clearing union proposals

Keynes's (1943/1969) ICU proposal, originally developed in the run-up to the post–Second World War Bretton Woods negotiations, continues to provide a promising basis for an important institutional step beyond the present organization of monetary and macroeconomic governance – with implications for trade and even existential risk governance as well. By now, many versions of the ICU – all building on Keynes's plan and broader Keynesian theorizing to varying degrees – have been proposed. Despite their largely shared intellectual origins, these ICU proposals also differ from each other in some crucial respects, including in terms of their ethical, political and economic theoretical commitments, as well as in terms of their implications for concrete institutional design. Some of the proposals have more promise than others in terms of providing resources for thinking about global (and not just international) governance.

In what follows, I will (1) outline central (a) *normative* underpinnings and (b) *institutional* elements of a few of the most prominent of the existing ICU proposals, and then (2) assess how promising their underpinnings and suggested institutional designs seem from the perspective of (a) *democratic*, (b) *ethico-social*, and (c) *existential* concerns humanity currently or soon faces – key criteria against which all contemporary attempts at developing macroeconomic governance further should be evaluated (or so I have argued; see Kotilainen 2024, Chapter 6). In this paper, my focus is on the ethical, political and related philosophical underpinnings of the ICU proposals.[17] Important questions about the feasibility of the proposals require a separate treatment and are thereby largely left for further work (for some initial ideas, see Kotilainen 2024: Chapter 9; see also many of the papers in this collection, including those by Patomäki and Kari and Holappa).

Given that most of the subsequent ICU proposals are modifications of Keynes's 1943 plan (and thereby inherit most of also its normative assumptions) it makes sense to start with, and focus much of the attention on, this proposal. To be sure, we should remember that Keynes's plan was far from the only plan concerning the reform of the international monetary system at the time of the Bretton Woods conference (and several of these other proposals were arguably even more cosmopolitan, at least in some important respects). Pioneering proposals were made also by for instance Kalecki and Raúl Prebisch. In fact, a very wide range of reform possibilities, many of them originating from the Global South, were discussed during the Bretton Woods negotiations (Helleiner 2014).

Keynes's plan

Keynes put forth his first detailed ICU plan in September 1941 and it went through several revisions during 1942–3. Along with the White Plan, the Keynes plan was published in April 1943 (Keynes 1943/1969: 19–36; see also Markwell 2006: 240). Both plans helped to shape the post-war Bretton Woods system,[18] but Keynes's ICU proposal was never implemented. Let us examine some of its key normative underpinnings and institutional elements.

(1a) Although Keynes's works contain deep ethical and political insights, he never provided fully fleshed-out theories of well-being, right action, (distributive) justice, just war, democracy, or related normative topics. It would be overly ambitious to try to reconstruct such theories from the somewhat scattered pieces he left. To guide us in gaining a broad picture of Keynes's normative views and assumptions, there are however many useful discussions on his beliefs about well-being and ethics (see e.g. Carabelli and Cedrini 2011; Mini 1991), as well as normative political theory, including questions relevant for International Relations (see e.g. Markwell 2006).[19]

In discussing commitments that may reasonably have underpinned Keynes's ICU proposal, we should arguably put most weight on the views he expressed publicly between his mature *General Theory* (1936) and the final published ICU proposal (1943) itself. As for instance Donald Markwell (2006) well documents, Keynes's thought about international (trade) governance evolved in different directions and in several phases from early 1900s to 1936 – reflecting the development of his own (attempted) revolution in economic theory. If we can find no textual evidence that Keynes *continued* to hold any one of his earlier views on these topics, we may often be wise to suppose that he did not (although the mature Keynes does occasionally refer back to his earlier writings also affirmatively).[20] No major further change of views on the basic approach to international governance (or economics) seems to have occurred during 1936–43.

Keynes's basic ethical views, by contrast, may have remained more constant, as for instance Anna Carabelli and Mario Cedrini (2011) argue – and as Keynes (1938/1972) partially confirms. This certainly allows us to cite for instance the 'Economic Possibilities for Our Grandchildren' (1930/1952: 358–73) and possible even some of his much earlier writings relevant for grasping the ethics of ICU.

Judging by a selected set of Keynes's writings between 1930–43, the *normative underpinnings* of his ICU proposal include (but are certainly not limited to):

Commitments to certain specific accounts of *human well-being* as well as *normative and practical ethics*[21] (and related notions and principles):

(i)　A rudimentary multidimensional *objective-list theory of human well-being* drawing for instance on Aristotle and G.E. Moore (see Carabelli and Cedrini 2011).[22] Keynes's (1930/1952) views about 'the real values of life' are clearly incompatible with competing hedonist and desire-fulfilment theories (on this standard threefold distinction between theories of well-being, see, for example, Crisp 2021; Parfit 1984: 493–502).

(ii)　Some further notion of the good of the *whole* society and, by extension, even humanity (and related ideas about social, global, and even long-term justice[23], see, for example, Keynes 1930/1952, 1936/2009: Chapters 23 and 24; Keynes 1943/1969). For Keynes, attempts at deriving 'general' interests from 'particular' interests often constitute fallacies of composition (Carabelli and Cedrini 2011). Repeated calls for a more impartialist perspective. A long-standing belief in 'a principle of organic unity through time' (Keynes 1938/1972: 436).

(iii) An ethical commitment to *pursuing* the good of the whole society /
       humanity (and justice), even if *not* in the hedonist utilitarian spirit of
       Jeremy Bentham, see Mini 1991; at the same time, this commitment to
       social action is also in tension with the largely contemplative spirit of G.E
       Moore (Carabelli and Cedrini 2011; Keynes 1938/1972).
(iv)   The related (partially economic theoretical) conviction that the good of
       the whole (or the demands of justice) cannot / should not be pursued
       solely through uncoordinated market actions of individuals (contra (neo)
       classical economists, individuals chasing their own perceived goods is
       unlikely to lead to the good of the whole).[24]
(v)   Notions of reciprocity, mutual advantage, and (although Keynes predated
       game theory) implicitly even the possibility of 'non-zero-sum' dynamics
       (despite the 'zero-sum' nature of balance-of-payments accounting) (see
       e.g. Keynes 1936/2009, Chapter 23; 1943/1969; Markwell 2006; on 'non-
       zero-sumness', see Wright 2000).
(vi)   A commitment to certain broad moral principles,[25] applicable
       both nationally and internationally (and a derivative non-legalistic
       commitment to the rule of law, both domestic and international; see
       Markwell 2006: 193–5).
(vii) An 'antimoralistic' ethic:[26] thrift, hard work, accumulation of wealth,
       status, or social conventions have no intrinsic worth. As the merely
       instrumental 'economic problem' is solved, humanity should start to
       concentrate on what is genuinely valuable, exciting, or interesting (Keynes
       1930/1952; see also Russell 1935/2004). Relatedly, a 'paradox of thrift'
       contributes to recessions and an 'euthanasia of the rentier' should be a
       key goal of policy (Keynes 1936/2009). ICU's novel onus on creditors –
       obligations on states with trade surpluses (see below) – arguably continues
       to reflect this ethic (as well as the related economic theory).[27]

**A tentative *social philosophy* stressing the need to eliminate involuntary
unemployment and arbitrary wealth and income inequalities** (Keynes
1936/2009, Chapter 24). Both are key objectives of ICU also (Keynes 1943/1969;
Keynes 1941–1943/1980; Markwell 2006, Chapters 5 and 6).

**A dissatisfaction with existing *political* alternatives and binaries (clear-cut
rejections of both Bolshevism and Fascism; critiques of both laissez-faire**

liberalism and Marxian socialism) (influences from varied sources, including Silvio Gesell) (Keynes 1936/2009: 234–6; Markwell 2006: 173–8).

At least an apparent *idealism about international relations*, stressing the possibility of peaceful developments in world affairs, especially through the means of rational economic governance (a recurrent theme in Keynes's writings from the 1910s to 1940s; see Markwell 2006[28]). This is well exemplified by the ICU proposal (Keynes 1943/1969). However, one may also read parts of Keynes's writings as compatible with classical IR realism, perhaps especially along the lines of E.H. Carr.

A broad *optimism about societal progress* through rational means and economic development (Keynes 1930/1952; Markwell 2006) combined with a more specific *Malthusian pessimism* about the trajectory and effects of population growth on quality of life and social stability, including for the prospects of peace (also a recurrent theme in Keynes's writings from 1910s until 1940s, see Markwell 2006: 165–9).

A *'mature' liberal institutionalist governance ideology*[29] (the last phase of Keynes's thinking about IR and global economic governance issues, according to Markwell 2006, Chapters 5 and 6) aspiring to

(i)   transcend both the doctrines of classical free trade liberalism and traditional mercantilist protectionism, and

(ii) develop institutional solutions that would allow for a *peaceful* liberal global trade regime combining a degree of national macroeconomic policy autonomy with certain international macroeconomic obligations.[30]

A commitment to some notion of *liberal democracy* (stressing for instance the importance of individual and/or democratic autonomy, as well as cultivation of public opinion; yet this in some ways quite limited notion of democracy remains open to charges of technocraticism; see below; Markwell 2006).

A certain nascent or restricted form of *ethico-political cosmopolitanism*,[31] clearly visible in the ICU proposal (Keynes 1943/1969; Keynes 1941–1943/1980; for a summary of Keynes's ambitious aspirations concerning supranational governance, see Markwell 2006: 259–61; see also Patomäki 2013: 138–93).

(1b) The key *institutional elements* of Keynes's ICU plan (Keynes 1943/1969: 19–36; Markwell 2006: 233–47), reflecting both his theoretical and normative commitments, include the proposals that all international trade transactions should be denominated in a new international currency, *bancor*, which ought to be issued by a similarly novel *International Clearing Union*. Bancor should replace all national currencies and gold for the purposes of international trade. The exchange rates between bancor and gold, on the one hand, and bancor and national currencies, on the other, should be fixed in the short term but adjustable in the long term. Countries who export more than they import during a certain period would *receive* bancor (and thereby run a positive bancor balance). Correspondingly, countries whose imports exceed their exports would *lose* bancor (and thereby run a negative bancor balance). The resulting bancor balances should be cleared multilaterally: all national central banks would have accounts in the ICU that would settle their balances at bancor par value. In settling the balances, the ICU should sanction both excessive trade deficits and – reflecting the guiding idea of creditor obligations – excessive trade surpluses (i.e. deficits or surpluses that exceed a certain threshold). Countries with a positive bancor balance should be incentivized to decrease their surpluses by spending more on the products and services of countries with negative balances. Alternatively, or in addition, these countries with positive balances should appreciate their currency and/or donate their excess balances to a special *reserve fund*. Excess balances would be directed to finance international efforts at reconstruction, investment, development, and aid (providing 'a link between international liquidity creation and aid' (Markwell 2006: 246)).[32] By contrast, the countries with a negative bancor balance would need to lower the exchange rate of their currency vis-à-vis bancor (which would lead to fewer imports and more exports). In addition, the ICU would have an allowance for overdraft facilities (proportional to the importance of a state's foreign trade) to slow down the speed of adjustments. It would also allow (and under certain circumstances require) capital controls.

The guiding idea of Keynes's proposal was that full employment and some limited degree of macroeconomic policy autonomy (including in exchange rate policy) within or for all states would allow for mutually beneficial free trade. Despite the special position granted to its founders, the United States and the United Kingdom, the (preferably worldwide) ICU would not operate in the name of any state but instead constitute a 'a genuine organ of truly international government' (Keynes 1943/1969: 35).

(2a) What are some of the normative merits and weaknesses of Keynes's proposal? From the perspective of (global) democratic theory, Keynes's proposal can be understood to seek to enhance state autonomy (autonomy of governments), and thereby potentially also democratic autonomy (autonomy of citizens) – to the extent that governments *are* democratic. Crucially, however, Keynes effectively insists that such autonomy should come with important conditions – the autonomy of any one state (or demos) must be made compatible with the autonomy of all other states (or demoi). 'Free development of each' needs to be combined with the 'free development of all', as Marx and Engels famously put a broadly similar conception of autonomy.[33] Held's (1995, 2006) 'principle of autonomy' extends this idea to global politics, including interstate relationships. At the very least, no state is allowed to exercise its autonomy to beggar its neighbour – that is to literally impoverish or more broadly undermine the interests and autonomy of the neighbour (near or far[34]).[35] This idea has obvious affinities also with the global (no-)harm principle (Linklater 2006, 2011; on cosmopolitan conditions on legitimate national macroeconomic policies, see Kotilainen 2024, Chapter 7; 2022).

Although Keynes's writings in general, and the motivation of the ICU proposal in particular, can be interpreted to reflect a restricted notion of cosmopolitanism, his preferred kind of supranational design of post-war institutions also contains problematic hints of technocraticism. Instead of a nationally organized and thereby explicitly political arrangement, Keynes sought to avoid politicization and favoured an 'objective', a technical and apparently non-political, supranational approach to the management of these institutions (Markwell 2006: 244–5).[36] While the aspiration to move beyond exclusive national control sits well with political theoretical cosmopolitanism, technocratic solutions clash with it. Relatedly, Keynes (1930/1952) seems to conceptualize the notion of rationality in terms of expertise of the few (rather than for instance in terms deliberative democracy – expertise of the many).

Moreover, Keynes's liberal cosmopolitanism is restricted by a kind of political or institutional Eurocentrism, reflected in the Anglo-American terms he favoured for international cooperation (including the special position of the United Kingdom and United States in his ICU proposals[37]). Also intellectually and culturally, Keynes drew almost exclusively on the European tradition (and the British tradition in particular). These elements, too, are in tension with the more fleshed out versions of cosmopolitanism developed in recent political and democratic theory (even if they remain partially Eurocentric in several respects as well; for a discussion, see Held and Patomäki 2006). Some of the normatively problematic aspects in Keynes's ICU design arise from his practical concerns about guaranteeing the feasibility of his proposal in the conditions of the Second World War – and especially about his concern for selling the plan to his home audience in the UK (Markwell 2006: 265).[38] In the conditions of 2020s, it is hard to see how an ICU-style arrangement granting special powers to a few leading states could be perceived as legitimate (if it ever was).[39] Indeed, the recent ideas on rendering the dollar system gradually more inclusive are likely to be viewed as illegitimate for the same reason. Why should one state have any special powers or privileges at all?

(2b) Keynes's rudimentary objective-list account of well-being sits very well with for instance the capability approach of Sen and Nussbaum (see Carabelli and Cedrini 2011; Martins 2014: 329–434; 2009; Sen 2015; relatedly, see Putnam and Walsh 2012). Both draw explicitly on Aristotle (especially *Nicomachean Ethics* (2014 [350–320 BC])). The capability approach is a defensible objective-list theory of well-being that is more explicit about the constituents of flourishing – and thereby also several issues of social justice – than Keynes (see e.g. Nussbaum 2006; Nussbaum and Sen 1993; Sen 2009; although according to strict criteria, the capability approach does not amount to a 'full' theory of justice either, see Robeyns and Byskov 2021).

(2c) Keynes's attitude towards the future has long been subject to considerable controversy. His (in)famous remark about all of us being dead in the 'long run' was clearly intended as a critique of (neo)classical economists' unhistorical conception of time rather than as an endorsement of myopia. However, Keynes's (1930/1952) anticipations about the possibilities of future generations do include a recommendation that people should start to care less about the future (vis-à-vis the present) *when* 'the economic problem' – the problem of subsistence – is solved (by about 2030 or so). At one level, Keynes evidently cares about the future – he hopes and believes that humanity can overcome the unnecessary problem(s) and backward morals of his own time.[40] At another level, his (carpe diem) idea about concentrating on the present easily conveys an impression about a disregard about the future.

In my diagnosis, the real issue in Keynes's (1930/1952) vision of the future is an empirical and epistemological (rather than an ethical) one – Keynes does not yet see that the economic problem will soon be replaced, or complemented with, an *even graver* 'existential problem' of humanity's long-term survival itself[41] – first in the form of nuclear weapons during the Second World War and soon also through ecological and other emerging anthropogenic existential risks (ranging from engineered pandemics to AGI, see e.g Ord 2020; Beard and Torres 2020). Just when humanity had developed the tools to overcome the primeval issue of *sufficient subsistence*, it encountered the novel issue of *continued existence*! While radical uncertainty about the future prevented Keynes from seeing these developments, it seems clear in retrospect that these new threats do not permit us to discount the relative value of future even if we could soon indeed overcome the economic problem. The existential problem does, however, reinforce Keynes's call to reject other aspects of the profit ethic.[42]

In general, one can raise legitimate questions about how systematic or even mutually consistent Keynes's normative commitments are (and how well or comprehensively they are reflected in his ICU proposal). At the same time, it is not easy to spot any obvious contradiction in his mature 1936–43 vision. Although both its normative and institutional outlook should be clarified further and partially rethought,[43] Keynes's plan provides a good starting point for most subsequent proposals.

The Brandt Commission's programme for survival

A few years after the Bretton Woods arrangement collapsed, the Independent Commission on International Development Issues, chaired by the former West German social democratic chancellor Willy Brandt (1913–92), produced an important and subsequently widely cited report on international development issues. The report, titled *North-South: A Programme for Survival* (1980), was written in the geohistorical context of a growing influence of the Global South. During the 1970s, the United Nations Conference on Trade and Development (UNCTAD) had been created, the Group of 77 (G77) formed, and the call for a New International Economic Order (NIEO) voiced. While much of the Global North rejected the call for NIEO, there was a growing recognition even among many Northerners that global reforms would be needed. The Brandt Report was perhaps the clearest testament of this. Yet, the late 1970s and early 1980s saw the rise of Thatcher and Reagan, and the economic order was transformed in a way that contradicted with what the South asked for. As with the Keynes plan, most of the Brandt Report's proposals were never implemented. (Lees 2021: 86–7)

The Brandt Report documented the existence of a deep global divide in standards of living between the affluent North and the poverty-stricken South.

The report also articulated a reasonable worry that this divide could trigger troubling political developments analogous to the 1930s. Very much in the spirit of Keynes,[44] the Commission warned that in the absence of shared values[45] and a global institutional response – including ICU-style elements – widespread poverty, unemployment, and related social curses could eventually lead to outright and mass-scale violence, including yet another world war. Worse still, some of the genuine risks to humanity's future survival were now evident.

(1a) The key normative commitment and primary objective of the Brandt Report – 'a programme for survival' – is indeed nothing less than avoiding an existential catastrophe. Throughout, the report puts heavy and explicit stress on survival: 'Our Report is based on what appears to be *the simplest common interest*: that mankind wants to survive, and one might even add has *the moral obligation to survive*' (Brandt 1980: 13, my emphases; Ord 2020: 42–57, argues that this obligation can derive from various sources, including obligations towards the present, future and past people, as well as more cosmic lines of thought; see Beard and Torres 2020; Bostrom 2013; see also Kotilainen 2024, Chapter 6).

The report views such global catastrophic and existential concerns as relevant even in the short term: 'our belief [is that] the two decades ahead of us [1980–2000] may be fateful for mankind' (Brandt 1980: 7). Moreover, '[m]ass starvation and the dangers of destruction may be growing steadily – if a new major war has not already shaken the foundations of what we call world civilization [by the year 2000]' (Brandt 1980: 11).

The report's secondary objective is a '[r]eshaping [of] worldwide North-South relations' to achieve global justice and well-being. The report also views this as a key means to enable survival itself (along with 'counteracting the dangers of the arms race') (Brandt 1980: 8).

The report largely shares Keynes's broad optimism and rationalism; despite all the great risks to the existence of future human civilization, the report's outlook is not bleak: 'the mortal dangers threatening our children and grandchildren can be averted' and 'we have a chance – whether we are living in the North or South, East or West – if we are determined to do so, to shape the world's future in peace and welfare, in solidarity and dignity' (Brandt 1980: 7).[46] As '[t]he debate between North and South has been continuing for some years', it is 'urgent that both sides should now work together in a programme based on action for a rational and equitable international economic order' (Brandt 1980: 270).

The report expresses a related belief in common visions despite initial differences. The members of the Commission themselves 'came not only from many parts of the world, but also carried with [them] differing convictions and different sums of experience, resulting from various fields of responsibility in political and economic life'. Yet, through explicit deliberation they nevertheless reached a 'remarkable' 'consensus' as they 'found that [they] had gradually come to share a common vision of the kind of world [they] hoped for, and of some of the major problems to be overcome if [these] hopes were to be realized' (Brandt 1980: 7–8).

Relatedly, the report stresses *common human interests* resulting from globally 'interlocked' communities, jobs, and lives (Brandt 1980: 11)[47] and the need for public education about these shared interests. More generally, it views the '*welfare of nations*' as 'interlocked' (Brandt 1980: 18). The report goes on to suggest several ideas about international or *global justice*[48] and to call for *a broad-based humanism* organized around 'a belief in man, in human dignity, in basic human rights; a belief in the values of justice, freedom, peace, mutual respect, in love and generosity, in reason rather than force' (Brandt 1980: 12). According to the report, this belief can draw on both religious and secular sources: '[t]he impulses from churches and religious communities as well as from humanism can strengthen worldwide solidarity and thus help resolve North-South problems' (Brandt 1980: 13).

(1b) The monetary and financial reforms proposed by the Brandt Report (Chapters 13–15), as the entire report, aim at a less chaotic and more equitable global governance architecture. The report proposes (i) *a system of stable exchange rates* (to ease cross-border trade and investment); (ii) *provision of adequate global liquidity* (to reduce cyclical fluctuations, disincentivize protectionism, and to assist producers); (iii) *a smooth process for adjustment of balance of payments* (to allow for expansion rather than contraction of global economic activity); (iv) *a new approach to development finance* (to meet disregarded global needs, especially in the South) based on the principles of *universality* and *automaticity* (rather than selectivity and case-by-case discretion) as well as an institutionalization of international development cooperation en route to *co-management of the world economy*; and (v) *a framework for large-scale transfer of resources* (to encourage global trade, growth, and employment, and thereby to foster the prospects of peace and survival) (Brandt 1980: 74–5).

(2a) The Brandt Report is clearly cosmopolitan in its basic outlook – the interests and values of all people(s) and nations should matter equally. Moreover, many interests are ultimately shared even across the North-South divide – not least because of the common issue of survival: 'Global questions require global answers; since there is now a risk of mankind destroying itself, this risk must be met by new methods' (Brandt 1980: 27).

The report demands the South to be included in the discussions, institutions and actual decision-making on global governance and development. In effect, the report overcomes much of the (explicit) Eurocentrism of Keynes's plan. In terms of its own organization, the membership of the Commission was balanced in terms of the North-South divide – although it was still chaired by a Northerner (see Brandt 1980: 293–304).

Curiously from a cosmopolitan perspective, however, the report is somewhat ambiguous in terms of (the nature of) its commitment democracy – 'democracy' is not mentioned in the entire document, even if in many contexts the report makes calls for increased 'participation' of either nations or people in different processes.[49] Of course, there may have been good practical, including (geo) political, reasons for avoiding the *word* 'democracy' as such. Be that as it may, one can plausibly argue that the 'consensus' reached by the Brandt Commission emerged largely out of *elite* deliberation,[50] albeit of a cross-cultural sort.

(2b) The report aspires to take human well-being, and related concerns for global and long-term justice, very seriously – indeed fostering them is the secondary objective of the report (next to survival itself, which demands a focus on the North-South issues). As a downside, it tends to employ these notions like politicians usually do, that is, with few or vague definitions. That said, I found no textual evidence that the report would contradict with the accounts of well-being and justice put forward by Keynes, Sen, Nussbaum, and others sympathetic to a broadly Aristotelian (capability) approach. It is, however, possible that the report does not contradict with some non-hedonist versions of for instance utilitarianism either – a logical contradiction is hard to come by. At least it seems clear that the report's broad base humanism is committed to value pluralism (multiplicity of basic values),[51] while it simultaneously rejects any simple value or (further) moral relativism (the idea that different people and/or cultures have their 'own' basic values or moral norms that do not apply to others).[52]

(2c) The report fares very well from the global catastrophic and existential risks perspective. It is clear from the outset that its primary objective is to warn about risks to humanity's future survival and try to address them. As mentioned, it even points out that humanity might have a moral obligation, and not 'merely' a shared interest, to survive. Connecting the issues of global development and macroeconomic governance to the issue of survival is arguably the main contribution of the report.

As potential existential risks (or their triggers), the report views large-scale (nuclear) warfare, but (a bit more vaguely) also 'chaos' possibly produced by for instance 'economic disasters, environmental catastrophes, and terrorism' (Brandt 1980: 13). Many or most risks are linked to 'world hunger, mass misery and alarming disparities between the living conditions of rich and poor' (ibid, 13). Economic and social developments are viewed as inexorably linked to foreign policies and military threats: 'Could one be content to call something a "new world economic order" if it did not include major progress towards disarmament?' (Brandt 1980: 14).

As a downside, the report does not attempt to assess the (evidential or Bayesian) *probability* of the risks it mentions (by contrast, see e.g. Ord 2020). Especially in retrospect one could easily argue that the report (implicitly) even suggests *too high* a probability for existential risks *in the short term* (1980–2000). In fact, the probability of such risks may remain relatively low even this or next century (2025–2200), which of course does not mean that the risks would not pose a serious threat in – and for – the long term (nor that they *could not* materialize in the short term – low probability events happen all the time).

Davidson's path to ICU and global economic prosperity

Paul Davidson's (1930–2024) proposal for an international monetary reform (see e.g. Davidson 1992–3, 2004, 2009) draws much more explicitly on the Keynes plan than the Brandt Report did. Davidson himself was a key American post-Keynesian[53] economist who made contributions for instance on the applicability of probability, uncertainty and non-ergodicity in economics and finance. While Davidson did not write explicitly on normative ethical or political theory, his work certainly touched on these topics as well (in one way or other, virtually all macroeconomic theorizing does). Davidson's ICU proposals at the turn of the millennium were obviously put forth in a geohistorical context very different from the circumstances of both Keynes's and the Brandt Commission's plans. If the so-called neoliberal transition had only just begun when the Brandt Report appeared, what John Williamson (1990) termed the 'Washington Consensus' had been well established by the time of Davidson's (1992–3) call for a monetary reform. By the release of Davidson's 2009 book, *The Keynes Solution*, a major financial crisis had erupted, and the wisdom of this consensus had been thoroughly contested.

(1a) Based on Davidson's very broad agreement with Keynes (see e.g. Davidson 2007, 2009), we can assume that Davidson's ICU proposal inherits, even if perhaps for feasibility reasons waters down, many of the normative underpinnings of Keynes's plan. Davidson (1992–3: 155; 2004: 596–7) explicitly stresses the importance of Keynes's idea of creditor obligations – shifting 'the *onus* of adjustment' from the debtor country to the creditor country. This indeed is perhaps the key normative principle of Keynes's ICU plan (which arguably reflects his long-standing 'antimoralistic' ethic discussed above).

(1b) Davidson (1992–3: 158; 2009: 136) presents his updated proposal as more 'modest' than Keynes's original plan. Most significantly, Davidson has had no need for a supranational central bank,[54] fiscal authority or a reserve fund. Instead of *taxation* of excess surpluses, his proposals have relied, at the first instance, on *voluntary* action on part of the creditor states to take responsibility for the adjustment of balance of payments. Only at the last instance – if the creditor states fail to comply altogether – their surpluses are 'confiscated' (Davidson 1992–3: 161). For perhaps the most detailed version of this relatively 'minimal' ICU proposal, see Davidson 2004: 597–604.

(2a) Davidson's proposal is arguably somewhat less committed to political theoretical cosmopolitanism than Keynes's plan or Brandt Commission's even more ambitious global programme for survival (or even the proposal by Stiglitz and Greenwald; see below). In addition to not including a supranational central bank, it 'does not require surrendering national control of local banking systems and fiscal policies' (Davidson 1992–3: 158). Both monetary and fiscal policies would remain under national control (Davidson 2009: 136).

From my point of view, Davidson's proposal suffers from a few of the same issues that the standard nation-state-centric interpretation of Modern Monetary Theory (MMT)[55] does, even if to a considerably lesser extent. For its credit, the proposal does look good in the light of the 'weak' formulation of what I, drawing on Held (2010) and Linklater (2006, 2011), have called the cosmopolitan condition on defensible national exercise of monetary sovereignty (Kotilainen 2024, Chapter 7; 2022). That is, Davidson's plan does require each state to exercise its rights to currency issuance and macroeconomic policy in a fashion that is *compatible* with some basic cosmopolitan values and norms (no right to 'bad-neighbourliness', to use Keynes's words) and does *not harm* or interfere with the ability of other states to conduct their own preferred versions of such policies. In Davidson's own very clear words, 'each nation still will be able to determine the best economic destiny for its citizens *provided* this destiny *does not negatively affect* employment and income-earning opportunities in trading partner nations' (Davidson 2009: 136, my emphasis).

While Davidson's ICU proposal effectively builds on, or at least seems to concur with, the weak formulation of the cosmopolitan condition, it does not live up to my 'strong' formulation of the condition which calls the national exercise of monetary sovereignty to *positively promote* cosmopolitan social democracy both at home and abroad (see Kotilainen 2024, Chapter 7). This shortcoming results from the evident empirical fact that nation-states rarely if ever seek out to meet this version of the condition (and standardly do not happen to meet it by chance either). For instance, the lack of an automatic tax on excess surpluses in Davidson's plan implies that it is the creditor states – instead of an emerging global community – that by default decide *how* the surpluses are employed. A democratically run supranational reserve fund – which Davidson's plan also does not include – would be in a much better position to use these excess surpluses (as well as newly created liquidity) to fund programmes that effectively promote broad and continued flourishing than national governments are.[56] Such programmes could for instance seek to alleviate global poverty, inequalities in capabilities, climate change and emerging existential risks. In other words, proposals that call for such a fund (and a supranational central bank) – including Keynes's original plan – do better than Davidson's updated proposal from the perspective of the strong version of the cosmopolitan condition (for a Keynesian statement of this version of the condition, see Tobin 1978: 159, final paragraph[57]).

I do not know whether the more national focus of Davidson's proposal results *solely* from his practical considerations of political feasibility or whether Davidson's underlying normative sympathies themselves were more national in orientation. Be that as it may, Davidson could certainly plausibly have countered that in the present conditions his plan is politically more realistic than any proposal with clearer supranational or global ambitions,[58] such as those suggested by Keynes, the Brandt Commission or a straightforward cosmopolitan reading of MMT. There often are trade-offs between normative ambition and political feasibility,[59] at least in the short term (although for instance Keynes's forced shift from bilateralism to multilateralism during the Bretton Woods negotiations (see Markwell 2006: 223–47) should remind us that bold or universalist proposals are sometimes *more* realistic than convenient or partialist alternatives). Feasibility considerations, in addition to normative criteria, should obviously be considered in final assessments of the relative merits of different ICU proposals, but it is also important to recognize that feasibility is not the *only* thing that matters. A prevailing system is always the most feasible system, but it may not be a system good enough. Or, as Davidson (1992–3: 178) put it, '[i]f we start with the defeatist attitude that it is too difficult to change the awkward system in which we are enmeshed, then no progress will be made'.

(2b)-(2c) See (2a) and the assessment of Keynes's original plan above.

Stiglitz and Greenwald's proposal

Joseph Stiglitz and Bruce Greenwald (2010; see also Stiglitz 2006: 245–68; 2003; Greenwald and Stiglitz 2010) have put forward another widely discussed twenty-first century ICU proposal. Given that they write in the same geohistorical context as Davidson, they describe the global monetary predicament in a broadly similar way as him – fixed exchange rates have been replaced by unstable floating rates and the United States has moved from being the main global creditor to being the main debtor on whose reserve currency assets other states rely on (and which allow and encourage them to run trade surpluses). For both Davidson and Stiglitz and Greenwald, these developments constitute part of the reason why Keynes's approach to global monetary reform needs to be updated for the changed circumstances, even if it remains sound in its basic normative principles.

(1a) As Davidson and Brandt, in terms of his basic normative commitments, Stiglitz is basically a Keynesian social democrat with cosmopolitan aspirations (in a broad sense of all these attributes).[60] As the first two, Stiglitz is not a professional ethical or political theorist (he was awarded the 2001 Nobel Memorial Prize for his contributions to economics of asymmetric information). That said, Stiglitz has occasionally entered into these areas of research (see e.g. Stiglitz 2012).

Stiglitz's work on international economics, globalization, and development issues, including as chief economist at the World Bank, suggests that his normative commitments include (i) a conception of well-being and global justice that stresses the need to address global poverty and inequality and to foster provision of 'global public goods', such as knowledge, development, climate change mitigation etc (with critical implications towards the Washington Consensus and dollar hegemony) (see Stiglitz 2006, 2002; Stiglitz and Greenwald 2010); (ii) a commitment to a more democratic form of globalization (see e.g. Stiglitz 2006, Chapter 10); and (iii) a concern about global catastrophic risks, especially climate change (see e.g. Stiglitz 2006, Chapter 6).

(1b) In terms of institutional design, Stiglitz's and Greenwald's proposal is not as detailed as Davidson's. However, the core institutional elements of Stiglitz and Greenwald's (2010: 17–18) 'preferred' proposal to establish a new global reserve system include creating a new global reserve currency. In their view, this global currency should ideally be seen as an instrument for active *global macroeconomic policy* – to be issued at higher quantities when the global economy is slowing down and at lower quantities when the global economy is expanding – as well as providing *funding for global public goods*. In addition, new incentives for states not to pile up excess surpluses should be created to reduce macroeconomic 'externalities' associated with insufficient global aggregate demand. According to Stiglitz and Greenwald, we need a rule-based system run by a new institution or a reformed IMF.

(2a) Despite their largely shared diagnosis of the flaws of the current architecture, compared to Davidson, Stiglitz and Greenwald seem somewhat more optimistic about what could be feasible in the current circumstances.[61] Also their normative ambitions appear to be higher. Whereas Davidson advocates a comparatively modest proposal, Stiglitz and Greenwald (2010: 17)

> strongly believe that it would be desirable to move towards the more ambitious frameworks, which simultaneously address the central problems posed by the dollar reserve system – as well as other key problems in globalization. Keynes – not surprisingly, given his focus on underemployment equilibria – argued for a system that taxed surplus countries. This could be implemented by reducing allocation of new reserves to countries with persistent surpluses. These amounts could then be reallocated, e.g. for climate change or development.[62]

Both the idea of global macroeconomic policy and funding of global public goods reflect cosmopolitan aspirations that are not far from those of Keynes, the Brandt Commission, or (even) Tobin. Stiglitz (2006: 269–92) also devotes a chapter to discussing how globalization could be democratized, which strengthens the impression that he subscribes to cosmopolitanism of a sort.

Relatedly, Stiglitz and Greenwald also notice that in addition to considerations of a proposal's short-term feasibility, one should pay attention to considerations of its eventual legitimacy and/or sustainability – what one could perhaps call the proposal's long-term viability. As Stiglitz and Greenwald (2010: 17) put it, the 'more ambitious versions may be harder to negotiate – though given the additional benefits that would be reaped, they might enjoy greater support'. This in an important point that again suggests that the trade-offs between normative ambition and political feasibility / viability are not as nearly as clear-cut as one might first believe.

Stiglitz's complaints about the monetary hegemony of the US dollar seem to stem from a mixture of economic and ethico-political concerns of a broadly cosmopolitan type. First, the dollar-centred system is inherently unstable (and monetary rivalry of other *national* currencies would just make things worse) (Stiglitz and Greenwald 2010). Second, 'to many, especially outside the United States, it seems peculiar that a twenty-first century global economy should be dependent on the currency of a single country' (Stiglitz and Greenwald 2010: 1). Third, the United States is suggested to benefit unfairly from its ability to borrow from developing states (Stiglitz 2006: 245; Stiglitz and Greenwald 2010: 2).

The third of these claims is arguably a confusion that follows from a (neo) classical theory of state finance – the United States does not borrow from abroad to finance its deficits, but rather the surpluses of net exporting countries that correspond to the US deficits keep the demand for dollar bonds high (this at any rate is the MMT position, see Bell 2000; Wray 2012: 125–47).[63] By contrast, the first two of Stiglitz's claims are compelling – a dollar-based system is not only macroeconomically suboptimal, but also normatively problematic (and certainly widely perceived as illegitimate by other states).

(2b) Stiglitz's conception of global justice is clearly not far from Keynes's, Davidson's or Brandt's Commission's conceptions. It is therefore probably well in line also with the capability approach of Sen and Nussbaum. Indeed, Stiglitz (2006: 50, 299; 2002: xxii) is explicit about the influence of Sen on his thinking.

(2c) Stiglitz articulates a clear concern for global catastrophic risks, in particular climate change (Stiglitz 2006, Chapter 6). He goes on to suggest that climate change could be tackled also through the means provided by an international monetary reform (including expansion of SDRs, taxation of excess surpluses, climate change fund etc.) (see also Stiglitz and Greenwald 2010). Stiglitz's conception of existential and catastrophic risks could be more expansive (along the lines discussed in Kotilainen 2024, Chapter 6; see also Beard and Torres 2020), even if climate change is undeniably an excellent focus now.

On the key promises of a Global Clearing Union

The above normative analysis of ICU proposals is of course far from exhaustive (for further discussions on related cosmopolitan and/or Keynesian reforms in broader terms, see e.g. Ocampo 2017; Patomäki and Teivainen 2004). To fully grasp the normative underpinnings and related institutional elements of even the existing proposals, a lot more work remains to be done. Moreover, despite their many merits, none of the existing proposals is fully satisfactory – important questions about for instance their underlying technocraticism, Eurocentrism and even anthropocentrism[64] need to be addressed. Conceptions of global democracy, well-being, and the value of long-term future themselves can potentially draw on much more diverse sources than they currently tend to (see Kotilainen 2024, Chapter 6; for a recent call for a more global IPE, see Helleiner 2023: 264–9).

An updated Global Clearing Union could go a long way towards combatting the new trade wars and geoeconomic conflicts, and even help to address growing concerns about survival as such. Escalating global catastrophic risks should indeed be taken increasingly seriously in all prospective clearing union proposals – perhaps especially with respect to the envisaged role of the global reserve fund. At the simplest level, the fund could allocate new resources to the prevention of these risks. To the extent that cosmopolitan conditions on national policies are indeed desirable and democratically accepted, one could also make the access to these funds conditional on for instance the existence of credible plans to the elimination of carbon emissions, ecosystem damage, and nuclear proliferation (rather than on the standard *un*cosmopolitan conditions on the public finances of debtors). Once a system for the taxation of excess trade surpluses is in place, it would be easier to move on to tax states that create other global 'externalities' that are at least as dangerous as those linked to insufficient global effective demand.

As one of its key normative promises in my view, an international or global clearing union could facilitate the transition away from a national or regional macroeconomic governance framework to a truly global architecture (see Kotilainen 2024, Chapter 9). Moreover, the functions of the union could ultimately expand well beyond clearing. In effect, a GCU of this kind could constitute a key institutional step towards democratic global governance or world statehood (see Patomäki 2023).

In addition to designing increasingly concrete, effective, and desirable GCU proposals, questions about feasibility and potential strategies forward need to be tackled head-on. GCU may be a (viable) institutional possibility but is it a (feasible) political possibility given how things stand? Do for instance the actions of the new Trump administration decrease or increase the probability of the union? Through which mechanisms exactly?

Notes

1 https://blogs.worldbank.org/en/voices/silent-debt-crisis-engulfing-developing -economies-weak-credit-ratings

2 https://www.ft.com/content/4ed9edc2-cdfe-43c5-8d95-e1842adc9e62

3 https://www.sipri.org/media/press-release/2024/global-military-spending-surges -amid-war-rising-tensions-and-insecurity

4 While increasing national or regional military spending can make sense for every actor individually, the resulting increase in global military spending implies that all actors will be worse off collectively – or, indeed, may not survive.

5 In this context, I employ the terms 'hegemon(y)' and 'hegemonic' in roughly the standard sense in which they tend to be used in International Relations and IPE/GPE. These literatures are divided on whether hegemony is, or could be, a good thing on balance (compare e.g. the so-called hegemonic stability theory with neo-Gramcian analyses).

6 The kind of exceptional power associated with hegemony is often conceptualized as either 'supremacy' or 'leadership' (depending on one's normative take on its benevolence vs. malevolency). Such power may also be understood as 'dominance' (and many employ e.g. the term 'dollar dominance' instead of, or in addition to, 'dollar hegemony').

7 We might therefore talk more specifically about *currency hegemony*, but the concept of monetary hegemony seems specific enough for the purposes of this paper.

8 Strictly speaking it is not currencies as such that would 'hegemonic' but rather their issuers.

9 Unsurprisingly, the geopolitically hegemonic power has tended to be a monetary hegemon as well.

10 In principle, these definitions allow for more than one *non*-global monetary hegemons (and hegemonic currencies). Yet, it is unclear whether it would make sense to use the term in, for instance, national or regional settings, where we may

rather talk about monetary sovereignty (and macroeconomic policy autonomy). At any rate, this paper concerns *global* monetary hegemony.

11 https://www.brasildefato.com.br/2024/05/29/global-south-considers-increasing-de -dollarization-but-trump-wants-to-punish-those-who-reduce-dependence-on-us -currency

12 Someone might complain that the GCU would itself become another monetary hegemon, even if not a national one (and the bancor or its equivalent a hegemonic currency). However, since a desirable kind of GCU would not exercise *unilateral* power over the other relevant entities, its power might be genuinely democratic and legitimate. The relevant powers could also be shared by other entities. This potential complaint underscores the need for the GCU to be a truly common institution rather than just another alliance or bloc that exercises unilateral power over non-members.

13 https://www.federalreserve.gov/monetarypolicy/bst_liquidityswaps.htm

14 https://www.ft.com/content/4ed9edc2-cdfe-43c5-8d95-e1842adc9e62

15 For instance, much of what the EU or the BRICS are doing to advance their autonomy as geopolitical and economic actors can be viewed as reasonable responses to the situation in which they cannot count on the current hegemon. Yet, once, or to the extent that, they are seeking themselves to become the new hegemon, their actions stop being defensible.

16 Chapters 6–9 of my doctoral dissertation *From Monetary Sovereignty to Macroeconomic Policy Autonomy? Examining Promises, Limitations, and Reform Possibilities of a Nation-State-Centric Macroeconomic Governance Architecture* (Kotilainen 2024) provide a more extensive discussion of many of the issued raised in this article.

17 In contrast to most of the later economists that have developed his plan further in mainly technical terms, Keynes wrote hundreds of pages on ethics, politics, and even more abstract branches of philosophy. As with Smith, Marx, and many of the classical political economists, Keynes's underlying interests and much of the training were in philosophy.

18 The eventual Bretton Woods conference of July 1944 famously led to the establishment of the International Monetary Fund (IMF) and the International Bank for Reconstruction and Development (IBRD), which later became part of the World Bank. ICU and International Trade Organization (ITO) were not established, although the latter was soon adopted in a watered-down form of the General Agreement on Tariffs and Trade (GATT), which eventually developed into the World Trade Organization (WTO) in 1995. By contrast, no ICU-style arrangement has yet ever existed (even if IMF's Special Drawing Rights, established in 1969, are in effect an early form of global reserve currency, potentially serving functions that Keynes's ICU proposal suggested for the bancor).

19 In addition, there are of course very thorough overall biographies of Keynes, such
    as those written by Robert Skidelsky. Also Keynes's own writings are for the most
    part very accessible.

20 Although all people obviously have beliefs that they do not (repeatedly) affirm in
    writing (or are even aware of), the epistemologically most cautious approach is to
    focus on the views we have clear evidence Keynes believed towards the end of his
    life. Of course, there are for instance important partial parallels between Keynes's
    approaches to the aftermaths of the First and Second World Wars, as also Markwell
    (2006: 268–70) recognizes.

21 In terms of *metaethics*, Keynes was, and in some ways always remained, profoundly
    influenced by G. E. Moore's *Principia Ethica* (1903/1993). Moore's famous
    metaethical attack on hedonism (1903/1993, Chapter 3) helps to account for
    Keynes's persistent anti-Benthamism that influenced even the *General Theory* (Mini
    1991). His reading of Moore also explains Keynes's early idiosyncratic distinction
    between 'speculative' and 'practical' ethics, parts of his long-standing interest
    in uncertainty and probability, and perhaps even his style of doing economics
    (Carabelli and Cedrini 2011; Davidson 2007: 5–6). As Keynes (1938/1972: 435)
    explains, Moore's Principia 'dominated, and perhaps still dominates, everything
    else', even if he now makes also important criticisms of Moore's views.

22 For Keynes, human well-being has definitive material preconditions but also calls
    for appreciation of friendship, love, beauty, truth, knowledge, and so on. Pleasure,
    goodness, and happiness should furthermore be distinguished from each other (all
    of which can be valuable but do not always coincide). In these respects, Keynes's
    value pluralism draws heavily on both Aristotle and G.E. Moore. Keynes also puts
    considerable weight on freedom in the sense of *autonomy* – both at the individual
    and social level (Carabelli and Cedrini 2011; Markwell 2006). This commitment
    to autonomy is reflected in his non-utilitarian political liberalism (which in some
    respects comes close to even Hayek whom Keynes knew well).

23 'Though the "children of man" are not yet born, their grandfathers should engage
    in the attempt to create a new international economic order able to combine
    sound thinking with the perspective of easing the "material burdens" of their
    grandchildren' (Carabelli and Cedrini 2011: 340).

24 Rather the 'market is often at the origins of problems of fallacies of composition
    between particular and general interests, and cannot be invoked to solve them'
    (Carabelli and Cedrini 2011: 350).

25 Some such principles are for instance the belief that it is not just to punish
    the offspring of wrongdoers for what their parents (or their rulers) have done
    (essentially a view delineating the scope of legitimate retributive justice) and a
    belief about the moral obligation of both authorities and majorities to respect the
    autonomy of individuals (see Markwell 2006: 192–5).

26 Initially, this ethic was greatly influenced by the orientation of the so-called
    Bloomsbury Group of artists and thinkers (to which Keynes belonged and which
    drew from Moore and Russell), and is in many ways the mirror image of the
    Victorian ethic of Keynes's youth (and even the 'Protestant ethic' and related 'spirit
    of capitalism' described by Max Weber (1905/2001)). Even the mature Keynes
    (1938/1972: 447) writes that he remains, 'and always will remain, an immoralist'
    although his view of human nature was now far more pessimistic (Freud was a key
    influence on Keynes's later thought).

27 A complete argument for creditor obligations, it seems to be, must include the
    following premises: (i) elementary accounting relationships hold (in double-entry
    bookkeeping, surpluses and deficits sum to zero); (ii) a causal account of global
    political economy according to which a simultaneous motivation of too many states
    to chase surpluses promotes trade wars and contractionary pressures on global
    demand, and thereby leads to sluggish growth, unemployment, and related political
    and social ills, including the threat of military conflict (here Keynes's ideas on
    macroeconomics and international relations are relevant); (iii) a normative premise
    according to which these outcomes would be undesirable (this follows from almost
    any view in ethics); and (iv) another normative premise according to which there is
    no adequate ethical reason *why debtors rather than creditors* should bear the (main)
    responsibility for the undesirable outcomes and thereby have the sole (or greater)
    obligation to address the problem (it is in justifying this last premise that Keynes's
    'antimoralistic' ethic can be very relevant).

28 According to Markwell (2006: 191), 'Keynes's – idealism may be seen in his attitude
    to nine issues: the possibility – indeed, the probability – of progress; pacifism;
    the rule of law; the League; the need to resist the "brigand powers" and uphold
    collective security; the importance of public opinion; disarmament; the process of
    international cooperation; and the utility of economic weapons, especially as an
    alternative to war. Keynes's beliefs were fundamentally similar to those of other
    idealists of his time, such as Zimmern, Murray, and Angell. Keynes had friendly
    dealings with these, and with many other of the prominent inter-war idealist
    writers, such as David Davies, Arnold Toynbee, Philip Noel-Baker, Leonard Woolf,
    Lord Lothian, and the American James T. Shotwell.'

29 Selected elements of this governance ideology were institutionally 'embedded' in
    the resulting post–Second World War order (Ruggie 1982).

30 For Keynes, state autonomy does *not* entail a right to 'bad-neighbourliness' – 'It
    is an advantage, and not a disadvantage, of the scheme that it invites the member
    States to abandon [the] license to promote indiscipline, disorder and bad-
    neighbourliness which, to the general disadvantage, they have been free to exercise
    hitherto' (Keynes 1943/1969: 36). On the other hand, the ICU should not be 'too
    grandmotherly' at the outset (Keynes 1941–1943/1980: 333).

31 For instance, during his work on the ICU plan, Keynes expressed a hope in 'the new democracy of nations which after this war will come into existence, heaven helping, to conduct with amity and good sense the common concerns of mankind' (Keynes 1941–1943/1980: 269–70).

32 Directly in terms of security, the ICU would contain an account for an international policy force as well as provisions for financial blockades (Keynes 1943/1969; Markwell 2006: 259).

33 As a long-standing liberal critic of Marxism, Keynes may have denied this similarity. Held (1995, 2006) points out important ways in which liberalism and Marxism are part of the same Western tradition, however. Freedom and autonomy themselves are among the key unifying concerns of these grand isms (similarly to J.S. Mill, Marx wrote under the influence of W.v. Humboldt who articulated an early version of the harm principle and later founded the University of Berlin, where also Marx studied). Of course, Marxism was subsequently rebranded as an authoritarian state ideology (partially also because of its internal ambiguities), while libertarian and democratic versions of socialism continued to draw on the antiauthoritarian thought of Humboldt, Mill, and Marx.

34 As Niina Kari helpfully alluded, the underlying idea here is (or should be) that the circle of moral and political concern ought to be expanded to people residing within the territory of *any* state. In other words, the term 'neighbour' should be understood in a cosmopolitan sense (which arguably has something to do with even the biblical use of the word).

35 As Markwell (2006: 140–1) puts it, '*The General Theory* suggested that the principal economic cause of war (the "competitive struggle for markets") could be eliminated, and "unimpeded" trade could be to "mutual (p.141) advantage", if countries were able to maintain full employment. This was best done by simultaneous pursuit of national policies for full employment within an international monetary system which, unlike the gold standard, did not pit the interests of one country against another.' Typical beggar-thy-neighbour macroeconomic policies include competitive devaluations and austerity measures. Countless different kinds of national policies with potential domestic benefits can of course have detrimental cross-border effects (careless climate policies or hostile foreign policies are some obvious examples). Arguably also the word 'beggar' should be understood in a broad sense.

36 The efforts at avoiding overt politicization that characterize the ongoing development that van 't Klooster (2022) calls 'technocratic Keynesianism' are therefore not completely alien even to Keynes's own orientation. However, van 't Klooster (2022: 773) is, of course, right to stress that the mid-twentieth century shift towards Keynesianism, as a broad political and legal process, was *not* technocratic: 'Although key technical decisions rested with unelected actors in central banks and

treasuries (one of whom was Keynes himself), their efforts resulted in legislative action. International treaties codified new ideas about the governance of money into the design of the Bretton Woods institutions. Following changes to the international structure, central bank and banking laws were redrafted and navigated through parliaments.' To my knowledge, Keynes was also in favour of this kind of democratic process.

37 Keynes suggested, for instance, that the founder states should have certain voting privileges over other members and that the key institutional bodies should be located in these states. 'In view of our experience and of our geographical and political position in relation to Europe, the United States and the British Commonwealth, we could justifiably ask that the head office should be situated in London with the Board of Managers meeting alternately here and in Washington' (1941–1943/1980: 134). '[T]here might be a provision, at any rate for the first five years, by which the British and American members when acting in agreement could outvote the rest of the Board' (ibid., 135).

38 As Markwell (2006: 264–5) points out, other countries, including even the United States, were less enthusiastic about the kind of Anglo-American dominance proposed by Keynes: 'Indeed, the White Paper said that the "management of the institution must be genuinely international without preponderant power of veto or enforcement to any country or group; and the rights and privileges of the smaller countries must be safeguarded"'. In several important respects, the overall British interest in issues faced by developing states was 'lukewarm and inconsistent', as Helleiner (2014: 208) describes it.

39 Overall, there are many signs that Keynes lacks an adequate theory of power, authority, and legitimacy.

40 Also in terms of more tangible projects, 'in the long run almost anything is possible' (Keynes 1942/1980: 268).

41 Keynes (1930/1952) rather anticipates that the economic problem will give way for a completely different kind of 'existential' problem: the question of what to *do* with one's life (basically the problem of the so-called existentialists, such as Jean-Paul Sartre and Albert Camus). Keynes learned about nuclear weapons during the Second World War at latest, but given that he passed away in 1946, he did not see the emergence of other existential threats. As a Malthusian pessimist, he would undoubtedly have taken them as seriously as Russell and others did.

42 I doubt whether capitalist action has ever been driven by a longtermist ethic, except in the narrow economic and religious senses described by Keynes (1930/1952) and Weber (1905). Most strikingly, there has been no interest in the long-term prospects of (this-worldly) human existence (let alone that of other species).

43 This diagnosis of course applies also to Keynes's economic theory that has been developed further by especially the post-Keynesians.

44 The report mentions Keynes only once, however: 'While the western powers were committed to intervention in their home economies, they were determined to avoid the protectionism and "beggar thy neighbour" policies of the 1930s, by creating a strong free-trade system; it was a combination of Keynes at home, and Adam Smith abroad' (Brandt 1980: 36).

45 There were hopes that the commission's work could 'contribute to the development of worldwide moral values' (as pointed by Brandt 1980: 7).

46 'One should not give up the hope that problems created by men can also be solved by men' (Brandt 1980: 10).

47 In a similar spirit, Held (2010: 36) talks about 'overlapping communities of fate'.

48 'International social justice should take into account the growing awareness of a fundamental equality and dignity among all men and women. Scientific, technological and economic opportunities should be developed to allow a more humane social and economic order for all people. Strong efforts should be made to further a growing recognition of human rights and of the rights of labour and international conventions for protecting them' (Brandt 1980: 25). There is also a commitment to the post–Second World War notion of *global responsibility for economic and social development* (Brandt 1980: 8), including for the sake of peace (an idea that Keynes had helped to shape), as well as a further call for equitable inclusion of the South in the post–Second World War framework of international institutions (reflecting its demand in early 1970s for a New International Economic Order).

49 The overall *spirit* of the report is very democratic, however: 'The shaping of our common future is much too important to be left to governments and experts alone. Therefore, our appeal goes to youth, to women's and labour movements; to political, intellectual and religious leaders; to scientists and educators; to technicians and managers; to members of the rural and business communities. May they all try to understand and to conduct their affairs in the light of this new challenge' (Brandt 1980: 29).

50 This same critique may be made of the Bretton Woods negotiations.

51 '[T]he new generations of the world – need a belief in man, in human dignity, in basic human rights; a belief in *the values of justice, freedom, peace, mutual respect, in love and generosity, in reason rather than force*' (Brandt 1980: 12, my emphasis).

52 '[N]ecessary political decisions – will not be possible without *a global consensus on the moral plane that the basis of any world or national order must be people and respect for their essential rights, as defined in the Universal Declaration of Human Rights*. Only if these ideas are sincerely accepted by governments, and especially by individuals, will the political decisions be possible and viable. This requires *an intensive process of education to bring home to public opinion in every country the vital need to defend the values without which there will be no true economic*

development and, above all, no justice, freedom or peace' (Brandt 1980: 268, my emphases).

53 Davidson preferred the spelling 'Post Keynesian' (as in the *Journal of Post Keynesian Economics*).

54 'At this stage of the evolution of world politics – a supranational central bank is not feasible' (Davidson 1992–3: 157–8.)

55 For an introduction to MMT, see Mitchell, Wray, and Watts 2019. For nation-state-centric versus cosmopolitan interpretations of MMT, see Kotilainen 2022; 2024.

56 Davidson's ICU proposal (2004: 597–604) includes the suggestion that '[i]f the deficit nation is a poor one, then surely there is a case for the richer nations that are in surplus to transfer some of their excess credit balances to support the poor nation'. I agree, but if there is no reserve fund or other supranational institution that would order the state to act in this way, this is merely an ethical plea.

57 In this paragraph, Tobin (1978: 159) points out that '[t]ogether the major governments and central banks are making fiscal and monetary policy for the world, whether or not they explicitly recognise the fact'. He goes on to call for 'a longer-range and more global view of their responsibilities' for states enjoying substantial macroeconomic policy autonomy (hypothetically thanks to the Tobin tax). This call captures the thrust of the strong version of my cosmopolitan condition. As pointed out, the empirical problem is that nation-states *tend not to* live up to such responsibilities – which is why moving beyond the national architecture altogether is arguably the difficult-to-achieve ideal (as also Tobin claims).

58 Analogously, the national neochartalists can plausibly argue that their vision is *even* more realistic than Davidson's plan.

59 Funnily enough, however, the notion of 'political feasibility' essentially reduces to questions about normative ambition *prevailing in a society at large* (or at least among its leaders). If the emerging global society becomes sufficiently normatively ambitious about an ICU proposal, the proposal *thereby* becomes also politically feasible.

60 The normative commitments of Bruce Greenwald might call for a separate assessment. From watching some of their joint panel sessions, I got the impression that he and Stiglitz by no means agree on all issues.

61 Stiglitz and Greenwald (2010: 20) recommend a 'portfolio approach' of 'moving forward on several forms simultaneously' combining regional and international action.

62 Stiglitz and Greenwald (2010: 17), too, realize that there are also more modest ways forward, '[t]he least ambitious [of which] is a simple extension of the current system of special drawing rights (SDRs) within the IMF'. This comes close to Stiglitz's (2003) own suggestion to offer 'global greenbacks' (basically SDR grants)

to countries that need them most. For Davidson (2004: 596), Stiglitz's global greenbacks would be 'merely palliatives and not the solution to the problem'. It is thus not true that Stiglitz's proposals on global monetary reform would have been more ambitious than Davidson's *across the board*, and certainly not in all aspects – indeed, in some respects, including in basic questions of macroeconomic theory, Davidson is probably closer to Keynes than Stiglitz is (reflecting the post-Keynesianism/New Keynesianism split), and thereby more ambitious about certain related economic reforms. By contrast, Stiglitz is arguably more ambitious than Davidson with respect to cosmopolitan politics and development. From the perspective of the emerging Helsinki approach (see Kotilainen and Patomäki 2022; 2020), economic, political, and philosophical commitments *all* matter for assessing relative merits of competing accounts.

63 In general, Stiglitz's (2006) and Stiglitz and Greenwald's (2010) basic economic theoretical assumptions remain New Keynesian, although Stiglitz may have more recently taken some steps towards post-Keynesianism.

64 As Matias Ingman helpfully commented, future proposals should arguably move beyond Brandt Report style broad-based humanism and towards an even broader based 'ecologism' or something along such lines (even if the Brandt Report does make several references to ecology). To some extent, also for instance the literature on global catastrophic and existential risks might need to move towards a similar direction – there has been an overemphasis on 'intelligent life'. The Anthropocene has been characterized by (what could perhaps be called) *existential risks for non-human species* that, in numerical terms, are often much higher than such risks for humans. Indeed, the risks for other species regularly materialize as extinction outcomes.

Bibliography

Aristotle. (2014), [350–320 BCE]. *Nicomachean Ethics* [Translated by C.D.C. Reeve], Indianapolis, IN: Hackett Publishing Company.

Beard, Simon, and Phil Torres. (2020), 'Ripples on the Great Sea of Life. A Brief History of Existential Risk Studies', https://ssrn.com/abstract=3730000.

Bell, Stephanie. (2000), 'Do Taxes and Bonds Finance Government Spending?', *Journal of Economic Issues,* 34 (3): 603–20.

Bostrom, Nick. (2013), 'Existential Risk Prevention as Global Priority', *Global Policy,* 4 (1): 15–31.

Bostrom, Nick, and Milan M. Ćirković. (2008), *Global Catastrophic Risks,* Oxford: Oxford University Press.

Brandt, Willy. (1980), *North-South: A Programme for Survival. The Report of the Independent Commission on International Development Issues under the Chairmanship of Willy Brandt,* London: Pan Books.

Carabelli, Anna, and Maro Cedrini. (2011), 'The Economic Problem of Happiness: Keynes on Happiness and Economics', *Forum for Social Economics*, 40 (3): 335–59.

Carranza, E. Mario. (2003), 'Can Mercosur Survive? Domestic and International Constraints on Mercosur', *Latin American Politics and Society*, 45 (2): 67–103.

Crisp, Roger. (2021), 'Well-Being', *The Stanford Encyclopedia of Philosophy* (Winter 2021 Edition), Edward N. Zalta (ed), forthcoming. https://plato.stanford.edu/archives/win2021/entries/well-being/.

Davidson, Paul. (1992–3), 'Reforming the World's Money', *Journal of Post Keynesian Economics*, 15 (2): 153–79.

Davidson, Paul. (2004), 'The Future of the International Financial System', *Journal of Post Keynesian Economics*, 26 (4): 591–605.

Davidson, Paul. (2007), *John Maynard Keynes*, New York: Palgrave Macmillan.

Davidson, Paul. (2009), *The Keynes Solution. The Path to Global Economic Prosperity*, New York: Palgrave Macmillan.

Drezner, Daniel W., Henry Farrell, and Abraham L. Newman. (eds) (2021), *The Uses and Abuses of Weaponized Interdependence*, Washington: Brookings Institution Press.

Farrell, Henry, and Abraham Newman. (2019), 'Weaponized Interdependence: How Global Economic Networks Shape State Coercion', *International Security*, 44 (1): 42–79.

Flanagan, Owen. (2013), *The Bodhisattva's Brain. Buddhism Naturalized*, Cambridge, MA: The MIT Press.

Goodhart, A. E. Charles. (1998), 'The Two Concepts of Money: Implications for the Analysis of Optimal Currency Areas', *European Journal of Political Economy*, 14 (3): 407–32.

Greenwald, Bruce, and Joseph E. Stiglitz. (2010), 'A Modest Proposal for International Monetary Reform', in S. Griffith-Jones, J.A. Ocampo, and J.E. Stiglitz (eds), *Time for a Visible Hand: Lessons from the 2008 World Financial Crisis*, 314–44, Initiative for Policy Dialogue Series, Oxford: Oxford University Press.

Hale, Thomas, David Held, and Kevin Young. (2013), *Gridlock: Why Global Cooperation Is Failing When We Need It Most*, Cambridge: Polity Press.

Helleiner, Eric. (2014), *Forgotten Foundations of Bretton Woods: International Development and the Making of the Postwar Order*, Ithaca, NY: Cornell University Press.

Helleiner, Eric. (2023), *The Contested World Economy: The Deep and Global Roots of International Political Economy*, Cambridge: Cambridge University Press.

Held, David. (1995), *Democracy and the Global Order: From the Modern State to Cosmopolitan Governance*, Cambridge: Polity Press.

Held, David. (2006), *Models of Democracy*, 3rd edn, Cambridge: Polity Press.

Held, David. (2010), *Cosmopolitanism. Ideals and Realities*, Cambridge: Polity Press.

Held, David, and Heikki Patomäki. (2006), 'Problems of Global Democracy. A Dialogue', *Theory, Culture & Society*, 23 (5): 115–33.

Keynes, John Maynard. (1930/1952), 'Economic Possibilities for Our Grandchildren', in *Essays in Persuasion*, 358–73, London: Rupert Hart-Davis.

Keynes, John Maynard. (1936/2009), *The General Theory of Employment, Interest and Money*, Orlando: Signalman Publishing.

Keynes, John Maynard. (1938/1972), 'My Early Beliefs', in *The Collected Writings of John Maynard Keynes. Volume X. Essays in Biography*, 433–50, London and Basingstoke: Macmillan.

Keynes, John Maynard. (1941–1943/1980), *The Collected Writings of John Maynard Keynes, XXV. Activities 1940–1944. Shaping the Post-War World: The Clearing Union*, Donald Moggridge (ed), Cambridge: Cambridge University Press.

Keynes, John Maynard. (1942/1980), *The Collected Writings of John Maynard Keynes, XXVII. Activities 1940–1944. Shaping the Post-War World: Employment and Commodities*, Donald Moggridge, Cambridge: Cambridge University Press.

Keynes, John Maynard. (1943/1969), 'Proposals for an International Clearing Union (April 1943)', in J. Horsefield (ed), *The International Monetary Fund 1945–1965. Twenty Years of International Monetary Cooperation. Volume III: Documents*, 19–36, Washington, DC: International Monetary Fund.

Kindleberger, P. Charles. (1981), *International Money. A Collection of Essays*, Abingdon: Routledge.

Klein, C. Matthew, and Michael Pettis. (2020), *Trade Wars Are Class Wars: How Rising Inequality Distorts the Global Economy and Threatens International Peace*, New Haven: Yale University Press.

Kotilainen, Konsta. (2022), 'A Cosmopolitan Reading of Modern Monetary Theory', *Global Society*, 36 (1): 89–112. https://www.tandfonline.com/doi/full/10.1080/13600826.2021.1898343.

Kotilainen, Konsta. (2024), *From Monetary Sovereignty to Macroeconomic Policy Autonomy? Examining Promises, Limitations, and Reform Possibilities of a Nation-State-Centric Macroeconomic Governance Architecture*. Doctoral Dissertation. Helsinki: University of Helsinki. https://helda.helsinki.fi/items/1924f0f8-e788-461d-a7c5-8c59aa2da136.

Kotilainen, Konsta, and Heikki Patomäki. (2020), 'Towards a Helsinki Approach to Global Political Economy. Integrating Pluralist Economic Theorisation and Critical IPE'. Helsinki Centre for Global Political Economy Working Paper, 01/2020, Helsinki: University of Helsinki. https://helda.helsinki.fi/server/api/core/bitstreams/6bce8402-b026-495d-a666-8d8e2e137587/content.

Kotilainen, Konsta, and Heikki Patomäki. (2022), 'From Fragmentation to Integration: On the Role of Explicit Hypotheses and Economic Theory in Global Political Economy', *Global Political Economy*, 1 (1): 80–107.

Lees, Nicholas. (2021), 'The Brandt Line After Forty Years: The More North–South Relations Change, the More They Stay the Same?', *Review of International Studies*, 47 (1): 85–106.

Linklater, Andrew. (2006), 'The Harm Principle and Global Ethics', *Global Society*, 20 (3): 329–43.

Linklater, Andrew. (2011), *The Problem of Harm in World Politics: Theoretical Investigations*, Cambridge: Cambridge University Press.

Markwell, Donald. (2006), *John Maynard Keynes and International Relations*, Oxford: Oxford University Press.

Martins, Nuno Ornelas. 2009. 'Sen's Capability Approach and Post Keynesianism: Similarities, Distinctions, and the Cambridge Tradition'. *Journal of Post Keynesian Economics*, 31 (4), 691–706.

Martins, Nuno Ornelas. (2014). *The Cambridge Revival of Political Economy*. Abingdon and New York: Routledge.

Mini, V. Peter. (1991), 'The Anti-Benthamism of J.M. Keynes: Implications for General Theory', *American Journal of Economics and Sociology*, 50 (4): 453–68.

Mitchell, William, Wray, L. Randall, and Martin Watts. (2019), *Macroeconomics*, London: Red Globe Press.

Moore, G. E. (1903/1993), *Principia Ethica*, Cambridge: Cambridge University Press.

Nussbaum, C. Martha. (2006), *Frontiers of Justice: Disability, Nationality, Species Membership*, Cambridge, MA: Harvard University Press.

Nussbaum, C. Martha, and Ameartya Sen. (1993), *The Quality of Life*, Oxford: Oxford University Press.

Ocampo, Antonio José. (2017), *Resetting the International Monetary (Non)System*, Oxford: Oxford University Press.

Ord, Toby. (2020), *The Precipice. Existential Risk and the Future of Humanity*, London: Bloomsbury.

Parfit, Derek. (1984), *Reasons and Persons*, Oxford: Oxford University Press.

Patomäki, Heikki. (2013), *The Great Eurozone Disaster. From Crisis to Global New Deal*, London and New York: Zed Books.

Patomäki, Heikki. (2018), *Disintegrative Tendencies in Global Political Economy. Exists and Conflicts*, London and New York: Routledge.

Patomäki, Heikki. (2023), *World Statehood. The Future of World Politics*, Cham: Springer.

Patomäki, Heikki, and Teivo Teivainen. (2004), *A Possible World. Democratic Transformation of Global Institutions*, London and New York: Zed Books.

Putnam, Hilary, and Vivian Walsh (eds) (2012), *The End of Value-Free Economics*, Abingdon & New York: Routledge.

Robeyns, Ingrid, and Morten Fibieger Byskov. (2021), 'The Capability Approach', *The Stanford Encyclopedia of Philosophy* (Fall 2021 Edition), Edward N. Zalta (ed.). https://plato.stanford.edu/archives/fall2021/entries/capability-approach/.

Ruggie, John Gerard. (1982), 'International Regimes, Transactions, and Change: Embedded Liberalism in the Postwar Economic Order', *International Organization*, 36 (2): 379–415.

Russell, Bertrand. (1935/2004), *In Praise of Idleness*, Abingdon & New York: Routledge.

Sen, Amartya. (2009), *The Idea of Justice,* London: Allen Lane.

Sen, Amartya. (2015), 'The Economic Consequences of Austerity'. https://www
.newstatesman.com/uncategorized/2015/06/amartya-sen-economic-consequences
-austerity.

Stiglitz, E. Joseph. (2002), *Globalization and Its Discontents,* New York and London:
W.W. Norton & Company.

Stiglitz, E. Joseph. (2003), 'Dealing with Debt. How to Reform the Global Financial
System', *Harvard Relations Council International Review,* 25 (1): 54–9.

Stiglitz, E. Joseph. (2006), *Making Globalization Work,* New York and London: W.W.
Norton & Company.

Stiglitz, E. Joseph. (2012), *The Price of Inequality. How Today's Divided Society
Endangers Our Future,* New York and London: W.W. Norton & Company.

Stiglitz, E. Joseph, and Bruce Greenwald. (2010) 'Towards A New Global Reserve
System', *Journal of Globalization and Development,* 1 (2): 1–24.

Tobin, James. (1978), 'A Proposal for International Monetary Reform', *Eastern Economic
Journal,* 4 (3): 153–9.

van 't Klooster, Jens. (2021), 'Technocratic Keynesianism: A Paradigm Shift Without
Legislative Change', *New Political Economy.* DOI: 10.1080/13563467.2021.2013791.

Weber, Max. (1905/2001), *The Protestant Ethic and the Spirit of Capitalism,* London:
Routledge.

Williamson, John (ed) (1990), *Latin American Adjustment: How Much Has Happened?,*
Washington: Institute for International Economics.

Wray, L. Randall. (2012), *Modern Money Theory. A Primer on Macroeconomics for
Sovereign Monetary Systems,* Basingstoke: Palgrave Macmillan.

Wright, Robert. (2000). *Nonzero: The Logic of Human Destiny.* New York: Pantheon
Books.

9

Designing the rules and principles of the International Clearing Union

Past and present debated issues

Adrien Faudot

Introduction

Once it has been established that the current international monetary system, based on the domination of the US dollar, is asymmetrical and unfair, penalizing one part of the world and reinforcing both the risk of economic crisis and its propagation, the search for structural reform is a step in the right direction. The relevance of Keynes' Clearing Union to solve the fundamental issues of our international monetary system has been illustrated many times over. Its objectives are appealing. The Union would unite national central banks and organize their mutual payments through a clearinghouse at its top. The latter would act like a central bank for central banks, that is, it would issue its own currency which would be the only accepted international money. Each participating country would recognize the International Clearing Union (hereafter, ICU) as a multilateral institution which would facilitate access to international means of payment, and each participant would have equal access to the payment system. It would preserve the existence of national currencies. The aim of this chapter is not to contest the conclusions of the supporters of the ICU but to bring some elements to be discussed. Although the ICU would solve several structural problems of the current USD-dominated international monetary system, the new institutional architecture underlying the ICU induces several major questions – which does not mean that the game is not worth the candle. In other words, the creation of the ICU has serious implications. Economists and policymakers of the 1930s and 1940s had anticipated some of them. It is useful to dig into the discussions of that time, when exchange controls and clearing agreements were much more topical than today, to understand the nature of these problems.

In this chapter, I discuss four major problems. The first one is the policy space of the member countries. I question the assumption according to which the ICU will necessarily increase the monetary and political sovereignty of the member countries and relieve them from outside external pressure. I argue that external pressure does not disappear – it cannot – but is redirected towards creditor countries in a more equitable way. The second problem is related to the exchange rate regime adopted by the ICU and more generally the long-term credibility of the whole institution. I assume that only a quite rigid fixed exchange rate regime would make sense for the ICU, with regard to its infrastructure and credibility. The third section is related to the question of cross-border financial flows, recorded by the balance of payment as short-term (portfolio investments) and long-term (foreign direct investments) investment flows. Some versions of the plan for an ICU ignore or reject the possibility of cross-border financial flows and assume a framework of financial deglobalization, while others include a financial infrastructure that allows potentially large financial flows – which admits the possibility of large disequilibrium within the system. The fourth question is related to the role of the State and economic planning. The establishment of the ICU involves the adoption of restrictions on businesses and individuals regarding currency matters, which can raise some objections in the business elite. To some extent, the State has to play a greater role in the economy with the ICU. This last section discusses the degree of State intervention and planning induced by the creation of the ICU.

Policy space in a rule-based world order

Economic policy space is a term used by economists interchangeably with macroeconomic policy autonomy or economic policy independence (Kotilainen 2024: 93). It can be defined as the ability of a country to pursue the relevant economic policies of its choice – at its discretion – especially monetary and fiscal policies to target some macroeconomic objectives (Ferrer and Kireyev 2023). The policy space is essential for a government willing to sustain Keynesian policies in a global deflationary environment or, for developing countries, industrial policies aiming at transforming in-depth the national economy.

Could the Clearing Union provide additional policy space to its member countries? This question is topical since in today's world economy, the dollar system is often accused of reducing the sovereignty of the countries that rely on the US dollar for their external economic transactions (Prates 2020). The more a country uses the US dollar instead of its national currency for its external transactions, the more it has to carefully follow 'sound' economic policies in order to keep a stable exchange rate with the US dollar. In addition, it has to follow the US foreign policy agenda with more or less autonomy to access the US dollar payments system (Faudot 2018). A country that desires to be sovereign may do its best to 'buy' its economic sovereignty through an export-led growth model and a large current account surplus on the model of China. However, this is a self-imposed harsh discipline and the economic and social price of this policy is high (Angrick 2018).

The argument of the loss of sovereignty with the US dollar dominance has to be nuanced. A country that is integrated into the global economy cannot pretend at any rate to be fully sovereign and independent. As emphasized by Paul Davidson (2006: 272), '[o]nce a nation decides to join a community of nations for both political and economic reasons then interdependence and feedback effects among the trading partners are inevitable'. This statement is true for all nations, although some of them may preserve a higher degree of sovereignty than others which remain dependent countries.

The International Clearing Union is often seen as the best alternative to US dollar dominance as it is supposed to be a compromise between global integration and national sovereignty. For instance, Einzig (1944) considers that Keynes' ICU allows the extension of the national banking system autonomy. The ICU allegedly allows great autonomy of monetary policy and at the same time protects the international monetary system from beggar-thy-neighbour policies of devaluation/depreciation. It is supposed to guarantee the supply of international liquidity up to certain limit. However, its general acceptance would rest *a priori* on strict mutually accepted rules and discipline – an international institution without rules being meaningless.

As emphasized by Meyer (1947) in his pre-war study of exchange controls in Germany,[1] one of the problems of the gold exchange standard was the fact that creditor countries recording inflows of gold (e.g. the United States) were not forced to adjust their monetary base and could continue to accumulate (and sterilize) large amounts of gold. Gold inflows in those countries were supposed to expand the monetary base of their economy, resulting in (reflationary) economic expansion and an increase in import from the rest of the world. The effective attitude of the creditor countries disrupts the imagined adjustment mechanism of the gold standard. Although in practice this above-described mechanism never worked as in theory (Bloomfield 1959), economists viewed the United States as well as French policies at the time as particularly harmful to Germany in the capacity of the latter to equilibrate its balance of payments. On the opposite, debtor countries applied deflationary adjustment policies (see Accominotti 2020). Therefore, the lack of any symmetrical rule or discipline in the gold exchange standard has contributed to growing asymmetries and the further development of disturbances, which resulted in exchange controls and bilateral clearings.

Keynes was also aware of this. His wish was to establish a rule-based world order. Keynes wrote that this dilemma between rules and discretion was the most difficult question to determine (Keynes 1980a: 73). In 1943, he discarded the gold standard on the ground that it was too rigid, stating that '[t]he error of the gold-standard lay in submitting national wage-policies to outside dictation' (Keynes 1980b: 33). However, he did not endorse the floating exchange rate regime. While freeing such 'wage-policies' from 'outside dictation' may result in full-employment policies, Keynes also recognized that exchange rate instability is a likely undesirable side-effect of the end of gold standard. He admitted that there was an inherent conflict between monetary sovereignty and the respect of a stable international monetary arrangement. Keynes (1980a: 181) thought that his proposals were about restoring a sort of gold standard without the disadvantages of the gold standard: 'we should not only return to the advantages of an international gold currency, but we might enjoy them more widely than was ever possible in practice with the old system under which at any given time only a minority of countries were actually working with free exchanges'.

According to Keynes, one of the main problems of the interwar gold exchange standard was that it lacked a symmetric externally imposed adjustment process, because

> the process of adjustment is *compulsory* for the debtor and *voluntary* for the creditor. If the creditor does not choose to make, or allow, his share of the adjustment, he suffers no inconvenience. (Keynes 1980a: 28, author's emphasis)

Keynes wanted to solve this asymmetry by introducing a symmetrical rule, the well-known fee on deficit and surplus beyond some levels. Hence, contrary to the most popular views, he did not want less rules. What he wanted was commonly agreed rules and fairly distributed burdens, alleviating – to some extent – the constraint on debtors and increasing the pressure on creditors. If policy space could be quantified, one may say that the global mass of 'policy space' would not increase with the Union. However, the new rules would have an expansionary effect, for the benefit of debtor countries.

In the August 1942 version of his proposal, Keynes wrote that '[w]e need an orderly and agreed method of determining the relative exchange values of national currency units, so that unilateral action and competitive exchange depreciations are prevented' (Keynes 1980a: 168). Therefore, it might be misleading to assert that Keynes openly assumed that his proposals were in favour of a greater policy space.

> It has been suggested that so ambitious a proposal is open to criticism on the ground that it requires from the members of the Currency Union a greater surrender of their sovereign rights than they will readily concede. [. . .] In the second place a greater surrender of sovereign rights must be in order in the post-war world than has been accepted hitherto. The arrangements proposed could be described as a measure of financial disarmament. (Keynes 1980a: 89)

Such set of rules applying to undisciplined or free-rider countries as planned in Keynes' ICU has also seduced some free-market economists leery of discretionary government policies. Keynes' plan was well acclaimed when it went. As reported by Patinkin (1979: 232), Henry Simons wrote a letter to Keynes after reading the proposals for an International Clearing Union. He stated, 'I have just finished reading the document itself and am pleased beyond even my high expectations. It strikes me not only as sound in its proposals, but as eminently judicious and statesmanlike in its whole argument.'[2]

In practice, the most successful experience of interstate clearing union in the twentieth century was the European Payments Union (1950–8), established at the level of Western Europe and including eighteen countries. The EPU was managed by a technocratic body of unelected economists and policymakers, all of them strictly following the policy objectives of Washington in the context of the Cold War. It successfully overcame post-war bilateral clearing through the creation of a regional multilateral clearing. It boosted intra-European trade. Washington needed to restore the industrial capacities of its Western allies against the Soviet Union and the threat of communism. The United States, was the leading power and conductor of the regional clearing union without being a member of the regional clearing union. Thanks to the US leadership, the national discrepancies within the EPU did not prevent the smooth functioning of the Clearing Union. Hence the United States was the *Deus Ex Machina*. The ability of the EPU members to design policies which would depart from the other member countries was very limited in this Union. But today's analysts have good reason to believe that this lack of room for manoeuvre contributed to the success of the EPU.

Although the ICU would not significantly improve member countries' policy space, it would put an end to the possibility of using the payment system for geopolitical purposes. It would not be possible to unilaterally deny a country the access to the bancor payments system, since it is shielded from national decisions. This move would represent an improvement in autonomy in terms of foreign policy for each member nation. Sanctions using the payment system can only exist if they are taken in concert by the Governing Board of the ICU. They can also survive in the form of secondary sanctions – which remain extremely powerful sanctions using, for example, the threat of being banned from a national market (see, e.g., McDowell 2023).

Long-term stability and credibility

This section extends the former and focuses more specifically on the problem of exchange rates between the members' currencies within the ICU. This problem is a fundamental one. It was debated at length during the 1930s and further discussed in the BW negotiations. This is not surprising, as economists had been discussing exchange rate regimes for decades, even before Bretton Woods. What should be the exchange rate regime of the ICU?

As a foreword, it is worth noting that on one hand, floating exchange rates are still associated with Friedman and the current neoliberal era. On the other hand, fixed exchange rate regimes are currently unpopular among post-Keynesian and progressive economists. As a result, the most recent ICU-like proposals emphasized the exchange rate flexibility of Keynes' proposal. The authors writing on Keynes' clearing union argue that Keynes was supporting 'fixed but adjustable exchange rates' (Whyman 2015: 404) or 'adjustable peg' (Iwamoto 1995: 40; see also Cedrini and Fantacci 2018). Such a formulation is convenient but not very clear, either in terms of policy recommendation or in terms of long-term credibility. When should a member country be authorized to devalue or revalue its currency?

In the first version of the plan (8 September 1941), Keynes wrote: 'Each national currency to have a fixed value (subject to what follows about provisions for change) determined when the Currency Union is set up in terms of the bank money of the Clearing Bank, which would be itself expressed in terms of a unit of gold' (Keynes 1980a: 34). A fixed value meant a fixed exchange rate.

It is true, however, that Keynes wanted some flexibility in the establishment of the exchange rates, allowing depreciation for countries experiencing current account deficits beyond a certain threshold. The extent of the depreciation was capped: 'A member state may not depreciate the rate of exchange of its local currency in terms of bancor, unless it is a Deficiency Country; and the amount of the depreciation within a year shall not exceed 5 per cent without the permission of the Governing Board' (Keynes 1980a: 79). A Deficiency country is a member country whose debit balance has exceeded a quarter of its quota (for a certain period, e.g. a year).[3]

Noteworthy, Keynes was himself not clear at all on the subject of exchange rate regime, as acknowledged by Cesarano (2015) and Cedrini and Fantacci (2018: 154). For instance, he celebrated the sterling departure from the gold exchange standard but proposed different types of fixity in various proposals during his career. He changed his mind several times regarding his recommendations, especially during the 1930s. One of Keynes' concerns, when he conceived the clearing union, was nevertheless to stabilize exchange rates to avoid the disastrous competitive depreciations of the 1930s.[4] The main adjustment mechanism of the ICU in case of disequilibrium was not the exchange rate adjustment but the reflationary (preferably) / deflationary (as a last resort solution) policies resulting from the incentives mechanism of the interest rates applying on bancor balances (negative for both the debtor and the creditor central bank beyond some threshold).

The main argument in favour of fixity is that the ICU is often compared to the central bank of the national central banks. The analogy has been popular among all the promoters of the ICU. Triffin (1960: 40–1), another strong supporter of the International Clearing Union, used this analogy to compare the national histories of banking systems which resulted in the creation of national central banking, and the parallel (hopefully) future perspective of the international monetary system, with the creation of a clearing fund. According to Keynes (1980a: 72), 'The idea underlying such a Currency Union is simple, namely to generalise the essential principle of banking, as it is exhibited within any closed system.' The principle of banking rests on the overdraft economy allowing endogenous money creation ultimately supervised by the central banks, which guarantee the functioning of the payments system over time. Kregel (2017: 67) writes that '[a]s long as all debtors are members of the clearing and settled within it, there can only be individual divergences between debts and credits, but not for the system as a whole'. However, the assumption holds only with the fixity of exchange rates between these members.

In the national banking system, the central bank supervises and unifies the whole banking system. A commercial bank has the discretionary power to create (private) money through overdraft as long as it can comply with the rules of the Central Bank. Only in this way, this commercial bank's money creation is accepted by the rest of the banking system, as an interoperable means of payment (Cipollone 2024). The central bank unifies the exchange rates of private banks' monies at par value. For central bankers, there is no question about devaluing or revaluing the exchange rate of a private bank's money – such a movement would result in harmful balance sheet effects. In addition, the logic of compensation rests on an expansion of trade over time, which means that any prospect for devaluation would involve an exchange rate risk borne by the clearinghouse (i.e. by the creditor members of the clearing house). As a result, devaluations and appreciations are possible but they weaken the entire structure.

The advantage of retaining national currencies and not transforming the Clearing Union into a monetary union lies in the possibility, in the event of a major problem, of modifying the bancor exchange rate of a member economy. However, this possibility must be exceptional. The participating countries would not easily tolerate exchange rate variation of the national currencies against the ICU unit (bancor or whatever the name of the unit of account). First, there would be no market for bancor, and foreign exchange markets would be suppressed so there would be no market-led process to assess the extent of the devaluation. Furthermore, the act of depreciation/ appreciation of national currencies induces a way of adjustment alternative to/in competition with the real adjustment desired by Keynes (the latter being mainly an expansionary adjustment of surplus countries through higher volumes of consumption/ imports).

Hence the use of the comparison between the national and international levels is interesting, but it has deep implications. It is doubtful that the exchange rate could be easily devalued even to the extent suggested by Keynes' plan. The fixity of the exchange rate, so dear to the banking principle and the functioning of the clearing house, could be saved by the introduction of cross-border financial flows into the institutional architecture of the ICU.

Financial account of the balance of payment

The concept of the Balance of Payment was coined by Hume in 1752 and has been elaborated by macroeconomists since then. When the first models of the International Clearing Union appeared, the concept of the balance of payments could therefore not be ignored. However, the flows that are recorded in those models were mostly limited to the international trade of goods. This is particularly true for the models of Clearing Unions that were elaborated in the 1930s (Milhaud 1933; Einzig 1935). The absence of cross-border financial flows in those models did not seem that international finance did not exist. International finance was already of great significance – although not as much as today. At this time, most of the reformers agreed that the amount of cross-border financial flows should be lowered even in times of peace because financial interdependence had been harmful to the world's economic stability in the 1920s and 1930s. The reformers promoted a sort of financial deglobalization. Keynes, in a sense, was also in 1941–3 in this *zeitgeist*.

In Keynes' Clearing Union, the emphasis is put on the current account transactions. Keynes proposed to calculate the ICU quota only with the amount of current account balance.[5] It would be dishonest to claim that Keynes had not thought about the issue of international investment flows at all. Regarding the possibility of allowing long-term finance and development finance, Keynes (1980a: 175) wrote that a surplus country could choose the option of recycling its surplus to finance the development of 'backward' countries. In parallel, Keynes relied on the creation of the International Investment Board alongside the Clearing Union. On the question of international investment, Keynes hoped that the United States, as the post-war largest creditor nation, would take the initiative of a proposal. Be that as it may, Keynes' ICU proposal is often – maybe in a too simplistic way – summarized as an institution whose desire is to reach current account equilibrium regardless of the financial need of the country.

As we will see in the following section, the ICU induces exchange controls, which means that cross-border capital flows should be controlled (Helleiner 2015). However, 'controlling' capital flows does not mean 'preventing' them to reach their destination. Should the flows be simply prohibited by the regulatory agency or should they be authorized – if not totally prohibited, under which criteria should they be prevented from reaching their destination? One may be tempted to conclude that the government could ban cross-border flows as finance could be entirely 'nationalized'. The domestic financial system could take over the role of the rest of the world and supply credit to the domestic economy, simply by endogenous money creation. However, while 'nationalization' of the financial system is seducing at first sight, it rapidly encounters problems when confronting the domestic economy with the rest of the world, especially when it becomes necessary to import goods from abroad. As developing countries often need to import capital goods and need to finance it, banning cross-border financial flows is rarely an option. The external constraint, already dealt with in the two previous sections, gets in back through the window.

According to several post-Keynesian authors (e.g. Toporowski 2018), the ICU to be created should facilitate cross-border flows as they are of utmost importance for economic development. If the ICU is designed according to these rules of cross-border financing, the current account equilibrium is no longer the targeted objective of the Union, at least in the short run. The main achievement of the Union would be the creation of an efficient structure of trade financing and investment financing for economic development and economic peace. We can mention the Schumacher-Kalecki proposal of 1943 (Kalecki and Schumacher 1943). The two Oxford economists proposed the differentiation between two categories of countries. The developing countries, on the one hand, and the advanced economies, on the other hand. The developing countries would be authorized to accumulate bancor deficits because the investment in these countries involves huge spending and disequilibrium of the current account for several years. The members of the Clearing Union could therefore neglect current account equilibrium except in the (very) long run if they experience a process of economic convergence leading to a similar level of economic development – and therefore they would belong to the same category of countries. The international institution should establish clear criteria to declare that countries are 'advanced' or 'developing', which is another difficult task subject to debate and arbitrary decisions. Once these countries are declared 'developing countries' they benefit from some advantages. They could even have the right to discriminate against advanced countries' exports to boost the mutual trade between developing countries.

According to Kalecki and Schumacher (1943), the surplus country (automatically financing the deficit country) should be rewarded by the ICU with a positive (not negative) rate of interest on its bancor balances. Otherwise, the surplus country will be encouraged to stop exporting goods and services to the deficit country as there would be no incentives to export. Kalecki & Schumacher warned that the exporting country could prefer a recessionist policy of contracting export rather than a policy of accumulating useless bancor balances. In a sense, the Clearing Union established by Nazi Germany experienced this problem during the war.[6] Germany ended the war with a large deficit recorded in the clearinghouse of Berlin, which encouraged some of its partners (allied and neutral countries) to stop exporting goods to Germany (BIS 1944). However, even a positive rate of interest should be accompanied by the perspective of an economic recovery of deficit countries to be able to 'convert' in the future the positive balance of bancor into imports of goods and services.

Economic planning and controls

In practice, all the experiences of international clearing have entailed exchange controls and a certain degree of planning. Exchange controls are 'the channeling of all foreign exchange operations through national central banks or ad hoc institutions' (Hirschman 1951: 61). The experiences of bilateral (e.g. during the 1930s in Continental Europe) or regional (e.g. during the 1950s in Europe) clearing have been characterized by more or less strict exchange controls and planning.

The first bilateral clearing agreements of 1931 followed the establishment in the summer of 1931 of exchange controls which were the desperate means to retain foreign exchanges in Austria, Hungary and Germany. In such a situation, exchange controls were tied to clearing agreements out of necessity: it was necessary to hoard gold and convertible currencies which were going to be exhausted. Clearing agreements were then conceived to 'free' trade which was blocked by exchange control. The reverse is also true: clearing agreements could not function properly without exchange controls.

The reason is that the foreign exchange market needs to be shut down and should not reappear in any private centres. The central bank must have a monopoly on foreign exchange dealings for the success of the clearing machinery. As inaugurated in 1930s Germany, 'Private dealings in foreign exchange are likewise prohibited', which should be accompanied by 'the obligation for a person to declare, deposit or surrender the currencies which he has or expects to have at his disposal', as described by Piatier (1939: 102–3). Transactions in the national currency abroad are forbidden too, which means that the export of currency is forbidden and punished. To make this measure effective, the government also forbids the reimportation of the national currency (Piatier 1939: 107).

During the 1930s, an increasing number of governments resorted to exchange controls and clearing agreements mainly because of severe balance of payments problems. The establishment of these measures, however, does not solve the balance of payments problems by themselves. As a result, the only option left to the government is to apply quantitative restrictions. Exchange controls often lead to quantitative restrictions preventing outward investments and imports, since all external transactions were subject to authorization and a large part of them were forbidden due to liquidity shortage (Triffin 1946a). In most practical cases, the establishment of quantitative restrictions involves the distribution of licences on imports (subject to regulations) and quotas. When discussing the international monetary reform in 1943, Keynes (1980b: 33) also recognized that '[a] communist country is in a position to be very successful'. In some cases, it is possible to imagine various techniques relying more on market-led mechanisms to avoid too heavy bureaucratic regulations. For instance, Triffin (1946b) proposed an auction mechanism to distribute the licences of importations for unessential imports (luxury products), while essential imports would be given the highest priority.

Assume that the ICU scheme is eventually adopted in our current world. With the ICU, the liquidity shortage disappears completely, since there are no limits to the ability to finance international trade. Bancor will be the transferable unit used to settle international transactions. Individuals and any private actors will not be allowed to use national currencies outside the national economy. However, the success of the ICU rests on the assumption that private actors will not develop private solutions to circumvent the public infrastructure (e.g. by using foreign national key currencies that are not part of the Clearing Union in their trade). The central bank's monopoly over foreign exchange dealings seems a prerequisite to prevent the development of any alternative to the ICU.

Exchange controls would be part of the institutional scheme in the sense that foreign exchange markets lead to the dominance of one or a handful of key national currencies when left free to operate, which is obvious in our current monetary system. The international monetary reform implementing the ICU must therefore prevent private agents from using national currencies. Therefore, even in the absence of an international liquidity shortage, controls would be necessary. Controls provide for the general acceptability of the bancor (i.e. the newly created monetary unit) and the exclusion of all the other national key currencies from international trade. Keynes (1980a: 129, author's emphasis) was aware of the fact that the ICU makes a 'machinery' necessary:

> It is widely held that control of capital movements, both inward and outward, should be a permanent feature of the post-war system-at least so far as we are concerned. If control is to be effective, it probably involves the *machinery* of exchange control for *all* transactions, even though a general open licence is given to all remittances in respect of current trade. But such control will be more difficult to work, especially in the absence of a postal censorship, by unilateral action than if movements of capital can be controlled *at both ends.*

Helleiner (2015) has insisted on controls 'at both ends' as an innovative and essential feature of Keynes' reform, making it easier to implement and more efficient. The defence of controls in 1943 was not shocking for many economists and even welcomed by H. D. White at Bretton Woods. Nevertheless, the proposal was watered down due to American domestic opposition, especially from the 'New York Financial community' (Helleiner 2015: 421). The need for exchange controls explains certainly partly the fact that free-market economists often opposed all forms of clearing agreements including the ICU. According to Sayers (1956: 230), the British Treasury was against the German-type exchange control system at least up to 1939 because of 'the high degree of state interference and control of every branch of economic life inevitably involved', and 'the large number of officials needed to work the system' – the estimate being circa 30,000 people employed in Germany at the end of the 1930s.

Keynes' opinion seems difficult to determine on the subject. On the eve of the war, he was still reluctant to recommend exchange controls. Writing on Nazi Germany's trade methods and exchange controls in 1939, 'their technique does not offer a good model for us. I have not reached a decided opinion on the point' (Keynes 1978: 12). He seems to have changed his mind only with the outbreak of the war and the worsening international position of Britain. But he was embarrassed by the exchange restrictions problem until the end of the conflict. During the Spring of 1944, he eventually defended in the British Parliament the result of the Bretton Wood conference, that is, the Anglo-American Joint Statement which planned to restore currency convertibility as soon as possible after the war. In 1944, he read Hayek's *Road to Serfdom* on the boat bringing him back to Britain. He wrote a letter to Hayek saying a lot of positive comments. Although he was not fully in line with Hayek, he expressed his distrust of planners who did not share the moral values that he and Hayek had in common.

For the same reason mentioned by Sayers, Hayek (1944) was clear in his opposition to any sort of exchange control.

> The extent of the control over all life that economic control confers is nowhere better illustrated than in the field of foreign exchanges. Nothing would at first seem to affect private life less than a state control of the dealings in foreign exchange, and most people will regard its introduction with complete indifference. Yet the experience of most continental countries has taught thoughtful people to regard this step as the decisive advance on the path to totalitarianism and the suppression of individual liberty.

Should the channelling of transactions be necessarily followed by quantitative restrictions, quotas, or other measures aiming at preventing some trade? Triffin, who was economist at the Federal Reserve, then at the IMF after the Second World War, assumed that controls could be permissive and compatible with capitalist societies (Faudot 2022). The necessity (or not) to adopt economic planning as a domino effect is difficult to assess. In today's world economy, we could assume that an international clearinghouse replaces the international operations of the US dollar banking system. The network of central banks would be necessarily established as a permanent infrastructure, at the top of which would reign the clearinghouse. This would need exchange controls, for the reasons detailed above.

In the twenty-first century, it might be possible to adopt efficient controls on financial flows which would not prevent both existing market mechanisms and instantaneity of capital flows through the creation of a monopolistic structure responsible for recording and carrying out financial flows and international payments.[7] We cannot distinguish any technical or logical impossibility for such a financial infrastructure involving central banks' monopoly over foreign exchanges. The digitalization and technical innovations applied to financial systems have facilitated the standardization of the financial system and, to some extent, its centralization.[8] It has improved transaction speed, reduced the cost of payment infrastructures, and simplified authentication and security procedures (Bindseil and Pantelopoulos 2022). All these features favour the use of the payment infrastructure as they make it even more attractive for private and public players. Such a monopoly also enables greater control over transactions. For the private agent willing to circumvent the monopolistic financial platform, the cost-benefit ratio of the evasion could be too high to be tested.

This scenario rests on the assumption that the ICU will be based on a system of overdraft recording large financial flows to ensure that all balance of payment disequilibrium will not provoke the end of the institution. If the structure is based on strict current account equilibrium, some degree of planning and protectionism is expected to be on the agenda each time a country is under threat of being sanctioned for a large deficit.

Conclusion

The International Clearing Union (ICU) is a highly desirable institution. It is desirable because the current international monetary system is deeply asymmetrical and creates unfair economic and financial conditions for a large part of the world economy. The establishment of the ICU will solve many problems, and, nevertheless, create several new challenges that must be addressed. This chapter argues that some of them have been neglected or understudied in most of the recent discussions of the Clearing Union.

First, the ICU is essentially a rule-based institution. It aimed to restore some kind of rule-based multilateral, fair, and symmetrical discipline in the international monetary system, instead of a gold exchange standard (until 1971) – in which the alleged discipline was easy to circumvent for several creditor countries – and the dollar standard (as of 1971). For the former reason as well as for the functioning of the clearinghouse at the centre of the ICU, the exchange rate regime of the ICU rests on fixed rates which help to cement and unify the international monetary system.

Second, the adjustment process of the members' economy should not pass through devaluation but other policies, expansionary when possible and desirable, as some post-Keynesian economists called for. This mode of adjustment is designed to make it easier to achieve full employment without resorting to devaluation, which in turn relies on the downward adjustment of real wages. Third, the whole structure should deal with financial flows, organizing the recycling of surplus for deficit countries, which involves to relinquish the concept of current account equilibrium. Fourth, the ICU should be prepared for the implementation of exchange controls, its main concern being that no other means of payment should compete with the bancor in order to preserve the functioning of the adjustment mechanism.

The chapter uses experiences and discussions in twentieth-century history to understand the fundamental issues that could emerge from the establishment of the ICU. The lessons are mainly drawn from the experiences of bilateral and regional clearing agreements from 1931 to the 1950s. These lessons have, however, some shortcomings. At the time of the bilateral and regional clearing experiences between 1931 and 1958 in Western Europe (and beyond), economists and policymakers had to face severe balance of payments problems and hard currency shortages. This situation has changed dramatically, as currency shortage is no longer a major threat. The context of the twenty-first century is therefore different concerning the incentives underlying the establishment of the Clearing Union, but we still have good reasons to call for it.

Notes

1 Dr Fritz Meyer was invited to contribute in 1939 to the twelfth conference of the International Institute for International Cooperation organized by John Condliffe,

on exchange controls. The reports of the conference (held in Bergen, Norway) were published in several volumes in 1947 (for the French version), after the war. Some of them are available online: https://atom.archives.unesco.org/documents-concernant -letude-des-politiques-economiques-et-la-paix-conference-de-bergen-1939

2　Henry Simons is well known for his essay on 'rules vs authorities in monetary policy' (Simons 1936).

3　The quotas refer to the sum of each country's exports and imports on the average of the pre-war years.

4　'I should be reluctant, apart from the small change suggested above, to give much more fluidity, because the atmosphere of settled exchange rates seems to me to be an important ingredient in achieving post-war stability. If money wage rates in a particular country have got thoroughly out of gear, there is nothing to be done but to alter the exchanges. In other contingencies the possible benefit to be gained is, I am sure, greatly exaggerated, and it would be exceedingly easy to do more harm than good. This is the lesson of nearly all the depreciations which took place after the last war' (Keynes 1980a: 106).

5　'The initial quotas might be fixed by reference to the sum of each country's exports and imports on the average of (say) the three pre-war years' (Keynes 1980a: 118).

6　Germany created a multilateral clearing centre in Berlin to allow the multilateralization of payments as of Fall 1940. The structure was perverted by Nazi's increasing exploitation of occupied and allied countries, but it was the most contemporary concrete experience that could help Kalecki and Schumacher to design a better plan.

7　According to Alfred Hirschman, more than seventy years ago, 'It is possible to imagine a situation in which convertibility in the most general sense prevails, with all foreign exchange freely bought from the central bank and all foreign exchange earnings sold to it against local currency' (Hirschman 1951: 61).

8　Some innovations may increase the likeliness of fragmentation of the payment system, which nuances the argument (see again Bindseil and Pantelopoulos 2022).

References

Accominotti, O. (2020), 'International Monetary Regimes: The Interwar Gold Exchange Standard', in S. Battilossi, Y. Cassis, and K. Yago (eds), *Handbook of the History of Money and Currency*, 633–64, Cham: Springer.

Angrick, S. (2018), 'Structural Conditions for Currency Internationalization: International Finance and the Survival Constraint', *Review of International Political Economy*, 25 (5): 699–725.

Bindseil, U., and G. Pantelopoulos. (2022), 'Towards the Holy Grail of Cross-Border Payments', ECB Working Paper, n° 2022/2693, European Central Bank.

BIS (1944), Annual Report. Basel: Bank for International Settlements.

Bloomfield, A. (1959). *Monetary Policy under the International Gold Standard: 1880-1914*. New-York: Federal Reserve of New York.

Cedrini, M., and L. Fantacci. (2018), 'The Clearing Union as Keynes's Intellectual Testament', in Rosselli, A., Naldi, N., & Sanfilippo, E. (eds), *Money, Finance and Crises in Economic History: The Long-Term Impact of Economic Ideas*, 145–57, London: Routledge.

Cesarano, F. (2015). Indian Currency and Finance: John Maynard Keynes's Prismatic View of the International Monetary System. *History of Political Economy*, 47 (2), 241–269.

Cipollone, P. (2024), 'Modernising Finance: The Role of Central Bank Money'. Keynote speech by Piero Cipollone, Member of the Executive Board of the ECB, at the 30th Annual Congress of Financial Market Professionals organised by Assiom Forex. https://www.ecb.europa.eu//press/key/date/2024/html/ecb.sp240209~d481464c19.en.html.

Davidson, P. (2006), 'A Framework for Analysing Dollarization', in M. Vernengo (ed), *Monetary Integration and Dollarization: No Panacea*, 259–75, Cheltenham: Edward Elgar.

Einzig, P. (1935), *The Exchange Clearing System*, London: Macmillan.

Einzig, P. (1944), *Currency After the War: The British and American Plans*, London: Nicholson & Watson.

Faudot, A. (2018), 'The US Dollar and its Payments System: Architecture and Political Implications', *Review of Keynesian Economics*, 6 (1): 83–95.

Faudot, A. (2022), 'Robert Triffin and the Case for Exchange Controls', *Cahiers d'économie politique* 81: 163–89.

Ferrer, J., and A. Kireyev. (2023), 'Policy Space Index: Short-Term Response to a Catastrophic Event', *Economic Analysis and Policy*, 79: 837–59.

Hayek, F. A. (1944), *The Road to Serfdom*, London: Routledge.

Helleiner, E. (2015), 'Controlling Capital Flows "at Both Ends": A Neglected (but Newly Relevant) Keynesian Innovation from Bretton Woods', *Challenge*, 58 (5): 413–27.

Hirschman, A. O. (1951), 'Types of Convertibility', *The Review of Economics and Statistics*, 33 (1): 60–2.

Iwamoto, T. (1995), 'The Keynes Plan for an International Clearing Union Reconsidered', *The Kyoto University Economic Review*, 65 (2): 27–42.

Kalecki, M., and E. F. Schumacher. (1943), 'New Plans for International Trade: International Clearing and Long-Term Lending', *Bulletin of the Oxford University Institute of Economics & Statistics*, 5 (S5): 29–32.

Keynes, J. M. (1978), 'Activities 1939–1945. Internal War Finance', in D. E. Moggridge (ed), *The Collected Writings of John Maynard Keynes*, XXI, London and Basingstoke: The Macmillan Press.

Keynes, J. M. (1980a), 'Activities 1940–1944. Shaping the Post-War World: The Clearing Union', in Moggridge Donald (ed), *The Collected Writings of John Maynard Keynes*, XXV, London and Basingstoke: The Macmillan Press.

Keynes, J. M. (1980b), 'Activities 1941–1946. Shaping the Post-War World: Bretton Woods and Reparations', in D. E. Moggridge (ed), *The Collected Writings of John Maynard Keynes*, XXVI, London and Basingstoke: The Macmillan Press.

Kotilainen, K. (2024), *From Monetary Sovereignty to Macroeconomic Policy Autonomy?: Examining Promises, Limitations, and Reform Possibilities of a Nation-State-Centric Macroeconomic Governance Architecture*, Doctoral Dissertation, University of Helsinki.

Kregel, J. (2017), 'The Clearing Union Principle as the Basis for Regional Financial Arrangements in Developing Countries', in *Debt Vulnerabilities in Developing Countries: A New Debt Trap?*, II. United Nations Conference on Trade and Development, 57–92.

McDowell, D. (2023), *Bucking the Buck: US Financial Sanctions and the International Backlash Against the Dollar*, Oxford: Oxford University Press.

Meyer, F. (1947), 'Le contrôle des changes en Allemagne', in *Le contrôle des changes. Tome II. Rapports nationaux: Allemagne, Amérique Latine, Argentine et Bulgarie*, Institut international de coopération intellectuelle, Paris, 11–97.

Milhaud, E. (1933), 'A Gold Truce', *Annals of Collective Economy*, 9 (1): 1–153.

Patinkin, D. (1979), 'Keynes and Chicago', *The Journal of Law and Economics*, 22 (2): 213–32.

Piatier, A. (1939), *Report on the Study of Exchange Control* (Vol. 1), Paris: International Institute of Intellectual Cooperation.

Prates, D. (2020), 'Beyond Modern Money Theory: A Post-Keynesian Approach to the Currency Hierarchy, Monetary Sovereignty, and Policy Space', *Review of Keynesian Economics*, 8 (4): 494–511.

Sayers, R. S. (1956), *Financial Policy, 1939–45*, London: HM Stationery Office.

Simons, H. C. (1936), 'Rules Versus Authorities in Monetary Policy', *Journal of Political Economy*, 44 (1): 1–30.

Toporowski, J. (2018), 'Multilateralism and Regional Trade and Payments', in N. Levy and J. Bustamante (eds), *Financialisation in Latin America: Challenges of the Export-Led Growth Model*, London: Routledge.

Triffin, Robert. (1946a), Exchange Control and Quantitative Trade Restrictions, *Review of Foreign Developments*. Board of the Federal Reserve, January 14. Retrieved from FRASER, Federal Reserve of St Louis (Accessed on October 24, 2021). https://fraser .stlouisfed.org/archival-collection/marriner-s-eccles-papers-1343/review-foreign -developments-465871.

Triffin, R. (1946b), 'National Central Banking and the International Economy', *The Review of Economic Studies*, 14 (2): 53–75.

Triffin, R. (1948), 'Exchange Control and Equilibrium', in *Foreign Economic Policy for the United States*, 413–25, Harvard: Harvard University Press.

Triffin, Robert (1960), *Gold and the Dollar Crisis: The future of convertibility*, New Haven: Yale University Press.

Whyman, P. B. (2015), 'Keynes and the International Clearing Union: A Possible Model for Eurozone Reform?', *JCMS: Journal of Common Market Studies*, 53 (2): 399–415.

10

The ecor as global special purpose money

Towards a green international monetary system to finance sustainable and just transformation

Nicolás Aguila, Paula Haufe and Joscha Wullweber

Introduction

Every country around the world is affected by the climate crisis. The sustainable transformation necessary to combat climate change is an all-encompassing process requiring deep economic, political, social, cultural and ecological changes in the way our society is organized. Recent reports from the UN Intergovernmental Panel on Climate Change (IPCC) highlight the fact that financing is a critical factor in the realization of sustainability (IPCC 2022). Hence, one of the required dimensions of the transformation process involves finding ways to ensure the availability of financial flows needed for sustainable investments. The financial means to pursue a sustainable transformation, however, are very unjustly distributed: While high-income countries have the capacity to create the money needed, middle and low-income countries do not (Löscher and Kaltenbrunner 2022). This state of affairs is particularly problematic considering that in general Global South countries contribute the least to worldwide carbon emissions while being the most affected by the adverse ecological and climate impacts thereof (Ghosh et al. 2022; Haag 2023). In particular, many of these countries are heavily exposed to losses from climate-change-induced extreme weather events such as floods, droughts and hurricanes, but also to other natural disasters (Perry 2021).

To date, developed countries continue to lag far behind the annual 100 billion US dollar climate finance commitment they made in 2009 at the fifteenth Conference of Parties (COP 15). Moreover, the UN recently called upon the Group of Twenty (G20) to increase affordable and long-term financing for sustainable development by at least 500 billion US dollars per year (United Nations 2023a). However, the actual financing need far exceeds that figure. The Grantham Research Institute on Climate Change and the Environment estimates that emerging and developing countries will need to spend an annual amount of around 1 trillion US dollars by 2025 and 2.4 trillion US dollars by 2030 in order to pursue investments crucial to limit global warming to the target of 1.5 degrees (Bhattacharya et al. 2022). The report issued by the Independent High-Level Expert Group on Climate Finance elaborates that such spending is especially needed across the following three areas: (1) transformation of the energy system, (2) strengthening the adaptation capacity and resilience of climate-vulnerable countries, and (3) fostering sustainable agriculture and restoring natural capital and biodiversity damaged by human activity (Songwe et al. 2022).

In other words, the level of global finance has fallen far too short to effectively finance the required transformation (Attridge and Engen 2019). The vast majority of current funding (82 per cent) stems from bilateral and multilateral public sources, while the scale of private finance compared with levels in 2019 is relatively low and decreasing (OECD 2022). Additionally, the cost of capital (the rate of return required by investors) is two to three times as large in the Global South as it is in the Global North (Persaud 2023). Recent research shows that for these reasons foreign financial investors are unlikely to finance the green investments lacking in the Global South (Dafermos et al. 2021). This is the case, above all, because particularly in areas such as environmental conservation, restoration and protection, many sustainable projects are inherently high risk with little or no profit potential (Kedward et al. 2020; Bolton and Kacperczyk 2021; Christophers 2022).

The shaping of global financial flows is a highly political matter. Money itself is a political construct permeated by unequal and hierarchical power relations, both on the national and international level (Weber 1978). Considering how to create global financing opportunities for sustainable transformation requires examining power relations inscribed in the global financial architecture. The US dollar holds a central place in the current international monetary system. Located at the very top of the global currency pyramid, it is the unit of account in which most global trade and finance are denominated, and the currency which is used for reserve accumulation (Cohen and Benney 2014; Kaltenbrunner and Lysandrou 2017; Gopinath et al. 2020). Most importantly in the context of this paper, the US dollar is the medium of payment in which international balances are settled. Accordingly, one of the largest hurdles to financing sustainable and just transformation is the need on the part of Global South countries to acquire

US dollars to import and pay for the goods, services and technologies they require but do not (yet) produce for the sustainable transformation (Löscher and Kaltenbrunner 2022). Although the ultimate aim of transformation processes is certainly to strengthen local production and markets, the import of certain goods and services is unavoidable and will likely remain so, at least for some time to come. To move towards renewable energy sources, for example, countries need to import solar panels, wind turbines and other commodities that they do not yet have the capacity to produce themselves.

Most Global South countries, however, either lack US dollar reserves or cannot obtain the amount they need because they do not have sufficient trade surpluses. Access to foreign currency credit is either not an option or very expensive, and many of these countries are already highly indebted. As a result, proposals to provide finance to the Global South will continue to fall short in ambition unless a new, non-hierarchical international monetary system is created in accordance with principles of global justice. Accordingly, to overcome one of the largest problems in terms of financing sustainable transformation, we propose the establishment of a new international monetary system: A Green Bretton Woods System,[1] based on a new special purpose money that would operate on a global scale. Building on and expanding Keynes' idea for an International Clearing Union (ICU), the Green Bretton Woods System would include a Green World Central Bank (GWCB). The GWCB would be allowed to create its own unit of account: the ecor – a supranational special purpose currency similar to the one Keynes called 'bancor'. It would only be credited to and debited from the central banks of countries for the specific purpose of financing the sustainable transformation.

The GWCB would be able to expand its balance sheet, thereby creating money to finance sustainable projects throughout the world. The funds for such projects would not come from creditors but, as with any other central bank, would be created in the act of lending. This would allow for financial elasticity towards green projects, alleviating the financial constraints that exist under today's monetary regime. In this way, the amount of ecors in the system would adjust to the real demands for sustainable transformation and would not be limited by previous holdings of US dollars or any other currency. The system would accordingly make a decisive contribution to sustainable and just transformation by allowing countries, especially in the Global South, to finance necessary imports.

As our proposal specifically focuses on special purpose money, it is meant to supplement rather than supersede the current international monetary system.

It could, however, be a first step in setting up the infrastructure required to completely overcome the current hierarchy and to ultimately replace the current international monetary system with a more globally just system. During the transformation to a sustainable economy, the area of circulation of ecors would gradually expand and eventually displace the US dollar and other currently dominant currencies. Our proposal aligns with and extends proposals to reform the international monetary system that are currently being considered, above all, by the UN and the Bridgetown Initiative.

The remainder of the article is organized as follows: In section 2, we explain how money creation works and how it is embedded in power relations, including at a world level. Section 3 explores the limits of the current international monetary system to finance a sustainable and just transformation in the Global South. In section 4, we discuss the main characteristics of Keynes' proposal for an international monetary system. Section 5 details our proposal for the ecor within a Green Bretton Woods System. A concrete illustration of how the ecor would work is presented in section 6, followed by concluding remarks in the final section.

Money creation, power and global hierarchies

Before developing our approach to special purpose money, we consider it worthwhile and relevant to our topic to briefly explain how money creation works and why an understanding of money creation is important for the overall discussion of local and global special purpose money and the challenges posed in that connection.

In today's world, the nation-state proclaims a particular form of credit to be money, thus converting it into legal tender. While in principle any person can issue a promissory note with the hope that it will be accepted by another person, only commercial banks and nation-states, mostly via their central banks, are allowed to issue generally and legally accepted promissory notes (money). Consequently, the system is the product of conflicts of interest and power struggles. The contemporary monetary system evolved from those struggles as a historical compromise that granted commercial banks the right to create money by issuing loans. When a commercial bank extends credit, the money involved does not stem from another bank account as many mainstream economics textbooks still explain. Banks are not intermediaries of existing deposits or funds (McLeay et al. 2014). Instead, when issuing a loan, they create new money. This is possible because the money form constitutes an asset and, at the same time, a liability. In other words, money represents a credit relation (Mitchell-Innes 2004). The credit form issued by commercial banks is recognized by the state as a legal means of payment (Knapp 1924). More precisely: Via its central bank, a nation-state guarantees that credit issued by commercial banks will be traded with central bank money at par on demand. Accordingly, commercial bank credit is treated as if it were state money. When commercial banks settle their payments among themselves, however, they have to resort to central bank money. In the hierarchy of money forms, central bank money is at the top, followed by credit issued by commercial banks (Bell 2001; Mehrling 2013). Other types of credit – especially credit forms originating in financial markets but also regionally created special purpose monies – are situated at the level below commercial bank money.

There are also hierarchical differences among central bank monies, depending on which country the central bank belongs to. As already stated, the US dollar occupies the highest level as the undisputed global currency (Mehrling 2015; Murau et al. 2022). The lower levels of the pyramid are occupied by the currencies of Global South countries. Particularly, these countries face serious financial problems in achieving sustainable transformation. Although they can issue their own currency to finance green projects, they need US dollars, or other leading currencies, such as the euro or the pound, to import goods, services and green technologies that they cannot or prefer not to produce on their own. Since many countries in the Global South are dependent on imports and are unable or insufficiently able to generate or earn the foreign currency necessary to finance the goods they need from abroad, they face a constant shortage of US dollars (Löscher and Kaltenbrunner 2022).

Important conclusions on the potentials and limits of special purpose monies can be drawn from this understanding of money. First, as money is a form of credit, there is no natural limit to the amount that can be created. In theory, any green project is fundable as long as necessary resources are available and the actors involved are willing to accept the special purpose money in question. Second, if there is a shortage of legal tender, whether for legal reasons (e.g. a constitutional debt brake), ideological reasons (e.g. the dogma of austerity), or political-economic reasons (e.g. danger of inflation, imposed structural adjustment programmes), special purpose money can offer an alternative to national currencies.

This is one reason why in recent decades several proposals for local or complementary currencies, including local exchange trading systems (LETS), time banks, currencies such as the Ithaca Hours, and other convertible local currencies have been elaborated and put into practice with the aim of fostering sustainable agendas (Dittmer 2013). The objectives include (1) improving economic sustainability through the localization of production chains and the creation of alternative values,

(2) fostering environmental sustainability through the reduced ecological footprint of localized production and consumption and (3) promoting social sustainability through community-building, incentivizing neighbourly support, stimulating new networks of friendships and fostering democratic participation (Seyfang and Longhurst 2013; Gerber 2015; Cabaña and Linares 2022).

In this respect, the introduction of special purpose money has promising potential for overcoming constraints to financing green projects. However, the implementation of such a money form faces several challenges (Dittmer 2013). Considering the restricted scope of their circulation, complementary local currencies are not designed to finance infrastructure projects on the massive scale required to achieve climate change adaptation and mitigation goals. Furthermore, local currencies face the problem of convertibility into legal tender. Accordingly, they are not able to satisfy an important part of the financing needed for sustainable transformation because they cannot be used to pay for imports such as green technologies. Local currencies also face the problem of how to ensure the stability of their value. The question, in other words, is how to gain sufficient trust in, and acceptance for, a special money form to convince the public to start using it with sustained confidence. Additionally, to supervise the creation of this money form there would have to be an appropriate security mechanism, a control system, and/ or an oversight authority. To effectively advance sustainable transformation, the system in charge of creating any form of special purpose money would have to be vested with significant power. This raises the question of how to ensure state acceptance for the respective money form. All these considerations suggest the existence of serious limitations in the ability of local currencies to provide the kind of financing needed for sustainable transformation. In this paper, we undertake to demonstrate that there is, however, a conceivable solution to developing a form of special purpose money capable of overcoming these problems. Before detailing the specifics of our proposal, we argue that, for a variety of reasons, the current international monetary system constitutes a key barrier to the financing of a sustainable and just transformation.

The limits of the dollar-centred international monetary system to financing sustainable and just transformation

Several authors suggest that the United States and countries with currencies such as the euro and the pound, which are close to the top of the global currency hierarchy, possess the capacity to create enough money to fund a sustainable transformation (Nersisyan and Wray 2019; Galvin 2020). These authors contend that countries with dominant currencies would simply have to break with the neoliberal corset that guides their policymaking. This is basically because they either produce key resources domestically or can import them, given that every participant in the international monetary system is willing to accept their currencies as means of payment. For this reason, these countries could issue a significant amount of new money, for example, to hire workers, buy means of production (regardless of whether they are produced locally or abroad), or green technologies, unless they face constraints such as inflation. This, however, does not imply the absence of problems, as the initial creation of money is not enough: Credits must be put to productive use over time, financial stability must be preserved (among other things by avoiding a possible 'green financial bubble'), and mechanisms must be developed to solve the problem of money destruction that comes with repayment of debt (Murau et al. 2023).

By contrast, countries whose currency is lower down on the global currency pyramid face significant challenges in financing sustainable transformation (Althouse and Svartzman 2022; Löscher and Kaltenbrunner 2022; UNCTAD 2019). Countries in the Global South do not have sufficient trade surpluses or US dollar reserves, or do not have them in the amount required to pay for the imports needed for sustainable investment. Access to dollar-denominated credit is either not an option or too expensive, and many Global South countries are already highly indebted. One major hurdle in Global South countries is thus a lack of capital and the resulting contractionary effects on their economies, factors which are incompatible with sustainable development objectives. This problem is echoed by development scholars who point to the detrimental effects of external lending, capital outflows and debt crises (Eradze 2023). These effects have become stronger since the beginning of neoliberal globalization in the 1970s (Chang 2008).[2] Furthermore, as Althouse and Svartzman (2022) argue, the currency hierarchy constraining the development of financially subordinated countries is intertwined with an ecological hierarchy: the need to acquire US dollars leads peripheral countries to specialize in low value-added natural resources and polluting activities, enabling core countries, in turn, to appropriate said resources with devastating socio-ecological consequences. This makes it clear that an all-encompassing global transformation towards sustainable development must be firmly based on the transformation of the global monetary and financial system.

Against this background, international political and financial organizations have advocated for the mobilization of private finance towards sustainable objectives on a global scale (Bayliss and Van Waeyenberge 2018). This form of financing, however, has been variously criticized on the grounds that it lacks transparency and accountability (Bracking and Leffel 2021), and, most importantly, that the funds raised are insufficient in quantity and unjust in their consequences (Attridge and Engen 2019; Gabor 2021). Dafermos et al. (2021: 238) argue that the most prominent among the climate finance policies pursued will increase 'financial vulnerability in the Global South while doing little to achieve climate-aligned development'. Further studies on energy transition financing in Senegal, South Africa, and Zambia find that it sidelines local ownership while deepening financial dependencies (Claar 2020; Haag 2023; Elsner et al. 2021).

The limits of existing models to finance sustainable transformation have led to a series of alternative proposals. To mobilize the necessary funding, suggestions have been made to grant debt relief to countries of the Global South (Volz et al. 2021), to provide them with additional external finance through instruments such as debt-for-nature or debt-for-climate swaps (Essers et al. 2021), climate reparations (Perry 2021), and partial FX guarantees (Persaud 2023), or to issue and distribute International Monetary Fund (IMF) Special Drawing Rights (SDRs) (Aglietta and Coudert 2019). Although such proposals would be a step towards improving financing conditions for the Global South, they do not challenge the hierarchical character of the international monetary system, the powerful position of top currencies, and the financial subordination that constrains peripheral countries. Consequently, they fall short of bringing about the changes needed to counter the climate crisis on a global scale (Gallagher and Kozul-Wright 2022; Löscher and Kaltenbrunner 2022; Pettifor 2022; Svartzman and Althouse 2022).

The proposal by Aglietta and Coudert (2019) to bypass dollar dominance by moving towards a system based on IMF SDRs does, however, point to a number of possibilities that would enable this system to fund the process of sustainable transformation. Options include the setting up of a trust fund, the granting of SDR loans to development banks for carbon emission reduction pledged programmes, and the issuance of SDRs to capitalize a green fund for developing countries. While we agree on the need to move towards a more equitable system, we see the transfer of responsibility to the IMF as equally problematic, given that this international organization remains committed to austerity and its policy recommendations frequently run counter to ecological considerations (Mariotti 2022). In addition, the amount of liquidity in an SDR-based system increases exogenously rather than endogenously based on decisions made by the IMF board, and ultimately, therefore, by the creditor countries. The financial needs for a global sustainable transformation, however, require flexibility which can only be granted if credit creation responds endogenously, according to financing needs. Moreover, given that SDRs are allocated on the basis of country quotas, the bulk of funds issued would go to high-income economies. Finally, SDRs are often considered tantamount to a currency. This, however, is not the case. Countries must pay interest on SDRs. Even when interest rates are significantly below market interest rates, SDRs still function as a loan (Pforr et al. 2022).

For these reasons, an economic and financial order capable of effectively financing sustainable and just transformation on a worldwide basis must entail the redesign of the international monetary system in order to circumvent US dollar dominance. An important historical precedent for such a process was set by the discussions that took place in preparation for and during the Bretton Woods Conference in July 1944, where delegates from forty-four countries met to shape the international monetary system. Our proposal builds on Keynes' plan for that conference, which specified the creation of an International Clearing Union and a unit of account he called the 'bancor'. Key elements of Keynes' plan were rejected in favour of an alternative version drafted by Harry Dexter White (2019), which led, in particular, to the US dollar becoming the quasi-world currency. Keynes' version, however, offers important insights on how a green global monetary system could work. Before outlining our proposal, we will analyse specific aspects and implications of Keynes' proposal.

Keynes' International Clearing Union and bancor proposal

In the early 1940s, John Maynard Keynes developed a proposal for shaping the post-war international monetary system in a way that would avoid financial crises in the long run and balance global trade, thereby introducing an element of global justice into the system (Steil 2013). His idea involved the creation of an International Clearing Union (ICU) that would allow deficit countries to temporarily hold debit balances with surplus countries (Keynes 2019). According to his plan, both deficit and surplus countries would be members of the ICU, which would have its own unit of account: the bancor. Bancors were designed to exist only for the purpose of settling international balances between monetary authorities (central banks, for example) and not for private use between individuals, companies or banks. All countries participating in the union were to have ICU accounts through which they could transfer bancors to one another so as to settle external balances. Membership in the union would likewise require countries to commit to accepting bancors as a means of payment. Accordingly, whenever one country incurred a deficit with another, the former would be debited with bancors from its account at the ICU and the latter would receive a corresponding bancor credit. This would automatically expand the system's bancor reserves. Implied in this arrangement is the assumption that the amount of money in the system would adjust endogenously to the real demands of trade and would not be exogenously determined by a pre-existing amount of money (Mehrling 2016). Viewed from a different angle, the arrangement was designed to give countries a certain amount of flexibility in financing their trade deficits while allowing them sufficient time to sort out their external accounts (Keynes 2019).

Under Keynes' proposal, credits or debits of participating countries would be booked with the ICU and not with other countries or the IMF. Accordingly, the creation of a debit to the account of a deficit country could be thought of as an overdraft (Skidelsky 2005; Costabile 2009). It would not occur at the expense of any other country because the account of the surplus country would be credited with the amount owed in bancors which the surplus country could then spend within the system. As one country's debit would equal another's credit, the net position of the ICU would not change as a result of an expansion or contraction of credit within the system. According to Keynes' plan, the maximum debit balance of a given country would not be allowed to exceed its quota, and the quota would be determined by a formula based on a set of variables including the sum of the country's exports and imports (Keynes 2019).

Keynes' proposal stipulated that the exchange rate of each country's currency would be fixed relative to the bancor to avoid competitive devaluations that might trigger currency wars, but also provided that rates could be adjusted with the permission of the ICU governing board. The bancor, in turn, was envisaged to have a fixed (but adjustable) exchange rate with gold. Member countries would have to agree to purchase gold only at that price, but they would be permitted to buy and sell gold at will and without limit. Keynes reasoned that allowing countries to hold gold reserves and use them to settle their balances would make the system more attractive to those, such as the United States, with large stocks of gold stocks, as such countries presumably would not want to demonetize their gold holdings (Keynes 2019).

Keynes' plan also specifically dealt with the question of how countries would restore equilibrium in their balance of payments. It opposed a contractionary adjustment that would burden deficit countries by reducing their balance of payments deficit through the reduction of imports, the devaluation of their currency, and the adjustment of their fiscal and monetary policy. Instead, it required both debtor and creditor countries to make adjustments in order to establish equilibrium. The key reason for proposing symmetric adjustment stems from the fact that the sum of all surpluses equals the sum of all deficits. As a result, if the latter is considered a problem, then the former should be as well (Richardson 1985). According to Keynes, contractionary adjustment is detrimental not only for deficit countries but also for surplus countries since the reduction of imports by a deficit country leads to a reduction in world trade. In such a situation, surplus countries face a reduction in exports with negative consequences for their output and employment. To remedy this detriment, Keynes advocates a 'socialization of trade', meaning the expansion of international trade to ensure that all economies produce at full employment (Clary 2017).

Keynes' model contains specific proposals for both deficit and surplus countries to make balance of payment adjustments. On the one hand, if the balances of deficit countries were to exceed a certain proportion of their quota, they would be charged an increasing interest rate. Beyond a certain threshold, they would be allowed to devalue their currency. In addition, they would be asked to post collateral and implement measures to reduce their deficit. Barring the effectiveness of these measures, they could eventually be declared in default. On the other hand, if the credit balances of surplus countries were to exceed a certain proportion of their quota, they would be asked to take steps to restore equilibrium, among other things, by appreciating their currencies, expanding domestic demand and reducing import barriers. Through these corrective mechanisms, Keynes' proposal aims to restore equilibrium by incentivizing surplus countries to boost their spending. Adjustment in this sense is expansionary. When spending is increased, credit balances do not lie idle in the coffers of the surplus countries, but are used to expand world trade for mutual benefit. Paul Davidson (1993) argues that there are three ways for surplus countries to spend their balances within the system: (1) by buying goods from deficit countries (2) by investing in deficit countries and/or (3) by providing aid to deficit countries. Keynes' plan, however, does not foresee a ceiling for credit balances that would prevent surplus countries from no longer accepting bancors, or force them to settle their trade balances in gold or another currency.

Kalecki and Schumacher (1943) criticized the notion of 'equilibrium' in Keynes' plan. They argued that there 'is no merit in a general policy aiming at Current Account equilibrium for all countries, because different countries are at different stages of economic development, and a regular flow of investment from the more highly developed to the more backward regions of the world may redound to the benefit of all' (Kalecki and Schumacher 1943: 29). In their view, forcing adjustment could prove counterproductive. They held that surplus countries should be allowed to maintain as many reserves (in gold or bancors) as they wished and that countries needing imports for 'reconstruction, readjustment, and industrialization' should be allowed to hold the deficits that they required. In particular, the authors proposed that the Keynes plan be complemented by attaching an international investment board to the ICU that could advance long term bancor loans to 'industrializing countries' with the request that said loans be spent in other deficit countries.

Towards a Green Bretton Woods with the ecor at the centre

Times of crises, like the situation that prompted the founding of the Bretton Woods System after the Second World War, often lead to critical conjunctures (Eckersley 2021) that mark the politicization of structures that would otherwise seem almost impossible to change. Such a scenario may once again develop in the foreseeable future if the climate crisis continues to escalate. Already we are witnessing growing political pressure to reform the current international monetary system. And as international organizations are becoming increasingly aware of the system's flaws, momentum for change is building. In June 2023, at the Paris Summit for a New Global Financing Pact, UN Secretary-General António Guterres characterized the global financial architecture as 'outdated, dysfunctional, and unjust'. He called for 'a new Bretton Woods moment – a moment for Governments to come together, re-examine and re-configure the global financial architecture for the twenty-first century'.[3] This is also the goal of the Bridgetown Initiative for the Reform of the Global Financial Architecture launched in 2022 by the Prime Minister of Barbados, Mia Mottley.[4] In 2023, Guterres and Mottley convened a meeting that resulted in the Bridgetown Initiative 2.0, which includes among its action areas the provision of liquidity to developing countries, the transformation of the governance of international financial institutions, and the creation of an international trade system that supports global green and just transformations (United Nations 2023b). These initiatives are evidence of growing urgency in the debate over how to reform the international monetary system. What is still largely lacking, however, are concrete concepts for alternative forms of an internationally just monetary system conducive to the financing of the investments needed for sustainable transformation. The present paper aims to address this gap.

Wright (2011, 2017) makes the case for 'real utopias' that are ideal in spirit but very attentive to questions of practical feasibility and design. His works explore the possibilities of better futures while remaining grounded pragmatically in the historical configuration of contemporary capitalism. Our proposal can be understood as part of the effort to 'develop strategies that enable us to make empirically and theoretically sound arguments about emancipatory possibilities' (Wright 2011, 2017). We build on Keynes' plan but with the overarching aim to develop a supranational arrangement that would provide countries especially, but not only, from the Global South with the financial leeway they need to import green goods, services and technologies essential to achieve the objectives of sustainable transformation. Towards this aim, we propose the creation of a Green World Central Bank (GWCB) embedded within a Green Bretton Woods System that could issue its own unit of account, which we call the ecor. The ecor would constitute a supranational special purpose unit of account inspired by Keynes' bancor and created specifically for the purpose of financing the worldwide sustainable transformation. Under our proposal, all participating countries would have an account at the GWCB. The GWCB would create ecors through the act of lending by digitally crediting a country's GWCB account. The country would then transfer them to the GWCB account of another country to pay for the imports that it needs. This would alleviate financial constraints and provide the elasticity necessary to finance sustainable projects.

As discussed above, all forms of special purpose money face similar challenges: How can trust be created in the money form? How should its value be determined? How should the exchange with other currencies be managed? What steps need to be taken to ensure that the special purpose money is only used for its specified purpose, in the present case for sustainable projects? Above all - and this is the problem faced by all forms of special purpose money that have existed to date: What mechanisms exist to make it possible for this form of money to emerge from its niche existence and develop a broad and sustainable impact?

Regarding the first question: Trust in the ecor would be established via the Green World Central Bank (GWCB) and the Green Bretton Woods System. As more and more countries come to accept and use the system, trust in the ecor would grow. With growing participation in the system, the number of trade partners to buy from or sell to would increase. Surplus countries, in particular, might be reluctant to join the Green Bretton Woods System if they were unable to find an attractive way to spend their credits. The larger the system were to become, however, the more possibilities there would be for surplus countries to use their ecor credits.

With respect to the second question: Various possibilities are conceivable for determining the value of the ecor against other currencies. One ecor, for example, could be set to equal one US dollar or defined as equivalent to an IMF SDR. Another option would be to peg the ecor to a basket of currencies, or to track the evolution of the value of a basket of commodities. For simplicity's sake, we shall assume that one ecor equals one US dollar. This assumption will lend clarity to our discussion for two reasons: First, since US dollars are the current unit of account for global trade and finance, defining ecors as equal to US dollars would bypass the inevitable redenomination problem involved in transferring commodity prices from US dollars into ecors. Second, because the exchange rates of all national currencies are quoted in terms of US dollars, their exchange rates to ecors would be readily available. However, we recognize that pegging the ecor to the US dollar would problematically imply the retention of the US dollar's privileged status, at least for the foreseeable future. Additionally, as exchange rates can potentially be overvalued or undervalued at any given point in time, they might not be the most expedient starting point for a system of fixed (even if potentially adjustable) exchange rates. Accordingly, while proceeding on this assumption is useful for capturing the essence of this proposal in simplified terms, it might not be desirable for the actual system.

The third question concerns the exchange of ecors with other currencies. Similar to the Bretton Woods System, the exchange rate of all national currencies would be fixed to the ecor but adjustable based on internationally agreed rules. This would avoid competitive devaluations that could trigger currency wars and culminate in the collapse of the system. Moreover, it would also prevent the overvaluation of a given country's currency, which could lead to trade deficits and negatively impact local production. Closely following Keynes' proposal of one-way convertibility between the bancor and gold, and to obviate any possibility of a run on ecors, our proposal would not permit the conversion of ecors into US dollars or other national currencies. Nevertheless, countries would be able to sell US dollars, or other currencies to the Green World Central Bank in exchange for ecors. The one-way convertibility of US dollars to ecors is important because, similar to Keynes' vision that bancors would replace gold as the international reserve currency, the symmetric treatment of all currencies vis-à-vis the ecor would eventually lead to the gradual replacement of the US dollar, or any other key currency, in that role (Skidelsky 2005; Alessandrini and Fratianni 2009;

Costabile 2009). Key currencies would lose much of their special status because the countries issuing them, just as any other country, would have to obtain ecors to settle their international imbalances, and because other countries would no longer need to hold US dollar reserves.

Regarding the special purpose issue posed in the fourth question, we propose a classical dual control method to be carried out by democratic institutions to ensure that ecors are only be spent on sustainability projects. Similar processes are already in place, example given, whenever funds are requested from the EU or the World Bank. In order to acquire ecors for sustainable projects, actors such as local communities, mayors, governments or private investors would have to prepare an application for submission first to a national institution and then, after a positive evaluation, to the GWCB. The initial evaluation could be performed either by a new institution established for that purpose, or by an existing institution such as the ministry of economy or the central bank of the country where the investors are located. These institutions would have to build up corresponding competences internally. Projects failing to meet sustainability standards agreed upon by the members of the GWCB would not be funded. At the same time, the procedure would guarantee that funding would only be provided for projects with promising prospects, thus limiting the system's creation of credit to ideas with adequate repayment capacity or to necessary, albeit unprofitable, investments. In this way, the system would avoid an uncontrolled creation of credit (both in ecors and national currencies) with destabilizing consequences. As is currently already the case with central banks, corresponding competences would have to be built up in the respective institutions. We are aware that conflicting definitions exist over what is or is not considered sustainable and what counts as 'promising'. However, all sustainable projects must struggle with this problem. In our opinion, it is important that the task of determining what qualifies as sustainable and promising should be delegated to democratic institutions and not to private investors. It would, of course, also be possible at this point to involve other security mechanisms and actors, such as a consortium comprised of representatives from civil society organizations and scientific institutions. Regardless of how the decision-making process is designed, care must be taken to ensure that actors with superior financial resources or opportunities to exert influence through lobbying, for example, do not gain unfair advantage over competitors. Each member country would be allowed to define the institutional setting that best suits their interests. In the second step, however, after approval of the project, the national institution would have to apply to the GWCB for the required amount of ecors. This would constitute a second control point to ensure that ecor creation in the system would be limited to sustainable projects. During this phase, locally approved projects would be reviewed and validated by the GWCB to eliminate the risk of corruption or corporate capture of local governments.

Unlike the ICU in Keynes' proposal, the GWCB in our model would not extend credit to already finalized transactions, but would intervene prior to the transaction to decide whether or not to extend credit. In this sense, credit creation by the GWCB would resemble a productive loan rather than an overdraft as outlined in the ICU model. It follows that the GWCB would require a dynamic, qualified and independent staff specialized in sustainability and creditworthiness analysis within a framework based on mutually agreed standards. Many national and international institutions, including development banks, the World Bank, the IMF and the UN, among others, are already staffing their teams with highly skilled personnel specialized in these areas. In addition to professional expertise, the GWCB staff would need to be provided with the appropriate infrastructure to enable them to expedite credit applications and reach timely decisions while resisting pressure from national governments.

The answer to the final question – whether the ecor could succeed in leaving a niche existence – depends on the size and composition of the system's membership. If it were possible to establish a Green Bretton Woods System on a scale similar to the former Bretton Woods System, the ecor could become a global and widely used currency. Without a majority of the world's countries integrated in the scheme, the degree to which the ecor could prevail would largely depend on the status and number of participant countries. The system would be capable of working as long as enough countries came to accept ecors as payment for their exports. As the sum of surpluses equals the sum of deficits, if there were few surplus countries, the system would remain small, as total deficits would be limited to the willingness of the few financiers to finance them. Theoretically, the system we propose could be launched already by just two states. In practice, however, we assume that a significantly larger number of participating states would be required to constitute a critical mass. A more even proportion between surplus and deficit countries would allow the system to accommodate larger balances and therefore enhance its capacity to grow. This is not to say that a perfect balance between high- and low-income countries would be required. An agreement could also be concluded among mostly low-income countries, making it possible to increase green demand in the Global South, which in turn would promote sustainable transformation. Arrangements of this nature are not uncommon. Several countries, including Bolivia, are already using the Chinese renminbi (RMB) to settle their cross-border trade. RMB transactions are increasing on the world stage even where China is not a trading partner – in the case of Argentina, for example, which uses RMB to repay IMF loans. Countries such as Argentina and Brazil also use their local currencies on a bilateral basis, and multilateral systems such as MERCOSUR, the Mercado Común del Sur (Southern Common Market) (Fritz et al. 2023), are gaining in importance. Although arrangements of this nature fall short of a more egalitarian international monetary system as we envisage it, they do show that various processes already underway are taking initial steps to circumvent the existing financial architecture. A coalition of these processes and countries with initiatives such as the UN-backed Bridgetown 2.0 would constitute a political moment towards a more just and sustainable financial architecture.

The ecor in practice

The following example is provided to demonstrate how our proposal could be operationalized in practice. As previously mentioned, one of the key problems of financially subordinated countries is the lack of US dollars necessary to acquire the means of production and green technologies essential for achieving a sustainable transformation. For the sake of illustration, we assume that local initiatives in Bolivia are planning to carry out a green project (e.g. a housing development with solar panels). They present the proposal to the Bolivian Central Bank. This first step is important as it serves as an initial filter to guarantee that ecors would actually be used for green purposes.

Local means of production and workers are to be employed in the implementation of the project, but other goods, services and technologies need to be imported. By creating money, the Bolivian Central Bank can finance the purchase of goods paid for in national currency, but imports such as solar panels have to be settled with international means of payment. Estimating that Bolivian local initiatives would need 1 million ecors to purchase solar panels, the Bolivian Central Bank would have to request that amount from the GWCB. Let us assume that the GWCB approves the project and creates a 1 million ecor debit (deposit) and credit (loan) to the account of the Bolivian Central Bank.[5] Once the ecor loan is granted, the Bolivian Central Bank would authorize the imports required by the local initiatives and would grant them a local currency equivalent loan (interest free, or with very low interest), which at a rate of 7 bolivianos to 1 ecor, would equal 7 million bolivianos. The local initiatives would then be authorized to buy solar panels worth 1 million ecors from, for example, a Chinese producer and would transfer the national currency equivalent (7 million bolivianos) to the Bolivian Central Bank. The latter would then transfer 1 million ecors from its account at the GWCB to the GWCB account of the People's Bank of China (PBoC). Once its GWCB account is credited accordingly, the PBoC would issue the national currency equivalent (650 renminbi at a 6.5 exchange rate) and transfer the amount to the solar panel producer.

In the end, the Bolivian local initiatives receive the imported goods. They owe the Bolivian Central Bank bolivianos in the amount of their loan. The Bolivian Central Bank, in turn, owes the GWCB said amount in ecors. The Chinese government receives an ecor deposit at the GWCB, and the Chinese exporter receives renminbi in exchange for the goods it has sold to the Bolivian investors. In this way, local sustainability initiatives that cannot buy solar panels under the prevailing system because they cannot raise 1 million US dollars would be able to effectively drive Bolivia's transformation towards reduced greenhouse emissions. Symmetrically, Chinese producers would benefit because they would now be able to sell solar panels that otherwise they would not have sold. The only necessary assumption is that they would be willing to accept local currency instead of dollars. However, this assumption does not seem problematic as a significant part of their expenditures are made in local currency. For their imports, however, they could ask their central bank for ecors. In this way, the ecor system would not only be attractive for deficit countries but also for surplus countries, as it would provide them with a way to increase the demand for their products.

As in the case of bancors, ecors would only be able to be spent within the system. It would not be possible, for instance, to use ecors to buy something in a grocery shop. The currency would constitute Green World Central Bank money to be used exclusively in transactions between central banks. In our example, the PBoC would then have a credit in the amount of 1 million ecors which it could use in a number of different ways. First, the bank could hold them as reserves. Incentives to keep reserves, however, would not exist, considering that countries would be able to procure new credits to finance imports and would not have to protect their exchange rates against runs. Second, the ecor credits could be used to buy green goods or services from other countries. As there are no incentives in our example for the PBoC to hold ecors, the central bank could make them available to Chinese residents with an interest in purchasing sustainable products abroad. The spending of ecors by surplus countries in deficit countries would expand green demand there, leading to the creation of jobs designed to promote sustainable transformation, which, in turn, would provide the deficit countries with the ecors they need to cancel their ecor debits. As this would be an ideal solution from an internationally just perspective, strong incentives would be required for its realization. Such incentives would have to be agreed upon internationally, but, as in the Keynes proposal, one potential option would be to impose interest rates on the balances of both creditors and debtors above a certain threshold. Third, surplus countries such as China in our example could invest the money in deficit countries. This would promote additional green demand and the creation of green employment as well as ecor credits. The fourth option for surplus countries in general, including China in our example, would be to simply forgive the debt and transfer their ecor credits to the deficit country as a form of aid. Since this option does not require funds that would otherwise not be available for domestic spending, as in the case of foreign aid financed from the national budget, it is also an attractive option for exporting countries.

Considering Kalecki and Schumacher's (1943) critique of Keynes' model, and assuming that the sustainable transformation will be a gradual and time-consuming process, the design of the system should take into account the fact that in some countries transformation is likely to be a lengthy process involving significant deficits, while in others there will be sustained periods of surplus. This should not be a problem since ultimately all countries will benefit from climate change mitigation, not least because of its money-saving potential. For the system to work in the long run, however, countries in need of funds in the short term would eventually have to reverse their foreign trade position to repay their debts. This, in turn, implies that the productive structure of deficit countries would have to become competitive enough so as to be able to export and earn the ecors needed for repayment. In options two through four above, this would be achieved by an international increase in demand, leading to an expansionary adjustment of imbalances. In order to avoid replication through the system of existing patterns of ecologically unequal exchange, mechanisms would be required to encourage surplus country spending on sustainable activities. This means that some of the projects financed by the GWCB would have to be geared towards activities with good export prospects. However, this would not necessarily apply to every approved project. In fact, spending would be desirable not only for non-competitive or non-tradable activities, but also for non-profit projects, including, for instance, efforts directed at mitigating the costs of loss and damage due to climate change. To be able to conduct projects of this nature, a deficit country would either have to develop highly competitive export sectors so as to attract ecors in sufficient amounts to cover all of its debts, or it would have to count on aid from surplus countries or their willingness to finance unprofitable projects. In this way, the system would contribute to addressing the fundamental productive and ecological imbalances that characterize the current state of world trade (Svartzman and Althouse 2022).

Conclusion

At the international Summit held in Paris in June 2023 around the theme 'Building a new consensus for a more inclusive international financial system', Mia Mottley, prime minister of Barbados, argued the need for 'a more responsive, fairer and more inclusive international financial system to fight inequalities, finance the climate transition, and bring us closer to achieving the Sustainable Development Goals'.[6] As shown in the paper, the political process to establish a new, more just, and sustainable global financial architecture is well underway. We maintain, however, that current approaches fall short in financing worldwide sustainable transformation. First, the significance and constraints of the global monetary hierarchy are underestimated. As long as this hierarchy holds, the countries of the Global South will remain dependent on the Global North and will not be able to generate funds at the level required for achieving sustainable transformation. Second, current approaches are based primarily on the mobilization of private funds. Private investors, however, are risk-averse and, above all, profit-oriented. Most of the investments needed to drive sustainable transformation cannot be financed with such funds. Third, existing approaches lack endogenous financial elasticity. This implies that funding is contingent on the goodwill of private investors or wealthy countries which always face domestic political pressure to invest their budgets internally. As a result, financial resources are always scarce. A Green World Central Bank with the ecor as its own unit of account would be able to use its balance sheets to finance the transformation. This would provide the elasticity necessary to adapt to the real needs of the transformation. Lastly, the proposed Green Bretton Woods System would facilitate democratization of the global financial architecture, thereby making the sustainable transformation more comprehensive and inclusive. Accordingly, we argued the need to rethink the overall international monetary structure. A Green Bretton Woods System with a Green World Central Bank and a supranational currency, the ecor, at its core would constitute a strong force with the potential of promoting sustainable and just transformation on a global scale.

Our example above demonstrates how the Green Bretton Woods System would make it possible for countries of the Global South to move towards sustainable investments and create green jobs, thus rendering their economies more sustainable. It introduces an enabling structure capable of overcoming current constraints on financing climate change adaptation and mitigation, while reducing loss and damage and driving the global transition towards zero greenhouse gas emissions (Svartzman and Althouse 2022). As we argue, without such a system, shortages of hard currencies such as the US dollar make necessary investments impossible. Furthermore, we describe how the proposal would allow producers of green goods and services to secure additional sources of demand, which would also benefit their domestic economies. Accordingly, the ecor system would benefit not only deficit but also surplus countries.

The example illustrates how a Global South country could procure an interest-free loan in foreign currency. The functionality of the system does not necessarily depend on a zero interest rate, but interest rates would definitely have to be kept low. Because ecors would not be convertible into US dollars or any other currency, they would only be valid within the system. This would eliminate any risk of a run on the GWCB. At the same time, it would incentivize surplus countries to spend their accumulated balances in other countries, creating further demand and positive loopback effects. In the system we propose, projects would need to be approved by both the national government and the GWCB. Therefore, only those meeting the internationally agreed sustainable standards would have access to funding. This would ensure a built-in limit to the quantitative expansion of ecors. More importantly, the Green Bretton Woods System would give deficit countries more autonomy to actively advance their national endeavours towards sustainable transformation without relying on the benevolence of international donors, conditional loans from international financial institutions, or private, profit-motivated financial institutions. This would contribute to the development of Southern sovereignty, allowing Global South countries to shape their own transformation.

There is no doubt that in coming years the increasingly catastrophic effects of the climate crisis will intensify the political debate on how to change the current financial architecture. Already we are seeing calls for change from both the United Nations (as evidenced, e.g. by the Bridgetown Initiative) as well as from countries seeking to circumvent US dollar dominance. Power struggles over a multitude of conflicting interests will certainly present a major challenge to the transformation process. However, possibilities for real change are bound to increase as recognition grows within society and among decision-makers over the inadequacy of the current international monetary system to facilitate the kind of sustainable transformation needed to prevent the world from becoming uninhabitable.

Notes

1 We use the reference to Bretton Woods to indicate the possibility of an international monetary system arising as a result of international coordination that achieves a certain level of financial stability. However, we acknowledge that the historical founding process excluded many countries of the Global South. Moreover, as we show in the following, the system that came about as the outcome of those negotiations is based on the US dollar, which already constitutes an inherent impediment to sustainable development. Finally, our concept is not in any way intended to replicate or supersede the currently remaining Bretton Woods institutions, the World Bank or the International Monetary Fund.

2 In line with this understanding of the problems faced by countries of the Global South, we diverge from approaches that see the failure of domestic policies as the root cause of development failure. Explanations based on this reasoning deflect attention away from the problematic nature of neoliberal globalization (Chang 2008) which has reinforced the monetary hierarchy outlined above.

3 https://press.un.org/en/2023/sgsm21855.doc.htm.

4 https://pmo.gov.bb/wp-content/uploads/2022/10/The-2022-Bridgetown-Initiative .pdf.

5 In the interest of simplicity, we shall assume a zero interest rate.

6 See https://nouveaupactefinancier.org/en.php.

References

Aglietta, M., and V. Coudert. (2019), The Dollar and the Transition to Sustainable Development: From Key Currency to Multilateralism, Policy Brief CEPII 26.

Alessandrini, P., and M. Fratianni. (2009), 'Resurrecting Keynes to Stabilize the International Monetary System', *Open Economies Review,* 20: 339–58.

Althouse, J., and R. Svartzman. (2022), 'Bringing Subordinated Financialisation Down to Earth: The Political Ecology of Finance-Dominated Capitalism', *Cambridge Journal of Economics*: 679–702.

Attridge, S., and L. Engen. (2019), Blended Finance in the Poorest Countries: The Need for a Better Approach, Overseas Development Institute, London. Available at: http://hdl.handle.net/10419/206745.

Bayliss, K., and E. Van Waeyenberge. (2018), 'Unpacking the Public Private Partnership Revival', *The Journal of Development Studies*, 54: 577–93.

Bell, S. (2001), 'The Role of the State and the Hierarchy of Money', *Cambridge Journal of Economics*, 25: 149–63.

Bhattacharya, A., M. Dooley, H. Kharas, and C. Taylor. (2022), Financing a Big Investment Push in Emerging Markets and Developing Economies for Sustainable, Resilient and Inclusive Recovery and Growth, London: Grantham Research Institute on Climate Change and the Environment, London School of Economics and Political Science, and Washington, DC: Brookings Institution.

Bolton, P., and M. Kacperczyk. (2021), 'Do Investors Care About Carbon Risk?', *Journal of Financial Economics*, 142: 517–49.

Bracking, S., and B. Leffel. (2021), 'Climate Finance Governance: Fit for Purpose?', *Wiley Interdisciplinary Reviews: Climate Change*, 12: 1–18.

Cabaña, G., and J. Linares. (2022), 'Decolonising Money: Learning from Collective Struggles for Self-Determination', *Sustainability Science*, 17: 1159–79.

Chang, H. J. (2008), 'The Lexus and the Olive Tree Revisited. Myth and Facts About Globalisation', in *Bad Samaritans. The Myth of Free Trade amd the Secret History of Capitalism*, 19–39, New York: Bloomsbury Press.

Christophers, B. (2022), 'Fossilised Capital: Price and Profit in the Energy Transition', *New Political Economy*, 27: 146–59.

Claar, S. (2020), 'Green Finance and Transnational Capitalist Classes: Tracing Vested Capital Interests in Renewable Energy Investment in South Africa', *Journal für Entwicklungspolitik*, 37: 110–28.

Clary, B. J. (2017), 'Keynes, the Socialisation of Trade, and International Monetary Institutions', *European Journal of the History of Economic Thought*, 24: 979–97.

Cohen, B., and T. M. Benney. (2014), 'What Does the International Currency System Really Look Like?', *Review of International Political Economy*, 21: 1017–41.

Costabile, L. (2009), 'Current Global Imbalances and the Keynes Plan. A Keynesian Approach for Reforming the International Monetary System', *Structural Change and Economic Dynamics*, 20: 79–89.

Dafermos, Y., D. Gabor, and J. Michell. (2021), 'The Wall Street Consensus in Pandemic Times: What Does it Mean for Climate-Aligned Development?', *Canadian Journal of Development Studies / Revue canadienne d'études du développement*, 42: 238–51.

Davidson, P. (1993), 'Reforming the World's Money', *Journal of Post Keynesian Economics*, 15: 153–79.

Dittmer, K. (2013), 'Local Currencies for Purposive Degrowth? A Quality Check of Some Proposals for Changing Money-as-Usual', *Journal of Cleaner Production*, 54: 3–13.

Eckersley, R. (2021), 'Greening States and Societies: From Transitions to Great Transformations', *Environmental Politics*, 30: 245–65.

Elsner, C., M. Neumann, F. Müller, and S. Claar. (2021), 'Room for Money or Manoeuvre? How Green Financialization and De-Risking Shape Zambia's

Renewable Energy Transition', *Canadian Journal of Development Studies / Revue canadienne d'études du développement,* 43: 276–95.

Eradze, I. (2023), *Unravelling The Persistence of Dollarization. The Case of Georgia,* Oxfordshire: Routledge.

Essers, D., D. Cassimon, and M. Prowse. (2021), 'Debt-for-Climate Swaps: Killing Two Birds with One Stone?', *Global Environmental Change,* 71: 102407.

Fritz, B., A. Kaltenbrunner, L. Mühlich, and B. Orsi. (2023), 'South-South Monetary Regionalism: A Case of Productive Incoherence?', *New Political Economy,* 28: 818–31.

Gabor, D. (2021), 'The Wall Street Consensus', *Development and Change,* 42: 429–59.

Gallagher, K., and R. Kozul-Wright. (2022), *The Case for a New Bretton Woods,* Cambridge, Oxford, Boston, New York: Polity.

Galvin, R. (2020), 'Yes, There is Enough Money to Decarbonize the Economies of High-Income Countries Justly and Sustainably', *Energy Research and Social Science,* 70: 101739.

Gerber, J. (2015), 'An Overview of Local Credit Systems and Their Implications for Post-Growt', *Sustainability Science,* 10: 413–23.

Ghosh, J., S. Chakraborty, and D. Das. (2022), 'Climate Imperialism in the Twenty-First Century', *Monthly Review,* 74: 1–17.

Gopinath, G., E. Boz, C. Casas, F. J. Díez, P. O. Gourinchas, and M. Plagborg-Møller. (2020), 'Dominant Currency Paradigm', *American Economic Review,* 110: 677–719.

Haag, S. (2023), 'Old Colonial Power in New Green Financing Instruments. Approaching Financial Subordination From the Perspective of Racial Capitalism in Renewable Energy Finance in Senegal', *Geoforum,* 145: 103641.

IPCC. (2022), Mitigation of Climate Change. Available at: https://report.ipcc.ch/ar6wg3/pdf/IPCC_AR6_WGIII_FinalDraft_FullReport.pdf.

Kalecki, M., and E. F. Schumacher. (1943), 'New Plans for International Trade: International Clearing and Long-Term Lending', *Bulletin of the Oxford University Institute of Economics & Statistics,* 5: 29–32.

Kaltenbrunner, A., and P. Lysandrou. (2017), 'The US Dollar's Continuing Hegemony as an International Currency: A Double-matrix Analysis', *Development and Change,* 48: 663–91.

Kedward, K., J. Ryan-Collins, and H. Chenet. (2020), Managing Nature-Related Financial Risks: A Precautionary Policy Approach for Central Banks and Financial Supervisors. UCL IIPP Working Paper 9.

Keynes, J. M. (2019), 'The Keynes Plan. Proposals for an International Clearing Union', in N. Lamoreaux and I. Shapiro (eds), *Bretton Woods Agreements, Together with Scholarly Commentaries and Essential Historical Documents,* Yale University Press.

Knapp, G. F. (1924 [1905]), *The State Theory of Money,* London: Macmillan & Company Ltd.

Löscher, A., and A. Kaltenbrunner. (2022), 'Climate Change and Macroeconomic Policy Space in Developing and Emerging Economies', *Journal of Post Keynesian Economics,* 1: 113–41.

Mariotti, C. (2022), Special Drawing Rights. Can the IMF's Reserve Currency Become a Transformative Financial Resource? Briefing Paper Eurodad, April. Available at: https://www.eurodad.org/sdr_transformative_resource.

McLeay, M., A. Radia, and T. Ryland. (2014), 'Money Creation in the Modern Economy', *Bank of England Quarterly Bulletin*, 54: 14–27.

Mehrling, P. (2013), 'The Inherent Hierarchy of Money', in L. Taylor, A. Rezai, and T. Michl (eds), *Social Fairness and Economics. Economic Essays in the Spirit of Duncan Foley*, 394–404, Oxfordshire: Routledge.

Mehrling, P. (2015), 'Elasticity and Discipline in the Global Swap Network', *International Journal of Political Economy*, 44: 311–24.

Mehrling, P. (2016), 'Beyond Bancor', *Challenge*, 59: 22–34.

Mitchell-Innes, A. (2004), 'The Credit Theory of Money', in R. Wray (ed), *Credit and State Theories of Money. The Contributions of A. Mitchell Innes,* 50–78, Cheltenham – Northampton, MA: Edward Elgar.

Murau, S., A. Haas, and A. Guter-Sandu. (2023), 'Monetary Architecture and the Green Transition', *Environment and Planning A: Economy and Space*, 56 (2): 382–401.

Murau, S., F. Pape, and T. Pforr. (2022), 'International Monetary Hierarchy Through Emergency US-Dollar Liquidity: A Key Currency Approach', *Competition & Change,* 27: 495–515.

Nersisyan, Y., and L. R. Wray. (2019), How to Pay for the Green New Deal, Levy Economics Institute Working Papers, 971.

OECD. (2022), Climate Finance Provided and Mobilised by Developed Countries in 2016–2020: Insights from Disaggregated Analysis, Climate Finance and the USD 100 Billion Goal, OECD Publishing, Paris, DOI https://doi.org/10.1787/286dae5d-en.

Perry, K. (2021), 'The New "Bond-Age", Climate Crisis and the Case for Climate Reparations: Unpicking Old/New Colonialities of Finance for Development Within the SDGs', *Geoforum,* 126: 361–71.

Persaud, A. (2023), 'Unblocking the Green Transformation in Developing Countries with a Partial Foreign Exchange Guarantee' Climate Policy Initiative Working Paper. Available at: https://www.climatepolicyinitiative.org/wp-content/uploads/2023/06 /An-FX-Guarantee-Mechanism-for-the-Green-Transformation-in-Developing -Countries.pdf.

Pettifor, A. (2022), 'Society Must Transform the International Financial System in Order to Stabilise the Ecosystem', in P. Arestis and M. Sawyer (eds), *Economic Policies for Sustainability and Resilience*, 179–222, London: Palgrave Macmillan.

Pforr, T., F. Pape, and S Murau. (2022), 'After the Allocation: What Role for the Special Drawing Rights System?' INET Working Paper, 180.

Richardson, D. R. (1985), 'On Proposals for a Clearing Union', *Journal of Post Keynesian Economics,* 8: 14–27.

Seyfang, G., and N. Longhurst. (2013), 'Growing Green Money? Mapping Community Currencies for Sustainable Development', *Ecological Economics,* 86: 65–77.

Skidelsky, R. (2005), 'Keynes, Globalisation and the Bretton Woods Institutions in the Light of Changing Ideas about Markets', *World Economics,* 6: 15–30.

Songwe, V., N. Stern, and A. Bhattacharya. (2022), *Finance for Climate Action: Scaling Up Investment for Climate and Development,* London: Grantham Research Institute on Climate Change and the Environment, London School of Economics and Political Science.

Steil, B. (2013), *The Battle of Bretton Woods. John Maynard Keynes, Harry Dexter White, and the Making of a New World Order,* Princeton: Princeton University Press.

Svartzman, R., and J. Althouse. (2022), 'Greening the International Monetary System? Not Without Addressing the Political Ecology of Global Imbalances', *Review of International Political Economy*, 29: 844–69.

UNCTAD. (2019), Trade and Development Report: Financing A Global Green New Deal. UNCTAD/TDR/2019, United Nations. Available at: https://unctad.org/system/ files/official-document/tdr2019fas_en.pdf.

United Nations. (2023a), Inter-Agency Task Force on Financing for Development, Financing for Sustainable Development Report 2023: Financing Sustainable Transformations. United Nations, New York. Available at: https:// developmentfinance.un.org/fsdr2023.

United Nations. (2023b), With Clock Ticking for the SDGs, UN Chief and Barbados Prime Minister Call for Urgent Action to Transform Broken Global Financial System, Press Release. Available at: https://www.un.org/sustainabledevelopment/ blog/2023/04/press-release-with-clock-ticking-for-the-sdgs-un-chief-and-barbados -prime-minister-call-for-urgent-action-to-transform-broken-global-financial -system/.

Volz, U., S. Akhtar, K. P. Gallagher, S. Griffith-Jones, J. Haas, and M. Kraemer. (2021), *Debt Relief for a Green and Inclusive Recovery: Securing Private-Sector Participation and Creating Policy Space for Sustainable Development,* Heinrich-Böll-Stiftung, SOAS, University of London, Boston University, June. Available at: https://www.boell .de/sites/default/files/2021-06/DRGR Report 2021 Endf.pdf.

Weber, M. (1978), *Economy and Society,* Berkeley: University of California Press.

White, H. (2019), 'The White Plan. Preliminary Draft Outline of a Proposal for an International Stabilization Fund of the United and Associated Nations', in N. Lamoreaux and I. Shapiro (eds), *Bretton Woods Agreements. Together with Scholarly Commentaries and Essential Historical Documents*, London: Yale University Press.

Wright, E. O. (2011), 'Real Utopias', *Contexts,* 10: 36–42.

Wright, E. O. (2017), *Reale Utopien. Wege Aus dem Kapitalismus,* Berlin: Suhrkamp.